Viewpoints

Readings Worth Thinking and Writing About

INSTRUCTOR'S EDITION

W. ROYCE ADAMS

Santa Barbara City College

D. C. Heath and Company
Lexington, Massachusetts   Toronto

Copyright © 1989 by D. C. Heath and Company.

Published simultaneously in Canada.

Printed in the United States of America.

International Standard Book Number: 0-669-20033-6

Library of Congress Catalog Card Number: 88-81148

10 9 8 7 6 5 4 3 2 1

ACKNOWLEDGMENTS

Thomas A. Arciniega. From "Bilingual Education in the Eighties: One Hispanic's Perspective," by Thomas A. Arciniega, *Educational Research Quarterly*, Fall 1981. Reprinted by permission of the publisher.

Russell Baker. From "School vs. Education," by Russell Baker, September 9, 1975. Copyright © 1975 by the New York Times Company. Reprinted by permission.

R. Richard Banks. "Presenting the Good News About Black College Students," from the *Los Angeles Times*, January 3, 1988, Part V, p. 5. Reprinted by permission of R. Richard Banks, Director of the Stanford Upward Bound Program.

Dave Barry. "Red, White, and Beer." Copyright © 1988 by the *Miami Herald*. From *Dave Barry's Greatest Hits* by Dave Barry. First published in the *Miami Herald*. Reprinted by permission of Crown Publishers, Inc.

Georgette Bennett. "TV's Crime Coverage Is Too Scary and Misleading" by Georgette Bennett, from *TV Guide*, January 5, 1985. Reprinted by permission of the author.

Janet Bodnar. "Your Brilliant Career" by Janet Bodnar. Reprinted from *Changing Times* magazine, © 1987 Kiplinger Washington Editors, Inc., November, 1987. This reprint is not to be altered in any way, except with permission from *Changing Times*.

Nien Cheng. Excerpt from *Life and Death in Shanghai*. Copyright © 1987 by Grove.

Frank D. Cox. "Romantic Love" from *Human Intimacy*, pp. 68–70. Reprinted by permission from *Human Intimacy* by Frank D. Cox. Copyright © 1987 by West Publishing Company. All rights reserved.

Cathleen Decker. "The L.A. Woman" from the *Los Angeles Times Magazine*, February 21, 1988.

Phil Donahue. "Beauty and the Beast" from *The Human Animal* by Phil Donahue, pp. 15–22. Copyright © 1985 by Multimedia Entertainment, Inc. & Woodward/White, Inc. Reprinted by permission of Simon & Schuster, Inc.

Nancy Friday. "Mother Love" by Nancy Friday from *My Mother/My Self*. Copyright © 1977 by Nancy Friday. Reprinted by permission of International Creative Management, Inc.

Rick Greenberg. "Escaping the Daily Grind for Life as a House Father" by Rick Greenberg, a Washington, D.C.-based writer. Reprinted by permission.

Pete Hamill. "The Wet Drug" as found in *San Jose Mercury News*, March 24, 1983. Copyright © 1983 Pete Hamill. Used with permission of the author.

L. Rust Hills. "How to Eat an Ice Cream Cone" from *How to Do Things Right: The Revelations of a Fussy Man.* Copyright 1972 by Doubleday.

Arlene B. Hirschfelder. "It Is Time to Stop Playing Indians" (editor's title) from the *Los Angeles Times*, November 25, 1987. Reprinted by permission of Arlene B. Hirschfelder, Education Consultant, Association on American Indian Affairs.

Langston Hughes. "Salvation" from *The Big Sea* by Langston Hughes. Copyright 1940 by Langston Hughes, renewed © 1968 by Arna Bontemps and George Houston Bass. Reprinted by permission of Hill and Wang, a division of Farrar, Straus and Giroux, Inc.

Jon D. Hull. "Slow Descent into Hell" by Jon D. Hull from *TIME*, February 2, 1987, p. 27. Copyright 1987 *TIME* Inc. All rights reserved. Reprinted by permission from *TIME*.

Rachel L. Jones. "What's Wrong with Black English" by Rachel L. Jones from *Newsweek*, December 27, 1982 from "My Turn" column. Reprinted by permission of the author, a 26-year-old reporter for the *St. Petersburg Times*.

Suzanne Britt Jordan. "Fun. Oh, Boy. Fun. You Could Die from It," by Suzanne Britt Jordan from the *New York Times*, December 23, 1979. Copyright © 1979 by the New York Times Company. Reprinted by permission.

Ken Keyes, Jr. Excerpt from *The Hundredth Monkey*. Copyright 1981 by Vision.

Coretta Scott King. "The Death Penalty Is a Step Back" by Coretta Scott King. Reprinted by permission of Joan Daves. Copyright © 1981 Cleveland Press Publishing Company and Coretta Scott King.

Arthur J. Kropp. "Let's Put an End to Mediocre Textbooks" from the *Houston Post*, May 2, 1987.

Lynette M. Lamb. "Censorship in Publishing" by Lynette Lamb from *Utne Reader* Jan/Feb 1988, 17–18. Reprinted with permission of *Utne Reader* magazine.

Ann Landers. Column which appeared in the *Los Angeles Times*. Reprinted with permission of Ann Landers and Los Angeles Times Syndicate.

Ken Lonnquist. "Ghosts" from *The Art of Public Speaking* by Stephen E. Lucas. Copyright 1983 by Random House.

Stephen E. Lucas. *The Art of Public Speaking*. Copyright 1983 by Random House.

Joyce Maynard. "His Talk, Her Talk" by Joyce Maynard. Copyright © 1985 by Joyce Maynard. Used by permission.

Phyllis McGinley. "Reflections Dental," *Times Three* by Phyllis McGinley. Copyright 1941 by Phyllis McGinley. Copyright renewed © 1969 by Julie Elizabeth Hayden and Phyllis Hayden Blake. All rights reserved. Reprinted by permission of Viking Penguin Inc.

Nickie McWhirter. "What You Do Is What You Are" from the *San Jose Mercury News*, March 8, 1982.

H. Bruce Miller. "Severing the Human Connection" by H. Bruce Miller from the *San Jose Mercury News*, August 4, 1981. Reprinted with permission from the *San Jose Mercury News*.

Barbara Mujica. "Bilingualism's Goal" by Barbara Mujica from the *New York Times*, February 26, 1984. Copyright © 1984 by the New York Times Company. Reprinted by permission.

Steven O'Brien. "One Son, Three Fathers" by Steven O'Brien from the *New York Times*, December 28, 1986. Copyright © 1986 by the New York Times Company. Reprinted by permission.

Roger von Oech. From *A Whack on the Side of the Head* by Roger von Oech, pp. 88–94. Copyright © 1983 by Roger von Oech. Reprinted by permission of Warner Books/New York.

Jay Olgilvy, Eric Utne, and Brad Edmondson. "What Makes a Baby Boomer?" from *Utne Magazine* May/June 1987, pp. 122–128. Reprinted with permission of *Utne Reader* Magazine.

Rosa Parks. "A Long Way to Go" by Rosa Parks from the *Los Angeles Times*, June 29, 1986. Reprinted by permission of the author.

Robert Pirsig. Excerpt from *Zen and the Art of Motorcycle Maintenance* by Robert Pirsig. Copyright © 1974 by Robert M. Pirsig. By permission of William Morrow and Company, Inc.

Maxine Phillips. "Needed: A Policy for Children When Parents Go to Work" from the *Los Angeles Times*, December 6, 1987. Reprinted by permission of Maxine Phillips, managing editor of *Dissent* magazine.

Letty Cottin Pogrebin. "Superstitious Minds" by Letty Cottin Pogrebin from *Ms.* magazine, February 1988. Reprinted by permission of the author, © 1988 by Letty Cottin Pogrebin.

Gary Provost. "The 8 Essentials of Nonfiction that Sells" from *Writer's Digest*, March 1988.

Murio Puzo. "Choosing a Dream: Italians in Hell's Kitchen" by Mario Puzo from *The Immigrant Experience* edited by Thomas Wheeler. Copyright © 1971 by Dial Press. Reprinted by permission of Doubleday, a division of Bantam, Doubleday, Dell Publishing Group, Inc.

Richard Reeves. "America Isn't Falling Apart" in *Richard Reeves* by Richard Reeves. Copyright 1987 Universal Press Syndicate. Reprinted with permission. All rights reserved.

Caryl Rivers. "The Issue Isn't Sex, It's Violence" by Caryl Rivers from the *Boston Globe*. Reprinted by permission of the author.

Albert Robbins. "Settling in the Cities" by Albert Robbins from *Coming to America*. Reprinted by permission of Visual Education Corporation.

Diana Robinson. "Recharging Yourself Through Meditation" from *The People's Almanac*. Copyright 1975 by Doubleday.

Richard Rodriquez. "Workers" from *Hunger of Memory* by Richard Rodriquez. Copyright 1981 by Richard Rodriquez. Reprinted by permission of David R. Godine, Publisher.

Theodore Roethke. "My Papa's Waltz" by Theodore Roethke. Copyright 1942 by Hearst Magazines, Inc. From *The Collected Poems of Theodore Roethke*. Reprinted by permission of Doubleday, a division of Bantam, Doubleday, Dell Publishing Group, Inc.

Mike Royko. "Death to the Killers" from *Chicago Sun Times*.

Vincent R. Ruggiero. From *The Art of Thinking* by Vincent R. Ruggiero. Copyright © 1984 by Harper & Row, Publishers, Inc. Reprinted by permission of the publisher.

William Shannon. "Shield Our Youth with Censorship" from the *Santa Barbara News-Press*, June 5, 1987.

Jean Shepherd. Excerpts from "The Endless Streetcar Ride into the Night" from *In God We Trust: All Others Pay Cash* by Jean Shepherd. Reprinted by permission of Doubleday, a division of Bantam, Doubleday, Dell Publishing Group, Inc.

Debra Sikes and Barbara Murray. "The Practicality of the Liberal Arts Major" by Debra Sikes and Barbara Murray. Reprinted by permission: Innovation Abstracts, Vol. IX, No. 8; Austin, Texas: The University of Texas and the National Institute for Staff and Organizational Development (NISOD).

Bonnie Smith-Yackel. "My Mother Never Worked" from *Women: A Journal of Liberation*, 1975.

Kirby W. Stanat. "How to Take a Job Interview" by Kirby W. Stanat from *Job Hunting Secrets and Tactics*, Raintree Publishers.

Brent Staples. "Night Walker" by Brent Staples from *Los Angeles Times Magazine*, December 7, 1986. Reprinted by permission of Brent Staples, Assistant Metropolitan Editor of the *New York Times*.

Ben Stein. "The Media's Regrettable Imitation of the *National Enquirer*" by Ben Stein from *Los Angeles Herald Examiner*, October 20, 1987. Reprinted by permission of the author.

James Thurber. "The Unicorn in the Garden" by James Thurber. Copyright © 1940 James Thurber. Copyright © 1968 Helen Thurber. From *Fables For Our Time*, published by Harper & Row.

Luis R. Torres. "Los Chinos Discover el Barrio" by Luis R. Torres from *Los Angeles Times*, November 14, 1987. Reprinted by permission of Luis R. Torres, journalist and associate professor of Journalism at California State University, Los Angeles.

Stanley N. Wellborn. "Birth" from *U.S. News & World Report*, November 11, 1985.

Sharon Whitley. "Students' Love Affair With Anne Frank" by Sharon Whitley from the *Los Angeles Times*, December 1, 1985. Reprinted by permission of the author.

David Whitman. "Trouble for America's 'Model' Minority" Copyright 1987, *U.S. News & World Report*. Reprinted from issue of Feb. 23, 1987.

Walt Whitman. "When I Heard the Learn'd Astronomer" from the *Heath Introduction to Poetry*, Third Edition. Copyright 1988 by D. C. Heath and Company.

Betty Anne Younglove. "The American Dream" from *U.S. News & World Report*, December 8, 1986. Reprinted by permission of the author.

To The Instructor

Viewpoints: Readings Worth Thinking and Writing About is a thematic collection of readings that have been used successfully with developmental students to stimulate ideas for discussions and their own compositions. None of the readings is very long; most are essays, but a few poems and stories appear.

The premise of this collection is that students who have difficulty writing compositions usually have not or do not read much beyond their assigned textbooks. To provide them merely with grammar drills is not enough. They need to know what to look for when they read; they need to understand what an essay is and how it is constructed; they need to be shown the relationship of reading and writing skills; they need to be exposed to various writing styles; they need to experience the range of emotions that good writing can convey; and they need to see how writers work and how that knowledge can work for them. But most importantly, they need to be introduced to and provoked by the world of ideas in readings that can stimulate their own thinking.

To reach these objectives, the text is divided into two parts. Part I, **Viewpoints on Reading and Writing Essays** gives an overview of the required skills for good reading and writing. Unit 1 on reading skills explains the basic essay structure, thesis, and arrangement of support. To aid reading comprehension, it shows how to separate main ideas from supporting details, how to distinguish fact from opinion, and how to draw inferences. It also provides methods for marking and notetaking while reading, along with suggestions for keeping a reading journal.

Unit 2 on writing skills covers the three basic stages of writing: prewriting, drafting, and revising. However, while students become familiar with these stages, they are reminded that writing is not a linear, step-by-step experience but rather a recursive one, with all stages occurring and recurring throughout the writing process.

Making a writing assignment one's own, finding and developing a working thesis, arranging supporting evidence, and revising and editing tasks are all explained. The writing section draws heavily upon the information in the reading section to reflect the reading-writing connection. Rhetorical patterns are explained as aids to both reading comprehension and writing.

Both units provide models and illustrations to make clear the concepts presented. Students are periodically required to interact with the text through various reinforcement activities. After every major concept is presented, a short **writing assignment** is given that can be collected or used as the basis for a journal entry.

Part II, **Readings Worth Thinking and Writing About** contains eight thematically organized reading units. These units present a collection of perspectives on learning, human behavior, cultural heritage, changing social values, family and relationships, work, the media, and controversial issues. The unit on controversial issues presents pro and con arguments on bilingual education, the death penalty, and handgun control. The viewpoints in all units are deliberately diverse and are intended to stimulate thinking as well as to inform. Attention has been given to include in these reading selections subjects that appeal to students of various ethnic backgrounds. Many of the reading selections have not been anthologized before, but all have been selected with a developmental student audience in mind. The selections provide a wide range of styles, from formal to informal, from narrative to documented pieces. Readability levels for each selection can be found in the **Instructor's Guide.** While an effort was made to select relatively short readings at a level appropriate for developmental students, some essays will be more difficult to read than others. But if students are to develop their reading and writing skills, they must be provided with both readings and assignments that will challenge them to rise above their present level. Rather than avoid what seems to be difficult reading, students need to be shown how to approach such material, a goal of this text.

Each essay is preceded by two or three questions to engage the reader's thoughts on the selection's content, as well as a list of vocabulary words and their definitions. Following each selection are four sets of activities: **Understanding the Content, Looking at Structure and Style, Evaluating the Author's Viewpoints,** and **Pursuing Possible Essay Topics.** The questions and suggestions in these four categories draw upon the information provided in Part I. The last essay in each unit is a **student essay** written in response to the theme of that particular unit and is followed by a brief critical commentary. In some cases, flawed student essays are used in order to illustrate both the problem and the correct revision approach needed.

As with the readings, the questions and suggestions for essays reflect a graduated range of difficulty in order to provide for and to challenge the diversity of ability usually found in developmental writing classes.

The Appendix contains information on the final essay form, some possible research sources for those students interested or required to read beyond this text, and a brief section on citing and documenting sources that follows the *Modern Language Association Handbook for Writers of Research Papers*. For those who prefer the rhetorical approach to the teaching of writing, an alternate rhetorical table of contents is provided.

Appreciation is extended to those reviewers who provided guidance and help during the various developmental stages of this text: Domenick Caruso, Kingsborough Community College; Robert Cosgrove, Saddleback College; Ian Cruickshank, St. Louis Community College—Florissant Valley; Kitty Dean Chen, Nassau Community College; Kathryn Fitzgerald, University of Utah; Eric P. Hibbison, J. Sargent Reynolds Community College; Myra J. Linden, Joliet Junior College; and Robert E. Yarber, San Diego Mesa College. In addition, my thanks go to Paul Smith, whose faith, support, and guidance in this project helped me keep balance. Finally, a special word of appreciation and recognition goes to Karen Potischman. Her editorial expertise and diligence go unequalled when compared with other editors with whom I've worked.

Contents

PART II
READINGS WORTH THINKING AND WRITING ABOUT

Rhetorical Table of Contents

Reading selections containing examples of several rhetorical modes appear under more than one category.

VIEWPOINTS

Readings Worth Thinking and Writing About

INSTRUCTOR'S EDITION

PART I

VIEWPOINTS ON READING AND WRITING ESSAYS

Viewpoints on Reading Essays

Take Time To Read... Together

"Reading is to the mind what exercise is to the body."
Joseph Addison

*T*HERE are a few poems and short stories in Part II, but most of the reading selections are essays. As a serious student, you will want to use the readings not only to provide ideas for essays of your own, but also to further your reading ability. This section shows you what to look for when you read essays and how to look more closely at the ways writers express their opinions, feelings, and experiences. As your reading improves, so will your writing.

The Structure of an Essay

A well-structured essay usually contains three basic ingredients: a thesis, sufficient support for the thesis, and a logical arrangement of that support.

Thesis

Every good essay has a **thesis,** which is the main idea or point an author wants to make about his or her topic. The **topic** of an essay is a broad or general subject, such as teenage drinking. A thesis, on the other hand, is the point the author wants to make about the subject of teenage drinking. A thesis might be "Teenagers should be allowed to drink when they reach age 19" or "Teenagers should not be allowed to drink." In other words, a thesis is what the author thinks or feels about the subject of the essay. It's the purpose for writing, the main point around which everything else is written. If you fail to recognize an author's thesis, you may miss the whole point of the essay.

To help clarify the difference between a topic and a thesis, look at the examples below. Notice that topics are broad, general categories, whereas thesis statements are more specific.

Topics	*Possible thesis statements*
Little League sports	Little League sports can be harmful to a child's sense of sportsmanship.
	The best years of my life were spent playing Little League baseball.
	The Little League soccer coach has a varied background in professional sports.
word processing	All college freshmen should be required to take a word processing course.
	Word processing may be helpful to some but not to me.
	Before buying a word processing program, consider the functions needed, the cost, and the manufacturer's support.
nuclear disarmament	It is too late to worry about nuclear disarmament.
	Everyone should be required to read Jonathan Schell's book on nuclear disarmament, *The Fate of the Earth*.
	Nuclear disarmament would open us up to World War III.

Notice that in each case the thesis statement is a viewpoint about the subject or topic. The thesis deals with a narrower view of the broader subject and makes the author's position clear. You may not agree with the viewpoint, but if the essay is well written, it will support the author's opinion in an effort to convince the reader. A key element in reading, then, is to make certain you understand an author's thesis or viewpoint on the subject of the essay.

Below are some thesis statements. Separate the topic from the writer's viewpoint. In the space provided, write a one-sentence statement that explains the topic and the point being made about it.

1. A college education may be important, but its value is overemphasized by many employers.

2. We humans have many strange and contradictory behaviors.

3. Our society seems afraid or ashamed of growing old and places too much emphasis on youth.

4. Most of the visuals shown on MTV distract from the music.

Compare the content of your sentences with the following chart.

Topic	*Viewpoint expressed*
1. college education	value overemphasized by employers
2. human behavior	strange and contradictory
3. aging, growing old	ashamed/afraid of aging, too much value placed on youth
4. MTV	visuals distract from music

Thesis statements are usually clearly stated within the essay; often you can find a sentence or two that directly states the author's views. Other times there is no one sentence you can point to that states the thesis, but the author's viewpoint becomes clear once you have read the supporting evidence. In those cases, it's necessary to form the author's thesis in your own words.

Supporting evidence

Once a writer has his or her thesis in mind, the next step is to provide **supporting evidence.** If a thesis is controversial, such as whether Little League sports are harmful in some way, then the writer must provide evidence that will at least cause someone who disagrees to look at Little League sports from a new angle. As a reader, you need to look for the reasons given to support the thesis. You may still disagree with the author when you have finished reading, but you will understand why the author feels as he or she does.

Of course, you have to be careful that your own feelings on the subject don't cause you to reject or accept the author's viewpoints without thinking carefully about the evidence presented. Say you coach a Little League team. Because of your own involvement, you immediately resent or reject the thesis that Little League is harmful. Your own bias or prejudice (feelings that keep you from seeing another view) could cause you to miss some valid points that you had never considered before, points that might make you a better coach. It's important to keep an open mind as you read supporting evidence.

In essays, support is given in the form of paragraphs. A paragraph is in some ways similar to a mini-essay. Just as every essay has an implied or stated thesis, a well-written paragraph has an implied or stated **topic sentence.** A topic sentence states the key point or idea of the paragraph. The rest of the sentences support it, just as paragraphs support a thesis.

Good writers use a variety of paragraph types to support their thesis statements. These types are sometimes called **rhetorical modes** or **patterns.** Because humans think in certain basic ways, we can sometimes communicate better with one another if we use these thinking patterns in our writing. Eight common patterns are presented here.

Description is a common writing pattern. This method is used when authors want to reach one or all of our five senses: sight, sound, smell, touch, and taste. See if you can visualize what's being described in this paragraph:

> Whack! A police baton slaps his legs and a voice booms, "Get the hell up, you're outta here. Right now!" Another police officer whacks his nightstick against a metal grating as the twelve men sprawled along the tunnel crawl to their feet. Red pulls himself up and walks slowly up the stairs to the street, never looking back.
>
> Jon D. Hull, "Slow Descent into Hell"

Even though there is no stated topic sentence in the paragraph, it is not difficult for us to understand the point the author wants to make about Red's situation. The author forces us to *hear* the whacks of the police nightstick, to *hear* the roughness and lack of concern in the voice yelling at the twelve men, to *see* Red and the men "crawl to their feet." Their slow movement up the stairs with no comment to the police implies that this event and this treatment are nothing new to Red and the others. The author makes us *feel* what it's like to be one of the homeless. No topic sentence could say what the description itself reveals. The author relies on our reactions to his description to imply (suggest or hint at) his message.

Another paragraph pattern frequently used by writers is **narration.** A paragraph using narration moves from one occurrence to another, generally in chronological order. Narration is often used when authors want to tell a story or relate an anecdote about something that has happened in their lives. Here is an example:

> I was saved from sin when I was going on thirteen. But not really saved. It happened like this. There was a big revival at my Auntie Reed's church. Every night for weeks there had been much preaching, singing, praying, and shouting, and some very hardened sinners had been brought to Christ, and the membership of the church had grown by leaps and bounds. Then just before the revival ended, they held a special meeting for children, "to bring the young lambs into the fold." . . . That night I was escorted to the front row and placed on the mourners' bench with all the other young sinners. . . .
>
> Langston Hughes, "Salvation"

Here the author uses first-person narration, which means that he tells us his story from his own point of view. He takes us back to his thirteenth year and then proceeds to narrate for us the story of how he was saved, "but not really." As readers we can expect the rest of the story to be told in a chronological fashion, moving from one incident to the next. We might say that the topic sentence is the first one, but to be more accurate the main idea of the paragraph is a combination of the first three sentences.

Still another paragraph pattern is **analysis.** An author may wish to take a subject and examine its parts. For instance, a writer could analyze a poem by looking at the way it is structured, examining the number of lines and stanzas, the rhyme scheme, or the reasons behind the use of certain words. Another author may wish to show how a rotary engine works, which would be called a **process analysis,** a step-by-step explanation of the way the engine works. A paragraph based on an analysis pattern reads like this:

> Let us move in for a closer look at how the campus recruiter operates. Let's say you have a 10 o'clock appointment with the recruiter from the XYZ Corporation. The recruiter gets rid of the candidate in front of you at about 5 minutes to 10, jots down a few notes about what he is going to do with him or her, then picks up your résumé or data sheet (which you have submitted in advance). . . . Although the recruiter is still in the interview room and you are still in the lobby, your interview is under way. You're on. The recruiter will look over your sheet pretty carefully before he goes out to call you. He develops a mental picture of you.
>
> Kirby W. Stanat, "How to Take a Job Interview"

The topic sentence in this paragraph is the first one and the subject is how a job interview works. The paragraph begins analyzing or examining the process. As a reader, we can expect each of the following paragraphs in the essay to continue explaining each part of the job interview process.

Another rhetorical method is the use of **illustration and example.** You probably use this method when you talk. If you are explaining something to someone who doesn't quite understand, you might say, "For instance, . . ." and then proceed to give an example or two to clarify what you mean. The same technique is used in writing. Here is a paragraph that uses the illustration and example pattern:

> Dr. Wayne Dyer, in his book *Your Erroneous Zones,* claims that we have grown up in a culture which has taught us that we are not responsible for our feelings even though the truth is that we always were. He claims we have learned a "host of sayings" to defend ourselves against the fact that we control our feelings. For example, here are some of the utterances that we use over and over to take the blame off ourselves and place it on others:
> "You hurt my feelings."
> "You make me feel bad."
> "I can't help the way I feel."
> "He makes me sick."
> "You're embarrassing me."
> "You made me look foolish."

Dyer feels that each of these sayings has a built in message that we are not responsible for how we feel, when in fact we are in charge of how we feel.

As is often the case, the topic sentence for the paragraph is the first one. Notice that the main point is to summarize for us what Dr. Wayne Dyer says in his book *Your Erroneous Zones* about growing up in our culture to think that we are not responsible for our feelings. As a reader, it's important to distinguish between what an author is saying and what someone being written about is saying. The author of the paragraph selects examples of sayings Dyer believes we use so frequently that we begin to believe others are responsible for how we feel when, according to Dyer, we are actually in charge. The examples are used to support Dyer's views. These are not the views of the paragraph writer. In fact, we don't know what the author thinks about Dyer's views.

Notice that the **transitional phrase** "for example" alerts us to what is coming. Transitional expressions such as *for instance, also, likewise, in addition, furthermore,* and *more than that* alert us that more examples of the same idea are about to be presented. Words such as *but, however, although,* and *rather* should make us aware that a point is about to be modified or contrasted. When we read *consequently, so, therefore, in conclusion, thus,* or *as a result,* we know that we are about to get a summary or the conclusion of a point. An author's use of transitional words is of great help when we read. Remember to use them in your own writing.

Before learning about any more paragraph patterns, read the paragraphs below. Underline the topic sentence of each, and then in the spaces provided write the paragraph pattern being used and its purpose. Some paragraphs may use more than one pattern.

1.   I looked around the room, and my heart sank. Cobwebs dangled from the ceiling; the once whitewashed walls were yellow with age and streaked with dust. The single naked bulb was coated with grime and extremely dim. Patches of the cement floor were black with dampness. A strong musty smell pervaded the air. I hastened to open the only small window with its rust-pitted iron bars. When I succeeded in pulling the knob and the window swung open, flakes of peeling paint as well as a shower of dust fell to the floor. The only furniture in the room was three narrow beds of rough wooden planks, one against the wall, the other two stacked one on top of the other. A cement toilet was built into one corner.

Nien Cheng, *Life and Death in Shanghai*

pattern used: _____

purpose: _____

2.   Americans, unlike people almost everywhere else in the world, tend to define and judge everybody in terms of the work they do, especially work performed for pay. Charlie is a doctor; Sam is a carpenter; Mary Ellen is a copywriter at a small ad agency. . . .

Nickie McWhirter, "What You Do Is What You Are"

pattern used: _____

purpose: _____

3.   It was at Stanford, one day near the end of my senior year, that a friend told me about a summer construction job he knew was available. I was quickly alert. Desire uncoiled within me. My friend said that he knew I had been looking for summer employment. He knew I needed some money. Almost apologetically he explained: It was something I probably wouldn't be interested in, but a friend of his, a contractor, needed someone for the summer to do menial jobs. There would be lots of shoveling and raking and sweeping. Nothing too hard. But nothing more interesting either. Still, the pay would be good. Did I want it? . . . I did. Yes, I said, surprised to hear myself say it.

Richard Rodriquez, "Workers"

pattern used: _____

purpose: _____

4.   Grasp the cone with the right hand firmly but gently between the thumb and at least one but not more than three fingers, two-thirds of the way up the cone. Then dart swiftly away to an open area, away from the jostling crowd at the stand. Now take up the classic ice-cream-cone-eating stance: feet from one to two feet apart, body bent forward from the waist at a twenty-five-degree angle, right elbow well up, right forearm horizontal, at a level with your collarbone and about twelve inches from it. But don't start eating yet! Check first to see what emergency repairs may be necessary. Sometimes a sugar cone will be so crushed or broken or cracked that all

one can do is gulp at the thing like a savage, getting what he can of it and letting the rest drop to the ground, and then evacuating the area of catastrophe as quickly as possible. . . .

L. Rust Hills, "How to Eat an Ice Cream Cone"

pattern used: _____

purpose: _____

The first paragraph primarily uses description, but it is told through first-person narration. The topic sentence is the first one, with the rest of the paragraph describing why her heart sank. The purpose of the paragraph is to describe the room. Paragraph 2 uses examples to support the topic sentence, which is the first one. The purpose is to show that Americans judge people by the work they do. The third paragraph uses first-person narration with the purpose of telling us about a summer job he accepted. It is difficult to point to any clearly stated topic sentence, but if there is one, it's the first one. The last paragraph uses analysis. Its purpose is to show us the step-by-step process of eating an ice cream cone. Description is also used to help explain the process. There is no stated topic sentence. Make certain you understand these patterns before going on.

Another paragraph pattern often used by writers is **definition.** This pattern is used to clarify words and terms by providing more explanation than a dictionary, or to explain the writer's interpretation of something.

First, let us get this [American] dream business—and business it now seems to be—straight. The word *dream* is not a synonym for *reality* or *promise*. It is closer to *hope* or *possibility* or even *vision*. The original American dream had only a little to do with material possessions and a lot to do with choices, beginnings and opportunity. . . .

Betty Anne Younglove, "The American Dream"

Here the author is defining the term *American dream* as she sees it. By comparing and contrasting, she defines what it is and is not, implying that there is a new, incorrect definition that has more to do with materialism than its true original meaning.

You will also frequently see a pattern that **divides and classifies** a subject under discussion. Classification is used to divide a subject into groups or parts on the basis of similarities. In the following paragraph, notice how the author divides and classifies "baby boomers," a term applied to those born between 1946 and 1964.

Understandably, the younger half of the baby boom is much more concerned with finances. Since 1967, UCLA has asked incoming students why they want to go to college; among the choices provided are "to become well off financially," or "to gain a meaningful life philosophy." In 1967, as the oldest boomers were entering college, nearly 85 percent said they were going to school for philosophical reasons, and less than half went to school to get rich. By 1985, as the youngest boomers were entering school, three-fourths said, "give me the money." Only 44 percent said they wanted a meaningful life philosophy.

Jay Olgilvy, et al., "What's a Baby Boomer?"

The topic sentence, the first one, states that the younger half of the baby boom generation is more concerned with finances. The rest of the paragraph divides the baby boom generation into older and younger groups. It then classifies the younger half as more interested in finances and the older half as more interested in a life philosophy. Support is provided through the UCLA questionnaire.

Comparing and contrasting items is another paragraph pattern that appears frequently in writing. An author uses this pattern to show similarities (comparison) and differences (contrast) in the subjects under discussion. For instance:

Bees get together and build hives, termites build mounds, beavers build dams, and spiders spin webs, but what other animal can change stone and glass into poetry? Other animals can alter their environment at the margins, but only we can set goals for ourselves and then pursue them. . . .

Phil Donahue, "Beauty and the Beast"

Here a comparison and contrast, mostly contrast, is made between what animals and humans can do. Notice the use of the word *but* to show contrast. Key transitional words often used to show comparisons are *similarly, likewise, compared with, both* _____ *and* _____, and *in the same way.* The words *although, however, but, on the other hand, instead of, different from,* and *as opposed to* are used to indicate contrast.

The last pattern we will discuss is that of **cause and effect.** A cause-effect paragraph explains why something happens or happened. Some key words that serve as clues in such paragraphs are *because of this, for this reason, as a result,* or *resulting in.* Sometimes the effects are presented first and the cause of the effects last; other times it is the other way around.

See if you can distinguish between the cause and the effect in the following paragraph:

> Television commercials brought a lot of fun and fun-loving folks into the picture. Everything that people in those commercials did looked like fun: taking Polaroid snapshots, swilling beer, buying insurance, mopping the floor, bowling, taking aspirin. We all wished, I'm sure, that we could have half as much fun as those rough-and-ready guys around the locker room, flicking each other with towels and pouring champagne. The more commercials people watched, the more they wondered when the fun would start in their own lives.
>
> Suzanne Britt Jordan, "Fun. Oh, Boy. Fun. You Could Die
from It."

The cause here is watching fun-loving folks in television commercials. The effect is that they made everything look like fun, causing still another effect: people wondered when they would begin having fun.

To make certain you can recognize the writing patterns you just learned about, read the paragraphs below. Underline the topic sentence of each, and then in the spaces provided write the paragraph pattern being used and its purpose. Some paragraphs may use more than one pattern.

1. If you're within a few miles of a nuclear detonation, you'll be incinerated on the spot! And if you survive the blast what does the future promise? The silent but deadly radiation, either directly or from fallout, in a dose of 400 rems could kill you within two weeks. Your hair would fall out, your skin would be covered with large ulcers, you would vomit and experience diarrhea and you would die from infection or massive bleeding as your white blood cells and platelets stopped working.

   Ken Keyes, Jr., *The Hundredth Monkey*

pattern used: _____

purpose: _____

2. An inference is a statement *about* the known made on the basis of what *is* known. In other words, an inference is an educated guess. If a woman smiles when a man tells her she is attractive, he can infer she is pleased. If she frowns and slaps him, he can guess she is not pleased. His inferences are

based on what is known: people generally smile when they are pleased and frown when displeased. However, to know for certain why she slapped him, we would have to ask her.

pattern used: _____

purpose: _____

3.   What do L.A. [Los Angeles] women want? According to the poll, their top two goals in life are having a happy marriage, named by 37%, and helping others, 21%. Those are followed by career and a desire to be creative. Power and fame rank low on the list, with 1% each. But among women who've never been married, career takes top priority, followed by marriage and helping others. Four percent chose fame. A happy marriage appears to be the least popular goal in the Valley and Southeast areas, where it was chosen by 46% of the women—about double the number on the Westside.

Cathleen Decker, "The L.A. Woman"

pattern used: _____

purpose: _____

4.   Every paragraph you write should include one sentence that's supported by everything else in that paragraph. That is the topic sentence. It can be the first sentence, the last sentence, the sixth sentence, or even a sentence that exists only in your mind. When testing your article for topic sentences, you should be able to look at each paragraph and say what the topic sentence is. Having said it, look at all the other sentences in the paragraph and test them to make sure they support it.

Gary Provost, "The 8 Essentials of Nonfiction that Sells"

pattern used: _____

purpose: _____

5.   A trend that began about 10 years ago in Lincoln Heights seems to have hit a critical point now. It's similar to the ethnic tug-of-war of yesteryear, but different colors, different words are involved. Today Chinese and Vietnamese are displacing the Latinos who, by choice or circumstance, had Lincoln

Heights virtually to themselves for two solid generations. . . . The bank where I opened my first meager savings
account in the late 1950s has changed hands. It's now the
East-West Federal Bank, an Asian-owned enterprise. The public library on Workman Street, where I checked out *Charlotte's
Web* with my first library card, abounds with signs of the new
times: It's called "La Biblioteca del Pueblo Heights," and on
the door there's a notice that the building is closed because
of the Oct. 1 earthquake; it's written in Chinese.

Luis Torres, "Los Chinos Discover El Barrio"

pattern used: _____

purpose: _____

Compare your responses to the paragraphs with these:

1. The topic sentence is the third one. The basic pattern is cause
   and effect, with description of the effects of the blast provided.
   The cause is the nuclear bomb and the effect is death. The purpose
   is to show that you will die from radiation even if the initial blast
   doesn't kill you.

2. The first sentence is the topic sentence. The pattern is definition,
   with the example of the man and woman used to clarify the
   definition. The purpose is to define *inference*.

3. There really isn't a topic sentence. The implied topic sentence is
   an answer to the question that begins the paragraph, such as
   "Here is the result of the polls showing what L.A. women want."
   To show us what they want, the author uses the classification
   "L.A. women" and divides or groups them according to poll per-
   centages. She further groups the women by areas: the Valley, the
   Southeast, and the Westside. The purpose is to reveal what L.A.
   women want, according to the polls.

4. The first sentence is the topic sentence. The author uses both
   definition and process analysis. He defines what a topic sentence
   is and its position in the paragraph. Then he shows how to test
   for an implied or directly stated topic sentence in each paragraph.
   The purpose is to stress the importance of the topic sentence in
   writing.

5. The topic sentence is the third one. The rest of the sentences
   contrast the differences in Lincoln Heights from the time he lived
   there to now. Examples such as the library and the bank are used

to show the contrast. The purpose is to show that what once was a Latino neighborhood is now being shared by Asians.

Make certain you understand what a topic sentence is and can recognize all eight paragraph patterns before reading on.

Order of Support

The third ingredient of a well-structured essay, in addition to thesis and supporting evidence, is the **order** (or **arrangement**) **of the thesis and its supporting evidence.** A good writer will arrange the supporting points for the thesis in a logical, progressive order. What you, the reader, see is the final product of the writer. What you do not see are all the different writing drafts the author went through in deciding which supporting point should go where or which paragraph method of development works best.

Most essays follow a basic order similar to the diagram below. While not every essay fits this pattern, it represents the traditional order or arrangement of an essay's structure.

Introductory Paragraph

- attempts to draw the reader's interest.
- usually states or hints at the subject.
- sometimes states or hints at the thesis.

Paragraph 2

- usually builds on or continues what was said in the introductory paragraph.
- sometimes contains the thesis if it's not in the introductory paragraph.
- uses varying methods of development depending on what point is being made.

Paragraph 3

- is connected to paragraph 2 by a transition.
- provides more support of the thesis.
- uses varying methods of development depending on what works best to clarify supporting point.

> *Paragraph 4* (plus more paragraphs if needed)
> - starts with a transition from paragraph 3 to 4
> - provides more support of thesis.
> - uses varying methods of development depending on what best clarifies the point.

> *Concluding Paragraph*
> - summarizes points made or draws a conclusion based on the points provided.
> - leaves the reader thinking about or reacting to the thesis.

The diagram above represents the basic structure of an essay. Longer essays will, of course, contain more paragraphs. Sometimes an author writes two or three paragraphs of introduction. There may be a dozen supporting paragraphs, and the conclusion may take more than one paragraph. Sometimes an author's thesis may not be clear until the last paragraph. The typical essay form, however, is much the way it is outlined above.

Before Going On

You have learned that three basic ingredients make up a good essay: a thesis, sufficient support of the thesis, and a logical order or **arrangement** of the supporting material. Good reading comprehension depends upon being able to identify an author's thesis based on the support that is provided. You have also learned eight different paragraph patterns or rhetorical modes that writers use to express their views: description, narration, analysis, illustration and example, definition, classification and division, comparison and contrast, and cause-effect relationships. Topic sentences are supported through the use of these patterns. In addition, you have learned the basic structure most essays follow to support the thesis. Applying this knowledge can enhance both your reading and writing skills.

Writing Exercise

On a separate sheet of paper, write a one-paragraph summary of the three basic elements found in a well-structured essay. Make certain you have a topic sentence to support. Your instructor may want to see it.

Understanding the Content

Let's look now at the skills needed to better understand what you read. To get the most from your reading, you need to be able to separate main ideas from supporting details, to distinguish fact from opinion and bias, and to draw inferences from implied statements. As you read, all of these skills work together, but for clarification purposes we'll look at each skill separately.

Separating Main Ideas from Supporting Details

The main idea in an essay is the thesis, which we've already discussed on pages 5–7. As you've seen, each paragraph in an essay supports that main idea. You've also learned that each paragraph is, in a way, a mini-essay. Paragraphs, too, have a main idea, expressed through the topic sentence and supported by the rest of the sentences.

Read the following paragraph and underline what you think is the main idea. Determine what paragraph pattern is used.

> There are almost as many definitions of meditation as there are people meditating. It has been described as a fourth state of consciousness (neither waking, sleeping, nor dreaming); as a way to recharge one's inner batteries; as a state of passive awareness, of "no mind." Some teachers regard meditation as the complement to prayer: "Prayer is when you talk to God; meditation is when you listen to God." Some say meditation teaches the conscious mind to be still.
>
> Diana Robinson, "Recharging Yourself Through Meditation"

The point of the paragraph is to show that there are many definitions of meditation. Each of the supporting sentences provides an example of a different definition of meditation to show just how varied they are. An outline of the paragraph might look like this:

Main idea: "There are as many definitions of meditation as there are people meditating."

Support: one definition: fourth state of consciousness (neither waking, sleeping, nor dreaming)

Support: second definition: recharging one's batteries

Support: third definition: state of passive awareness, no mind

Support: fourth definition: complement to prayer

Support: fifth definition: teaches mind to be still

What we see are five different definitions that support the statement made in the first sentence. The first sentence, then, is the topic sentence.

Looking for the main idea in the first sentence of a paragraph is a good place to begin, but as you've already seen, it doesn't always appear there. Read and then underline the main idea in the following paragraph:

> In one year, about $3.5 billion is spent for television commercial time. Where does all this money come from, and where does it go? Suppose Ford Motor Company buys $1 million worth of air time from NBC to introduce its new models in the fall. First it hires an advertising agency to actually produce the commercials. Of the $1 million, 15% goes to the agency for its services, and 85% goes to the network. The network in turn uses some of its 85% to pay program costs and some to pay local stations who broadcast the shows on which Ford commercials are carried. This latter payment usually equals about one-third of the local station's base rate (the amount a station would receive for commercial time bought by a local advertiser).

In the above paragraph, the first sentence is not the main idea. Most of the paragraph provides an example of what would happen to one million dollars spent by the Ford Motor Company on television advertising. The example is used to provide a breakdown of where the money spent on television advertising comes from and where it goes, providing an answer to the question in the second sentence of the paragraph: "Where does all this money [$3.5 billion spent on TV advertising] come from, and where does it go?" In a way, then, the main idea is really a combination of the first two sentences of the paragraph. An outline of the paragraph might look something like this:

Main idea: Here's an example of where the $3.5 billion a year spent on advertising comes from and where it goes.

Support: If Ford Motor Company spent $1 million on TV ads:

    1. 15% would go to an advertising agency

    2. 85% would go to the network, which would pay

       a. program costs

> b. local stations that broadcast the shows on which ads appear (about one-third of the local station's base advertising rate)

In this paragraph, then, there is no one topic sentence expressing the main idea, but by combining the first two sentences, we can form a topic sentence of our own.

Here is another paragraph. Underline what you think is the main idea.

> The Upjohn Company is studying anti-cholesterol therapy that would actually reverse some coronary artery injury. They are also doing some exciting research in combating hypertension. In addition, they are working on important advances against deadly heart arrhythmias, or irregular heartbeat rhythms, plus a new way to zero in on blood clots with fewer side effects. These are just a few of the research projects against heart disease that Upjohn is working on.

The main idea in the paragraph is the last sentence. It sums up the purpose of each of the other sentences—to provide examples of the research projects Upjohn is working on in the area of heart disease. An outline of the paragraph might look like this:

Main idea: Here are a few examples of Upjohn's research projects against heart disease.

Support: anti-cholesterol therapy to reverse coronary artery injury

Support: ways to combat hypertension

Support: advances against heartbeat irregularities (arrhythmias)

Support: ways to treat blood clots with fewer side effects

Thus, we see that it doesn't matter where a topic sentence is placed; it will always contain the main idea of the paragraph.

When you have difficulty separating main ideas from the details of a paragraph, you may need to stop and outline the passage that is giving you trouble. Remember that reading entails a combination of skills, only one of which is separating main ideas from supporting details. But finding the main idea, whether in a paragraph or an essay, is crucial to good comprehension.

Separating Fact from Opinion

Once you have identified the main ideas from supporting details, you need to separate facts from opinions. A **fact** is usually defined as something that can be proven. We accept something as a fact only when many different people come to the same conclusion after years of observation, research, and experimentation. Evidence that supports a fact is generally arrived at objectively. An **opinion,** on the other hand, is a belief, feeling, or judgment made about something or someone that a person may hold as fact but cannot prove. Evidence that supports an opinion is usually subjective. *Beautiful/ugly, wonderful/terrible, nice/disgusting, greatest/worst* are examples of subjective words writers often use to express their views. When you see them, you're reading opinions, even if you agree with the author.

But separating facts from opinions is not always easy. One reason is that facts change. At one time in history, it was a "fact" that the earth was flat (members of the Flat Earth Society still believe it); it was a "fact" that the sun revolved around the earth; it was a "fact" that the atom couldn't be split; it was a "fact" that no one would ever walk on the moon. Today, enough evidence has been gathered to prove that these and many other "facts" are wrong. Who knows what "facts" of today may be laughed at by future generations?

Another reason that separating fact from opinion is difficult is that statements can be made to sound factual. We might read in one anthropology book that the first inhabitants of North America arrived "around 25,000 years ago." Another book might say North America was first inhabited "over 35,000 years ago." Which is the correct figure? Since no one who lived back then kept records, and since anthropologists disagree on the exact date the first native Americans came, we have to be careful that we don't accept such information as actual fact. We could take the trouble to read several anthropology journals and textbooks in order to get an overview of what various anthropologists believe, but until there is more factual evidence, we can't accept either date as fact. In the future, there may be enough evidence gathered to prove a particular date.

Another reason for the difficulty in separating fact from opinion is our personal bias or prejudice. Frequently, we allow our feelings and beliefs to interfere with our acceptance of facts. Certain ideas and thoughts are instilled in us as we grow up. Family, friends, and people we admire all influence our thinking. Sometimes we unknowingly accept someone's opinion as fact simply because of our faith in that person.

Let's look now at some statements of fact and opinion. In the following paragraph, underline any verifiable facts (those statements that can be supported with objective evidence).

In the U.S., 1 in 6 couples has difficulty conceiving or bearing a child. About 27 percent of women between ages 15 and 44 can't have children because of physical problems. The sperm count of U.S. males has fallen more than 30 percent in 50 years. Some 25 percent of men are considered functionally sterile. Experts suspect that environmental pollution is a cause.

Stanley N. Wellborn, "Birth"

In this case the entire paragraph should have been underlined. You may have hesitated marking the last sentence as fact. But the sentence doesn't say that environmental pollution *is* a cause; it merely says that experts suspect it is, and it can be verified that experts do suspect it is a cause. All of the paragraph can be accepted as factual. The author of the paragraph does not offer his opinion; he merely presents objective, statistical data.

Read the following paragraph and underline any statements in it that seem to be factual or that could be verified as fact:

It's hard to believe, but in the ninth decade of the 20th Century, *The Catcher in the Rye*, *Of Mice and Men*, *Huckleberry Finn*, and *The Diary of Anne Frank*, among other books, are still the objects of censorship in the nation's public schools. And the incidence of book bannings is going up, according to a report by People for the American Way, the liberal watchdog group. In the last year, the study found, there were efforts to ban books in schools in 46 of the 50 states, including California. Many of them succeeded.

Editorial, *Los Angeles Times*

The opening four words, "It's hard to believe . . . ," constitute a statement of opinion, but the majority of the paragraph can be verified as fact. We could do research on censorship to see if the books mentioned are "still objects of censorship in the nation's public schools." We could read the study mentioned by People for the American Way to see if the numbers quoted are correct. We can investigate the group that did the study to see if they are "liberal." If we disagree with the statement because we don't want to believe it, that's because of personal bias; basically, there's no reason we shouldn't accept the statement as verifiable.

Now read this paragraph and underline any statements that appear to be facts:

The purpose of education is to teach students to think, not to instill dogma or to train them to respond in predictable ways. Far from being banned, controversial material should be welcomed in schools. Students should be taught the critical ability to evaluate different ideas and to come to their own conclusions. It is a disservice to them and to society to restrict instructional material to a single viewpoint.

Editorial, *Los Angeles Times*

If you underlined anything in the above paragraph, you didn't underline any facts. Regardless of how true or false you think the ideas in the paragraph are, they are all opinions. On a personal level, we may agree with the statements made, but that doesn't make them facts. Not everyone agrees with the purpose of education as stated above; many people do not want controversial materials presented to their children. In fact, some parents select certain schools for their children *because* only one viewpoint is taught.

Here's one more statement on censorship. Again, read it and underline any statements that seem to be factual.

Everyone older than 50 grew up in a time when Hollywood films were strictly censored by the industry itself to exclude explicit sexual scenes, gruesome violence, and vulgar language. The Supreme Court in the 1950s struck down movie censorship. It extended to film makers the First Amendment protection traditionally enjoyed by newspapers and book publishers. The court also redefined the anti-pornography and anti-obscenity statutes into meaninglessness.

Those decisions were praised as liberal advances, but their consequences were unforeseen and disastrous. . . . Unless they are reversed, the coarsening and corrupting of the nation's youth will continue.

William Shannon, "Shield Our Youth with Censorship"

A mixture of fact and opinion appear here. At one time, the film industry did censor itself; in the 1950s the Supreme Court did rule against movie censorship by expanding the interpretation of the First Amendment; some people did praise this as a liberal advance. This can all be verified. The last sentence, however, is opinion. There is no verifiable proof that the lack of censorship in the movies is the cause for the "coarsening and corrupting of the nation's youth," nor is there verifiable proof that unless the decisions the author cites are reversed, the corruption of youth will continue. He uses facts to make his opinions appear true.

As a careful reader, you will want to use the essays in Part II as a means of practicing the separation of facts from opinions.

Drawing Inferences

Another reading skill to practice is that of **drawing inferences.** Sometimes writers don't state directly what they mean; they imply or suggest their meaning. When that happens, we have to draw inferences from what they do say.

Drawing an inference is sometimes called "making an educated guess." Based on what an author tells us, we can often guess what other thoughts, feelings, and ideas the author may have that are not stated directly. For instance, what are some things you can tell about the writer of the following paragraph, although they are not directly stated?

> In 1987, we commemorated the 100th anniversary of Sherlock Holmes's "birth." The great sleuth made his first appearance in 1887, and right from the start was so popular that when his creator killed him off after twenty-four adventures, followers eventually forced Conan Doyle to bring him back to life. Even today, the intrepid duo of Holmes and his stalwart companion Dr. Watson continue to delight each new generation of readers.

The author doesn't say it straight out, but we can infer from what is said that the writer is very knowledgeable about the Sherlock Holmes stories because of the facts that are presented. We also suspect that the author has probably read most or all of the stories and likes them very much; notice the use of the phrases "great sleuth," "intrepid duo," and "continues to delight." Finally, based on the vocabulary and structural organization used, we can infer that the writer is fairly literate. These inferences help us get a sense of the person writing, a sense that goes beyond what is actually written. We may not always be right, but our inferences are good educated guesses.

Read the following paragraph and see what inferences you can draw about the author. In the space that follows, write what you infer.

> We say that it is our right to control our bodies, and this is true. But there is a distinction that needs to be made, and that distinction is this: Preventing a pregnancy is controlling a body—controlling your body. But preventing the continuance of a human life that is not your own is murder. If you attempt to control the body of another in that fashion, you become as a slave master was—controlling the lives and

bodies of his slave, chopping off their feet when they ran away, or murdering them if it pleased him.

Ken Lonnquist, "Ghosts"

You probably can infer that the author of the paragraph is against abortion. While he agrees with pro-abortionists that we have a right to control our bodies, he draws the line after conception. We can infer, then, that he defines human life as beginning at the moment sperm and egg fuse. We can also infer he is opposed to slavery. We might even suspect that his use of the unpleasant image of slave masters cutting off the feet of runaways in connection with abortion is done deliberately to win readers to his way of thinking. If we are pro-abortionists, we might still disagree with him, but we will better understand the reasons for his views.

Now let's put together all of this section on understanding content. Read the next paragraph, underline what you think is the main idea, and see what you can infer about the author:

> Controversy—the heart of politics—has gotten a bad name in the textbook business, and publishers have advised their writers to avoid it. This fear of controversy is distorting our children's education, leaving us with biology texts that neglect evolution history and texts that omit the important influence of religion. Similarly, in civics and government texts, it is treatment of such volatile events as the Vietnam war, the Watergate scandal, the civil rights movement, and the school prayer debate that is "dulled down" to the point of tedium, or minimized to the point of evasion.

Arthur J. Kropp, "Let's Put an End to Mediocre
Textbooks"

If you underlined the first sentence as the main idea, you are partly right. But there are parts of the second sentence that also apply. The paragraph method used here is cause-effect: the cause, the fear of publishers to deal with controversial issues in textbooks; the effect, a distortion of children's education. While the author mentions that publishers have advised their writers to avoid certain issues in text-books, the paragraph does not support that point. The support state-ments that are provided are examples of issues that are either left out or watered down in textbooks, which the author believes distorts children's education. Thus, the paragraph uses a combination of cause-effect and illustration-example. Here is a possible outline of the paragraph:

Main idea: Fear among publishers to deal with controversial is-sues has resulted in a distortion of children's edu-cation. (cause-effect)

Support: biology texts that neglect evolution history

Support: omission of the important influence of religion

Support: civics and government texts that "dull down" or minimize
a. Vietnam war
b. Watergate scandal
c. civil rights movement
d. school prayer debate

Though he does not directly state it, we can infer that the author is against censorship and that he believes children should be exposed to controversy. We can infer that he does not want everything in textbooks to be watered down to show only the "smooth" side of life. We can also infer that the author believes publishers are responsible for producing books that do not challenge students. This, we might guess, is from the fear that controversial subjects in textbooks might offend some people who would then put pressure on the schools not to buy those books.

As written, most of what is stated is opinion. To prove what he says and implies, we would need to examine textbooks in many of the areas he mentions, or do further research on the subject of text-book censorship.

Use the following passage to practice all of the reading skills you have learned.

Adaptability and lifelong learning are now the corner-stones of success. What direction does a person take to prepare for a lifetime of change? The one degree which provides train-ing which never becomes obsolete is the liberal arts degree; it teaches you how to think. It also teaches you how to read, write and speak intelligently, get along with others, and conceptualize problems. For the first time in several decades, the liberal arts degree is coming to the forefront of the employment field.

Growing ranks of corporate executives are lamenting that college students are specializing too much and too early. What corporate America really needs, according to chief executive officers of major corporations, is students soundly grounded in the liberal arts—English, especially—who then can pick up more specific business or technical skills on the job. Few students, however, seem to be listening to this message. Today's best selling courses offer evidence that students want to take the courses that provide direct job related skills rather than the most basic survival skills in the workplace: communication and thinking skills. They want courses they can parlay into jobs—and high paying ones at that. . . .

Debra Siles and Barbara Murray, "The Practicality of the
Liberal Arts Major"

In the spaces provided, answer the following questions. You may look back if you need to do so.

1. What writing pattern is used in the first paragraph?

2. In your own words, write a one-sentence statement of the main idea of the first paragraph.

3. List the support provided for the main idea of the first paragraph.

4. In your own words, write a topic sentence for the second paragraph.

5. What inference can you draw regarding the authors' attitude toward a liberal arts degree?

6. Is the passage mostly fact or opinion? Explain.

7. What does the passage imply about most of today's college students?

Wording will be different, of course, but compare your answers with these:

1. Examples of the benefits of a liberal arts education make up the bulk of the paragraph, thus the illustration and example pattern is used.
2. A combination of the first three sentences is needed to cover the major point of the paragraph, so the main idea is "The one degree which provides adaptability and lifelong learning skills is the liberal arts degree."
3. The liberal arts degree (1) teaches you how to (a) think, (b) read, write, and speak intelligently, (c) get along with others, and (d) conceptualize problems; and (2) it is coming to the forefront of the employment field.
4. The basic idea is "Corporate executives feel that college students are coming into business too specialized, but students don't seem to be listening."
5. The authors seem in favor of the degree.
6. The passage is mostly opinion. (However, you should be aware that the passage is taken from an article that is based on the findings of research conducted with corporate executives.)
7. The last two sentences imply that most of today's college students are more interested in obtaining job skills that they think will

land them high-paying jobs. They are more interested in making money than preparing for lifelong change and adaptability.

Make your goal be the ability to read well enough to answer correctly these types of questions when you read. Part II will provide ample practice.

Before Going On

You have learned that reading critically requires the ability to distinguish main ideas from supporting details, to separate fact from opinion, and to draw inferences when authors imply something not directly stated.

✍️ Writing Exercise

On a separate sheet of paper, write a one-paragraph statement explaining what major field of study you have selected, why you selected it, and what you hope to learn. If you have not yet selected a major, write a paragraph that discusses areas of study you are considering and why. Make certain that you have a clearly stated topic sentence and adequate support. Your instructor may want to see this exercise.

Marking as You Read

Our minds tend to wander when we read, so it's a good idea to read with a pen in hand, making notations in the margins of books. Marking as you read slows you down; it forces you to get engaged with the author, to catch your thoughts and put them in writing before you forget them. How you mark or take notes as you read is up to you, but you might want to consider doing all or some of the following:

1. Underline only major points or statements. Don't underline almost everything as some students do. Force yourself to read so carefully that you are sure of what the key statements are before you mark them. Identifying the paragraph method used may help you see the difference between supporting points and main ideas.

2. Use numbers in the margins when a series of points are made. This, too, will help you distinguish the main ideas from supporting points.

3. Circle key words or phrases that you need to learn or that strike you as important.

4. Think about and react to what you are reading. In the margins, write your reactions, such as "Good point!" or "Never thought of that" or "Where's the proof?"

5. If there's not much room in the margins, create your own kind of shorthand: Use an exclamation mark [!] when a statement surprises you, a question mark [?] when you don't understand a point, or abbreviations, such as "ex" for example or "prf" for proof—anything that will remind you of what it means.

6. Write a one-paragraph summary of the reading selection. If you can't, then you may need to read it again.

These are just suggestions. You or your instructor may have other methods for marking. Feel free to mark your books in any way that will help your reading concentration. Whatever the method, the reasons for marking are to gain control of concentration and to force close, analytical reading.

Try to create an interest in the assigned readings. If you don't know anything about the subject of the reading selection, keep asking questions as you read, such as: "What does the author mean by this statement?" and "How do I know if this is true?" and "What's the point of this statement?" Asking questions about what you are reading will keep you alert. You'll be less likely to nod off when reading selections that don't interest you. Don't try to read for too long a period of time. And don't try to read assignments when you are tired; you won't concentrate very well. Good reading requires a fresh mind.

Here's a reading selection typical of the kind in Part II of this book. Read it through once. Then read it again, marking it up as directed above.

The Wet Drug

PETE HAMILL

Among the worst bores in the Western world are religious converts and reformed drunks. I have never been knocked off a horse on the way to Damascus, but I did give up drinking more than a dozen years ago. This didn't make me feel morally superior to anyone. If asked, I would talk about going dry but, from the first, I was determined to preach no sermons and stand in judgment of no human being who took pleasure in the sauce.

But I must confess that lately my feelings have begun to change. Drinking and drunks now fill me with loathing. Increasingly, I see close friends—human beings of intelligence, wit and style—reduced to slobbering fools by liquor. I've seen other friends ruin their marriages, brutalize their children, destroy their careers. I've also reached the age when I've had to help bury a few people who allowed booze to take them into eternity.

In the past few weeks, two ghastly episodes have underlined for me the horror that goes with alcohol. In New Bedford, Mass., a 21-year-old woman was beaten and repeatedly raped by a gang of drunks in a bar called Big Dan's. There were at least 15 onlookers to her violation; they did nothing to prevent it. All of them were drunk or drinking.

In New York, four teen-age boys were killed when a car driven by a fifth kid smashed into a concrete wall at 90 mph. They were all under the legal drinking age of 19; nevertheless, they had managed to spend a long night drinking in a public bar, and got drunk enough to die. When it was over, and they had pried the human pieces out of the torn rubber and steel, the driver was charged with four counts of manslaughter. His worst punishment may be that he lived.

These are not isolated cases. This year more than 25,000 Americans will die in auto accidents caused by alcohol. And the roads are not the only site of the horror. Studies indicate that alcohol is a factor in 86 percent of our homicides, 83 percent of our fatal fires, 72 percent of robberies, 52 percent of wife-beatings, 38 percent of cases of child abuse. We can never be certain how many on-the-job accidents are caused by drinking, how many drownings, how many suicides.

All of this is bizarre. We live in a culture that certifies alcohol as an acceptable drug and places marijuana smokers or coke dealers in jail. Presidents and statesmen toast each other with the wet drug. It's advertised on radio and TV. Popular music is full of references to it. But when the mellow moments, the elegant evenings are over, there are our kids, smashing themselves into eternity with the same drug.

I'm not suggesting here any bluenose return to Prohibition. But I wish we would begin to make it more and more clear that drinking to drunkenness is one of the more disgusting occupations of human beings.

For every beer commercial showing all those he-men getting ready to drink, we should show footage of destroyed teenagers, their bodies broken and bleeding, beer cans filling what's left of the back seat. For every high fashion couple toasting each other with wine, show men and women puking on their shoes, falling over tables, sliding away into violence.

If cigarette advertising could be banned from TV, so should commercials for the drug called alcohol. Cigarette smokers, after all, usually kill only themselves with their habit. Drunks get behind the wheels of their cars and kill strangers.

At night now, driving along any American road, you come across these vomiting slaughterers, slowly weaving from lane to lane, or racing in confused fury to the grave at 90 mph. They don't know the rest of us exist and, what's more, they don't care. They are criminal narcissists, careening around until they kill others and themselves.

We Americans should begin immediately to remind ourselves that when we drink we are entering the company of killers and fools.

Here again is the essay you just read. Compare your markings with those below. Your markings will be different, but compare what you underlined as main ideas and what you marked as supporting points with those marked in the model. They should be similar.

The Wet Drug   what's a? wet drug?

PETE HAMILL

Among the worst bores in the Western world are religious converts and reformed drunks. I have never been knocked off   *ask instructor what this means*
? a horse on the way to Damascus, but I did give up drinking more than a dozen years ago. This didn't make me feel morally superior to anyone. If asked, I would talk about going dry but, from the first, I was determined to preach no sermons and   *changed his mind why?* stand in judgment of no human being who took pleasure in the sauce. Booze? Ah, the wet drug!

transition But I must confess that lately my feelings have begun to   *1. foolish acting* change. Drinking and drunks now fill me with loathing. In-   *2. ruined marriages* creasingly, I see close friends—human beings of intelligence,   *3. child beating* wit and style—reduced to slobbering fools by liquor. I've seen   *4. ruined careers* other friends ruin their marriages, brutalize their children,   *5. death* destroy their careers. I've also reached the age when I've had to help bury a few people who allowed booze to take them into eternity.

In the past few weeks, two ghastly episodes have under-   *example of drunks in bar— beating/raping woman* lined for me the horror that goes with alcohol. In New Bed-ford, Mass., a 21-year-old woman was beaten and repeatedly raped by a gang of drunks in a bar called Big Dan's. There were at least 15 onlookers to her violation; they did nothing to prevent it. All of them were drunk or drinking.

In New York, four teen-age boys were killed when a car   *example of teenage deaths 4 teenage from drunk driving* driven by a fifth kid smashed into a concrete wall at 90 mph. They were all under the legal drinking age of 19; nevertheless, they had managed to spend a long night drinking in a public bar, and got drunk enough to die. When it was over, and they had <u>pried the human pieces</u> out of the <u>torn rubber and steel</u>, the driver was charged with four counts of manslaughter. His worst punishment may be that he lived.

[margin: Yuk! (descriptive)]

These are not isolated cases. This year more than 25,000 Americans will die in <u>auto accidents</u> caused by alcohol. And the roads are not the only site of the horror. Studies indicate that alcohol is a factor in 86 percent of our <u>homicides</u>, 83 percent of our <u>fatal fires</u>, 72 percent of <u>robberies</u>, 52 percent of <u>wife-beatings</u>, 38 percent of cases of <u>child abuse</u>. We can never be certain how many on-the-job accidents are caused by drinking, how many drownings, how many suicides.

[margin: statistics on damage from drinking problems / 1. auto accidents / 2. homicides / 3. fires / 3. robberies / 4. wife beating / 5. child abuse]

All of this is bizarre. <u>We live in a culture that certifies alcohol as an acceptable drug and places marijuana smokers or coke dealers in jail.</u> Presidents and statesmen toast each other with the wet drug. It's advertised on radio and TV. Popular music is full of references to it(But)when the mellow moments, the elegant evenings are over, there are our kids, <u>smashing themselves into eternity</u> with the same drug.

[margin: good point / if alcohol is so damaging why legal? / examples of acceptability contrasted with problem]

I'm not suggesting here any bluenose return to Prohibition.(But)I wish we would begin to make it more and more clear that drinking to drunkenness is one of the more disgusting occupations of human beings.

For every beer commercial showing all those he-men getting ready to drink, we should show footage of destroyed teenagers, their <u>bodies broken and bleeding</u>, beer cans filling what's left of the back seat. For every high fashion couple toasting each other with wine, show men and women <u>puking</u> <u>on their shoes</u>, <u>falling over tables</u>, sliding away into violence.

[margin: Compare/contrast / strong images / wants to counter all "acceptable" drinking images in media with negative, unmadded, "realistic" ones]

If cigarette advertising could be banned from TV, so should commercials for the drug called alcohol. Cigarette smokers, after all, usually kill only themselves with their habit. Drunks get behind the wheels of their cars and kill strangers.

[margin: wants to ban alcohol ads]

At night now, driving along any American road, you come across these <u>vomiting slaughterers</u>, slowly weaving from lane to lane, or racing in confused fury to the grave at 90 mph. They don't know the rest of us exist and, what's more, they don't care. They are criminal(narcissists)careening around until they kill others and themselves.

[margin: strong image]

We Americans should begin immediately to remind ourselves that when we drink we are entering the company of killers and fools.

[margin: forceful ending! sounds fed up.]

- ask teacher about "... way to Damascus" in first ¶
- look up <u>narcissist</u>
- strong argument -- uses personal appeal, emotional appeal, facts & figures
- guess booze is a wet drug - never thought about it before

If you aren't used to this type of reading, it may take one or two practices before you feel confident about what you are doing. But it's a practice worth your time.

Keeping a Reading Journal

Psychologists tell us that unless we keep notes and review what we learn on a regular basis, within two weeks we forget over 80 percent of what we thought we learned. That's a big waste, considering the time, energy, and money put into learning.

Keeping a reading journal for this class is a good way to make certain that you don't lose what you have learned or forget the questions that come up when you are studying. Buy an $8^{1}/_{2}'' \times 11''$ spiral notebook that you will use only for journal entries. Don't use it to take lecture notes for this or other classes. Your journal should be used for at least three basic functions: (1) writing **summaries** of the essays you read; (2) recording any **reflections** you may have after reading, such as reactions, questions, and ideas prompted by the reading topic; and (3) keeping a list of **vocabulary** words from the readings that you need to learn.

Writing Summaries

A good habit to develop is to write a one-paragraph summary in your journal of each essay you are assigned to read. Doing so requires that you put to use all the reading skills discussed earlier. To write a good summary, you need to recognize the main idea of the essay (the thesis), identify its supporting points, separate fact from opinion, and draw inferences. You then use this information to write an objective summary, including only what the author says, not your opinions. When you write a summary in your journal, follow these steps:

1. Think about what you want to say first. Try writing down the author's thesis in your own words and then listing the supporting points. Use this as an outline for your summary.

2. Don't write too much, about 200 words or less. One paragraph is usually enough, although there may be times when two paragraphs are needed. The idea of a summary is to present only the main idea and supporting points.

3. Be objective; that is, don't give your own opinions or value judgments.

4. In your first sentence, provide the author's name, the title of the work, and an indication of what the essay is about. Once you have stated the author's name, you don't need to repeat it in your summary.

5. Use your own words, except for phrases you feel are important to include for clarity of a point. These phrases should have quotation marks around them.

6. Avoid using phrases such as "the author believes" or "another interesting point is." Just state what the author says.

As practice, try writing a one-paragraph summary of what you just read, Pete Hamill's essay, "The Wet Drug." You will probably want to look over your markings or reread it first. Limit yourself to the following space:

Naturally, your wording will be different, but see if your summary contains the same basic points as this one:

Excessive drinking is disgusting and harmful, says Pete Hamill in his essay, "The Wet Drug." Although he had vowed not to moralize or pass judgment on those who still drank after he quit, Hamill has changed his mind after witnessing the harm he has seen from the "drinking to drunkenness" of friends and others. As support, Hamill provides examples of what excessive drinking has done to some of his friends, such as acting foolish, ruined marriages and careers, child beating, and even death. He then cites two recent news accounts of harm from excessive drinking, one regarding a woman who was beaten and raped by a gang in a bar, another of four teens killed in an auto accident. Finally, the author presents some national statistics on the effects drinking has on auto accidents, homicides, fatal fires, wife-beatings, child abuse, and on-the-job accidents. Because we live in a society that "certifies alcohol as an acceptable drug," we should counter all acceptable images of drinking with more realistic images of the results of drunkenness. Commercials for alcohol, like those for cigarettes, should be banned from TV.

Notice that the summary's first sentence includes the author, title, and thesis of the essay. It includes the evidence Hamill uses to support his thesis: examples of the effects drinking has had on Hamill's friends, recent "horror stories" in the news of crime and violence related to drinking, and statistics on the harm caused by drinking. The summary concludes with Hamill's suggestion for countering the "acceptable" media images of drinking with more realistic ones.

The summary is objective; the only opinions used are those of Hamill, the author of the essay. Notice, too, that when the summary uses words from the essay, those words are identified with quotation marks.

You can write a good summary only when you truly understand what you have read. Writing good summaries in your journal ensures that you have read carefully. In addition, the summaries serve as good resources if you ever need to go back to review what you've read.

Writing Reflections

Writing your reflections on what you read is another useful type of journal entry to consider. Since writing summaries requires objectivity, you need some place to capture your subjective reactions, ideas, and questions that arise from the reading selections assigned. Here is where you write whatever you want. There's no right or wrong. You might, for instance, disagree with Pete Hamill's thesis that commercials for alcoholic beverages be banned. Write it down in this section of your journal before you forget your reaction. Or, maybe you agree with Hamill because his essay reminds you of someone who was harmed physically or mentally because of drinking problems. Maybe the essay causes you to wonder why "the wet drug" is legal when other drugs, such as marijuana, are not. Write it down. You might be able to use your entry as the basis for an essay of your own. Write down any reactions you have or ideas that the essay causes you to think about—even those that don't directly relate to the essay. The point is not to lose any good ideas while they are on your mind.

This is also a good place to write down some examples of the way writers work. For instance, maybe you like some of Hamill's use of language, such as: "I've had to help bury a few people who allowed booze to take them to eternity," ". . . these vomiting slaughterers, slowly weaving from lane to lane," or ". . . when we drink we are entering the company of killers and fools." On the other hand, if you think these statements are too dramatic, write them down as examples of overdramatic writing. Such entries help you pay more attention to a writer's style and use of language. In turn, you will be more conscious of your own word choices when you write.

This is also a good place for questions you might want to pursue later or ask your instructor. Some of the questions might come from your marking as you read; others might come after you have finished reading. As you were reading the first paragraph in "The Wet Drug," you might have marked as a question "What does 'knocked off a horse on the way to Damascus' mean?" Maybe you don't understand what Hamill means in paragraph 7 when he uses the phrase "bluenose." Write down, "What is a 'bluenose'?" Perhaps you've heard much about Prohibition, but don't really know what it was or when it occurred. Write it down. Some of your questions can be answered by asking your instructor; others can be answered by using a dictionary or doing a little research in the library. Some sources for library research appear in the Appendix at the back of this book.

It's important to capture our thoughts, ideas, and questions in writing while we are thinking about them. If we don't, chances are we'll forget them when we get involved in another assignment. Making journal entries of this type right after reading prevents the loss of our thoughts and questions.

Collecting Words to Learn

It is a good idea to set aside a section in your journal where you keep a list of the words you should learn. The only way you're going to enlarge your vocabulary is to take the time to expand it. You need a strong vocabulary not only to handle sophisticated reading, but also to express yourself in your own writing.

How you can best develop your vocabulary is something only you know, but just collecting a list of words is not going to help you learn them. You need to do something with the list.

As you know, words often have more than one meaning; their definitions depend on their contextual usage; that is, how they are used in the sentence. So don't merely keep a list of unknown words from the reading selections. Write down the entire sentence or at least the phrase in which the word appears. That way, when you look up the word in a dictionary, you can pick from among the various meanings given the definition that fits. Once you have looked up the word to learn, write a sentence of your own using it in the proper context. Show your sentences to your instructor to make certain you are using the word correctly. Then use as many as possible in your own writing until they become as familiar as the words you already use. Yes, this takes time, but how else are you going to develop your vocabulary?

Before Going On

In order to understand better what you read, and remember it longer, be an active reader by carrying on a dialogue with the author. Make brief notations and marks in your books as you read. In addition, keep a reading journal where you can write objective summaries of the readings. Also use the journal as a place to record your reactions, ideas, and questions prompted by the reading selections. Finally, in order to enlarge your vocabulary, keep a list of new words from the readings and learn as many as you can.

Writing Exercise

On a separate sheet of paper, make a brief outline of pages 5–19, stating the main idea and listing the major support. Then write a one-paragraph summary of those pages. Make certain you have a clearly stated topic sentence. Your instructor may want to see this.

Viewpoints on Writing Essays

By the year 2000, 2 out of 3 Americans could be illiterate.

"Writing is manual labor of the mind:
a job, like laying pipe."
John Gregory Dunne

*I*N THE previous unit "Viewpoints on Reading Essays," you looked at some methods and qualities required of a good essay reader. Now you'll learn what it takes to be a good essay writer. What you learned about an essay's thesis, supporting paragraphs, and organization will be useful in writing essays. In fact, much of that information will sound familiar. The difference is that you will now look at the essay from a writer's point of view rather than a reader's. As a reader, you see only the final efforts of a writer; in this section, you'll see each of the various writing stages that lead to the finished product.

Three basic writing steps are presented here: how to get started, how to get your ideas in writing, and how to rewrite or polish what you write. But good writing is seldom a quick one-two-three process. It involves starting and stopping, eagerly writing away and angrily throwing away, moving along and stalling, feeling pleased and feeling frustrated, thinking you're finished and then realizing you need to start again. Sometimes a writing assignment may seem to come effortlessly; more often you will have to work at it.

Writers go about writing in various ways. Hundreds of books exist on how to write, each one offering "the right way." But regardless of their differences, most of them cover at least three basic stages of writing: methods for getting started, methods for writing a first draft, and methods for revision and editing. These three stages in the writing process will be presented in that order in this section, but the order in which you follow them may vary with each essay you write. Once you increase your knowledge of what goes into writing an essay, you may modify the stages to suit you.

This basic three-step approach should make writing easier for you. It will give you a sense of direction and an understanding of what is expected of you as a writer. Let's look at each of these steps more closely.

Getting Started: Finding a Working Thesis (Stage 1)

As you learned in the section on reading, essays are structured around a thesis, the main idea an author wants to develop. The thesis is what the author wants to say about the topic or subject of the essay. Sometimes an instructor gives you a topic for an essay. In that case, you have to decide what you want to say about it and what thesis will guide what you want to say. Sometimes you are left on your own and must come up with both an essay topic and a thesis.

Once you've been given a writing assignment, make the topic interesting for yourself. Finding a slant that interests you will make it easier to write about the subject assigned. Also, unless the assignment requires research, think about the assignment in terms of what you already know. Depending upon the topic, that's not always easy, but here are some methods for selecting and making a topic your own.

Using Your Reading Journal

Your reading journal is one of the best places to start searching for a topic and thesis. If your instructor asks you to write an essay dealing with the general topic of an assigned reading selection, you may have already written down some reactions, ideas, or questions that you can use as a starting point. So look over your journal entries. Also, look over any textbook markings you made when you read the assignment. Just by keeping in mind that you have to write on something from that particular reading selection, you might see other essay possibilities in your markings that didn't occur to you before. By using your reflections on what you read, you will have not only a possible topic and working thesis, but also an essay that is based on your feelings.

Let's say you are assigned to read Pete Hamill's "The Wet Drug" from Unit 1. The writing assignment is to agree or disagree with the author's opinion that advertisements for alcoholic beverages should be banned from television. In this case, both your topic and thesis have been given to you. By checking your journal entry for the essay, you discover you wrote down your reaction, a notation that you agree (or disagree) with the author. You might begin by writing down a working thesis: "I agree (or disagree) with Pete Hamill in his essay

'The Wet Drug' when he says advertisements for alcoholic beverages should be banned from television." Then look again at each of Hamill's supporting points and show why you agree or disagree with his points. Such an approach at least gets you started. You may even change your mind once you begin. That's why the term *working thesis* is used at this stage. It's quite normal to discover you want to go in a different direction after writing several hundred words. Just accept that as part of the writing process.

At other times you may be assigned a broader topic that you must write about. Let's say that an instructor wants you to write a 500-word essay on some aspect of television commercials. A review of your journal entry on Hamill's essay shows you wrote some questions: "Where did Hamill get his statistics?" "Doesn't Hamill know that hard liquor ads are already banned on TV?" "How much of an effect do beer and wine ads on TV have on teens? adults?" "Why should such ads be banned on TV but allowed in magazines?" Looking for answers to your own questions is also a good place to find a topic and a thesis. You can see how important thoughtful journal entries can be to stimulate your own writing.

Brainstorming

When the topic is too big for a short essay, you have to narrow it down. How do you whittle down a topic to something you can handle if you can't even think of something to write about? There are at least two ways to come up with an idea, or *brainstorm*. One way is to create a list of your ideas, and another is to cluster them. Let's look at **creating a list** first.

You've probably participated in brainstorming sessions at one time or another. If so, you know it is important to follow the rules. Done correctly, brainstorming can be used to help you select a topic. For instance, if the general writing assignment is to write about television commercials, then take a sheet of paper and start writing down whatever ideas about the topic pop into your head. The trick here is not to be critical as you jot down your thoughts; just put your ideas on paper even if you don't like them at the time. It's important not to interrupt the flow of thoughts by stopping to ask yourself if what you've written is a good idea or not; you can decide that later. Just let your brain "storm." Once you have exhausted all your thoughts about the topic, then look at your list and see which ones are useful.

Sometimes it's helpful (and fun) to work with other classmates as a team. Getting together with two or three others to brainstorm brings out ideas for the assigned topic that you might not have thought about on your own.

Here's an example of a brainstorming list a student wrote on television commercials:

TV Commercials

pretty stupid
miller lite bar scenes
lots of automobile ads
seem louder than program
    being watched
repetitive, get boring
Some seem sexy
have you driven a Ford
    lately?
hate the interruptions
what does an ad cost?
Doublemint gum twins
Some are funny (Isuzu)
truck splashing through
    rivers, up hills

I just called to say
    I love you
are they necessary?
music used is hot
    sometimes
one after the other
obnoxious but memorable
attractiveness of some
    makes you want to
    buy
causes dissatisfaction
    with what you don't
    have
Saturday moring kids'
    ads

As you can see, some of these provide a sense of direction for an essay on television commercials. Some of the items are slogans and scenes from TV commercials that she remembers. Other items are her opinions about commercials. A closer look at the list may reveal that some items are dated or unusable. It doesn't matter. Making the list got her to think about the assigned subject.

It may be that once you decide upon a topic, such as Saturday morning kids' ads, you may need to do more brainstorming on that. Another brainstorming session dealing with the topic should provide more specific ideas on it. If few ideas occur, it may be that the topic shouldn't be used. The usefulness of making a brainstorming list is that it helps prevent writer's block and gets ideas flowing. Discovering and narrowing down a possible topic through brainstorming saves you from false starts.

Try a little brainstorming. In the following space, brainstorm for three minutes on the topic "my neighborhood." Remember to write down everything that comes to your mind, even if it doesn't seem related. Don't be critical of any ideas; just list as many as you can in the time allowed.

Now look over your brainstorming list. Your topic was "my neighborhood," a broad subject. Circle any items that could serve as *narrower* topics for an essay on your neighborhood. For instance, you might have listed "plants" because you were thinking about the neighbors' trees and gardens. A possible narrower topic would be "neighborhood plants." You might have listed "Mrs. Little," a neighbor you like. Writing about her would be a narrower topic than "my neighborhood."

Once you've found a narrower topic from your brainstorming list, place a check mark by all the items that could support such a topic. (If there's not much on your list, you might need to brainstorm more on the new topic.) Then, in the spaces below, write down the topic and a working thesis statement for it.

topic: _____

working thesis: _____

Another brainstorming method is called **clustering.** In her book *Writing the Natural Way*, Gabriel Rico claims that we have two minds, our "Design mind" and our "Sign mind." Most of us have learned to write through our Sign mind, the part of the brain that deals with rules and logic. Our Sign mind criticizes, censors, and corrects errors. Because most of our training in writing deals with the Sign mind, our Design mind—the creative, less critical side of our brain—doesn't get developed much. This often leaves our creative side blocked and unused. A good piece of writing requires that both minds work together. Using an analogy with music, Rico says our Sign mind "attends to the notes," whereas our Design mind "attends to the melodies."

Clustering is a way to tap into the Design mind, the part of the brain that doesn't care about rules. It helps bring out our more creative side. A type of brainstorming, clustering brings to the surface our hidden thoughts. Rather than merely making a list of ideas, clustering creates a design, a pattern of thought.

Here's how clustering works. By writing down a word or phrase in the center of a page (the **nucleus thought**), allow your mind to flow out from the center, like ripples created by a stone thrown into water. Rapidly write down and circle whatever comes to mind, connecting each new word or phrase with a line to the previous circle. When a new thought occurs, begin a new "ripple," or branch.

An example of a clustering done on the topic "language" appears on the next page. Notice that there are six branches stemming from television commercials: "dumb," "funny," "costly," "emotional appeal," "harmful," and "none [of the above]." Each one of these leads the writer closer to a subject. If one of these branches seems interesting enough to write about, that branch can become the nucleus for a new clustering to gain more specific details. A few minutes of clustering on an assigned topic frequently provides a sense of direction that is truly your own. Chances are your essay will be different from the norm because you will have found ideas in your mind that your usual approach to writing would not have touched.

Give clustering a try. On a separate sheet of paper, use the clustering technique for three minutes on the topic "making changes." Write the nucleus thought "making changes" in the middle of the space and draw a circle around it. Then begin branching and clustering your ideas on the subject.

Look over your clustering. Pick one of the branches from the cluster that could serve as a narrower essay topic than "making changes." For instance, you might have a cluster on "physical changes," whose branches deal with changes you've made in diet and exercise. (If you don't have anything that might serve as a topic, you might need to cluster some more.) In the spaces below, write in the narrower topic you select from your clustering and a working thesis statement for it.

topic: _____

working thesis: _____

Freewriting

In his book *Writing with Power,* Peter Elbow recommends freewriting as still another way to focus on a writing topic or to break writer's block. Elbow claims that practicing freewriting for ten minutes a day increases writing skills within a few weeks. Freewriting isn't polished writing, but it helps open you up to the thinking-writing process without worrying about mechanical errors that often block thinking. As Elbow states in his book, what's important about freewriting is not the end product, but the process.

To freewrite, simply start writing words on a page and see what comes out. There are only two rules: don't stop to think about what you are saying, and don't stop to worry about errors in writing. Just try to write down as fast as you can exactly what's going through your mind. If you can't think of anything, write, "I can't think of anything." Repeat the phrase until you do think of something. It won't take long. You'll be surprised to see how many useful ideas for topics often come out.

Here's an example of freewriting done by a student who was asked to freewrite about television commercials for a few minutes without stopping. The errors aren't important here; the ideas are.

Freewrite about Tv commercials, huh? O.K. I'll que it a try but I don't know what to say, what am I suppose to say about Tv commercials, anything I guess. But I don't watch much television and I hate commercials. maybe I could write about how much I hate commercials. I always watch them because I'm to lazy to get up and turn them off or down wish we had a gizmo— what its called— remote box or something that you just press a button and the sound goes off or you could change the channel. Channel 10 is that public station, they don't have any commercials but I don't like much of what I see on it always animals or nature or lots of talking. I did see a TV commercial I liked the one with the guy who lies about the car, don't remember the name of the car, but its kind a funny. Could I write about that ad? probably not, but maybe I need to watch some TV commercials and relly look at them.

Notice that the student didn't stop to fix spelling or grammatical mistakes made during the freewriting. What matters in freewriting is *what* is being said. If you look carefully at the sample, you'll notice that after a bit of spinning around and going nowhere, some ideas started to come out: the advantage of owning a remote control device, the programming on stations that don't air commercials compared with programming on those that do, writing about funny ads, and the need to watch some television commercials closely before trying to write. Even the last idea provides a sense of direction for the writing assignment. At least four ideas for possible essays surfaced from just a few minutes of freewriting.

A ten-minute freewriting session is also useful for reasons other than finding a topic. A freewriting session before you begin to write an essay can get you warmed up to writing. It can discipline you to write when you don't feel like it. It helps you get words on paper without worrying about the writing process itself. And it helps bring out ideas and thoughts buried in your subconscious.

Some students like to freewrite for a few minutes in their journals after completing a reading assignment. It helps them capture ideas, experiences, feelings, and reactions prompted by the reading assignment and exercises. You might want to make this a part of your assignment, too.

Freewriting is an especially good technique to use if you work with a word processor. You can turn off the monitor light and, since you won't see anything on the screen, you can concern yourself only with writing your thoughts. When finished, turn up the monitor light and read what you have written. Chances are that you will have found a topic you can handle.

To see how freewriting works, write for just three minutes on the topic "automobiles." Remember, keep writing the *whole time*. Don't worry about or change any mistakes. Use a separate sheet of paper so you will have plenty of room. Come back here when you're finished.

Now look over your freewriting. In the space below, write down all the possible essay topics that came from it.

Before Going On

You now know some approaches for finding an essay topic on your own. One way is to look over your journal entries for possible topics. Another is to brainstorm for topics, either by making a list or by clustering. Still another is to freewrite. If you experience difficulty selecting a topic for an essay, try one or all of these approaches. Feel free to modify them to fit your style of thinking and writing.

✍ Writing Exercise

On a separate sheet of paper, write a paragraph that summarizes one of the four methods for finding an essay topic: using journal entries, listing, clustering, or freewriting. In a second paragraph, explain which one you prefer and explain why. Your instructor may want you to turn this in.

Getting It on Paper: Supporting Your Thesis (Stage 2)

Refining Your Thesis

Sometimes it's possible to sit down and write an essay from beginning to end. But more often than not, you'll find yourself surrounded by crumpled sheets of paper containing false starts, because you tried to write before you and your thesis were ready.

Here's a more practical and productive way to get your ideas on paper. Let's say that after clustering for ideas on the broad topic of television commercials, you narrow it to harmful television commercials. That branch of your cluster contains three reasons you think they are harmful: "create desires," "poor role models," and "numbs the mind." You realize now that when you wrote "numbs the mind" you were really thinking about television in general, not just commercials. So that leaves only two points.

Now you are wondering what you meant exactly about "role models" and decide it's not something you could easily write about. That leaves only one point: "creates desires." You consider forgetting the whole idea, but you scribble down a possible working thesis: "Television advertisements create desires for things we don't need and often can't pay for." That, you think, is something you can write about because you have experienced it.

Had you gone ahead and started writing a draft on the three items of the cluster "leg," you would have eventually realized you couldn't do it. Much time, effort, and paper would have been wasted. In most cases, it pays to think before you write.

Even now, with a working thesis, you still aren't ready to write a first draft. The way your thesis is stated, you have to show that TV ads create a desire for things we don't need and sometimes can't pay for. Do all television ads do this? No, so you change your thesis: "*Some* television advertisements create desires for things we don't need and often can't pay for." Now, which ones do that? You remember a television advertisement you saw for the Mazda pickup truck. The ad made the truck look so good that you went out and bought one, even though there was nothing wrong with your old car, and even though you really couldn't afford it. In fact, you had to get your parents to cosign the loan. Further, you bought new speakers for the truck's stereo, which you didn't need.

As you think about your working thesis, it dawns on you. You use a toothpaste and after-shave lotion because you've been influenced by commercials on television! You never used after-shave lotion until that ad appeared. Even last night, you called in to order a collection of 1950s rock-and-roll music advertised on television. Suddenly your thesis really applies to *you*! You don't actually know about everyone else, so you change your working thesis again: "Some television advertisements create desires *in me* for things I don't really need and often can't pay for." But the thesis sounds awkward, so you refine it: "Sometimes I am influenced by television advertisements and buy things I don't need and often can't afford." Now you can see why the term *working thesis* is used at this stage of essay writing.

In the process of developing a thesis, the ideas used to form it often become part of the support:

> **Working thesis:** Sometimes I am influenced by television advertisements and buy things I don't need and often can't afford.
>
> **Support:** the Mazda truck I bought
>
> **Support:** the toothpaste I use
>
> **Support:** the after-shave lotion I started using
>
> **Support:** the rock-and-roll records I bought

Rather than writing a draft at this point, it would be better to brainstorm a bit more. What other ads have given you the "wants"? You soon come up with these:

> **Support:** subscription to *TIME* magazine (a free watch came with it)
>
> **Support:** subscription to *Sports Illustrated* (a free videotape came with it)
>
> **Support:** new speakers for the truck
>
> **Support:** Reebok tennis shoes
>
> **Support:** a survival knife I didn't need

By now, you are embarrassed by the growing list; that's enough support to prove your point.

Before going on, make certain you understand what is meant by a working thesis and support. Some of the statements below are working thesis statements, others are not. Circle the letter of any thesis statements and then explain in the space provided what the topic is and what support would be needed.

1. First impressions of people can be misleading.

2. Smaller colleges are better.

3. The value of pets

4. Participating in college athletics builds character.

5. The problems of today's students

6. Making mistakes has an educational value.

Compare your answers with these. Item 1 could be used as a working thesis. The essay topic is first impressions of people. The key word requiring support is "misleading." Examples are needed to support how first impressions can be misleading. Item 2 is also a possible working thesis. The topic is smaller colleges and support must be given to show why they are better. Item 3 should not have been circled. The value of pets is a topic, but there is no statement about the value of pets. Item 4 is usable. The subject is participation in college athletics; the support required is evidence that it builds character. Item 5 is only a topic, not a thesis statement. What about the problems of today's student? Are there any? If so, what? Item 6 should have been circled. The subject or topic is making mistakes; the support must reveal its educational value.

Grouping Your Ideas

Even after deciding on a working thesis, you're not quite ready to begin your first draft. You can't simply go down the list of supporting ideas and write about each one. You need to organize the list in some way. So you group the items this way:

Group 1	Group 2	Group 3	Group 4
truck	toothpaste	*TIME* subscription	records
truck's stereo speakers	after-shave	*Sports Illustrated* subscription	knife
	tennis shoes		

Group 1 deals with the truck; Group 2, personal items; Group 3, magazine subscriptions; and Group 4, miscellaneous items.

Outlining Your Support

Using the reasoning behind your grouping, you must now write down an **informal outline** to follow when you begin your first draft.

> **Thesis:** Sometimes I am influenced by television advertisements and buy things I don't need and often can't afford.
>
> **Major support:** unnecessary truck purchase
> —didn't need it; old car OK
> —parents had to cosign
> —didn't need new speakers either
>
> **Major support:** unnecessary personal items
> —changed toothpaste
> —started using after-shave
> —bought Reebok tennis shoes; already had new Pumas
>
> **Major support:** unnecessary magazine subscriptions
> —subscribed to *TIME* for the watch; already have one
> —subscribed to *Sports Illustrated* for the free videotape of sports events
>
> **Major support:** unnecessary miscellaneous purchases
> —rock-and-roll records, could have borrowed them from friends and made tapes
> —survival knife, for what?

This informal outline provides a structure for getting your ideas on paper. Following it ensures organized support of the thesis.

There may be times when an instructor requires a more **formal outline** attached to your essay. In that case, you should submit something along these lines:

> **Main idea:** Sometimes I am influenced by television advertisements and buy things I don't need and often can't afford.
>
> I. Unnecessary truck purchase
>   A. didn't need it; old car fine
>   B. couldn't afford it
>   1. parents had to cosign
>   2. stuck with payments
>   C. spent even more on unnecessary new speakers
>
> II. Unnecessary changes in personal items
>   A. switched brand of toothpaste
>   B. started using after-shave lotion
>   C. bought Reebok tennis shoes because of ad

    III. Unnecessary magazine subscriptions
        A. subscribed to *TIME* for the free watch
        B. subscribed to *Sports Illustrated* for the free videotape

    IV. Unnecessary miscellaneous purchases
        A. rock-and-roll records
        B. survival knife

Regardless of what form an outline takes, it is, like a thesis, usually a working outline. Once you start writing, new ideas may surface and you may add, delete, or change what you have on your outline. Until the final essay draft, nothing written should be considered permanent.

For practice, pick one of the topics you got from brainstorming on pages 47 and 48. In the space provided, write a working thesis and list your support. If you don't have at least eight supporting points, do more brainstorming or clustering.

topic: _____

working thesis: _____

support: _____

support: _____

support: _____

support: _____

support: _____

support: _____

support: _____

support: _____

In the space provided, group your support into some type of organizational pattern you could follow to write your first draft.

Nutshell Statement

You could begin writing your first draft at this point, but first you might want to write a nutshell statement. A nutshell statement is a one-paragraph statement of the **purpose** of your essay, the **support** to be used, and the **audience** to whom you are writing. A nutshell statement for an essay based on the outline on pages 57–58 might read:

> The purpose of my essay is to show how I am influenced by television commercials to buy things I don't need and often can't pay for. As support, I will reveal some of the items I have purchased recently because of ads I have seen, such as my new truck, personal items, magazine subscriptions, and other miscellaneous things. My intended audience will be other buyers like myself, who have yet to realize the power television ads have on us.

Notice that the statement of purpose contains the thesis. The statement regarding support summarizes the major groups or categories to be used. The statement about audience provides a real or imaginary picture of the people interested in the subject or those you want to make more aware of your subject.

Even though your ultimate "audience" is your instructor who will read and grade your essay, you should write for an audience that either is interested in your thesis or needs to be made aware. Thinking about audience before you write can help you determine the type of vocabulary to use, what arguments to present, and what to assume your audience may know about the subject. For instance, if your intended audience is fifth-grade students, you will have to write at a level they can understand. The words you use, your sentence structure, and the content will have to be geared to that group. On the other hand, if you are writing to convince anti-abortionists to change their minds, you will need to understand their reasoning and provide counterarguments. You will have to imagine what they might say in reaction to what you say. You will have to decide what approach will get them to even listen to your views. Should you use sarcasm? sympathy? medical terms?

A nutshell statement requires that you have your purpose, support, and audience in mind before you begin writing. If you can complete a nutshell statement, then you are ready to begin your first draft.

In the space provided, write a one-paragraph nutshell statement for an essay based on the outline you completed on pages 58–59.

Once you have your thesis, support, and audience in mind, you're ready to start your first draft.

Patterning Your Paragraphs

As a means for better reading comprehension, Unit 1 presented some paragraph methods that writers use. Now let's look at those same paragraph patterns from the writer's angle.

Recall that the **topic sentence** in a paragraph serves the same function as the thesis statement in an essay. Just as what you say in your essay depends on the point of your thesis, what you say and how you say it depend on the topic sentence of your paragraph. Here are some possible topic sentences for paragraphs. Notice that the way they are written requires that you follow a certain paragraph pattern:

Topic sentence	*Best pattern*
The Mazda truck commercial was very appealing.	**description** Descriptive details should be provided to create an image in the reader's mind of the commercial's appeal.
Yesterday, I went from one truck dealership to the next looking for the best deal.	**narration** A narrative would take the reader from one dealership experience to the next relating what happened at each.
I now realize I buy many things I don't really need for three reasons.	**analysis** Each of the three reasons for the buying problem need to be examined.

I recently bought several things I don't need.

illustration-example
Evidence needs to be provided to illustrate the unnecessary items purchased. Examples of the things not needed or a narrative about the buying of unnecessary items is required.

Pat's mother says he is the perfect example of an impulsive buyer.

definition
The term *impulsive buyer* needs to be defined so readers understand what Pat is an example of.

The commercial showed the four basic types of auto stereo speakers.

division-classification
The topic sentence divides the speakers into four basic types, each of which needs to be named and discussed.

The Mazda truck commercial appealed to Jim more than the one for Chevrolets.

comparison-contrast
While some description of the two truck ads may be needed, the topic sentence calls for a comparison of the two ads to show why Jim prefers one over the other.

Because the Mazda commercial was so well done, I bought one of their trucks.

cause-effect
The cause here is the ad, and the effect is the purchase; description of the well-done ad may be needed to help explain the cause.

It is important to see here that the way a topic sentence is stated requires that you structure your paragraph with a pattern that supports it. Of course, all the examples above are "working" topic sentences. After you have developed your support, you may need to change the wording of the topic sentence to fit what you wrote. You may decide that the topic sentence is best placed at the end of the paragraph or in the middle, or that it should be implied rather than stated. Remember, revision does not come at any particular stage. It occurs at all points during the writing process. But if writing does not come easy for you, try writing a topic sentence that you can use as the first sentence in the paragraph and work from there.

Here are some topic sentences taken from the reading selections in this book. In the space provided, write a one-sentence statement that tells what pattern or method should be used to develop the paragraph and why.

1. "Compared to the animals around us, there's no doubt we are a remarkable phenomenon."

2. "I will never forget that Sunday as long as I live."

3. "Behind a Dumpster sits a man who calls himself Red enjoying the last drops of a bottle of wine called Wild Irish Rose."

4. "There are four reasons for practicing freewriting."

5. "After the dishes have soaked in water hot enough to deform small plastic implements, I begin my attack."

6. "We humans live with contradictions in our behavior."

7. "Irony is not easy to explain."

8. "Television journalism has recently stimulated political conservatism."

Compare your statements with these. Wording may be different, but the explanations should contain the same ideas.

1. The **comparison-contrast** method will show why humans are a phenomenon compared with other animals.
2. A **narration** will tell us about that unforgettable Sunday.
3. The topic sentence introduces us to Red and calls for more **description** of him.
4. **Division-classification** is required to show each of the four reasons for practicing freewriting.
5. The "attack" on the dishes is a process calling for a **step-by-step analysis.**

6. **Examples and illustrations** of contradictory behavior are needed for support.

7. An extended **definition** of irony is needed to show why it isn't easy to define.

8. Television journalism has stimulated political conservatism requiring some proof or support of this **cause-effect** relationship.

If you had trouble with these, you may want to review the section on paragraph patterns in Unit 1. Otherwise, move on to the next step—writing the first draft.

First Draft

Let's say that you decide to follow the formal outline on pages 57–58 about the effect of television commercials. The first draft might look something like this:

First Draft

I have a tendency to buy things I see on television commercials even though I don't need them and often can't pay for them. The other night I was putting myself to sleep by watching a late movie on TV when an ad with a fast-talking announcer began describing a new collection of rock-and-roll records. You've probably seen the kind I mean. You get to hear little pieces of music with famous singers singing one or two lines then they cut to the next song. Anyway, I like all of the songs they played, and when the announcers said, "Call this 800 number now and get these fabulous songs not sold in any record store," I called and ordered the record set. This is not unusual behavior for me.

I bought my Mazda truck because of a TV commercial. It seemed like every time I watched TV I'd see the same ad for the truck. It showed the truck going through mud, climbing hills, and carrying heavy loads. Then it showed a guy and his girlfriend all dressed up pulling up in front of some fancy restaurant in the truck all shined up. The girl was something else and every time the ad came on I caught myself looking at her and not the truck.

Anyway, the next thing I knew I had talked my folks into cosigning the loan for me even though they tried to talk me out of it. Banks don't loan money to college students to buy trucks. There wasn't anything wrong with my old car. But I came up with this crazy idea I could get some parttime work hauling or something to help make the payments. I think that's what convinced them to help out. Anyway, now I can't afford to take a girl out because I'm too busy with classes, homework, and an evening job I have to keep to make my truck payments.

I also have two magazine subscriptions that I don't even have time to read. When **TIME** showed an ad on TV for a good deal on a subscription, plus a free watch, I called their toll-free number. Then Sports Illustrated ran an ad for their magazine offering a free videocassette of famous sports plays if you subscribed to them. Of course, I called their toll-free number. Now unread magazines are stacking up around my room. Not only that, they sent me a Beta videocassette and we've got VHS.

I realize now that I have even been persuaded by TV ads to buy items I never used before. My family has always used Crest. After seeing all those ads for Closeup and having kissable breath, I got mom to buy some for me. I even use an after-shave lotion now because of ads. I use to do like my dad and just put on a little of mom's skin cream after I shaved. And even though I didn't need them, I bought a new pair of Reebok tennis shoes because a TV commercial for a local shoe store had them on sale.

Last night there was a commercial on TV for a good deal on a neat looking survival knife. It looked like something the commandos use. It had a big blade, a compass in the handle, with a fish hook and line, matches and the sheath had a little pocket with a sharpening stone in it. Naturally, I ordered one.

When my mom heard about this she called me an "impulsive complusive buyer." When I asked her what she meant, she just yelled look it up. After looking it up, I realize she's right. I need to belong to a "buyers anonymous" group or something.

Even though the outline wasn't followed exactly, it served to get the ideas into a rough draft in essay form. Of course, this is just the first draft. There's more to be done.

This is a good place to make another pitch for word processing. If you don't know how already, you should learn to write on a word processor. Making changes, doing revisions, and producing neat essays is so much easier once you learn word processing. In a recent study done by a professional organization of English teachers, it was discovered that students who submitted typed papers usually got a letter grade higher than those who submitted handwritten papers. But more importantly, word processing enables you to make changes without having to retype your entire essay. It's something to think about.

Whatever you use for your first drafts—pencil, pen, typewriter, or word processor—don't worry about mistakes in punctuation, word choice, spelling, and the like as you write your first draft. At this point, you want to get your essay ideas into words on paper. If you stop to make too many corrections as you write, you may lose your train of thought. You can worry about the nitty-gritty later. On the other hand, if it's an error you can quickly change, go ahead and do it, but never at the expense of thoughtful content.

Before Going On

Remember that a working thesis statement is open to changes based on your supporting ideas. Before writing a first draft, make certain you have sufficient support to develop your thesis. Once you are satisfied you do, organize or outline the support as a writing guide. Writing a nutshell statement before you begin your draft helps you focus on your thesis, support, and audience. As you write your draft, be aware that all paragraphs should have an implied or directly stated topic sentence. The wording of your topic sentence can often provide a clue as to the best paragraph pattern to use. However, don't let concern over paragraph patterns or mechanical errors get in the way of getting your ideas on paper. Changes and corrections can be made during the revision and editing process.

Look again at the student essay on television commercials. Apply the information on reading essays from Unit 1. Mark and take notes as you read. Then, on a separate sheet of paper, write what you would tell the student about the essay, offering your suggestions and indicating errors that should be changed. Your instructor may want to see your paper.

Getting It Right: Revising and Editing (Stage 3)

It can't be said too often that good writing frequently requires many rewrites. Don't be impatient. Revision is necessary, expected, and part of the writing process. A final draft of an essay may look nothing like the first draft. There's much to do before turning in your masterpiece.

Revising

Here's a checklist of questions to ask yourself when you begin revision of your first draft:

1. *Have you made your point?*
   Make sure your thesis is clear. Your purpose should be clear to the reader, whether it's stated or implied. Have someone read your draft; if he or she doesn't understand the point you're trying to make, rewrite until it becomes clear. It's even possible that you will need to change your entire thesis once a first draft is completed.

2. *Does your support move smoothly from one point to the next?*
   Rearrange what you have written so that the ideas flow easily from one to the next. You may need to "cut and paste," or move a sentence or paragraph from one place to another. Use scissors and literally cut up your draft, moving parts around where you want them. (Here again, word processing helps. With a word processor you can easily move whole paragraphs around without having to cut or retype.) To move smoothly and logically from one point to the next, use transitional words and phrases such as:

however	thus	in addition
although	on the other hand	first
therefore	in conclusion	next
furthermore	in other words	finally

moreover	for instance	as a result
consequently	for example	also

3. *Have you developed each paragraph fully?*
   Look closely at the topic sentence of each paragraph. Do you provide enough support to fully develop the topic sentence? You may need to add more information or to take out information that does not relate to the topic sentence. You may need to rewrite your topic sentence to fit the content of the paragraph.

4. *Will your essay interest your audience?*
   Try to make your essay interesting for your audience. Your opening paragraph should grab the reader's attention and make him or her want to read on. Try to get a picture in your mind of your audience and talk to them in writing. Sometimes the opening paragraph isn't written until several drafts are completed.

5. *Is the tone of your essay consistent?*
   Use the same **tone of voice** throughout your essay. For instance, the tone of the student's rough draft on television commercials is personable and friendly. Using contractions (such as *don't* instead of *do not*) is acceptable in informal writing. The essay is not written for the audience of a scholarly or professional journal. If it were, it would need more formal language, less personal narrative, and a thesis that dealt more broadly with television commercials and cited sources other than personal ones.

6. *Have you said everything you want and need to say and nothing else?*
   Make certain you have said everything necessary to support your thesis. On the other hand, you may need to cut out passages that aren't relevant or repeat what you've already said.

Let's apply the above checklist to the rough draft on television commercials. Here's what it might look like:

I have a tendency to buy things I see on television commer- *move to the end*
cials even though I don't need them and often can't pay for them.

The other night I was putting myself to sleep by watching a late
movie on ~~TV~~ *television* when a~~n ad~~ *commercial* with a fast-talking announcer began describing a new collection of rock-and-roll records. You've probably
seen the kind I mean. ~~You get to hear~~ *They play* little ~~pieces~~ *snippets* of ~~music with~~
of a song you recognize
famous singers singing one or two lines∧then they cut to the next
song. ~~Anyway,~~ I like all of the songs they played, ~~and~~ *so* when the

announcer~~s~~ said, "Call this 800 number now and ~~get these~~ fabu- *operators on duty,* *order this* lous ~~songs~~ not sold in any ~~record~~ store," I ~~called and ordered the~~ *record set* *did.* ~~record set.~~ This is not unusual behavior for me. (For *instance,*) *start new ¶*

I bought my Mazda truck because of a TV commercial. It seemed like every time I watched TV I'd see the same ad for the truck. It showed the truck going through mud, climbing hills, and *at work during the day* carrying heavy loads. Then it showed ~~a guy and his girlfriend all~~ *the truck at night cleaned and polished,* ~~dressed up~~ pulling up in front of ~~some fancy~~ restaurant ~~, in the~~ *a plush* *As the driver got* *out, a smiling doorman helped the woman out. Both of them looked elegant, but she* ~~truck all shined up. The girl was something else~~ and every time *really* *got to me.* the ad came on I caught myself looking at her and not the truck. *I realize now it wasn't the truck I wanted.* ¶ Anyway, the next thing I knew I had talked my folks into cosign- *a* *a new truck since* ing ~~the~~ loan for ~~me even though~~ (they tried to talk me out of it *since*) ~~Banks don't loan money to college students to buy trucks.~~ There wasn't anything wrong with my old car. But I came up with this *delivering* crazy idea I could get some parttime work hauling or ~~something~~ to help make the payments. I think that's what convinced them to *I wish I hadn't been so convincing.* help out. ~~Anyway, now~~ I can't afford to take a girl out because I'm too busy with classes, homework, and an evening job I have to keep to make my truck payments.

Thanks to TV commercials,
I also have two magazine subscriptions that I don't even have *I saw a commercial* *reduced price* time to read. When ~~TIME showed an ad on TV~~ for a ~~good deal~~ on a *for TIME* subscription plus a free watch, I called their toll-free number. The *offered a low-priced subscription and* Sports Illustrated ~~ran an ad for their magazine offering~~ a free videocassette of famous sports plays if you subscribed to them. Of course, I called their toll-free number. Now unread magazines are stacking up around my room. Not only that, they sent me a Beta videocassette and we've got VHS.

I realize now that I have even been persuaded by TV ads to buy items I never used before. My family has always used Crest. *the need for* After seeing all those ads for Closeup and ~~having~~ kissable breath,

I got my mom to buy some for me. I even ~~use~~ began using an after-shave lotion now because of ~~ads.~~ the influence of commercials, I use to do like my dad and just put on a
little of mom's skin cream after I shaved. And even though I
didn't need them, I bought a new pair of Reebok tennis shoes because a TV commercial for a local shoe store had them on sale.

Last night there was a commercial on TV for a good deal on an
interesting ~~neat~~ looking survival knife, similar to the ones ~~It looked like something~~ the commandos use. It has a big blade, a compass in the handle, with a fish
hook and line, matches and the sheath had a little pocket with a
sharpening stone in it. Naturally, I ordered one. *end here*

When my mom heard about this she called me an "impulsive
complusive buyer." When I asked her what she meant, she just
move up yelled look it up. After looking it up, I realize she's right. I need to
belong to a "buyers anonymous" group or something.

Look more closely at some of the changes being considered for the
next draft. Sentences are to be moved or removed. Wording has been
changed, in some cases to keep from repeating words, in others to be
more descriptive or clear. New paragraphs have been started in different places, and the last paragraph has been moved. While none of
the support has changed, more attention has been paid to the flow
of support with smoother transitions from one idea to the next. Attention to such things is the basis for another draft. And even after
that draft is completed, it may be necessary to write still another.

After applying the revision check list to several different drafts,
you might have something resembling this:

About to doze off while watching an old movie on television
the other night, a commercial caught my eye. The sound came up
as a fast-talking announcer began describing a new collection of
rock-and-roll records. You've probably seen the kind I mean. They
play little snippets of singers singing one or two seconds of a
song that made them famous, cutting quickly from one to the
next. I like all the tunes they played, so when the announcer

urged, "Call this toll-free number now ... operators are standing by ... order this fabulous set of records not available in any store," I did.

This, I'm sorry to say, is not unusual behavior for me. For instance, when I saw a television commercial offering a free digital watch along with a reduced price on a subscription to TIME, I called their toll-free number. Then Sports Illustrated offered a low price subscription along with a free videocassette of some famous sports plays. Of course, I had to call their toll-free number too. Now I have unread magazines stacking up around my room. Not only that, the videocassette they set me is for a Beta machine, we've got VHS.

TV commercials have influenced me so much that I even use personal items I have never used before, my family has used Crest toothpaste ever since I can remember. But after all those ads for Close-up (I think its the kissable breath idea) I had my mom buy some just for me. And, like my dad, I used to just apply a little of moms skin cream on my face after I shaved. But now, thanks to the influence of television commercials, I have tried several beands of after-shave lotion.

The biggest purchase I ever made because of a TV commercial is my truck. It seemed like every time I watched TV I'd see the same ad for Mazda pickup trucks. It showed the truck at work during the day going through mud, climbing hills, and carrying heavy loads. Then it showed the truck at night, cleaned and polished, pulling up in front of a plush restaurant. As the driver got out, a doorman helped his date step out. Both of them looked elegant. But it was the woman that got me. Every time the commercial comes on, I caught myself looking at her, not the truck. Anyway, the next thing I knew I had talked my folks into cosigning a loan for a new truck, since banks don't loan money to un-employed college students to buy new trucks. They tried to talk me out of it because there wasn't anything wrong with my old one. But you know how it is when you really want something. I rationalized that I could get part-time work hauling or delivering to help make payments. I think that's what convinced my mom and dad to help out.

Now I wish I hadn't been so convincing. I can't afford to go out on a date because I'm too busy with classes, homework, and an evening job. If I don't make my truck payments, my parents said they would sell my truck. They don't want to be stuck with the payments. I can't blame them.

Recently a local shoe store announced on television that Ree-bok tennis shoes were on sale. The next day, I bought a pair, even though I had just bought a pair of Pumas a week before. When my mom heard, she called me an "impulsive compulsive buyer". When I asked her what she meant, she yelled, "Look it up!" and mum-bled something about my need to join a "buyers anonymous" group or quit watching so much TV.

She's right I have a tendency to buy things I see on television even though I don't need them or can't really afford them. Even last night, there was a commercial for a survival knife similar to the type commandos use. The knife has a big blade, a hollow han-dle with a fish hook, some line, a few matches, a compass that screws on top of the knife handle, and the sheath has a little pocket on the side with a sharpening stone, I just couldn't resist calling there toll-free number.

This draft still retains the same thesis and support, but it is struc-tured differently. The position of the thesis has been moved from the opening paragraph to the end. The first draft opened with the thesis statement and then provided examples of "impulsive compulsive" buying. This draft opens with a narrative anecdote that reflects the subject and thesis of the essay, rather than directly stating it. The narrative now builds on one purchase after the other and ends with the thesis statement. This seems to work better because the thesis itself doesn't deal with any resolution of the problem, only an awareness of the influence of television commercials on the author.

Other changes in the position of the supporting materials have been made. The largest purchase, the truck, has been moved toward the end of the essay, with smaller purchases leading up to it. The placement of the Reebok purchase after the truck purchase works well because it reflects the mother's exasperation with her son's buying habits. It also serves as a transition to the last paragraph which now contains the thesis and an acknowledgement that the author's mother is right: another needless purchase, the survival knife, is made. The essay ends with a touch of humor, yet leaves the reader with a feeling of pity for the author.

While the student essay is not perfect, it is an honest essay based on experience and it fits the assignment given: to write an essay on some aspect of television. Had the assignment been more specific, such as one requiring research on the effects of television advertising, then this first-person essay would not do.

But there is still more to do before this essay can be turned in. It needs editing.

Editing

Once you are satisfied that your essay's organizational structure and thesis are clear and fully developed, you need to edit your essay for errors in punctuation and mechanics. Of course, as you do this you may also see other problems or errors that need revision. Revision is a continual process, even though you may be focusing on something more specific.

Here is a list of questions to ask yourself when you edit your latest draft:

1. *Have you given yourself some time off between drafts?*
   Put your essay aside for at least a couple of hours before editing. In fact, it's a good idea to do this between each draft. You need to get away from what you've written so you can come back to it with "fresh eyes."

2. *Have you read each sentence aloud to hear how it sounds?*
   Begin editing by reading aloud the *last* sentence of your essay. Once you're satisfied it is the best you can do, read aloud the next-to-last sentence and do the same thing. Gradually work your

way to the beginning of the essay sentence by sentence. It sounds odd, but doing so forces you to look at each sentence out of context, as a separate piece of writing. Listen to the way the sentence sounds. If it is difficult to read or sounds awkward, rewrite it. Make certain each sentence is complete, not a fragment or piece of a sentence.

3. *Have you used proper punctuation?*
   Don't form a comma splice by putting a comma [,] between two sentences. If you aren't sure where a comma belongs, it's probably best to leave it out. Place periods [.] at the ends of sentences, not at the end of phrases or introductory clauses. Use apostrophes ['] to show possession (Tom's house, the Jones' house). Watch for *you're* (you are) as opposed to *your* (belonging to), and *it's* (it is) as opposed to *its* (belonging to it).

4. *Do your verbs agree with their subjects?*
   Watch for sentences that contain singular subjects and plural verbs. For instance, in the following sentence the subject is singular, but a plural verb is used:

   A set of books are missing.

   Because *set* is the subject, not *books*, the verb *is* should be used. Look also for sentences that contain plural subjects but singular verbs, such as:

   Boxes of computer software was everywhere.

   The sentence should use the verb *were* to agree with the subject *boxes*. Such mistakes are easy to make.

5. *Are your pronoun references correct?*
   Look at each pronoun (his, her, their, its, etc.) and make sure it agrees with what it refers to. For instance, it's incorrect to write:

   Everyone in the group must buy their own lunch.

   Since *everyone* is singular, the plural pronoun *their* can't be used. It should read:

   Everyone in the group must buy his or her own lunch.

   [Note: Avoid sexist usage. Don't use *his* when the reference being made is to a group containing both men and women.] Don't confuse *there* (not here), *they're* (they are), and *their* (belonging to them).

6. *Have you repeated the same word too often?*
   If you don't own a thesaurus, a dictionary of synonyms (words that mean the same thing), you should buy one. There are several published in paperback editions. A good thesaurus will not only define words for you, but will also provide synonyms and antonyms (words that are opposite in meaning). When you notice that you are repeating a word, look it up and use a synonym.

7. *Do you have a title that reflects your thesis?*
   A title, like a thesis, should not be too general. It should reflect the purpose and the content of your paper. A title should fit the tone of your essay. If your essay is serious in tone, it's probably best to have a title that is direct; if your essay is light or humorous, try a catchy title.

For practice in editing, apply the steps of the preceding editing checklist to the last draft of the student essay on pages 71–73. Change any errors you find and give it an appropriate title.

✍️ Writing Exercise

Write a one-paragraph summary of the editing checklist. Make certain you have a topic sentence that allows you to discuss all the steps. Your instructor may want to see your paper.

Here is what the next draft of the essay might look like after editing and minor revisions. Compare your markings with those below.

About to doze off while watching an old movie on television the other night, ~~the sound of~~ a commercial caught my ~~eye~~. The *awk. change opening* attention sound came up as a fast-talking announcer began describing a new collection of rock-and-roll records. You've probably seen the kind I mean. They play little snippets of singers singing one or two seconds of a song that made them famous, cutting quickly from one to the next. I like all the tunes they played, so when the announcer urged, "Call this toll-free number now ... operators are standing by ... order this fabulous set of records not available in any store," I did.

This, I'm sorry to say, is not unusual behavior for me. For instance, when I saw a television commercial offering a free digital watch along with a reduced price on a subscription to <u>TIME</u>, I called their toll-free number. Then *underline magazine titles* <u>Sports Illustrated</u> offered a low-price subscription along with a free videocassette of some famous sports plays. Of course, I had to call their toll-free number too. Now I have unread magazines stacking up around my room. Not only that, the videocassette they set me is for a Beta machine, we've got VHS.

[margin: comma splice, replace comma with semicolon.]

TV commercials have influenced me so much that I even use personal items I have never used before, my family has used Crest toothpaste ever since I can remember. But after all those ads for Close-up (I think it's the kissable breath idea), I had my mom buy some just for me. And, like my dad, I used to just apply a little of mom's skin cream on my face after I shaved. But now, thanks to the influence of television commercials, I have tried several brands of after-shave lotion.

[margin: comma splice. Replace comma with period. Cap M.]
[margin: comma after intro phrase]
[margin: possessive]

The biggest purchase I ever made because of a TV commercial is my truck. It seemed ~~like~~ *that* every time I watched TV I'd see the same ad for Mazda pickup trucks. It showed the truck at work during the day going through mud, climbing hills, and carrying heavy loads. Then it showed the truck at night, cleaned and polished, pulling up in front of a plush-*looking* restaurant. As the driver got out, a doorman helped his date ~~step out~~ *his date was helped by a doorman*. Both of them looked elegant. But it was the woman ~~that~~ *who* got me. Every time the commercial ~~comes~~ *came* on, I caught myself looking at her, not the truck. Anyway, the next thing I knew I had talked my ~~folks~~ *parents* into cosigning a loan for a new truck, since banks don't loan money to unemployed college students to buy new trucks. They tried to talk me out of it, because there wasn't anything wrong with my old one. But you know how it is when you really want something. I rationalized that I could get part-time work hauling or delivering to help make payments. I think that's what convinced my mom and dad to help out.

[margin: use who to refer to people]
[margin: past tense]

Now I wish I hadn't been so convincing. I can't afford to go out on a date because I'm too busy with classes, homework, and an evening job. If I don't make my truck payments, my parents said they would sell my truck. They don't want to be stuck with the payments. I can't blame them.

Recently a local shoe store announced on television that Reebok tennis shoes were on sale. The next day I [*necessary?*] bought ~~a pair~~ [*them*], even though I had just bought a pair of [*pair used twice*] Pumas a week before. When my mom heard, she called me an "impulsive compulsive buyer" [*end punctuation, goes inside quotation marks.*] When I asked her what she meant, she yelled, "Look it up!" and mumbled some- thing about my need to join a "buyers anonymous" group or quit watching so much TV.

She's right I [*run on needs period.*] have a tendency to buy things I see on television even though I don't need them or can't really af- ford them. Even last night, there was a commercial for a survival knife similar to the type commandos use. The knife has a big blade, a hollow handle with a fish hook, some line, a few matches, a compass that screws on top of the knife handle, and the sheath has a little pocket on the side with a sharpening stone, I just couldn't resist calling ~~their~~ ~~there~~ toll-free number. [*wrong word*]

At this point you are ready to type up the final draft to submit to your instructor.

Proofreading

Once you write, type, or print out your final draft, you should proof- read your paper for typing and spelling mistakes. It's possible that even then you might notice changes that have to be made. Remember that revising and editing, even though presented here as Stage 3, can happen at any stage of the writing process.

If the final copy of your essay has many mistakes, you may need to recopy or retype it. However, if it only has a few corrections necessary, use the proofreading guide in the Appendix to make your corrections. Your final copy might be marked like this after proofreading:

Trouble with Toll-Free Numbers

The other night I was about to doze off while watching an old movie on television when the sounds of a commercial caught my attention. A fast-talking announcer began describing a new collection of rock-and-roll records. You've probably seen the kind I mean. They play little snippets of singers singing one or two seconds of a song that made them famous, cutting quickly from one to the next. I like all the tunes they played, so when the announcer urged, "Call this toll-free number now ... operators are standing by ... order this fabulous set of records not available in any store," I did.

This, I'm sorry to say, is not unusual behavior for me. For instance, when I saw a television commercial offering a free digital watch along with a reduced price on a subscription to TIME, I called their toll-free number. Then Sports Illustrated offered a low-priced subscription along with a free videocassette of famous sports plays. Of course, I had to call their toll-free number, too. Now I have stacks of unread magazines around my room. Not only that, the cassette they sent me is for Beta; we have VHS.

TV commercials have influenced me so much that I even use personal items I never used before. My family has brushed with Crest toothpaste ever since I can remember. But after all those ads for Close-up (I think it's the kissable breath idea), I had mom buy some just for me. And, like my dad, I used to just apply a little of moms skin cream on my face after I shaved. But now, thanks to the influence of television commercials, I have tried several bands of after-shave lotion.

The biggest purchase I ever made because of a TV commercial was my truck. Almost every time I watched TV, I'd see the same ad for Mazda pickup trucks. It showed the truck at work during the day going through mud, climbing hils, and carrying heavy loads. Then it showed the truck at night, cleaned and polished. Neon signs reflected off the truck as it pulled in front of a plush-looking restaurant. As the driver, now dressed in his finest, got out, a doorman helped ~~his~~ the driver's elegant-looking date step from the truck. But it was the woman who got me. Every time the commercial came on, I caught myself looking at her, not the truck.

Anyway, the next thing I knew I had talked my parents into cosigning a loan for a new truck, since banks don't loan money to unemployed college students to buy new trucks. They tried to discourage me because there wasn't anything wrong with my old one. But you know how it is when you think you really want something. I rationalized that I could get part-time work hauling or delivering to help make payments. I think that's what convinced my mom and dad to help out.

Now I wish I hadn't been so convincing. I can't afford to go out on a date because of my truck payments. After attending classes, doing my homework, and working an evening job, I'm too tired to do anything but watch TV. If I don't make my Mazda payments, my parents said they ~~would~~ will sell my truck. They don't want to be stuck with the payments. I can't blame them.

But my buying hasn't stopped there. Recently a local shoe store announced on television that Reebok tennis shoes were on sale. The next day, I bought them, even though I had just bought a pair of Pumas a week before. When my mom heard, she called me an "impulsive compulsive buyer." When I asked her what she meant, she yelled, "Look it up" and mumbled something about my need to join a "buyers anonymous" group or quit watching so much TV.

She's right; I have a tendency to buy things I see on television even though I don't need them or can't really affod them. Even last night, there was a commercial for a survival knife similar to the type commandos use. It has a big blade, a hollow handle with a fish hook, some line, a few matches, a compass that screws on top of the handle, and the sheath has a little pocket on the side with a sharpening stone. When their toll-free number was announced, I just couldn't resist calling.

Using the proper proofreading marks relieves you of retyping or recopying your entire essay. One of the reasons for double spacing each page is to leave room to make corrections neatly. Of course, if there are so many corrections that the paper is too messy to read, you will have to redo it.

As a means to understanding the use of proofreading marks, use the symbols provided to mark the corrections in the paragraph below.

to remove a letter	reallly
to insert a word or letter	libary
to insert punctuation	professors book
to insert space	the model essay
to reverse letters	revrese
to change a word	a little larger
to close up space	re verse

Lets say you are assigned to do research on what critics have said abuot John Updikes novel The Witches of Eastwick. In such a case secondary sources will be called for in your pa per. If, on the other hand the assignment calls for your own analysis of the novel, you will neeed to stick to the primary source, the novel Reading secondarysources on the novel, however, may provide you with ideas arguments that could be useful in supporting your own analysis of the book.

Compare your markings with the following to see how well you did.

Let's say you are assigned to do research on what critics have said about John Updike's novel <u>The Witches of Eastwick</u>. In such a case, secondary sources will be called for in your paper. If, on the other hand, the assignment calls for your own analysis of the novel, you will need to stick to the primary source, the novel. Reading secondary sources on the novel, however, may provide you with ideas *and* arguments that could be useful in supporting your own analysis of the book.

Before submitting it, you should retype an essay that has this many corrections in one paragraph. The corrections get in the way of the reading content.

Your instructor may require that you follow a particular form regarding size of margins, position of name, title, and page numbers, and so on. If not, you will find information on form and style beginning on page 417 in the Appendix.

Before Going On

Remember that revising and editing are necessary and vital to good writing. Use the revision stage to make certain your essay makes its point, that the point is supported adequately, that each paragraph is developed fully, that your tone is consistent, and that you have done your best to make the essay interesting to your audience. When editing, look at each sentence separately. Make certain each sentence is complete and that it sounds correct. Check for correct punctuation, subject-verb agreement, pronoun agreement, and overuse of certain words. Consult the Appendix for the proper essay format and proofreading guide.

Writing Exercise

On a separate sheet of paper, write three paragraphs summarizing the major points of each of the three stages of writing presented in this section. Make certain each paragraph has a topic sentence and that each paragraph is developed fully. Apply the three writing stages to this writing exercise. Your instructor may want you to turn in this exercise.

Brief Version of the Revision Checklist on Pages 68–69

When you revise the various drafts of an essay, ask yourself the following:

_____ 1. Have you made your point? Is your thesis clear?

_____ 2. Does your support move smoothly from one point to the next? Is your support logically arranged? Do you use transitional words and phrases to aid the reader?

_____ 3. Have you fully developed each paragraph? Does each paragraph have a topic sentence? Have you added or cut information if necessary?

_____ 4. Will your essay interest your audience? Does your opening paragraph grab the reader's attention?

_____ 5. Is the tone of your essay consistent? Do you use the same tone throughout? Is the language appropriate for your audience?

_____ 6. Have you said everything you need to say? Is your thesis fully developed? Does everything relate to the thesis?

Brief Version of the Editing Checklist on Pages 74–76

When you edit the various drafts of an essay, ask yourself the following:

_____ 1. Have you given yourself some time off between drafts? Have you put your essay aside for at least two hours?

_____ 2. Have you read each sentence aloud to hear how it sounds? Did you read each sentence from last to first?

_____ 3. Have you used proper punctuation?

_____ 4. Do your subjects and verbs agree in tense and number?

_____ 5. Are your pronoun usages correct?

_____ 6. Have you avoided repeating the same word too often?

_____ 7. Do you have a title that reflects your thesis or subject?

PART II

READINGS WORTH THINKING AND WRITING ABOUT

Viewpoints on

Learning

DOONESBURY

G. B. TRUDEAU

*"Most teachers would agree that
the primary goal of education
is to teach students
how to learn on their own."*
Kenneth Graham and H. Alan Robinson

*I*MAGINE what your life would be like if you woke up one morning and everything you had ever learned was gone. You wouldn't be able to get out of bed, dress yourself, feed yourself, or find the bathroom, much less know how to use it. You wouldn't be able to talk, read, or write. You wouldn't know what a television was, how to drive a car, or how to use a telephone. In other words, you'd be helpless.

We all know that learning is important. But what exactly is it? A dictionary might tell you that learning is acquiring knowledge through experience or study (sounds all right); a teacher might tell you that it's memorizing what she/he wants you to know for a test (we could argue that one); your boss might tell you that it's mastery of the task you're hired to do (OK, if the pay's good); a psychology book might tell you that learning is a relatively permanent change in behavior due to past experience (that one could use some examples); your parents may tell you that learning is achieved by a "Do as I say, not as I do" approach (no comment).

Obviously, learning takes place in many ways and forms. Hardly a day goes by that we don't learn something, either directly or indirectly. For instance, from television you will "learn" that minorities are generally criminals, victims, service workers, or students (come on, now!) and you might "learn" from a friend that smoking is "cool" (but what about the surgeon general?). The tendency, however, is to link learning with school. Then, of course, we can think about the definition of school. Is it a building labeled elementary, junior, or senior high school? Is it the ivy-walled institution called college or university? Is it the warehouse converted into an adult education center? Is it Sunday school, the synagogue, or church? Is it the media—from television to the *National Enquirer?* Is it the city streets? Some type of schooling certainly occurs in all these places.

This unit does not provide any answers to what learning and schooling are. Instead, reading selections with various viewpoints on learning are offered. As you practice your reading skills, let your reactions to the ideas and the exercises provide some ideas for essays of your own.

📖 Preparing to Read

Take a minute or two to look over the following reading selection. Note the title and author, read the opening paragraph, and check the length. Make certain you have the time now to read it carefully and to do the exercises that follow it. Then, in the spaces provided, answer the following questions.

1. What will the essay have to say about school vs. education? _____

_____

_____

2. What might you learn from reading this essay? _____

_____

_____

3. Do you think this selection will be serious or humorous? _____

Vocabulary

Good comprehension of what you are about to read depends upon your understanding of the words below. The number following each word refers to the paragraph where it is used.

armaments (2) weapons

violate (3) break (a law, for example)

social cohesion (5) group togetherness (here, of parents who share the same concerns)

pigmentation (5) skin coloration (refers here to racial differences)

nightstick (5) a club used by policemen

subduing (5) overpowering, bringing under control

incentive (8) drive, desire, motivation

the bar (13) jargon for the legal profession, law practice

"the race is to the cunning and . . . the unprincipled" (13) the "winners" are crafty, shrewd, and without morals (a possible allusion or reference to John Davidson's poem "War Song": "The race is to the swift;/The battle to the strong.")

emerges (14) comes out

melodrama (14) plays or movies that rely heavily on sensational events, sentimentality, or coincidence instead of strong characterization

porcelain (15) a hard, white ceramic

inclination (15) desire

Now read the essay.

School vs. Education

RUSSELL BAKER

1   By the age of six the average child will have completed the basic American education and be ready to enter school. If the child has been attentive in these preschool years, he or she will already have mastered many skills.

2   From television, the child will have learned how to pick a lock, commit a fairly elaborate bank holdup, prevent wetness all day long, get the laundry twice as white, and kill people with a variety of sophisticated armaments.

3   From watching his parents, the child, in many cases, will already know how to smoke, how much soda to mix with whiskey, what kind of language to use when angry, and how to violate the speed laws without being caught.

4   At this point, the child is ready for the second stage of education, which occurs in school. There, a variety of lessons may be learned in the very first days.

5   The teacher may illustrate the economic importance of belonging to a strong union by closing down the school before the child arrives. Fathers and mothers may demonstrate to the child the social cohesion that can be built on shared hatred by demonstrating their dislike for children whose pigmentation displeases them. In the latter event, the child may receive visual instruction in techniques of stoning buses,

cracking skulls with a nightstick, and subduing mobs with tear gas. Formal education has begun.

6   During formal education, the child learns that life is for testing. This stage lasts twelve years, a period during which the child learns that success comes from telling testers what they want to hear.

7   Early in this stage, the child learns that he is either dumb or smart. If the teacher puts intelligent demands upon the child, the child learns he is smart. If the teacher expects little of the child, the child learns he is dumb and soon quits bothering to tell the testers what they want to hear.

8   At this point, education becomes more subtle. The child taught by school that he is dumb observes that neither he, she, nor any of the many children who are even dumber, ever fails to be promoted to the next grade. From this, the child learns that while everybody talks a lot about the virtue of being smart, there is very little incentive to stop being dumb.

9   What is the point of school, besides attendance? the child wonders. As the end of the first formal stage of education approaches, school answers this question. The point is to equip the child to enter college.

10   Children who have been taught they are smart have no difficulty. They have been happily telling testers what they want to hear for twelve years. Being artists at telling testers what they want to hear, they are admitted to college joyously, where they promptly learn that they are the hope of America.

11   Children whose education has been limited to adjusting themselves to their schools' low estimates of them are admitted to less joyous colleges which, in some cases, may teach them to read.

12   At this stage of education, a fresh question arises for everyone. If the point of lower education was to get into college, what is the point of college? The answer is soon learned. The point of college is to prepare the student—no longer a child now—to get into graduate school. In college, the student learns that it is no longer enough simply to tell the testers what they want to hear. Many are tested for graduate school; few are admitted.

13   Those excluded may be denied valuable certificates to prosper in medicine, at the bar, in the corporate boardroom. The student learns that the race is to the cunning and often, alas, to the unprincipled.

14   Thus, the student learns the importance of destroying competitors and emerges richly prepared to play his role in the great simmering melodrama of American life.

15   Afterward, the former student's destiny fulfilled, his life rich with Oriental carpets, rare porcelain, and full bank accounts, he may one day find himself with the leisure and the inclination to open a book with a curious mind, and start to become educated.

Understanding the Content

Feel free to reread all or parts of the selection to answer the following questions.

1. What does Baker see as the difference between school and education?

2. What are each of the "stages of education"? What is learned in each stage?

3. What is Baker's thesis? Is it stated or implied?

4. Describe Baker's attitude toward school. What early passages reflect this attitude?

5. Is Baker's tone serious or humorous? How do you know?

6. What can we infer about Baker's attitude toward television? toward parents? toward schools? toward American life?

Looking at Structure and Style

1. Divide Baker's essay into each "stage of education." What transitional techniques does he use to move from one stage to the next? Are they effective?

2. What is the topic sentence of paragraph 5? What paragraph pattern is used?

3. Explain or rewrite in your own words the following passages from the essay:
   a. paragraph 5, second sentence
   b. "... The child learns that success comes from telling testers what they want to hear." (6)
   c. paragraph 11
   d. paragraph 14

4. Explain Baker's conclusion in paragraph 15. How effective is it?

5. What suggestions for revision, if any, would you offer the author?

Evaluating the Author's Viewpoints

1. How strong is Baker's support for his thesis? Look again at each "stage." Are his viewpoints on television, parents, and school balanced or has he overlooked something?

2. Do you agree that "during formal education, the child learns that life is for testing"? (6) Explain.

3. Do you agree or disagree with paragraph 10? Why?

4. Explain what Baker means in paragraphs 13 and 14. Do you agree with him?

5. Baker's tone is very cynical in this essay. Do you think he means what he says? Explain.

Pursuing Possible Essay Topics

1. Agree or disagree with one of Baker's "stages of education."

2. Summarize Baker's definition of education and defend or argue against his position.

3. Discuss what children learn from watching television. You may want to narrow this down to what they learn from commercials, cartoons, soap operas, crime shows, or whatever. Don't try to cover too much.

4. Discuss what preschool children learn from their parents, directly or indirectly, that schools don't teach. You might want to use yourself as your subject.

5. Baker says that students learn that "destroying competitors" is the way to win. In what ways do schools teach students the importance of winning?

6. Brainstorm or freewrite on one or more of the following:
   a. learning to read
   b. learning to win
   c. learning to lose
   d. learning prejudice

7. Write a reaction to the following quotation:

   Thank God there are no free schools or printing; . . . for learning has brought disobedience and heresy into the world, and printing has divulged them. . . . God keep us from both.

   Sir William Berkeley
   Governor of Virginia, 1677

8. Write about the first educational experience you can remember. What did you learn? Where? Why is it memorable?

9. If you don't like these, try your own topic related to learning.

Preparing to Read

Take a minute or two to look over the following reading selection. Note the title and author, read the opening paragraph, and check the length. Make certain you have the time now to read it carefully and to do the exercises that follow it. Then, in the spaces provided, answer the following questions.

1. What do you think the title means? What is a liberal arts major?

   _____

   _____

2. What is the difference between the way our fathers prepared for their careers and the way entering college freshmen will prepare?

   _____

   _____

3. What might you learn about preparing for your own career? _____

   _____

Vocabulary

Good comprehension of what you are about to read depends upon your understanding of the words below. The number following each word refers to the paragraph where it is used.

trends (1) movements, tendencies to go in a certain direction

apprenticed (1) placed under a skilled craftsman to learn a trade

obsolete (2) no longer useful

lamenting (3) complaining, regretting, showing sorrow

grounded (3) based

parlay (3) use an asset to its greatest advantage (from gambling lingo)

ivory tower (4) a place or attitude of retreat from the practical world where one is more occupied with intellectual considerations

extolling (4) praising highly

diversity (5) variety

validate (5) verify, prove

plethora (5) an excessive amount, more than enough

all encompassing (5) all inclusive, touching all bases

augment (5) supplement, add to

vehicle (7) means

steeped (8) saturated, subjected thoroughly

voluminous (9) of great volume

alluded (9) referred

smorgasbord (9) a wide variety

Now read the essay.

The Practicality of the Liberal Arts Major

DEBRA SIKES and BARBARA MURRAY

1   Current trends indicate that by the year 2000 the average person will change careers at least twice during a lifetime. How does the entering college student prepare for career mobility which has never before been necessary? Our fathers decided what they wanted to do in life, which was very often what their fathers had done—went to college or apprenticed themselves, and pursued the same career until retirement. Our mothers assumed one of the nurturing roles in society, if they assumed a role outside of the home at all. Things have certainly changed. No longer is life so simple.

2   Adaptability and lifelong learning are now the cornerstones of success. What direction does a person take to prepare for a lifetime of change? The one degree which provides training which never becomes obsolete is the liberal arts degree; it teaches you how to think. It also teaches you how to read, write and speak intelligently, get along with others, and conceptualize problems. For the first time in several decades, the liberal arts degree is coming to the forefront of the employment field.

3   Growing ranks of corporate executives are lamenting that college students are specializing too much and too early. What corporate America really needs, according to chief executive officers of major corporations, is students soundly grounded in the liberal arts—English, especially—who then can pick up more specific business or technical skills on the job. Few students, however, seem to be listening to this message. Today's best selling courses offer evidence that students want to take courses that provide direct job related skills rather than the most basic survival skills in the workplace: communication and thinking skills. They want courses they can parlay into jobs—and high paying ones at that. Certainly, we can understand this mentality when we consider trends indicating that this generation will be the first who will not be able to do better economically than their parents. They don't want to leave anything to chance. Historically, the liberal arts degree was good insurance for a poverty level existence. Students are looking to history to provide some answers it simply cannot give. They would do well to examine the present.

4   One of the big problems in the liberal arts community is that we do not market what we have to offer. Students very often fail to see the practicality of studying Shakespeare as preparation for a career in the business community. Perhaps some of us have locked ourselves in the ivory tower a little too long extolling the virtues of a liberal education as preparation for citizenship and life only to the neglect of it as preparation for career or careers. Education for education's sake is noble but impractical to today's college student who is facing a competitive and rapidly changing job market. They want and deserve to know how their courses will help them get a job. We as educators owe them some answers; we must be accountable not only for learning but also for providing information regarding the transferability of classroom skills into the workplace.

5   In an attempt to provide answers, we conducted a research project in the Dallas metroplex last year, assuming the role of the liberal arts graduate seeking employment in the fields of government, banking, business, and industry. Using informational interviewing as our method of job hunting and obtaining data, we conducted twenty-five interviews with a diversity of executive officers, ranging from personnel directors to the chairman of the board of an exclusive department store and the state governor. We wished to validate, through practical and current research, that not only does the liberal arts degree provide the best preparation for a lifetime of change, but it also provides a plethora of employment opportunities. We do not claim our research to be all encompassing, but we do feel its practicality was rewarding. We gathered data as to how the liberal arts major should present himself on paper and in person, where her best chances for employment are, and what he can do to augment the liberal arts degree. We were able to draw several conclusions as to how the liberal arts community could better prepare students for professional mobility.

The liberal arts degree is marketable.

6   Ninety percent of those interviewed responded they would hire a liberal arts major for an entry level position which could lead to the executive suite if the position itself were not executive level. The chairman of the board of a major department store in Dallas responded to the question, "For what position would you hire a liberal arts graduate?" with a direct, "Any position in the company." When asked if a buyer wouldn't need to have special skills, he replied, "Taste is acquired or learned, and the liberal arts major could certainly learn this skill on the job." This interview is typical of the responses.

Skills acquired with a liberal arts background are most desired by employers.

7   We were not at all surprised to learn that the skills cited as the most desirable in an employee are those skills acquired from a liberal arts background. The cited skills are listed below in order of importance.

1. Oral communication
2. Written communication
3. Interpersonal
4. Analytical thinking
5. Critical thinking
6. Leadership

Although these skills are not solely acquired through the mastery of an academic discipline, the discipline serves as a vehicle for developing or refining these skills.

Liberal arts majors can enhance their credentials.

8   Adaptability and lifelong learning are the cornerstones of success in today's complex and rapidly changing society. No longer can the person who is steeped in one academic discipline, but knows nothing about anything else, meet today's demands. Based on the data we accumulated, our recommendations for the liberal arts major are the following:

1. A basic knowledge of accounting
2. Computer literacy
3. Second major in a business field
4. Multiple minors
5. Advanced degree in another field

The key here is adaptability and diversity. Contrary to what most people believe, the higher a skill level an individual can claim, the more marketable he is. About those individuals who complain that they are "overeducated" we can only assume that they are marketing themselves on the wrong level. "Overeducation" is a term whose time will not come in the foreseeable future. The problem many individuals will face is a narrowness of education rather than "overeducation."

9   Unlike Aristotle who is believed to have known everything there was to know at the time he lived, it is impossible for us to deal with the voluminous amounts of information which are produced daily.

The lifelong learning which we have alluded to will not always be acquired through the traditional sixteen-week college course. We in the community college need to provide a smorgasbord of opportunities for individuals who wish to increase their mobility and options.

10   The time has come to rethink what education really is and how it relates to the functions of society. Perhaps what a liberal education does for an individual, which is more important than anything else, is to prepare him for more learning. The liberal arts background equips one with thinking skills; and those, coupled with the desire to learn, are the best preparation for career and life that any of us can possess.

Understanding the Content

Feel free to reread all or parts of the selection to answer the following questions.

1. By the year 2000 (judging from current trends), how many times will the average person change careers during a lifetime? How does this differ from past generations?

2. The authors claim that lifelong learning and adaptability are now the cornerstones of success. What do they mean? What degree provides training that is never obsolete?

3. According to the authors, what does corporate America want and need from its college graduates?

4. Upon what evidence have the authors based their information? Are their sources good?

5. What are the skills cited as the most desirable in an employee?

6. Based on their findings, what recommendations do the authors make for the liberal arts major to consider?

7. Do the authors believe it is possible to be "overeducated"? Explain.

Looking at Structure and Style

1. How do paragraphs 1 and 2 work together to establish the subject and thesis of the essay?

2. What is the basic function of paragraphs 3 and 4? How do they support the essay's thesis?

3. Why are paragraphs 5 and 6 important for thesis support? How strong would the essay be without these two paragraphs?

4. Paragraphs 7 and 8 both use lists. Is this effective? Explain.

5. To what audience do you think the authors direct their essay? How do paragraphs 4, 9, and 10 help reveal audience?

6. How would you describe the essays's tone and attitude toward the subject? What words or phrases reveal tone and attitude?

Evaluating the Authors' Viewpoints

1. Do the authors convince you that a liberal arts education is important to your future career? Explain.

2. In paragraph 2, the authors state that the most basic survival skills in the workplace are communication and thinking skills. Why would these be more important than, say, learning how to program a computer if your goal is to be a computer programmer?

3. Look again at the skills listed in paragraph 7. Do these skills seem important to you? How are your skills in those areas? Do you feel you need to improve in those areas?

4. Look again at the list in paragraph 8 of the basic knowledge a liberal arts major should have. Discuss how you feel about the importance of each item.

5. The authors conclude by stating that perhaps the best thing a liberal arts education can do is to prepare one for more learning. How does such a statement fit your definition of what you think education is all about?

Pursuing Possible Essay Topics

1. Argue for or against the need for a liberal arts education.

2. Discuss what you think are the most important job skills necessary for the career you have chosen or are thinking of entering. Explain why you think each is important.

3. Define what is meant by a liberal arts major. You may want to consult your college catalog for information on the course work required or talk with a counselor on campus.

4. Explain your reasons for wanting to attend college.

5. Discuss some aspect of yourself as a student: your study skills, your attitude, your self-image, your best learning style, your needs, your expectations, and so on.

6. Explain what you consider "the best preparation for career and life that any of us can possess."

7. Brainstorm or freewrite on one or more of the following:

   a. college life
   b. your favorite class
   c. high school vs. college

   d. a good teacher
   e. student responsibility
   f. life-long learning

8. Ignore these and find a topic of your own related to learning.

📖 *Preparing to Read*

Take a minute or two to look over the following reading selection. Note the title and author, read the opening paragraph, and check the length. Make certain you have the time now to read it carefully and to do the exercises that follow it. Then, in the spaces provided, answer the following questions.

1. What does the title mean to you?_____

_____

_____

2. What do you think this selection will have to say about making mistakes?

_____

_____

3. How do you feel about making mistakes? _____

_____

_____

Vocabulary

Good comprehension of what you are about to read depends upon your understanding of the words below. The number following each word refers to the paragraph where it is used.

plateau (1) an elevated, stable state

embedded (3) planted, fixed firmly

cultivates (3) fosters, nurtures

incentive (3) drive, desire, motivation (in this case, the grading system)

penalizes (4) subjects to penalty, places a disadvantage on

garners (4) acquires, gains

stigma (4) mark of shame or disgrace

adherence (8) desire to stick with or cling to

germinal phase (8) beginning or earliest stage

erroneous (9) mistaken, based on error

exemplifies (10) serves as an example

phenomenon (10) a perceivable occurrence or fact

combust (11) burn

analogous (11) alike in certain ways

Brittany (16) an area on the northern coast of France across the English Channel from England

precedence (18) awareness of prior existence, priority

innovators (18) creators or introducers of something new

diverging (24) branching out, departing from the norm

deleterious (25) damaging, harmful

amoeba (25) shapeless microscopic one-celled organism

atrophy (26) waste away

Now read the essay.

To Err Is Wrong

ROGER VON OECH

Hits and Misses

1   In the summer of 1979, Boston Red Sox first baseman Carl Yastrzemski became the fifteenth player in baseball history to reach the three thousand hit plateau. This event drew a lot of media attention, and for about a week prior to the attainment of this goal, hundreds of reporters covered Yaz's every move. Finally, one reporter asked, "Hey Yaz, aren't you afraid all of this attention will go to your head?" Yastrzemski replied, "I look at it this way: in my career I've been up to bat over ten thousand times. That means I've been unsuccessful at the plate over seven thousand times. That fact alone keeps me from getting a swollen head."

2   Most people consider success and failure as opposites, but they are actually both products of the same process. As Yaz suggests, an activity which produces a hit may also produce a miss. It is the same with creative thinking; the same energy which generates good creative ideas also produces errors.

3   Many people, however, are not comfortable with errors. Our educational system, based on "the right answer" belief, cultivates our thinking in another, more conservative way. From an early age, we are taught that right answers are good and incorrect answers are bad.

This value is deeply embedded in the incentive system used in most schools:

Right over 90% of the time = "A"
Right over 80% of the time = "B"
Right over 70% of the time = "C"
Right over 60% of the time = "D"
Less than 60% correct, you fail.

From this we learn to be right as often as possible and to keep our mistakes to a minimum. We learn, in other words, that "to err is wrong."

Playing It Safe

4   With this kind of attitude, you aren't going to be taking too many chances. If you learn that failing even a little penalizes you (e.g., being wrong only 15% of the time garners you only a "B" performance), you learn not to make mistakes. And more important, you learn not to put yourself in situations where you might fail. This leads to conservative thought patterns designed to avoid the stigma our society puts on "failure."

5   I have a friend who recently graduated from college with a Master's degree in Journalism. For the last six months, she has been trying to find a job, but to no avail. I talked with her about her situation, and realized that her problem is that she doesn't know how to fail. She went through eighteen years of schooling without ever failing an examination, a paper, a midterm, a pop-quiz, or a final. Now, she is reluctant to try any approaches where she might fail. She has been conditioned to believe that failure is bad in and of itself, rather than a potential stepping stone to new ideas.

6   Look around. How many middle managers, housewives, administrators, teachers, and other people do you see who are afraid to try anything new because of this fear of failure? Most of us have learned not to make mistakes in public. As a result, we remove ourselves from many learning experiences except for those occurring in the most private of circumstances.

A Different Logic

7   From a practical point of view, "to err is wrong" makes sense. Our survival in the everyday world requires us to perform thousands of small tasks without failure. Think about it: you wouldn't last very long if you were to step out in front of traffic or stick your hand into a pot of boiling water. In addition, engineers whose bridges collapse,

stock brokers who lose money for their clients and copywriters whose ad campaigns decrease sales won't keep their jobs very long.

8   Nevertheless, too great an adherence to the belief "to err is wrong" can greatly undermine your attempts to generate new ideas. If you're more concerned with producing right answers than generating original ideas, you'll probably make uncritical use of the rules, formulae, and procedures used to obtain these right answers. By doing this, you'll by-pass the germinal phase of the creative process, and thus spend little time testing assumptions, challenging the rules, asking what-if questions, or just playing around with the problem. All of these techniques will produce some incorrect answers, but in the germinal phase errors are viewed as a necessary by-product of creative thinking. As Yaz would put it, "If you want the hits, be prepared for the misses." That's the way the game of life goes.

Errors As Stepping Stones

9   Whenever an error pops up, the usual response is "Jeez, another screwup, what went wrong this time?" The creative thinker, on the other hand, will realize the potential value of errors, and perhaps say something like, "Would you look at that! Where can it lead our thinking?" And then he or she will go on to use the error as a stepping stone to a new idea. As a matter of fact, the whole history of discovery is filled with people who used erroneous assumptions and failed ideas as stepping stones to new ideas. Columbus thought he was finding a shorter route to India. Johannes Kepler stumbled on to the idea of interplanetary gravity because of assumptions which were right for the wrong reasons. And, Thomas Edison knew 1800 ways *not* to build a light bulb.

10   The following story about the automotive genius Charles Kettering exemplifies the spirit of working through erroneous assumptions to good ideas. In 1912, when the automobile industry was just beginning to grow, Kettering was interested in improving gasoline-engine efficiency. The problem he faced was "knock," the phenomenon in which gasoline takes too long to burn in the cylinder—thereby reducing efficiency.

11   Kettering began searching for ways to eliminate the "knock." He thought to himself, "How can I get the gasoline to combust in the cylinder at an earlier time?" The key concept here is "early." Searching for analogous situations, he looked around for models of "things that happen early." He thought of historical models, physical models, and biological models. Finally, he remembered a particular plant, the trailing arbutus, which "happens early," i.e., it blooms in the snow ("earlier" than other plants). One of this plant's chief charac-

teristics is its red leaves which help the plant retain light at certain wavelengths. Kettering figured that it must be the red color which made the trailing arbutus bloom earlier.

12   Now came the critical step in Kettering's chain of thought. He asked himself, "How can I make the gasoline red? Perhaps I'll put red dye in the gasoline—maybe that'll make it combust earlier." He looked around his workshop, and found that he didn't have any red dye. But he did happen to have some iodine—perhaps that would do. He added the iodine to the gasoline and, lo and behold, the engine didn't "knock."

13   Several days later,, Kettering wanted to make sure that it was the redness of the iodine which had in fact solved his problem. He got some red dye and added it to the gasoline. Nothing happened! Kettering then realized that it wasn't the "redness" which had solved the "knock" problem, but certain other properties of iodine. In this case, an error had proven to be a stepping stone to a better idea. Had he known that "redness" alone was not the solution, he may not have found his way to the additives in iodine.

Negative Feedback

14   Errors serve another useful purpose: they tell us when to change direction. When things are going smoothly, we generally don't think about them. To a great extent, this is because we function according to the principle of negative feedback. Often it is only when things or people fail to do their job that they get our attention. For example, you are probably not thinking about your kneecaps right now; that's because everything is fine with them. The same goes for your elbows: they are also performing their function—no problem at all. But if you were to break a leg, you would immediately notice all of the things you could no longer do, but which you used to take for granted.

15   Negative feedback means that the current approach is not working, and it is up to you to figure out a new one. We learn by trial and error, not by trial and rightness. If we did things correctly every time, we would never have to change direction—we'd just continue the current course and end up with more of the same.

16   For example, after the supertanker *Amoco Cadiz* broke up off the coast of Brittany in the spring of 1978, thereby polluting the coast with hundreds of thousands of tons of oil, the oil industry rethought many of its safety standards regarding petroleum transport. The same thing happened after the accident at the Three Mile Island nuclear reactor in 1979—many procedures and safety standards were changed.

17   Neil Goldschmidt, former Secretary of Transportation, had this to say about the Bay Area Rapid Transit (BART):

> It's gotten too fashionable around the country to beat up on BART and not give credit to the vision that put this system in place. We have learned from BART around the country. The lessons were put to use in Washington, in Atlanta, in Buffalo, and other cities where we are building mass transit systems. One of the lessons is not to build a system like BART.

We learn by our failures. A person's errors are the whacks that lead him to think something different.

Trying New Things

18   Your error rate in any activity is a function of your familiarity with that activity. If you are doing things that are routine and have a high likelihood of correctness, then you will probably make very few errors. But if you are doing things that have no precedence in your experience or are trying different approaches, then you will be making your share of mistakes. Innovators may not bat a thousand—far from it—but they do get new ideas.

19   The creative director of an advertising agency told me that he isn't happy unless he is failing at least half of the time. As he puts it, "If you are going to be original, you are going to be wrong a lot."

20   One of my clients, the president of a fast-growing computer company, tells his people: "We're innovators. We're doing things nobody has ever done before. Therefore, we are going to be making mistakes. My advice to you: make your mistakes, but make them in a hurry."

21   Another client, a division manager of a high-technology company, asked his vice president of engineering what percentage of their new products should be successful in the marketplace. The answer he received was "about 50%." The division manager replied, "That's too high. 30% is a better target; otherwise we'll be too conservative in our planning."

22   Along similar lines, in the banking industry, it is said that if the credit manager never has to default on any of his loans, it's a sure sign he's not being aggressive enough in the marketplace.

23   Thomas J. Watson, the founder of IBM, has similar words: "The way to succeed is to double your failure rate."

24   Thus, errors, at the very least, are a sign that we are diverging from the main road and trying different approaches.

Nature's Errors

25   Nature serves as a good example of how trial and error can be used to make changes. Every now and then genetic mutations occur—errors in gene reproduction. Most of the time, these mutations have a deleterious effect on the species, and they drop out of the gene pool. But occasionally, a mutation provides the species with something beneficial, and that change will be passed on to future generations. The rich variety of all species is due to this trial and error process. If there had never been any mutations from the first amoeba, where would we be now?

Summary

26   There are places where errors are inappropriate, but the germinal phase of the creative process isn't one of them. Errors are a sign that you are diverging from the well-traveled path. If you're not failing every now and then, it's a sign you're not being very innovative.

Tip #1:
If you make an error, use it as a stepping stone to a new idea you might not have otherwise discovered.

Tip #2:
Differentiate between errors of "commission" and those of "omission." The latter can be more costly than the former. If you're not making many errors, you might ask yourself, "How many opportunities am I missing by not being more aggressive?"

Tip #3:
Strengthen your "risk muscle." Everyone has one, but you have to exercise it or else it will atrophy. Make it a point to take at least one risk every twenty-four hours.

Tip #4:
Remember these two benefits of failure. First, if you do fail, you learn what doesn't work; and second, the failure gives you an opportunity to try a new approach.

Understanding the Content

Feel free to reread all or parts of the selection to answer the following questions.

1. Does von Oech believe "to err is wrong"? Why?

2. How does von Oech feel about the traditional grading system in schools? Why?

3. According to the author, what is wrong with "playing it safe"?

4. What are some of the "useful purposes" of making mistakes?

5. Explain what von Oech means when he says we should differentiate between errors of "commission" and those of "omission"?

6. What does the author feel are the two benefits of failure?

7. To what audience do you think the author is writing? Why?

8. Is there an implied or stated thesis? What is it?

Looking at Structure and Style

1. How does von Oech use the first two paragraphs to lead us into his subject and thesis?

2. What is the cause-effect relationship discussed in paragraph 4?

3. What is the function of paragraphs 5 and 6?

4. What is being compared/contrasted in paragraphs 7 and 8?

5. Is this essay mostly formal or informal? Pick out some words or phrases that support your answer.

6. For what purpose does the author use paragraphs 9–13? Are they effective?

7. What writing pattern is used in paragraphs 14, 16, and 17?

8. How would you describe the author's attitude and tone?

Evaluating the Author's Viewpoints

1. Do you agree or disagree with von Oech's comments regarding the traditional educational grading system? Why?

2. In paragraph 6, the author says, "Most of us have learned not to make mistakes in public. As a result, we remove ourselves from many learning experiences except for those occurring in the most private of circumstances." Is this true? Is it true of you?

3. Respond to paragraph 25. What does von Oech mean? Do you agree?

4. Do you agree with von Oech that we should take at least one risk every twenty-four hours? Why? What kind of risks does he mean?

5. Where and when are errors inappropriate?

Pursuing Possible Essay Topics

1. Make a list of von Oech's arguments for the positive side of making errors. Write an essay that agrees with his thesis, but provide examples of your own. Or, write an essay that disagrees with him.

2. Write about a time when you learned from an error you made.

3. Discuss your viewpoints on the traditional grading system. What are the pros and cons? How has it affected your learning?

4. Use this statement from the essay as the thesis for your own essay: "Most people consider success and failure as opposites, but they are actually both products of the same process."

5. In his book *Escape from Childhood*, John Holt states:

> Young people should have the right to control and direct their own learning, that is, to decide what they want to learn, and when, where, how, how much, how fast, and with what help they want to learn it. To be still more specific, I want them to have the right to decide if, when, how much, and by whom they want to be *taught* and the right to decide whether they want to learn in a school and if so which one and for how much of the time.

   Write an essay that supports or refutes Holt's statement about learning. How would his ideas work? How would such an approach change the present educational system?

6. Write an essay about your own learning style. How do you learn best? What kind of teaching seems to help you learn best?

7. Freewrite or brainstorm on one or more of the following:
   a. making mistakes
   b. famous errors
   c. grades
   d. nature's errors
   e. negative feedback
   f. trying new things

8. Ignore these and find your own topic on some aspect of learning.

Preparing to Read

Take a minute or two to look over the following reading selection. Note the title and author, read the opening paragraph, and check the length. Make certain you have the time now to read it carefully and to do the exercises that follow it. Then, in the spaces provided, answer the following questions.

1. With what experience in the life of the author will this selection deal?

   _____

   _____

2. What will the tone of the selection be (funny, sad, serious, etc.)? Why do

   you think so? _____

   _____

   _____

Vocabulary

Good comprehension of what you are about to read depends upon your understanding of the words below. The number following each word refers to the paragraph where it is used.

revival (1) a meeting for the purposes of reawakening religious faith

fold (1) a fenced enclosure for sheep; here, a group gathered for the same purposes

dire (3) dreadful, warning of disaster

work-gnarled (4) misshapen and swollen from work

rounder (6) a dishonest person

deacons (6) assistants to a minister

knickerbockered (11) wearing loose pants gathered just below the knees

ecstatic (14) very enthusiastic

Now read the essay.

Salvation

LANGSTON HUGHES

1   I was saved from sin when I was going on thirteen. But not really saved. It happened like this. There was a big revival at my Auntie Reed's church. Every night for weeks there had been much preaching, singing, praying, and shouting, and some very hardened sinners had been brought to Christ, and the membership of the church had grown by leaps and bounds. Then just before the revival ended, they held a special meeting for children, "to bring the young lambs to the fold." My aunt spoke of it for days ahead. That night I was escorted to the

front row and placed on the mourners' bench with all the other young sinners, who had not yet been brought to Jesus.

2   My aunt told me that when you were saved you saw a light, and something happened to you inside! And Jesus came into your life! And God was with you from then on! She said you could see and hear and feel Jesus in your soul. I believed her. I had heard a great many old people say the same thing and it seemed to me they ought to know. So I sat there calmly in the hot, crowded church, waiting for Jesus to come to me.

3   The preacher preached a wonderful rhythmical sermon, all moans and shouts and lonely cries and dire pictures of hell, and then he sang a song about the ninety and nine safe and in the fold, but one little lamb was left out in the cold. Then he said: "Won't you come? Won't you come to Jesus? Young lambs, won't you come?" And he held out his arms to all of us young sinners there on the mourners' bench. And the little girls cried. And some of them jumped up and went to Jesus right away. But most of us just sat there.

4   A great many old people came and knelt around us and prayed, old women with jet-black faces and braided hair, old men with work-gnarled hands. And the church sang a song about the lower lights are burning, some poor sinners to be saved. And the whole building rocked with prayer and song.

5   Still I kept waiting to *see* Jesus.

6   Finally all the young people had gone to the altar and were saved, but one boy and me. He was a rounder's son named Westley. Westley and I were surrounded by sisters and deacons praying. It was very hot in the church, and getting late now. Finally Westley said to me in a whisper: "God damn! I'm tired o' sitting here. Let's get up and be saved." So he got up and was saved.

7   Then I was left all alone on the mourners' bench. My aunt came and knelt at my knees and cried, while prayers and songs swirled all around me in the little church. The whole congregation prayed for me alone, in a mighty wail of moans and voices. And I kept waiting serenely for Jesus, waiting, waiting—but he didn't come. I wanted to see him, but nothing happened to me. Nothing! I wanted something to happen to me, but nothing happened.

8   I heard the songs and the minister saying: "Why don't you come? My dear child, why don't you come to Jesus? Jesus is waiting for you. He wants you. Why don't you come? Sister Reed, what is this child's name?"

9   "Langston," my aunt sobbed.

10   "Langston, why don't you come? Why don't you come and be saved? Oh, Lamb of God! Why don't you come?"

11   Now it was really getting late. I began to be ashamed of myself, holding everything up so long. I began to wonder what God thought

about Westley, who certainly hadn't seen Jesus either, but who was now sitting proudly on the platform, swinging his knickerbockered legs and grinning down at me, surrounded by deacons and old women on their knees praying. God had not struck Westley dead for taking his name in vain or for lying in the temple. So I decided that maybe to save further trouble, I'd better lie, too, and say that Jesus had come, and get up and be saved.

12   So I got up.

13   Suddenly the whole room broke into a sea of shouting, as they saw me rise. Waves of rejoicing swept the place. Women leaped in the air. My aunt threw her arms around me. The minister took me by the hand and led me to the platform.

14   When things quieted down, in a hushed silence, punctuated by a few ecstatic "Amens," all the new young lambs were blessed in the name of God. Then joyous singing filled the room.

15   That night for the last time in my life but one—for I was a big boy twelve years old—I cried. I cried, in bed alone, and couldn't stop. I buried my head under the quilts, but my aunt heard me. She woke up and told my uncle I was crying because the Holy Ghost had come into my life, and because I had seen Jesus. But I was really crying because I couldn't bear to tell her that I had lied, that I had deceived everybody in the church, and I hadn't seen Jesus, and that now I didn't believe there was a Jesus any more, since he didn't come to help me.

Understanding the Content

Feel free to reread all or parts of the selection to answer the following questions.

1. For what reason is Langston Hughes at the revival?

2. Why didn't Hughes go to the altar with the rest of the children to be saved?

3. Why does Westley finally go down to the altar? What effect does this have on Hughes?

4. What kind of pressure was put on Hughes to be saved?

5. Why does Hughes cry that night? What has he learned?

6. What is the thesis? Is it implied or stated?

Looking at Structure and Style

1. Why are the first three sentences of the essay important? What information is provided that is necessary to understanding what happens?

2. How important is the information in paragraph 2? How does it prepare us as readers for the last paragraph?

3. Paragraphs 3 and 4 are basically descriptive. What senses are mostly used in the description? How do these passages serve to explain the emotional pressure put on the children to be saved?

4. Paragraphs 8–10 use dialogue. What is their use? How effective are they in helping us feel the pressure being put on the author?

5. How important to the story is paragraph 11? For what purpose is the description of Westley used?

6. What is the effect of having paragraphs 5 and 12 consist of just one sentence?

7. Hughes is writing as an adult about his experience as a twelve-year-old. How does he manage to develop a tone and an attitude that fits the experience?

8. In the last paragraph, is it the adult or the twelve-year-old talking?

Evaluating the Author's Viewpoints

1. How do you think Hughes's adult attitude toward revivals differs from when he was "going on thirteen"?

2. Hughes didn't believe he could tell his Auntie Reed the truth about why he was crying. Do you think he was right? Explain.

3. Compare the young Hughes's literal definition of "seeing Jesus" with that of his adult aunt's. In your view, is he making fun of himself, of adults, of both, of neither? Explain.

4. Explain what attitudes are revealed in the following phrases from the essay:
   a. "I believed her. I had heard a great many old people say the same thing and it seemed to me they ought to know." (2)
   b. "The preacher preached a wonderful rhythmical sermon, all moans and shouts and lonely cries and dire pictures of hell. . . ." (3)
   c. "Suddenly the whole room broke into a sea of shouting, as they saw me rise. Waves of rejoicing swept the place." (13)
   d. "That night for the last time in my life but one—for I was a big boy twelve years old—I cried." (15)

Pursuing Possible Essay Topics

1. Write an essay about an experience you had that caused you to become hurt or disillusioned. What did you learn from the experience that changed you?

2. Describe a time in your life when you could not tell your parents how you really felt because you didn't think they would understand. Were you right?

3. Write a new ending for the essay that allows Hughes to say what you think he wants to say to his Auntie Reed.

4. Write a narrative essay that recalls a time when you went along with the crowd and did not follow your true convictions. What did you learn from the experience?

5. Discuss whether or not disillusionment is a necessary part of learning about life.

6. If you don't like these, find a topic of your own on some aspect of learning.

📖 *Preparing to Read*

Take a minute or two to look over the following reading selection. Note the title and author, read the opening paragraph, and check the length. Make certain you have the time now to read it carefully and to do the exercises that follow it. Then, in the spaces provided, answer the following questions.

1. What do you think the title means? _____

   _____

2. Do you think the author believes in book censorship, especially *The Diary*

   of Anne Frank? Explain. _____

   _____

3. With which of the books mentioned, if any, are you familiar? _____

   _____

Vocabulary

Good comprehension of what you are about to read depends upon your understanding of the words below. The number following each word refers to the paragraph where it is used.

deprived (2) underprivileged, needy

migrant (2) moving about, not permanent

offhand (2) not well thought out, on the spur of the moment

plight (7) difficult situation or condition

optimistic (7) having a bright outlook, positive

cropping up (8) appearing unexpectedly

empathy (11) sympathy, understanding

multitude (12) great number (of individuals)

tyranny (12) dictatorship, a government where the power rests in one individual

Now read the essay.

Students' Love Affair with Anne Frank

SHARON WHITLEY

1   There it was, among books listed as "objectionable, filthy, dirty and inappropriate" by several groups: *The Diary of Anne Frank.* I couldn't believe it. The list of books facing censorship in some public schools (which included *The Catcher in the Rye* by J. D. Salinger, *Of Mice and Men* by John Steinbeck, Mark Twain's *Huckleberry Finn,* and William Shakespeare's *Romeo and Juliet*) was recently published in a New York Times News Service article. According to the article, the groups objecting to use of these books in schools include Phyllis Schlafly's Eagle Forum, Jerry Falwell's Moral Majority, the national Pro-Family Forum, and a few with "other political perspectives."

2   All I could think of was the fifth-grade class I taught 10 years ago in the dusty, hot, socially and economically deprived desert town of Coachella, Calif. The 36 Latino children in my class, mostly from migrant farming families, were a handful. Eleven couldn't speak English, and I was a young and inexperienced teacher. I'll never forget that scorching September day when my charges trooped noisily into the classroom after lunch. I made an offhand remark that they could never keep as quiet as Anne Frank had for more than two years.

3   "Anne Frank? Who's that? Does she go here?"

4   As they settled down into the after-lunch routine and placed their hands, grimy from play, on the desks, I told them the story of Anne Frank: how she hid with her family from Hitler's Nazis, how she was persecuted because she was Jewish (none of my Mexican-heritage Roman Catholic students had ever heard of a Jew), how Anne wrote a diary, and about her death in the Bergen-Belsen concentration camp.

5   I had just returned from a summer vacation in Europe, and the highlight for me was seeing the small rooms in the Amsterdam factory where Anne and her family had hidden. I described them to the children: the yellowed wallpaper, the tiny kitchen sink, the photos of movie stars and Queen Elizabeth and Princess Margaret as children; the pencil markings on the doorway where Anne's mother measured the growth of Anne and her sister, Margot; the attic where Peter, Anne's first love, stayed; the bookcase that hid the stairs leading up to the secret hide-out. I told them about the guest register at the Anne Frank Museum next door where visitors from all over the world had written their feelings and thoughts, and that when it was my turn I picked up the pen but was too overwhelmed to put any words down.

After-Lunch Ritual

6   The children were wide-eyed and quiet as I told them the tale of Anne. But that was not enough: "Read the diary to us!" they excitedly demanded.

7   So that became our ritual every day after lunch for the next several weeks. With heads on their desks, the only sound in the class was the whir of the fan on the hot September afternoons and my reading from the yellowed, torn copy I had owned since sixth grade. Stopping only now and then to clarify some of Anne's sophisticated vocabulary, I was prodded on by the children who wanted to hear more and more. The diary opened up a whole new world for these children in the Coachella Valley. They understood prejudice. Now they knew there were many different kinds. They identified with Anne and her plight. They grew to love her as she described her pre-war birthday parties, receiving her first diary, her friends, falling in love, and her still optimistic view of the world: "In spite of everything, I still believe that people are really good at heart."

8   As I continued reading the diary every afternoon, I soon noticed more of the diaries cropping up in class. One by one, the children had bought their own copies of the book—even Spanish versions— and were quietly following along with me, or looking intently at the sad-eyed picture of Anne on the cover. When we completed reading the diary, they wanted more. "Please help us write a play about Anne that we can put on!" they begged.

9   So for the next month, in a flurry of excitement over the class project, we spent several hours after school, rehearsing our condensed version of *The Diary of Anne Frank*. (The Broadway version in 1955 was awarded the Pulitzer Prize, the New York Drama Critics Circle Award and the Antoinette Perry Award.) The night we performed our amateur version in the school auditorium, 100 members of the community turned out to see it.

10   Several years later, when I had moved to San Diego to teach high school special education, one of my former Coachella fifth-graders—then in high school—called excitedly to tell me that *The Diary of Anne Frank* was on television that night. I was thrilled that she had remembered our special class project from years before.

11   To this day, *The Diary of Anne Frank* continues to be an important teaching tool in my classes. It is the ultimate in lesson plans—teaching listening skills, silent and oral reading, vocabulary, history, religion and customs, race relations, thoughts for the future, boy-girl relationships, empathy for others, comparison of our experiences with Anne's and the experiences of others, drama and role play, and understanding ourselves, our friends, and parents.

Tribute from Kennedy

12   As John F. Kennedy wrote Sept. 15, 1961: "Of the multitude who throughout history have spoken for human dignity in times of great suffering and loss, no voice is more compelling than that of Anne Frank. . . . Her words, written as they were in the face of a monstrous tyranny, have significant meaning today as millions who read them live in the shadow of fear of another such tyranny. . . . It is indeed a gift for all mankind to receive from a child growing into womanhood the greatest truth of all—that as man rises from the brute, the kind and hopeful and the gentle are the true makers of history."

13   And Eleanor Roosevelt had commented, "This is one of the wisest and most moving commentaries on war and its impact on human beings that I have ever read."

14   As Anne wrote, "I can feel the sufferings of millions and yet, if I look up into the heavens, I think that it will all come right, that this cruelty too will end, and that peace and tranquility will return again" (July 15, 1944).

15   More than 10 million copies of *The Diary of Anne Frank* have been printed in 38 different languages in 48 countries. We *must* keep Anne in the classroom.

Understanding the Content

Feel free to reread all or parts of the selection to answer the following questions.

1. Who was Anne Frank? What do you learn about her life?

2. What groups object to the use of *The Diary of Anne Frank* in the classroom? To what other books do they object?

3. How did Whitley get her students interested in *The Diary of Anne Frank?* Describe her students at the time.

4. Why does Whitley feel that *The Diary of Anne Frank* is an important teaching tool, "the ultimate in lesson plans"?

5. What is Whitley's thesis?

Looking at Structure and Style

1. How is the opening paragraph used to introduce the subject of the essay? How is the author's attitude toward her subject revealed?

2. Paragraph 2 serves as a "flashback" to Whitley's past. How is this done?

3. Whitley carefully describes her students in paragraphs 2, 4, and 7. Is it important to her discussion of Anne Frank? Why? What inferences might we draw from this?

4. In paragraph 9, Whitley mentions the prizes the Broadway version of *The Diary of Anne Frank* won. What function does this serve? Why does she put this information in parentheses?

5. What function do paragraphs 12–13 serve? Are these important to her viewpoint?

6. How does Whitley's concluding paragraph bring us back to her opening remarks?

7. To whom is Whitley writing? Explain.

Evaluating the Author's Viewpoints

1. Whitley is shocked to see *The Diary of Anne Frank* listed by some groups as an "objectionable, filthy, dirty and inappropriate" book. Does she convince you it is not? Explain.

2. Look at paragraph 11. Do you feel that all of the items listed should be taught and discussed in the classroom? Explain. What items on Whitley's list might some persons or groups not want discussed or taught in class? Would you agree with them? Why?

3. In paragraph 12, John F. Kennedy, is quoted as saying of Anne Frank, "It is indeed a gift for all mankind to receive from a child growing into womanhood the greatest truth of all—that as man rises from the brute, the kind and hopeful and the gentle are the true makers of history." Explain what he means. Do you agree? Why?

4. Respond to the quote from Anne Frank's diary in paragraph 14. Do you hold such an optimistic view of life? Explain.

Pursuing Possible Essay Topics

1. Write an essay about a book or play you have read that had a profound effect on your life. Why is it memorable? What did you learn? What

emotions were aroused? Why would you recommend it be taught to others?

2. Some parents feel that schools should only teach what are often called "the basic skills"—reading, writing, and math. Agree or disagree with such a viewpoint.

3. Pretend that some parents in Whitley's classroom are demanding that she stop using *The Diary of Anne Frank* in her classes. Choose a side and write a defense of your argument.

4. Find a copy of *The Diary of Anne Frank* or one of the other books listed as objectionable by some in Whitley's opening paragraph, and read it. Argue for or against its being taught in schools.

5. What is the role of public education today? What skills should the schools emphasize? Should such subjects as sex education, race relations, facing moral dilemmas, communism, marriage and the family, and driver's education be required? Are we asking too much of our schools and teachers?

6. Brainstorm or freewrite on one or more of the following:

   a. reading to learn
   b. book censorship
   c. keeping a diary

   d. loving to learn
   e. the real basic skills
   f. stimulating teaching

7. Forget these and find your own topic on some aspect of learning.

Preparing to Read

Take a minute or two to look over the following reading selection. Note the title and author, read the opening paragraph, and check the length. Make certain you have the time now to read it carefully and to do the exercises that follow it. Then, in the spaces provided, answer the following questions.

1. What do you think the title means? _____

   _____

   _____

2. What will be the subject of this essay? _____

   _____

3. What might you learn from reading it? _____

_____

_____

Vocabulary

Good comprehension of what you are about to read depends upon your understanding of the words below. The number following each word refers to the paragraph where it is used.

disparagement (1) the act of making someone feel inferior

Bozeman (2) a city in Montana

drudge (4) one who does boring, mechanical work

dutifully (6) filled with a sense of duty

infinity (7) an indefinitely large number

hypotheses (7) explanations or assumptions that account for a set of facts and can be tested (plural of hypothesis)

Now read the essay.

Seeing Freshly*

ROBERT M. PIRSIG

1   . . . He'd been having trouble with students who had nothing to say. At first he thought it was laziness but later it became apparent that it wasn't. They just couldn't think of anything to say.

2   One of them, a girl with strong-lensed glasses, wanted to write a five-hundred-word essay about the United States. He was used to the sinking feeling that comes from statements like this, and suggested without disparagement that she narrow it down to just Bozeman.

3   When the paper came due she didn't have it and was quite upset. She had tried and tried but she just couldn't think of anything to say.

4   He had already discussed her with her previous instructors and they'd confirmed his impressions of her. She was very serious, disciplined and hardworking, but extremely dull. Not a spark of creativity in her anywhere. Her eyes, behind the thick-lensed glasses, were the eyes of a drudge. She wasn't bluffing him, she really couldn't think of anything to say, and was upset by her inability to do as she was told.

---

* Editor's title

5   It just stumped him. Now *he* couldn't think of anything to say. A silence occurred, and then a peculiar answer: "Narrow it down to the *main street* of Bozeman." It was a stroke of insight.

6   She nodded dutifully and went out. But just before her next class she came back in *real* distress, tears this time, distress that had obviously been there for a long time. She still couldn't think of anything to say, and couldn't understand why, if she couldn't think of anything about *all* of Bozeman, she should be able to think of something about just one street.

7   He was furious. "You're not *looking!*" he said. A memory came back of his own dismissal from the University for having *too much* to say. For every fact there is an *infinity* of hypotheses. The more you *look* the more you *see*. She really wasn't looking and yet somehow didn't understand this.

8   He told her angrily, "Narrow it down to the *front of one* building on the main street of Bozeman. The Opera House. Start with the upper left-hand brick."

9   Her eyes, behind the thick-lensed glasses, opened wide.

10   She came in the next class with a puzzled look and handed him a five-thousand-word essay on the front of the Opera House on the main street of Bozeman, Montana. "I sat in the hamburger stand across the street," she said, "and started writing about the first brick, and the second brick, and then by the third brick it all started to come and I couldn't stop. They thought I was crazy, and they kept kidding me, but here it all is. I don't understand it."

11   Neither did he, but on long walks through the streets of town he thought about it and concluded she was evidently stopped with the same kind of blockage that had paralyzed him on his first day of teaching. She was blocked because she was trying to repeat, in her writing, things she had already heard, just as on the first day he had tried to repeat things he had already decided to say. She couldn't think of anything to write about Bozeman because she couldn't recall anything she had heard worth repeating. She was strangely unaware that she could look and see freshly for herself, as she wrote, without primary regard for what had been said before. The narrowing down to one brick destroyed the blockage because it was so obvious she *had* to do some original and direct seeing.

Understanding the Content

Feel free to reread all or parts of the selection to answer the following questions.

1. While no name is given for the "he" in the selection, it might help to know it is the author, Robert Pirsig, talking about himself in the third person. Through inference, what do we learn about him?

2. What is the girl's problem?

3. How does Pirsig help her solve her problem?

4. What attitude does Pirsig have toward the girl?

5. What did Pirsig learn? What did the girl learn?

6. What is the point of this selection? What does it have to do with the subject of learning?

Looking at Structure and Style

1. How does paragraph 2 serve to support paragraph 1?

2. Explain how paragraphs 5–8 develop both the teacher's and the student's frustration.

3. For what effect does Pirsig make paragraph 9 only one sentence long?

4. What paragraph method is used in paragraph 4? Why is this important to the point of the essay?

5. Throughout the selection, Pirsig italicizes certain words. Why?

6. What might be the advantages of Pirsig's writing about himself in the third person?

Evaluating the Author's Viewpoints

1. Why is the teacher upset when the girl wants to write a 500-word essay on the United States? Is his reaction valid?

2. "For every fact there is an *infinity* of hypotheses. The more you *look* the more you *see*." (7) Is this true? Explain.

3. Read the last sentence. Is his conclusion correct? Explain.

Pursuing Possible Essay Topics

1. Recall a time when you had difficulty writing about a topic. How did you solve the problem? What was the outcome?

2. Offer advice to a student audience on how to overcome writer's block. You might want to review some of the suggestions in Unit 2, "Viewpoints On Writing Essays."

3. Summarize what the girl in the reading selection learned. Explain how other student writers might benefit from her experience.

4. Go to a place that is familiar to you. Sit for a while and look for things you never noticed before. Take some notes on what you observe and feel. Go there again in a day or two. Take more notes on what you observe and feel. What did you learn about your perception of things?

5. Find a brick building or wall somewhere. Start writing about the first brick on the bottom left, then the next, and the next, and so on to experience what the student in the reading selection did. Write about what you learned from that experience.

6. Brainstorm or freewrite on one of the following:

   a. learning to drive
   b. learning to write
   c. learning moral values

   d. learning manners
   e. learning to dance
   f. learning to play _____

7. Ignore these and find your own topic on some aspect of learning.

Preparing to Read

Here's something different to read—a poem. Read it two or three times. Read it aloud at least once. Then answer the questions that follow it.

When I Heard the Learn'd Astronomer

WALT WHITMAN

When I heard the learn'd astronomer,
When the proofs, the figures, were ranged in columns
　　before me,
When I was shown the charts and diagrams, to add, divide,
　　and measure them,
When I sitting heard the astronomer where he lectured
　　with much applause in the lecture-room,
How soon unaccountable I became tired and sick,
Till rising and gliding out I wander'd off by myself,
In the mystical moist night-air, and from time to time,
Look'd up in perfect silence at the stars.

Understanding the Content

1. Explain what happens in the poem.

2. Why does Whitman "unaccountable" become "tired and sick"?

3. What is the theme or point of the poem?

4. What does the poem say about learning?

Looking at Structure and Style

1. Why does Whitman spell *learned, wandered,* and *looked* the way he does?

2. What purpose or effect is served by beginning the first four lines with the same word?

3. For what purpose does Whitman use words such as *proofs, figures, ranged in columns, charts, diagrams, add, divide,* and *measure?* How are they contrasted against the words *mystical moist night-air,* and *perfect silence of the stars?*

4. What visual images does Whitman create? What word arrangements help us "see" what goes on?

5. In a sense this poem shows cause and effect. What are the cause and the effect? What does this have to do with the way the poem is structured?

Evaluating the Author's Viewpoints

1. How does the author feel about the "learn'd astronomer"? Why? Would he be part of the "much applause in the lecture-room"?

2. What seems to interest Whitman more than the lecture? What might we infer about Whitman's attitude toward learning? Do you agree with him?

3. With what other subjects besides astronomy might Whitman feel the same? Explain. About what subjects do you feel this way? Why?

Pursuing Possible Essay Topics

1. Summarize the theme or point of this or any other poem you have read.

2. Write about a time when you were listening to a "learn'd" professor and felt the way Whitman does in his poem. Did your mind "glide out" to something else? Why was it difficult to pay attention?

3. Discuss the difference between reading and understanding a poem with reading and understanding an essay. From which can you learn more? Which is more demanding?

4. Brainstorm or freewrite on one or more of the following:

   a. learning from lectures
   b. vocabulary power
   c. listening skills
   d. taking lecture notes
   e. your wandering mind
   f. astrology vs. astronomy

5. Ignore these and find your own topic on some aspect of learning.

🖎 *Student Essay*

For an assignment to write on some aspect of learning, a student submitted the following essay. As you read it, look for answers to these questions:

1. Does the essay fit the assignment?

2. Does the writer show an understanding of the subject?

3. How well does the author follow the writing suggestions provided in Unit 2, "Viewpoints On Writing Essays"?

Stargazing with Whitman

Linda Klouzal

1   In Walt Whitman's poem "When I Heard the Learn'd Astronomer," he contrasts the stark division between the formal, organized approach to learning about the stars and the natural, personal feeling he has when he looks at the astral bodies. We gather that he prefers the mystery of the universe to the "proofs," "figures," and "charts" of the "learn'd astronomer."

2   To show these two distinct views, Whitman divides his eight-line poem into two parts. The first part consists of the first four lines, each line beginning with "when." These lines all reflect the formal, academic approach to learning about the stars. Whitman, sitting with a group of people, was listening to a lecture. The learned "astronomer where he lectured with much applause," used visual aids: "... I was shown the charts and diagrams." The "proofs, the figures" were all scientifically "arranged in columns."

3   The second part of the poem begins with line 5: "How soon unaccountable I became tired and sick." While Whitman says his negative reaction to the lecture was "unaccountable," we get the feeling he is being sarcastic. Something was missing in the astronomer's discussion of the stars, so Whitman, "gliding out" of the lecture hall, "wander'd off by himself" (in contrast to the audience), preferring to gaze "up in perfect silence at the stars."

4   At this point, no more words are necessary, for now there is the mystery of the universe. The stars shine with their own signif-

icance, and we can almost feel ourselves breathe a sigh of relief because this is where Whitman has left us. It appears as if in this poem the scientific approach to astronomy threatens to take the romance, beauty, and simple appreciation out of stargazing. The poem reveals an awe for those beautiful stars which lose their twinkle when they become figures, charts, and diagrams. What can be learned seems less important than what can be felt.

Reaction

In the space below, write your reaction to the student essay. What would you tell this student about her essay?

Commentary

Linda was assigned the broad subject of writing about some aspect of learning. She says this final essay is a far cry from her original draft. In fact, she had no intention of writing about the Whitman poem when she started. She began by freewriting about her negative reaction to lectures as a way of learning. When she was assigned the Whitman poem to read, she felt it said what she was unsuccessfully trying to say in her own essay. Since Linda felt the poem said it well, she decided to write about it and Whitman's feelings about lectures. However, after several drafts that kept taking her away from the poem itself, she decided to use the key lines from the poem to show not only what she feels Whitman is saying but also how he goes about saying it.

In her opening line, Linda correctly provides both the author and the title of the poem she is writing about. Too often, students begin an essay such as Linda's with "This poem . . . " or "This essay . . . " and forget to identify the subject for the audience. Such opening lines indicate that the student is writing only for the instructor and that since the instructor gave the assignment, the instructor will know what the subject of the essay is. Linda does not write to the instructor. She provides enough information to let anyone who reads her essay know her subject and thesis.

In her earlier drafts, Linda forgot some of the points mentioned in Unit 2. For instance, she used for her own essay title the title of Whitman's poem. Now she has one that is more appropriate and ties in with her own thesis. She also failed originally to use lines and quotes from the poem to back up her explanations and interpretations. In this final draft, Linda does an excellent job of incorporating lines and words from the poem as she explains what they mean to her and identifies them appropriately with quotation marks.

At first Linda did not notice that the poem was eight lines long and divided into two parts. But as she read and reread the poem, she noticed more and more about its structure and about Whitman's careful use of certain words, both of which helped her to better infer Whitman's meaning. She says she was worried that the final product might not be acceptable for the assignment on some aspect of learning. To the contrary, it serves as a fine example of narrowing a topic down to something that is personally interesting to the author and still says something about the topic—in this case, learning.

*V*iewpoints on

Human
Behavior

*"What a piece of work
is man!"*
William Shakespeare

DEAR ANN: For most of the 14 years that my wife and I have been married she has been undressing in the closet. At first it bothered me, but I never said anything because I knew she was shy by nature and I didn't want to upset her. Well, last week she started to sleep in the closet and this is more than I can take.

I don't understand how she can be comfortable in there, but she says it is just fine and that I shouldn't worry about her.

I ought to tell you that we have two beautiful children and a good marriage. We love and respect each other even though our sex life isn't terrific. Her mother told her when she got married that sex was a duty and to lie back and think of England.

I feel guilty in a nice, comfortable bed while my wife is on the floor with a shoe rack and a laundry bag. Please advise.

GARY, IND.

WHAT makes us behave the way we do? Sociologists and psychologists are still trying to find an answer to this question. Some answers have been found. It's clear that humans have the ability to reason and make choices. But many aspects of our physical and social environment limit the choices available. Still, sociologists claim that given our options and our preferences, we choose to do what we expect will be most rewarding. Whether the rewards are candy, fame, money, a better life in the future, or affection, we act or choose for self-interest.

The idea of self-interest as a way to explain human behavior is still one that social scientists use to try to explain our actions. Economists believe that we seek a variety of goods for ourselves. Their theories of supply and demand come from this belief. And the success of advertising seems to bear this out. Psychologists believe that behavior is shaped by reinforcement. That is, we repeat actions or behaviors that produce the results we desire. If our parents praise us for certain actions, we continue to act to please. Our reward is the praise we get from their pleasure. Sociologists believe that we seek what we perceive to be rewards and avoid what we perceive to cost us. Making our parents angry "costs" us; touching a hot fire "costs" us. If we are "normal," then we learn to behave based on these norms.

According to social scientists, we learn to see ourselves as others see us. In a sense, we look at ourselves from the outside. As infants and young children, we are not able to understand the meaning of the behavior of those around us. As we grow, we learn to know what we are like by seeing ourselves in others. We form an idea of what others want and expect and how they react to us. We settle into a pattern of behavior through interactions with others; we learn the "rules" of behavior for our particular environment. And even though we have choice, our behavior is frequently influenced by what those around us want or expect us to do.

Of course, we don't always follow the norm. Those who regularly don't want to follow the rules are considered abnormal. Some abnormal behavior is funny, some sad, some self-destructive, some dangerous to others. The essays in this unit deal with a variety of behavior: the good and the bad, the misunderstood, the so-called abnormal, the funny, and the unexplainable. You will recognize some behavioral actions described and wonder at others, but they are all part of the complex creatures called humans. It is hoped that you will both learn from the variety of readings and be stimulated by them to write your viewpoints on the subject.

Oh, in case you're interested, here is Ann Landers's reply to the behavior described in the letter above from Gary, Indiana:

> DEAR GARY: I've heard of shy women undressing in the closet, but sleeping there is a new one on me.
>
> Is it possible that you aren't as careful about your personal hygiene as you might be? Do you snore? Are your sexual demands excessive or kinky?
>
> If you can answer no to all of the above I suggest that you sit down with your wife and have a quiet talk. A woman who prefers the closet floor to a bed needs to explain herself.

📖 *Preparing to Read*

Take a minute or two to look over the following reading selection. Note the title and author, read the opening paragraph, and check the length. Make certain you have the time now to read it carefully and to do the exercises that follow it. Then, in the spaces provided, answer the following questions.

1. What do you think is meant here by the title "Beauty and the Beast"?

_____

_____

_____

2. What do you think will be the point of this essay? _____

_____

_____

_____

3. What might you learn from reading this selection? _____

_____

_____

_____

Vocabulary

Good comprehension of what you are about to read depends upon your understanding of the words below. The number following each word refers to the paragraph where it is used.

phenomenon (1) a perceivable, often unusual occurrence or fact

reciprocating machine (1) a type of engine in which the piston rod and piston move back and forth in a straight line, unlike a rotary engine

cyclotron (1) a device used to accelerate atomic particles in a spiral path

bridge (1) a card game involving four players

Charles Lindbergh (2) the first man to fly across the Atlantic Ocean alone

scores (2) large numbers

"solitary, poor, . . . and short" (3) quotation from seventeenth century English philosopher Thomas Hobbes's work *Leviathan*

Chartres (4) a city in north central France (In 1194, the old cathedral burned down and the people of Chartres replaced it with what some people call the most beautiful of all Christian churches.)

luminous (4) full of light

skeptical (4) doubting, questioning

consecrated (4) declared as sacred

guild (5) a medieval type of union or association

legions (5) a great many

sublime (7) impressive, supreme, majestic

vaults (8) arched structures forming ceilings

infidel (8) without religious beliefs (Here Donahue is being sarcastic and trying to show the attitude the Crusaders had toward those who were not Christians.)

noncombatants (8) those not involved in a fight or war

erratic (10) irregular, inconsistent

catechism (10) an instructional summary of the basic principles of a religion in question-answer form; here, a reference to Catholic instruction

machismo (11) an exaggerated sense of masculinity (This is where we get the word *macho*.)

entitlement (11) a right to something

Now read the essay.

Beauty and the Beast

PHIL DONAHUE

1   Compared to the animals around us, there's no doubt we are a remarkable phenomenon. Someone once referred to us as the "superdeluxe model": we walk, we talk, we smell, we taste, we touch, we think. All this in a relatively small and attractive package. We're also very good with our hands. In the comparatively brief time we've been available in the current form—about 50,000 years—we've invented the wheel, the alphabet, the clock, the reciprocating machine, the cyclotron, and everything in between. When we weren't busy making progress, we invented more playful things like music, art, baseball, and bridge. Over the years, we've demonstrated an admirable willingness to cooperate with each other. We assemble in big

groups to form towns and cities; we get together in twos to discover love. We've also shown a lot of individual spunk. The wheel wasn't invented by a committee, and Albert Einstein, by himself, revolutionized our understanding of the universe.

2   Of course, most of our uniquely human accomplishments are the result of a combination of cooperation and individual achievement. Even Charles Lindbergh had a ground crew. Beethoven composed the *Ninth Symphony* in the solitude of deafness, but scores of musicians are needed to bring it to life. Neil Armstrong had to have personal courage to step out on the surface of the moon, knowing that he might sink into 15 feet of "moondust," but he had an army of people to help put him there and bring him back.

3   We can only imagine what it must have felt like to stand on the moon; look back at the earth, suspended like a blue-and-white marble in space; and think how far we humans have come in such a short time. That feeling itself—the tightening in the throat, the tingle up the spine, the tear of pride—is unique to the human animal. Throughout most of our history, that feeling belonged exclusively to religion. When most people's lives were "solitary, poor, nasty, brutish, and short," religion was the only thing that made them feel dignified, special, proud of being human.

4   The peasants who gazed for the first time at the stained glass in the cathedral at Chartres undoubtedly experienced that same feeling—the most human of emotions—wonder. Most of them had never been inside anything bigger than a thatched hut and never seen anything more colorful than a piece of dyed cloth. Even today, the sight of this huge, arched space with those luminous windows suspended high in the darkness is almost enough to make a believer of even the most skeptical. In 1260, when the church was consecrated, the peasants who shuffled through those doors must have thought they had died and gone to heaven.

5   In fact, Chartres cathedral, like dozens of other cathedrals built in the same period, is the medieval equivalent of the modern effort to put a man on the moon. Both represent the perfect combination of individual achievement and group cooperation in the pursuit of something beautiful and lasting. The space program would never have gotten off the ground if Wernher von Braun hadn't made his discoveries in the field of jet propulsion, and the arches of Chartres would never have soared if an anonymous French architect hadn't devised a system of buttresses to support a two-ton block of stone 120 feet in the air and keep it there for a thousand years. But there would have been no stones to support if the wealthier townspeople hadn't dug deep into their pockets and come up with the money needed for construction. The glass in the openings would be clear

instead of stained if merchant guilds, members of the nobility, and even the French king hadn't contributed money for the windows. And all the money would have been worthless if legions of craftsmen hadn't been willing to dedicate their skills and often their lives to making this not just another building, but a monument to human achievement.

6   Bees get together and build hives, termites build mounds, beavers build dams, and spiders spin webs, but what other animal can change stone and glass into poetry? Other animals can alter their environment at the margins, but only we can transform our environment so completely that we reshape our destiny. Alone in the animal kingdom, we can set goals for ourselves and then pursue them. The dream of the medieval craftsmen who built Chartres was to secure a place for themselves in heaven. By lavishing love on this stone and glass, they glorified God and hoped to be rewarded in the next life. But in the process, they changed this life, made it more beautiful and more worth living.

7   A place like Chartres makes us proud to be human. We can stand tall and hold our heads high. Certainly no other creature could conceive and create something of such sublime beauty. Case closed? Hardly. There is, unfortunately, another side to the human animal that's nothing to be proud of. At places like Chartres, it's easy—and tempting—to overlook this other side, the ugly side, of our nature. But we can't begin to understand the human animal without it. Surely there's beauty inside us—but there's also a beast, a part of us that we'd like to deny but can't, a part that gives us a knot in the stomach instead of a lump in the throat.

8   Even the God-loving people who fashioned the soaring vaults and delicate windows of Chartres had murder on their minds. Some of the workers may well have been veterans of the First Crusade, an expedition to save the Holy Land from the infidel Muslims that was part religious frenzy, part military adventure, and part social fad. On that excursion, begun four years after work on Chartres began, the Crusaders slaughtered thousands of noncombatants, leveled whole communities, and finally "saved" the holy city of Jerusalem by massacring all its inhabitants—men, women, children, Muslims, Jews: everybody. Muslims, after all, were only infidels, not humans, so it wasn't like killing your next-door neighbor.

9   After the shrines of Christianity were in "safe" hands, many Crusaders returned home and turned their attention to other things, like the cathedral at Chartres.

10   How could the same hands that carved these stones and stained this glass have wielded swords and butchered women and children? How could so much beauty and so much brutality exist side by side?

This is the great contradiction of the human animal. We can be both noble and petty, sublime and savage, beauty and beast. We can pray one minute and kill the next, create one minute and destroy the next, even love and hate simultaneously. We like to think that our erratic behavior is a thing of the past, that we've outgrown the excesses of the Crusades. But nothing could be further from the truth. There are people in Belfast today who will repeat the catechism, then go toss a bomb into a crowded pub; people who grieve for the victims of crime, then pay good money to see it reenacted on a movie screen. The same technological wizardry, individual bravery, and group effort that put us on the moon have also given us weapons that can blow our whole planet into permanent winter.

11   Far from having disappeared with the last Crusade, the human animal's strange capacity for contradictory behavior still affects our daily lives. As parents, we desperately want our kids to grow up emotionally healthy, able to love and be loved; then our culture teaches them that sex is dirty and they should be ashamed of their sexual desires. Women say they want to marry a nice person who will respect them and communicate with them; then they melt for *machismo* and fall for the strong, silent type. They want a man who will share the housework and feed the baby at three in the morning, but they live in a society in which few bosses grant time off to men who want to share parenting. Cops throw drunken drivers in jail while television sells beer as though it were an American entitlement. The message to teenage males: "You're not a man without a beer can in your hand." But there are millions of teenage drivers and thousands of cloverleaves out there, and the phone rings every day, in homes across America, and it's the hospital calling—or the morgue.

12   Why do we do the things we do? Why, after thousands of years of personal tragedies and group catastrophes, do we continue to make the same mistakes? Why do we persist in the same contradictory behavior day after day, century after century, alternating between Chartres and the Crusades, between grief and gore, between moonwalks and megatons?

13   These questions aren't just for the historians and the sociologists. They're for everyone who wrestles with these contradictory drives in his or her own life. The impulse that sends a society back to war, despite the knowledge that children will die and mothers will grieve, is the same impulse that leads you to light up another cigarette or have "one more for the road," despite the knowledge that it may kill you. We live with contradictions in our own behavior—and the behavior of others—every day. It's about time we tried to understand those contradictions. Are they a permanent part of the human condition, or can we do something about them?

Understanding the Content

Feel free to reread all or parts of the selection to answer the following questions.

1. What does Donahue call "beauty" and what does he call "beast"?

2. What, according to Donahue, are some of the things that make man "a remarkable phenomenon" and different from the rest of the animal kingdom?

3. How is man's contradictory behavior in the past similar to man's behavior today?

4. Why does Donahue feel that the building of the cathedral in Chartres is similar to putting a man on the moon today?

5. What does Donahue call the most human of emotions? Do you agree? Explain your answer.

6. Can we infer that Donahue feels man will eventually lose his dark or "beast" side?

7. What is the thesis of this selection? Is it implied or stated?

Looking at Structure and Style

1. Make a list of the major examples of behavior Donahue uses to support the beauty and the beast in man. How and where does he switch from one to the other?

2. What is the topic sentence of paragraph 2? How is it supported?

3. Why does Donahue spend so much time discussing Chartres and the Crusades? How effective is this technique?

4. Explain the effectiveness of paragraphs 12 and 13.

5. In what paragraph is the thesis best stated or implied?

6. Select some sentences from the selection that use comparison-contrast. How much of the essay uses this technique?

7. Explain or rewrite the following passages from the selection:
   a. "The wheel wasn't invented by a committee. . . ." (1)
   b. ". . . The peasants who shuffled through those doors must have thought they had died and gone to heaven." (4)
   c. ". . . But what other animal can change stone and glass into poetry?" (6)
   d. ". . . and finally 'saved' the holy city of Jerusalem by massacring all its inhabitants." (8)
   e. "Cops throw drunken drivers in jail while television sells beer as though it were an American entitlement." (11)

8. What suggestions for revision, if any, would you give the author?

Evaluating the Author's Viewpoints

1. Donahue states that "most of our uniquely human accomplishments are the result of a combination of cooperation and individual achievement." (2) Do you agree? Why?

2. Does Donahue use mostly facts or opinion? With what statements do you agree or disagree? Why?

3. Donahue says, "Surely there is beauty inside us—but there is also a beast, a part of us that we'd like to deny but can't, a part that gives us a knot in the stomach instead of a lump in the throat." (7) In addition to some of the things Donahue discusses, give some examples of human behavior that puts a knot in your stomach. Are these the types of behavior to which Donahue refers? Would he agree with you?

4. "As parents, we desperately want our kids to grow up emotionally healthy, able to love and be loved; then our culture teaches them that sex is dirty and they should be ashamed of their sexual desires." (11) Is this true in your view? Explain.

Pursuing Possible Essay Topics

1. Think about a behavior trait you have that you would like to change. Discuss how that trait developed, what effect it has had on you, and how you might change it.

2. Discuss your pet peeve(s) of the "human animal."

3. Write your own essay about the beauty and the beast in humans. What are achievements that can be classified as beauty and what as beast? Try not to repeat what Donahue says in his essay.

4. Answer the question Donahue raises: "Why, after thousands of years of personal tragedies and group catastrophies, do we continue to make the same mistakes?" (12)

5. If you had the opportunity to redesign the human animal, what changes would you make? Why?

6. Answer the question Donahue raises in the last sentence of the essay.

7. Brainstorm or freewrite on one or more of the following:
   a. beautiful behavior
   b. beastly behavior
   c. silly behavior
   d. warlike behavior
   e. peaceful behavior
   f. _____ behavior

8. Come up with your own topic that deals with human behavior.

📖 *Preparing to Read*

Take a minute or two to look over the following reading selection. Note the title and author, read the opening paragraph, and check the length. Make certain you have the time now to read it carefully and to do the exercises that follow it. Then, in the spaces provided, answer the following questions.

1. What attitude toward superstitions do you think the author has?

   _____

2. How would you define a "superstitious mind"? _____

   _____

3. Are you superstitious? Why? _____

   _____

Vocabulary

Good comprehension of what you are about to read depends upon your understanding of the words below. The number following each word refers to the paragraph where it appears.

   amulets (1) lucky charms

   incantations (1) words believed to have magic powers to cast spells

   occult (2) supernatural, unearthly, mystical

   excising (3) removing, ridding

   evasion (4) avoidance

   deference (4) honor, respect

   shroud (5) a cloth used to wrap a person for burial

   pinafore (5) a young girl's dress

   idiom (6) an expression of speech having a meaning different from the literal meaning of the words

   melodramatic (6) exaggeratedly emotional

   prolong (7) extend

   ironically (8) oppositely or differently from what is expected

   matrilineal heritage (8) those things inherited from the mother's side of the family

   askew (9) crooked

Now read the essay.

Superstitious Minds

LETTY COTTIN POGREBIN

1   I am a very rational person. I tend to trust reason more than feeling. But I also happen to be superstitious—in my fashion. Black cats and rabbits' feet hold no power for me. My superstitions are my mother's superstitions, the amulets and incantations she learned from *her* mother and taught me.

2   I don't mean to suggest that I grew up in an occult atmosphere. On the contrary, my mother desperately wanted me to rise above her immigrant ways and become an educated American. She tried to hide her superstitions, but I came to know them all: Slap a girl's cheeks when she first gets her period. Never take a picture of a pregnant woman. Knock wood when speaking about your good fortune. Eat the ends of bread if you want to have a boy. Don't leave a bride alone on her wedding day.

3   When I was growing up, my mother often would tiptoe in after I seemed to be asleep and kiss my forehead three times, making odd noises that sounded like a cross between sucking and spitting. One night I opened my eyes and demanded an explanation. Embarrassed, she told me she was excising the "Evil Eye"—in case I had attracted its attention that day by being especially wonderful. She believed her kisses could suck out any envy or ill will that those less fortunate may have directed at her child.

4   By the time I was in my teens, I was almost on speaking terms with the Evil Eye, a jealous spirit that kept track of those who had "too much" happiness and zapped them with sickness and misery to even the score. To guard against this mischief, my mother practiced rituals of interference, evasion, deference, and above all, avoidance of situations where the Evil Eye might feel at home.

5   This is why I wasn't allowed to attend funerals. This is also why my mother hated to mend my clothes while I was wearing them. The only garment one should properly get sewn *into* is a shroud. To ensure that the Evil Eye did not confuse my pinafore with a burial outfit, my mother insisted that I chew a thread while she sewed, thus proving myself very much alive. Outwitting the Evil Eye also accounted for her closing the window shades above my bed whenever there was a full moon. The moon should only shine on cemeteries, you see; the living need protection from the spirits.

6   Because we were dealing with a deadly force, I also wasn't supposed to say any words associated with mortality. This was hard for a 12-year-old who punctuated every anecdote with the verb "to die," as in "You'll die when you hear this!" or "If I don't get home by ten,

I'm dead." I managed to avoid using such expressions in the presence of my mother until the day my parents brought home a painting I hated and we were arguing about whether it should be displayed on our walls. Unthinking, I pressed my point with a melodramatic idiom: "That picture will hang over my dead body!" Without a word, my mother grabbed a knife and slashed the canvas to shreds.

7   I understand all this now. My mother emigrated in 1907 from a small Hungarian village. The oldest of seven children, she had to go out to work before she finished the eighth grade. Experience taught her that life was unpredictable and often incomprehensible. Just as an athlete keeps wearing the same T-shirt in every game to prolong a winning streak, my mother's superstitions gave her a means of imposing order on a chaotic system. Her desire to control the fates sprung from the same helplessness that makes the San Francisco 49ers' defensive more superstitious than its offensive team. Psychologists speculate this is because the defense has less control; they don't have the ball.

8   Women like my mother never had the ball. She died when I was 15, leaving me with deep regrets for what she might have been—and a growing understanding of who she was. *Superstitious* is one of the things she was. I wish I had a million sharp recollections of her, but when you don't expect someone to die, you don't store up enough memories. Ironically, her mystical practices are among the clearest impressions she left behind. In honor of this matrilineal heritage— and to symbolize my mother's effort to control her life as I in my way try to find order in mine—I knock on wood and I do not let the moon shine on those I love. My children laugh at me, but they understand that these tiny rituals have helped keep my mother alive in my mind.

9   A year ago, I awoke in the night and realized that my son's window blinds had been removed for repair. Smiling at my own compulsion, I got a bed sheet to tack up against the moonlight and I opened his bedroom door. What I saw brought tears to my eyes. There, hopelessly askew, was a blanket my son, then 18, had taped to his window like a curtain.

10   My mother never lived to know David, but he knew she would not want the moon to shine upon him as he slept.

Understanding the Content

Feel free to reread all or parts of the selection to answer the following questions.

1. Pogrebin says that she is a rational person, but superstitious in her own way. In what way is she superstitious?

2. The author mentions several of her mother's superstitions. What were some of them?

3. What was the reason Pogrebin's mother would never mend her clothes while she was wearing them?

4. The term "Evil Eye" is used several times. How would the author's mother define the term?

5. Pogrebin says that she now understands her mother's superstitions. How does she explain them?

6. How does Pogrebin explain away her own practice of some of her mother's "tiny rituals" if she is a "rational person"?

Looking at Structure and Style

1. How well does the opening paragraph establish the author's subject and her attitude toward that subject? What do we know after reading it?

2. What writing pattern is used in paragraph 2? Explain it.

3. What writing pattern is used in paragraph 3? Explain it.

4. What is the function of paragraph 7?

5. What is the function of paragraph 9? What inferences can you draw from it?

6. Explain or rewrite the following passages from the essay:
   a. "By the time I was in my teens, I was almost on speaking terms with the Evil Eye, a jealous spirit that kept track of those who had 'too much' happiness and zapped them with sickness and misery to even the score." (4)
   b. "This was hard for a 12-year-old who punctuated every anecdote with the verb 'to die,' as in 'You'll die when you hear this!'. . ." (6)
   c. "Experience taught her that life was unpredictable and often incomprehensible." (7)
   d. "Women like my mother never had the ball." (8)

7. How would you describe the tone of this essay?

Evaluating the Author's Viewpoints

1. Pogrebin says that her mother's "desire to control the fates sprung from the same helplessness that makes the San Francisco 49ers' defensive more superstitious than its offensive team. Psychologists speculate this is because the defense has less control; they don't have the ball." (7) Is this a good analogy?

2. Do you get the feeling that the author is as superstitious as her mother was? Explain.

3. For what reason do you think Pogrebin chose to write about her mother's superstitions? Is she embarrassed or ashamed of them? What is her point?

Pursuing Possible Essay Topics

1. Write about a superstition of your own or a family member's. How strong is it? Where does it come from?

2. Talk to someone from another country about superstitions. Are their superstitions similar to those you know?

3. Go to the library and look under "superstitions" in the card catalogue. Find some of the references listed in the library. Look through one or two references that seem interesting. You may get some ideas for an essay.

4. Brainstorm or freewrite on one or more of the following:
   a. black magic
   b. voodoo
   c. the occult
   d. silly superstitions
   e. ESP
   f. astrological forecasts

5. Attempt to explain why many people like to view movies that frighten them.

6. Ignore these and write on some aspect of strange human behavior.

Preparing to Read

Take a minute or two to look over the following reading selection. Note the title and author, read the opening paragraph, and check the length. Make certain you have the time now to read it carefully and to do the exercises that follow it. Then, in the spaces provided, answer the following questions.

1. What is suggested by the title? _____

   _____

2. What do you think the essay will be about? _____

   _____

3. Does the opening paragraph make you want to read on? Why?

   _____

   _____

Vocabulary

Good comprehension of what you are about to read depends upon your understanding of the words below. The number following each word refers to the paragraph where it is used.

affluent (1) wealthy, well-to-do

impoverished (1) drained of wealth, poor

discreet (1) cautious, careful

uninflammatory (1) not arousing anger or emotion

unwieldy (2) difficult to handle

quarry (2) a hunted animal, prey

dismayed (2) unnerved, rattled, taken aback

accomplice (2) one who aids a criminal

tyranny (2) absolute power, usually unjust and cruel; here, the power muggers have to terrorize women

elicit (3) bring out or cause

avid (4) enthusiastic, eager

taut (4) strained, tense

warrenlike (5) describing a *warren*, a place where small animals live, but also referring to places overcrowded with people

bandolier-style (5) like a soldier's bullet belt

perpetrators (5) those who commit crimes

solace (5) comfort

in retrospect (6) looking back on the past

bravado (6) false bravery

perilous (7) dangerous

ad hoc posse (7) *ad hoc* refers to the formation of a group for a special purpose (in this case, to chase him)

skittish (9) nervous

congenial (9) friendly, cooperative

constitutional (10) a healthy walk

Now read the essay.

Night Walker

BRENT STAPLES

1 My first victim was a woman—white, well dressed, probably in her early 20s. I came upon her late one evening on a deserted street in Hyde Park, a relatively affluent neighborhood in an otherwise

mean, impoverished section of Chicago. As I swung onto the avenue behind her, there seemed to be a discreet, uninflammatory distance between us. Not so. She cast back a worried glance. To her, the youngish black man—a broad six feet two inches with a beard and billowing hair, both hands shoved into the pockets of a bulky military jacket—seemed menacingly close. She picked up her pace and was soon running in earnest. Within seconds she disappeared into a cross street.

2   That was more than a decade ago. I was 22 years old, a graduate student newly arrived at the University of Chicago. It was in the echo of that terrified woman's footfalls that I first began to know the unwieldy inheritance I'd come into—the ability to alter public space in ugly ways. It was clear that she thought herself the quarry of a mugger, a rapist, or worse. Suffering a bout of insomnia, however, I was stalking sleep, not defenseless wayfarers. As a softy who is scarcely able to take a knife to a raw chicken—let alone hold one to a person's throat—I was surprised, embarrassed, and dismayed all at once. Her flight made me feel like an accomplice in tyranny. It also made it clear that I was indistinguishable from the muggers who occasionally seeped into the area from the surrounding ghetto. I soon gathered that being perceived as dangerous is a hazard in itself: Where fear and weapons meet—and they often do in urban America—there is always the possibility of death.

3   In that first year, my first away from my hometown, I was to become thoroughly familiar with the language of fear. At dark, shadowy intersections, I could cross in front of a car stopped at a traffic light and elicit the *thunk, thunk, thunk, thunk* of the driver—black, white, male, female—hammering down the door locks. On less traveled streets after dark, I grew accustomed to but never comfortable with people crossing to the other side of the street rather than pass me. Then there were the standard unpleasantries with policemen, doormen, bouncers, cabdrivers, and others whose business it is to screen out troublesome individuals *before* there is any nastiness.

4   I moved to New York nearly two years ago and I have remained an avid night walker. In central Manhattan, the near-constant crowd covers the tense one-on-one street encounters. Elsewhere, things can get very taut indeed.

5   After dark, on the warrenlike streets of Brooklyn where I live, I often see women who fear the worst from me. They seem to have set their faces on neutral, and with their purse straps strung across their chests bandolier-style, they forge ahead as though bracing themselves against being tackled. I understand, of course, that the danger they perceive is not a hallucination. Women are particularly vulnerable to street violence, and young black males are drastically overrepre-

sented among the perpetrators of that violence. Yet these truths are no solace against the alienation that comes of being ever the suspect, an entity with whom pedestrians avoid making eye contact.

6   It is not altogether clear to me how I reached the ripe old age of 22 without being conscious of the lethality nighttime pedestrians attributed to me. Perhaps it was because in Chester, Pa., the small, angry industrial town where I came of age in the 1960s, I was scarcely noticeable against a backdrop of gang warfare, street knifings, and murders. I grew up one of the good boys, had perhaps a half-dozen fistfights. In retrospect, my shyness of combat has clear sources. As a boy, I saw countless tough guys locked away; I have since buried several, too. They were babies, really—a teen-age cousin, a brother of 22, a childhood friend in his mid-20s—all gone down in episodes of bravado played out in the streets. I chose, perhaps unconsciously, to remain a shadow—timid, but a survivor.

7   The fearsomeness mistakenly attributed to me in public places often has a perilous flavor. The most frightening of these confusions occurred in the late 1970s and early 1980s, when I worked as a journalist in Chicago. One day, rushing into the office of a magazine I was writing for with a deadline story in hand, I was mistaken for a burglar. The office manager called security and, with an ad hoc posse, pursued me through the labyrinthine halls, nearly to my editor's door. I had no way of proving who I was. I could only move briskly toward the company of someone who knew me.

8   Relatively speaking, however, I never fared as badly as another black male journalist. He went to nearby Waukegan, Ill., a couple of summers ago to work on a story about a murderer who was born there. Mistaking the reporter for the killer, police officers hauled him from his car at gunpoint and but for his press credentials would probably have tried to book him. Such episodes are not uncommon. Black men trade tales like this all the time.

9   Over the years, I learned to smother the rage I felt at so often being mistaken for a criminal. Not to do so would surely have led to madness. I now take precautions to make myself less threatening. I move about with care, particularly late in the evening. I give a wide berth to nervous people on subway platforms during the wee hours. If I happen to be entering a building behind some people who appear skittish, I may walk by, letting them clear the lobby before I return, so as not to seem to be following them. I have been calm and extremely congenial on those rare occasions when I've been pulled over by the police.

10   And on late-evening constitutionals I employ what has proved to be an excellent tension-reducing measure: I whistle melodies from Beethoven and Vivaldi and the more popular classical composers.

Even steely New Yorkers hunching toward nighttime destinations seem to relax, and occasionally they even join in the tune. Virtually everybody seems to sense that a mugger wouldn't be warbling bright, sunny selections from Vivaldi's "Four Seasons." It is my equivalent of the cowbell that hikers wear when they are in bear country.

Understanding the Content

Feel free to reread all or parts of the selection to answer the following questions.

1. What point is Staples making in his essay? Is his thesis implied or stated?

2. What happened that caused Staples to learn that "being perceived as dangerous is a hazard in itself" (2)? What does he mean?

3. How old was the author at the time? What was his reaction?

4. What other events have occurred that have made him "thoroughly familiar with the language of fear" (3)?

5. Why does Staples feel that he is "often being mistaken for a criminal" (9)?

6. What tactics or precautions does he take to avoid being mistaken for a potential criminal?

Looking at Structure and Style

1. How effective is the author's first paragraph? Does it create an interest in the essay? Why?

2. Why does Staples wait until the middle of paragraph 2 to explain what was actually happening, that he was merely taking a walk?

3. What is the function of paragraph 3?

4. What attitude do you think is expressed in paragraph 9? Can you draw any inferences from the author's statements?

5. Rewrite or explain the following passages from the essay:
   a. "It was in the echo of that terrified woman's footfalls that I first began to know the unwieldy inheritance I'd come into. . . ." (2)
   b. "Where fear and weapons meet—and they often do in urban America—there is always the possibility of death." (2)
   c. ". . . I could cross in front of a car stopped at a traffic light and elicit the *thunk, thunk, thunk, thunk* of the driver—black, white, male, female—hammering down the door locks." (3)
   d. "They seemed to have set their faces on neutral, and with their purse straps strung across their chests bandolier-style, they forge ahead as though bracing themselves against being tackled." (5)

    e. "It is my equivalent of the cowbell that hikers wear when they know they are in bear country." (10)

6. How effective is the title? Explain.

7. What suggestions for revision, if any, would you offer the author?

Evaluating the Author's Viewpoints

1. In paragraph 2, Staples says that he learned at twenty-two that he had "the ability to alter public space in ugly ways." Explain what he means. Might the woman he describes in the opening paragraph be just as afraid of a white man in the same situation?

2. Reread the last sentence in paragraph 3. What attitude does the author reflect when he cites examples of "standard unpleasantries"? Is he exaggerating?

3. In paragraph 5, Staples says that "young black males are drastically overrepresented among the perpetrators of . . . violence." Where do you think he believes this overrepresentation takes place? Do you agree?

4. Staples reveals to his audience negative attitudes toward black males that he has experienced firsthand and does not deserve. What is your reaction to the way he has responded?

Pursuing Possible Essay Topics

1. Write about a time when your identity was questioned or you were mistakenly accused of something. How were you made to feel? How did you react?

2. Write about a time when you were frightened or felt threatened by someone. Was the fear or threat real or imagined? What caused the situation? How was it resolved?

3. Brainstorm or freewrite on one or more of the following:

    a. fear   d. gangs
    b. anger   e. danger
    c. prejudice   f. tension

4. Skim through a newspaper for two or three days to see how many episodes of street violence are reported. What effect do these reports have on people's fears? Is street violence exaggerated?

5. Staples believes that violence committed by black males is exaggerated. Write an essay about another ethnic group that has negative characteristics attributed to it that are false or exaggerated. Try to touch upon why this happens.

6. Examine a characteristic of yourself or someone you know that you don't like. How did it develop? What harm has it caused? What can you do about it?

7. Ignore these and come up with your own topic on some aspect of human behavior.

📖 *Preparing to Read*

Take a minute or two to look over the following reading selection. Note the title and author, read the opening paragraph, and check the length. Make certain you have the time now to read it carefully and to do the exercises that follow it. Then, in the spaces provided, answer the following questions.

1. Explain your reaction to the title. _____

_____

_____

2. What do you think will be the point of the essay? _____

_____

_____

3. What is your reaction to the opening paragraph? _____

_____

Vocabulary

Good comprehension of what you are about to read depends upon your understanding of the words below. The number following each word refers to the paragraph where it is used.

Dumpster (1) a huge trash container

gaunt (2) thin and bony

incisor (2) the sharp, pointed tooth used for cutting and tearing

maze (3) a confusing series of pathways

canine unit (4) a patrol group using dogs

recesses (4) alcoves

baton (5) a club or nightstick

acrid (6) bitter, harsh

Now read the essay.

Slow Descent into Hell

JON D. HULL

1   Behind a Dumpster sits a man who calls himself Red enjoying the last drops of a bottle of wine called Wild Irish Rose. It's 1 a.m., and the thermometer hovers around 20°, with a biting wind. His nickname comes from a golden retriever his family once had back in Memphis, and a sparkle comes to his eyes as he recalls examples of the dog's loyalty. One day he plans to get another dog, and says, "I'm getting to the point where I can't talk to people. They're always telling me to do something or get out of their way. But a dog is different."

2   At 35, he looks 50, and his gaunt face carries discolored scars from the falls and fights of three years on the streets. An upper incisor is missing, and his lower teeth jut outward against his lower lip, giving the impression that he can't close his mouth. His baggy pants are about five inches too long and when he walks, their frayed ends drag on the ground. "You know something?" he asks, holding up the bottle. "I wasn't stuck to this stuff until the cold got to me. Now I'll freeze without it. I could go to Florida or someplace, but I know this town and I know who the creeps are. Besides, it's not too bad in the summer."

3   Finishing the bottle, and not yet drunk enough to sleep out in the cold, he gathers his blanket around his neck and heads for the subways beneath city hall, where hundreds of the homeless seek warmth. Once inside, the game of cat-and-mouse begins with the police, who patrol the maze of tunnels and stairways and insist that everybody remain off the floor and keep moving. Sitting can be an invitation to trouble, and the choice between sleep and warmth becomes agonizing as the night wears on.

4   For the first hour, Red shuffles through the tunnels, stopping occasionally to urinate against the graffiti-covered walls. Then he picks a spot and stands for half an hour, peering out from the large hood of his coat. In the distance, the barking of German shepherds echoes through the tunnels as a canine unit patrols the darker recesses of the underground. Nearby, a young man in a ragged trench coat stands against the wall, slapping his palms against his sides and muttering, "I've got to get some paperwork done. I've just got to get some paperwork done!" Red shakes his head. "Home sweet home,"

he says. Finally exhausted, he curls up on the littered floor, lying on his side with his hands in his pockets and his hood pulled all the way over his face to keep the rats away. He is asleep instantly.

5   Whack! A police baton slaps his legs and a voice booms, "Get the hell up, you're outta here. Right now!" Another police officer whacks his nightstick against a metal grating as the twelve men sprawled along the tunnel crawl to their feet. Red pulls himself up and walks slowly up the stairs to the street, never looking back.

6   Pausing at every pay phone to check the coin-return slots, he makes his way to a long steam grate whose warm hiss bears the acrid smell of a dry cleaner's shop. He searches for newspaper and cardboard to block the moisture but retain the heat. With his makeshift bed made, he curls up again, but the rest is short-lived. "This s.o.b. used to give off more heat," he says, staring with disgust at the grate. He gathers the newspapers and moves down the block, all the while muttering about the differences among grates. "Some are good, some are bad. I remember I was getting a beautiful sleep on this one baby and then all this honking starts. I was laying right in a damn driveway and nearly got run over by a garbage truck."

7   Stopping at a small circular vent shooting jets of steam, Red shakes his head and curses: "This one is too wet, and it'll go off sometimes, leaving you to freeze." Shaking now with the cold, he walks four more blocks and finds another grate, where he curls up and fishes a half-spent cigarette from his pocket. The grate is warm, but soon the moisture from the steam has soaked his newspapers and begins to gather on his clothes. Too tired to find another grate, he sets down more newspapers, throws his blanket over his head and sprawls across the grate. By morning he is soaked.

Understanding the Content

Feel free to reread all or parts of the selection to answer the following questions.

1. What is the subject of the essay?

2. What is the thesis or point of the essay? Is it stated or implied?

3. Can you infer where the incident takes place? How?

4. What is the "the game of cat-and-mouse" people like Red play?

5. For how long has Red been living as he is?

6. Why does Red stay when he could "go to Florida or someplace" (2)?

7. Describe Red.

Looking at Structure and Style

1. What is the author's attitude toward Red?

2. Is the essay told mostly subjectively or objectively? Explain. Is this an effective approach in this case? Why?

3. On occasion, the author lets Red speak for himself. How does hearing Red's own words help us get a better picture of him in paragraph 1? paragraph 2? paragraph 4? paragraph 6?

4. Describe the transition used between paragraphs 4 and 5.

5. Pick out some passages from the essay that you think are particularly well written. What makes them good?

6. What is the basic writing mode used in this essay? How else might the author have chosen to write about Red? Would it have the same effect?

7. Explain the significance of the title.

8. What suggestions for revision, if any, would you offer the author?

Evaluating the Author's Viewpoints

1. Hull does not directly state his viewpoints, but a look at his title implies a point of view toward Red's existence. What is it? Do you agree?

2. What seems to be Red's attitude toward his own lifestyle?

3. What seems to be the attitude of the police as Hull portrays them?

4. What do you think are Hull's feelings toward Red and others like him? Sympathy? Disgust? Concern? Interest? Explain.

Pursuing Possible Essay Topics

1. Pretend you are Red. Write a narrative that explains why you are living where you are and as you are. Be as descriptive as you can.

2. Investigate your city's laws and its attitude toward the homeless. Go to the city hall or ask your librarian for information. Write an analysis of your findings.

3. Go to the library to do some research on the homeless. Look in the latest issues of the *Reader's Guide to Periodical Literature* under the heading "homeless." It will direct you to any recent articles or essays appearing in current magazines. Do some reading and then react to what you read in an essay of your own.

4. Explain what you would do about the homeless situation if you had the power.

5. Visit an organization such as the Salvation Army that attempts to help the homeless. Interview someone who works for the organization and report their viewpoints on homeless people's behavior. How do they see the situation?

6. Brainstorm or freewrite on one or more of the following:

   a. runaways
   b. drunks
   c. street people
   d. shelters
   e. the human bond
   f. destitution

7. Ignore these and find your own topic on some aspect of human behavior.

📖 *Preparing to Read*

Take a minute or two to look over the following reading selection. Note the title and author, read the first *two* paragraphs, and check the length. Make certain you have the time now to read it carefully and to do the exercises that follow it. Then, in the spaces provided, answer the following questions.

1. What do you think is the author's attitude toward fun? _____

   _____

2. Do you think the essay is serious or humorous? Why? _____

   _____

3. Guess what you think is the thesis of the essay. _____

   _____

Vocabulary

Good comprehension of what you are about to read depends upon your understanding of the words below. The number following each word refers to the paragraph where it appears.

   Puritans (3) those who practice strict moral rules and regard luxury and fun as sinful

   fetish (5) an object to which one is overattached or obsessed

   traipsing (8) walking about idly

   licentiousness (9) immorality, lustfulness

epitome (11) perfect example

blaspheme (13) speak irreverently of

Now read the essay.

Fun. Oh, Boy. Fun. You Could Die from It.

SUZANNE BRITT JORDAN

1   Fun is hard to have.

2   Fun is a rare jewel.

3   Somewhere along the line people got the modern idea that fun was there for the asking, that people deserved fun, that if we didn't have a little fun every day we would turn into (sakes alive!) Puritans.

4   "Was it fun?" became the question that overshadowed all other questions: good questions like: Was it moral? Was it kind? Was it honest? Was it beneficial? Was it generous? Was it necessary? And (my favorite) was it selfless?

5   When pleasure got to be the main thing, the fun fetish was sure to follow. Everything was supposed to be fun. If it wasn't fun, then by Jove, we were going to make it fun, or else.

6   Think of all the things that got the reputation of being fun. Family outings were supposed to be fun. Sex was supposed to be fun. Education was supposed to be fun. Work was supposed to be fun. Walt Disney was supposed to be fun. Church was supposed to be fun. Staying fit was supposed to be fun.

7   Just to make sure that everybody knew how much fun we were having, we put happy faces on flunking test papers, dirty bumpers, sticky refrigerator doors, bathroom mirrors.

8   If a kid, looking at his very happy parents traipsing through that very happy Disney World, said, "This ain't no fun, ma," his ma's heart sank. She wondered where she had gone wrong. Everybody told her what fun family outings to Disney World would be. Golly gee, what was the matter?

9   Fun got to be such a big thing that everybody started to look for more and more thrilling ways to supply it. One way was to step up the level of danger or licentiousness or alcohol or drug consumption so that you could be sure that, no matter what, you would manage to have a little fun.

10   Television commercials brought a lot of fun and fun-loving folks into the picture. Everything that people in those commercials did

looked like fun: taking Polaroid snapshots, swilling beer, buying insurance, mopping the floor, bowling, taking aspirin. We all wished,
I'm sure, that we could have half as much fun as those rough-and-
ready guys around the locker room, flicking each other with towels
and pouring champagne. The more commercials people watched, the
more they wondered when the fun would start in their own lives. It
was pretty depressing.

11   Big occasions were supposed to be fun. Christmas, Thanksgiving
and Easter were obviously supposed to be fun. Your wedding day
was supposed to be fun. Your wedding night was supposed to be a
whole lot of fun. Your honeymoon was supposed to be the epitome
of fundom. And so we ended up going through every Big Event we
ever celebrated, waiting for the fun to start.

12   It occurred to me, while I was sitting around waiting for the fun
to start, that not much is, and that I should tell you just in case you're
worried about your fun capacity.

13   I don't mean to put a damper on things. I just mean we ought to
treat fun reverently. It is a mystery. It cannot be caught like a virus.
It cannot be trapped like an animal. The god of mirth is paying us
back for all those years of thinking fun was everywhere by refusing
to come to our party. I don't want to blaspheme fun anymore. When
fun comes in on little dancing feet, you probably won't be expecting
it. In fact, I bet it comes when you're doing your duty, your job, or
your work. It may even come on a Tuesday.

14   I remember one day, long ago, on which I had an especially good
time. Pam Davis and I walked to the College Village drug store one
Saturday morning to buy some candy. We were about 12 years old
(fun ages). She got her Bit-O-Honey. I got my malted milk balls,
chocolate stars, Chunkys, and a small bag of M&M's. We started back
to her house. I was going to spend the night. We had the whole day
to look forward to. We had plenty of candy. It was a long way to
Pam's house but every time we got weary Pam would put her hand
over her eyes, scan the horizon like a sailor and say, "Oughta reach
home by nightfall," at which point the two of us would laugh until
we thought we couldn't stand it another minute. Then after we got
calm, she'd say it again. You should have been there. It was the kind
of day and friendship and occasion that made me deeply regret that
I had to grow up.

15   It was fun.

Understanding the Content

Feel free to reread all or parts of the selection to answer the following
questions.

1. Jordan's essay subject is fun. What is her thesis?

2. What are some examples Jordan provides to support her thesis?

3. What are some of her objections to the idea of fun?

4. How does Jordan define fun?

Looking at Structure and Style

1. Jordan opens and closes with very short one-sentence paragraphs. How effective is this technique? Explain.

2. How does the use of "(sakes alive!)" in paragraph 3 help create the author's tone? What are some other examples of her use of certain words or phrases to create tone?

3. What is the function of paragraphs 4–11?

4. What is the function of paragraphs 12 and 13?

5. How does Jordan use paragraph 14 to help her define fun? Is it effective? Explain.

6. How appropriate is her title?

7. Explain or rewrite the following passages from the selection:
   a. "Just to make sure that everybody knew how much fun we were having, we put happy faces on flunking test papers, dirty bumpers, sticky refrigerator doors, bathroom mirrors." (7)
   b. "The more commercials people watched, the more they wondered when the fun would start in their own lives. It was pretty depressing." (10)
   c. "I don't mean to put a damper on things." (13)
   d. "The god of mirth is paying us back for all those years of thinking fun was everywhere by refusing to come to our party." (13)
   e. "It [fun] may even come on a Tuesday." (13)

Evaluating the Author's Viewpoints

1. Does Jordan convince you that her views on fun are correct? Explain.

2. In paragraph 4, Jordan supplies some questions she feels we should ask in place of "Was it fun?" Do you agree with her? Why?

3. Look through paragraphs 6–11 at the many examples of what she says we have come to expect to be "fun." With how many of these items do you agree? Why?

4. Do you agree with Jordan's definition of fun? Explain.

Pursuing Possible Essay Topics

1. Write your own essay defining fun. Avoid dictionary definitions and try to use examples to explain your definition.

2. Look closely at some television commercials. Is Jordan right? Is there a seeming attempt to make everything look like fun? Analyze the behavior portrayed in a particular commercial.

3. Write about a time when you expected to have fun and were disappointed. What did you learn?

4. What was the most fun you have ever had? Why was it fun? What does it say about you and your values?

5. "Are we having fun yet?" (commonly seen bumper sticker)

6. Brainstorm or freewrite on one or more of the following:
   a. the pursuit of happiness   d. jokes
   b. Is everybody happy?   e. pleasure vs. fun
   c. the funniest person alive   f. funny behavior

7. If these aren't fun enough, come up with your own topic on some aspect of human behavior.

Preparing to Read

Take a minute or so to look over the following reading selection. Note the title and author, read the first *two* paragraphs, and check the length. Make certain you have the time now to read it carefully and to do the exercises that follow it. Then, in the spaces provided, answer the following questions.

1. What is your reaction to the title of the reading selection?

   _____

   _____

2. With what subject do you think the reading selection will deal?

   _____

   _____

Vocabulary

Good comprehension of what you are about to read depends upon your understanding of the words below. The number following each word refers to the paragraph where it appears.

   torrent (1) a turbulent, overwhelming flow

   Castoria (1) a laxative

ciphers (1) those without influence or value

purported (2) professed, rumored, alleged, supposed

sidled (2) moved along sideways

ribald (6) vulgar, indecent

feckless (6) ineffective, careless

sartorial (8) having to do with clothing

eaves (8) the parts of the roof that hang over the building

voluminously (8) with great fullness and size

bilge-green (21) the color of the water that collects in the bottom of a boat (not a pretty color!)

bluchers (23) high laced shoes or half-boots

nonchalantly (29) casually, in a carefree way

car cards (30) advertisements on cardboad posters in streetcars

thorax (32) chest

crescendo (40) a gradual increase in sound

Now read the essay.

The Endless Streetcar Ride into the Night, and the Tinfoil Noose

JEAN SHEPHERD

1   When I was fourteen, Life was flowing through me in a deep, rich torrent of Castoria. How did I know that the first rocks were just ahead, and I was about to have my keel ripped out on the reef? Sometimes you feel as though you are alone in a rented rowboat, bailing like mad in the darkness with a leaky bailing can. It is important to know that there are at least two billion other ciphers in the same boat, bailing with the same leaky can. They all think they are alone and are crossed with an evil star. They are right.

2   I'm fourteen years old, in my sophomore year at high school. One day Schwartz, my purported best friend, sidled up to me edgily outside of school while we were waiting on the steps to come in after lunch. He proceeded to outline his plan:

3   "Helen's old man won't let me take her out on a date on Saturday night unless I get a date for her girlfriend. A double date. The old coot figures, I guess, that if there are four of us there won't be no

monkey business. Well, how about it? Do you want to go on a blind date with this chick? I never seen her."

4   Well. For years I had this principle—absolutely *no* blind dates. I was a man of perception and taste, and life was short. But there is a time in your life when you have to stop taking and begin to give just a little. For the first time the warmth of sweet Human Charity brought the roses to my cheeks. After all, Schwartz was my friend. It was little enough to do, have a blind date with some no doubt skinny, pimply girl for your best friend. I would do it for Schwartz. He would do as much for me.

5   "Okay. Okay, Schwartz."

6   Then followed the usual ribald remarks, feckless boasting, and dirty jokes about dates in general and girls in particular. It was decided that next Saturday we would go all the way. I had a morning paper route at the time, and my life savings stood at about $1.80. I was all set to blow it on one big night.

7   I will never forget that particular Saturday as long as I live. The air was as soft as the finest of spun silk. The scent of lilacs hung heavy. The catalpa trees rustled in the early evening breeze from off the Lake. The inner Me itched in that nameless way, that indescribable way that only the fourteen-year-old Male fully knows.

8   All that afternoon I had carefully gone over my wardrobe to select the proper symphony of sartorial brilliance. That night I set out wearing my magnificent electric blue sport coat, whose shoulders were so wide that they hung out over my frame like vast, drooping eaves, so wide I had difficulty going through an ordinary door head-on. The electric blue sport coat that draped voluminously almost to my knees, its wide lapels flapping soundlessly in the slightest breeze. My pleated gray flannel slacks began just below my breastbone and indeed chafed my armpits. High-belted, cascading down finally to grasp my ankles in a vise-like grip. My tie, indeed one of my most prized possessions, had been a gift from my Aunt Glenn upon the state occasion of graduation from eighth grade. It was of a beautiful silky fabric, silvery pearly colored, four inches wide at the fulcrum, and of such a length to endanger occasionally my zipper in moments of haste. Hand-painted upon it was a magnificent blood-red snail.

9   I had spent fully two hours carefully arranging and rearranging my great mop of wavy hair, into which I had rubbed fully a pound and a half of Greasy Kid Stuff.

10   Helen and Schwartz waited on the corner under the streetlight at the streetcar stop near Junie Jo's home. Her name was Junie Jo Prewitt. I won't forget it quickly, although she has, no doubt, forgotten mine. I walked down the dark street alone, past houses set back off

the street, through the darkness, past privet hedges, under elm trees, through air rich and ripe with promise. Her house stood back from the street even farther than the others. It sort of crouched in the darkness, looking out at me, kneeling. Pregnant with Girldom. A real Girlfriend house.

11   The first faint touch of nervousness filtered through the marrow of my skullbone as I knocked on the door of the screen-enclosed porch. No answer. I knocked again, louder. Through the murky screens I could see faint lights in the house itself. Still no answer. Then I found a small doorbell button buried in the sash. I pressed. From far off in the bowels of the house I heard two chimes "Bong" politely. It sure didn't sound like our doorbell. We had a real ripper that went off like a broken buzz saw, more of a BRRRAAAAKKK than a muffled Bong. This was a rich people's doorbell.

12   The door opened and there stood a real, genuine, goldplated Father: potbelly, underwear shirt, suspenders, and all.

13   "Well?" he asked.

14   For one blinding moment of embarrassment I couldn't remember her name. After all, she was a blind date. I couldn't just say:

15   "I'm here to pick up some girl."

16   He turned back into the house and hollered:

17   "JUNIE JO! SOME KID'S HERE!"

18   "Heh, heh. . . ." I countered.

19   He led me into the living room. It was an itchy house, sticky stucco walls of a dull orange color, and all over the floor this Oriental rug with the design crawling around, making loops and sworls. I sat on an overstuffed chair covered in stiff green mohair that scratched even through my slacks. Little twisty bridge lamps stood everywhere. I instantly began to sweat down the back of my clean white shirt. Like I said, it was a very itchy house. It had little lamps sticking out of the walls that looked like phony candles, with phony glass orange flames. The rug started moaning to itself.

20   I sat on the edge of the chair and tried to talk to this Father. He was a Cub fan. We struggled under water for what seemed like an hour and a half, when suddenly I heard someone coming down the stairs. First the feet; then those legs, and there she was. She was magnificent! The greatest-looking girl I ever saw in my life! I have hit the double jackpot! And on a blind date! Great Scot!

21   My senses actually reeled as I clutched the arm of that bilge-green chair for support. Junie Jo Prewitt made Cleopatra look like a Girl Scout!

22   Five minutes later we are sitting in the streetcar, heading toward the bowling alley. I am sitting next to the most fantastic creation in

the Feminine department known to Western man. There are the four of us in that long, yellow-lit streetcar. No one else was aboard; just us four. I, naturally, being a trained gentleman, sat on the aisle to protect her from candy wrappers and cigar butts and such. Directly ahead of me, also on the aisle, sat Schwartz, his arm already flung affectionately in a death grip around Helen's neck as we boomed and rattled through the night.

23   I casually flung my right foot up onto my left knee so that she could see my crepe-soled, perforated, wing-toed, Scotch bluchers with the two-toned laces. I started to work my famous charm on her. Casually, with my practiced offhand, cynical, cutting, sardonic humor I told her about how my Old Man had cracked the block in the Oldsmobile, how the White Sox were going to have a good year this year, how my kid brother wet his pants when he saw a snake, how I figured it was going to rain, what a great guy Schwartz was, what a good second baseman I was, how I figured I might go out for football. On and on I rolled, like Old Man River, pausing significantly for her to pick up the conversation. Nothing.

24   Ahead of us Schwartz and Helen were almost indistinguishable one from the other. They giggled, bit each other's ears, whispered, clasped hands, and in general made me itch even more.

25   From time to time Junie Jo would bend forward stiffly from the waist and say something I could never quite catch into Helen's right ear.

26   I told her my great story of the time that Uncle Carl lost his false teeth down the airshaft. Still nothing. Out of the corner of my eye I could see that she had her coat collar turned up, hiding most of her face as she sat silently, looking forward past Helen Weathers into nothingness.

27   I told her about this old lady on my paper route who chews tobacco, and roller skates in the backyard every morning. I still couldn't get through to her. Casually I inched my right arm up over the back of the seat behind her shoulders. The acid test. She learned forward, avoiding my arm, and stayed that way.

28   "Heh, heh, heh. . . ."

29   As nonchalantly as I could, I retrieved it, battling a giant cramp in my right shoulder blade. I sat in silence for a few seconds, sweating heavily as ahead Schwartz and Helen are going at it hot and heavy.

30   It was then that I became aware of someone saying something to me. It was an empty car. There was no one else but us. I glanced around, and there it was. Above us a line of car cards looked down on the empty streetcar. One was speaking directly to me, to me alone.
                    DO YOU OFFEND?

31   Do I *offend?!*

32   With no warning, from up near the front of the car where the motorman is steering I see this thing coming down the aisle directly toward *me*. It's coming closer and closer. I can't escape it. It's this blinding, fantastic, brilliant, screaming blue light. I am spread-eagled in it. There's a pin sticking through my thorax. I see it all now.

33   *I* AM THE BLIND DATE!

34   *ME!!*

35   *I'M* the one they're being nice to!

36   I'm suddenly getting fatter, more itchy. My new shoes are like bowling balls with laces; thick, rubber-crepe bowling balls. My great tie that Aunt Glenn gave me is two feet wide, hanging down to the floor like some crinkly tinfoil noose. My beautiful hand-painted snail is seven feet high, sitting up on my shoulder, burping. Great Scot! It is all clear to me in the searing white light of Truth—My friend Schwartz, I can see him saying to Junie Jo:

37   "I got this crummy fat friend who never has a date. Let's give him a break and. . . ."

38   *I* AM THE BLIND DATE!

39   They are being nice to *me*! She is the one who is out on a Blind Date. A Blind Date that didn't make it.

40   In the seat ahead, the merriment rose to a crescendo. Helen tittered; Schwartz cackled. The marble statue next to me stared gloomily out into the darkness as our streetcar rattled on. The ride went on and on.

41   *I AM THE BLIND DATE!*

42   I didn't say much the rest of the night. There wasn't much to be said.

Understanding the Content

Feel free to reread all or parts of the selection to answer the following questions.

1. How old was the author, Shepherd, when the events of the narrative took place? Why is this important?

2. What was Shepherd's attitude when Schwartz asked him to go on a blind date?

3. Describe the way Shepherd dressed for the date.

4. What was his reaction upon seeing his blind date, Junie Jo? Why? What was Junie Jo's reaction to Shepherd? Why?

5. Shepherd had a sudden revelation or awareness on the streetcar ride. What was it and how did it occur?

6. What is the implied thesis?

Looking at Structure and Style

1. Except for the first paragraph, the reading selection is a first-person narrative. What is the purpose of the first paragraph? How does it help set the tone of the essay?

2. How do paragraphs 8 and 9 help us to understand some of Junie Jo's reaction to Shepherd?

3. What function do paragraphs 23, 26, 27, and 28 serve?

4. Why does Shepherd make paragraphs 31, 33, 34, and 35 so short?

5. What is the effect of capitalizing and repeating "*I* AM THE BLIND DATE!" three times, in paragraphs 33, 38, and 41?

6. Explain the effectiveness of the following descriptive passages from the selection:
   a. "Sometimes you feel as though you are alone in a rented rowboat, bailing like mad in the darkness with a leaky bailing can." (1)
   b. "The inner Me itched in that nameless way, that indescribable way that only the fourteen-year-old Male fully knows." (7)
   c. "The door opened and there stood a real, genuine, gold-plated Father: potbelly, underwear shirt, suspenders, and all." (12)
   d. "On and on I rolled, like Old Man River, pausing significantly for her to pick up the conversation. Nothing." (23)

7. Pick out some descriptive phrases or passages that you think are particularly effective. What makes them so?

8. How well does the title fit? Why?

Evaluating the Author's Viewpoints

1. How does Shepherd view being fourteen years old? Do you agree with him?

2. At the end of paragraph 1, Shepherd says, "It is important to know that there are at least two billion other ciphers in the same boat, bailing with the same leaky can. They all think they are alone and are crossed with an evil star. They are right." What does he mean? Do you agree?

3. How different would this selection be if it were told from the viewpoint of Schwartz? Junie Jo?

Pursuing Possible Essay Topics

1. Brainstorm or freewrite on one or more of the following:

a. blind dates	d. teenage friendship
b. Do you offend?	e. first date
c. fourteen-year-olds	f. my usual topics of conversation

2. Pretend you are Junie Jo. Write your version of the "endless streetcar ride."

3. Write an essay about a time when you had a sudden discovery about yourself, something that startled you or made you more aware of yourself.

4. If you have ever had a blind date, write about how you got into it, what it was like, how it turned out, and so on.

5. Write an essay about the difficulties of being an early teenager. What changes occur both physically and mentally? What does life seem to be all about at that age? Are there typical behavioral patterns at that age?

6. Write an essay that prepares parents for dealing with fourteen-year-old behavior.

7. These don't do it for you? Then try your own ideas.

 **Student Essay**

The following student essay was written in response to an assignment to write on some aspect of human behavior. As you read it, look for answers to these questions:

1. Does the essay fit the assignment?

2. How well does the author know her subject?

3. Does the author provide good support and transitions?

Man and Woman: A Soap Opera with Real Soap

Cindy Evans

1   Anyone who doesn't believe in aggressiveness in the gentle sex and gentleness in the aggressive sex has never watched the two sexes do housework.

2   Take washing dishes at my house, for example. No gladiator ever entered the arena with more grim determination than I have before I plunge into the dinner dishes. First, with firm jaw and a steely-eyed glint, I don my pink rubber gloves. Not the cheap kind you see your fingernails through. Oh, no. Nothing but heavy-duty, industrial-strength, cotton-lined Playtex gloves can protect these hands from the counterful of foes mustered before them. From my

arsenal under the sink, I draw at least three weapons of germ destruction: the grease-cutting dishwashing detergent, a sponge
with two textures, and the ubiquitous nylon net ball, that kitchen
staple so often praised by Heloise in her household hints column.

3   After the dishes have soaked in water hot enough to deform
small plastic implements, my attack begins. Wielding the scratchy
side of my sponge, I aim first at my opponents' weakest link—the
glasses. I dig at the rim for lipmarks, scrape the insides for milk
rings, and feverishly rub the outside for fingerprints. Weakened,
they are then subjected to a severe rinsing. For silverware, the
strategy is to divide and conquer. Each individual piece gets
scraped, soaked, scratched, and scrubbed until no germ would
dream of polluting that shiny metal surface. Then the plates are
treated like an automatic sander gone mad. By the time I get to
the pans, the sink is a rolling cauldron of flying suds and steam-
ing metal. My hair snakes around my face and the swoosh of steel
wool against metal underscores the fanatical gleam in my eyes as
the pot-rubbing reaches a frenzied crescendo. In the end, the drip-
ping survivors of the massacre are left hanging in the drying
rack, glistening and quivering in the dark.

4   Compare this domestic Dante's Inferno to an Easter sunrise
service and you get some idea of how my husband approaches
this selfsame task of doing the dinner dishes. The acts of the Pope
blessing the crowd, Mother Teresa tending the sick, and Buddha
contemplating his navel pale in comparison to the tender rites
my beloved performs over our dirty dishes. It is truly a transcen-
dent experience to even watch him approach the sink, as he
moves reverently toward the unwashed masses awaiting him on
the counter. First, as though divinely inspired, he slowly turns on
the tap, adjusting the temperature equal to that of, say, day-old
communion wine. Then with a beneficent wave of his hand, he
casts drops of detergent onto the tepid waters. Gazing with kind
eyes, he begins the ritual by gently blessing our encrusted crock-
ery with the soft side of the sponge.

5   With a trembling hand, he brings up a palmful of silverware,
being careful not to separate them during washing and rinsing,

lest they get lonely for their metallic mates before they reach their resting place.

6   No mother bathing a newborn was ever more tender with her baby than my husband is when washing our pots. Mind you, this is the same bearded brute who smashed innocent fuzzy tennis balls so hard his racket strings broke. And this is the same man of iron who rode 60 miles uphill on a bicycle and called it "fun." My hairy leviathan, who thought nothing of repeatedly carrying his own weight in boxes on his bride's moving day, turns into a moon-struck mystic over a sinkful of dirty dishes, gazing at them lovingly, caressing them gently and making sure the rinse water is neither too hot nor too cold for the delicate Corningware. In another generation, he would have found a devout following among my grandmother's fine bone China.

7   So, under the care of St. Michael of the Dishes, our plates end up resting contentedly on the drying rack with their little souls cleansed—but not much else. Whoever says men can't be gentle and women aggressive should buy a ringside ticket to our sink. Group discounts available.

Reaction

In the space below, write your reaction to the student essay. What would you tell this student about her essay?

Commentary

Cindy's essay is a good example of making a topic your own. Assigned to write an essay on some aspect of human behavior, she uses something she knows well. By comparing the way she washes dishes with the way her husband does, Cindy uses as the basis for her essay something most readers can relate to. She puts a twist on the human behavior aspect by describing herself as the more aggressive sex instead of "the man of the house"—at least when it comes to doing dishes.

Some students try to write about things they have not experienced or don't really know enough about. The results are usually flat, uninteresting, forced pieces of writing churned out in time for an assignment deadline. Cindy takes a very simple task, doing dishes, and by describing the way two different people approach the task, makes a statement about human behavior. She shows that you can write interesting, readable essays by writing about what you know.

In doing her comparison of the dishwashing approaches, Cindy also uses description well. Notice in paragraph 2 how she equates herself with a gladiator with "grim determination . . . firm jaw . . . and a steely-eyed glint." Her "pink rubber gloves" are "nothing but heavy-duty, industrial-strength." The dishes are her "foes." From her "arsenal under the sink," she chooses "three weapons of germ destruction." In paragraph 3, her "attack begins," as she "digs . . . scrapes . . . and feverishly rubs" the dishes clean "until no germ would dream of polluting" her kitchenware. She's "an automatic sander gone mad."

In paragraph 4, she begins the comparison of her approach which she calls a "domestic Dante's Inferno" (a reference to a classical work by Alighieri Dante in which he depicts various levels of punishment suffered by people damned to Hell) to her husband's methods, which are more like the "Pope blessing the crowd, . . . Mother Teresa, . . . or Buddha. . . ." Against her rough methods, he "slowly turns on the tap," adjusting the temperature "equal to that of . . . day-old communion wine." Unlike her, he is "beneficent," has "kind eyes" and makes the whole process more like a gentle blessing than a gladiator fight. Yet, in paragraph 6 she provides ample evidence of her "bearded brute's" ability to smash "innocent fuzzy tennis balls," ride a bike 60 miles, and lift heavy weights. She lets us know he's no wimp, despite his gentle approach to the dishes.

Because the subject matter (washing dishes) is familiar to her, Cindy says she had more time to devote to her use of language, rather than needing to investigate or learn more about a new subject. Her attention to word choice helps make this an amusing look at a very basic level of human behavior.

iewpoints on

Cultural Heritage

"Give me your tired, your poor
Your huddled masses yearning to breathe free,
The wretched refuse of your teeming shore.
Send these, the homeless, tempest-tost to me,
I lift my lamp beside the golden door!"
Emma Lazarus

THE HISTORY of the United States is filled with accounts of people who came from all over the world to settle here. Many came willingly to find a better life, some were forced to come as slaves or to be used as cheap labor, some were driven from their homelands for political reasons, some fled from war, and still others came hoping to get rich quickly and then go back home. Immigration, especially of people from western and southern Europe, was high between 1870–1920. Between the years 1880–1900 alone, a half million people came to this country *each year*. During the next fourteen years, over a million people immigrated to America *each year*. Whether born here or an immigrant, everyone living in America felt widespread cultural and institutional changes. The rise of an urban-industrial way of life that attracted thousands of people to cities, the growing interest in scientific knowledge and research, and the variety of new cultures that the immigrants brought with them all had an effect on education, science, fashion, food, music, art, literature, publishing, and politics. People referred to America as "a melting pot," a place where people of all types could blend together.

Whereas immigration was somewhat restricted during the 1940s and 1950s, another surge in immigration occurred in the 1970s. According to Charles M. Dollar's *America: Changing Times*, estimates of illegal aliens arriving during this ten-year period matched the number of legal aliens, four million.

171

Most of the "new" immigration of the seventies came from the Western hemisphere and Asian nations. Statistics showed Mexico to be the leading source, with over 550,000 legal entrants from 1970–1978; the Philippines and Korea each accounted for about 300,000 in the same period, and Cuba, over 250,000. Other sources of more than 100,000 immigrants (1970–1978) included China (Taiwan), India, the Dominican Republic, Jamaica, and Vietnam. These immigrants, as well as hundreds of thousands of illegal newcomers every year . . . put great strains on the ability of the American Government to cope with such numbers. . . .

Because it is difficult to determine the number of illegal entries to the United States, these figures are probably low.

What will be the make-up of America's population by the year 2000? By the mid-1980s, it was estimated that there were between twelve and fifteen million people of Spanish origin here. The United States is now the fifth largest Spanish-speaking country in the world, following Mexico, Spain, Argentina, and Colombia. Hispanics, three out of every five from Mexico, are the second largest and fastest growing minority group in this country. In addition, Asian immigration is also on the rise. By the year 2000, it is estimated that as many as twelve million Asians will have immigrated here.

Some sociologists are concerned that America is no longer "a melting pot," but "a salad bowl." Unlike most earlier immigrants who were willing to learn English and wanted to "melt" into American life, many of today's immigrants don't see the need. How will all this affect America's future?

The reading selections in this unit reflect various viewpoints on this country's rich cultural heritage. Broad in scope and attitude, they will provide you with information on this country's cultural heritage and get you to think about your own.

📖 Preparing to Read

Take a minute or two to look over the following reading selection. Notice the title and author, read the opening paragraph, and check the length. Make certain you have the time now to read it carefully and to do the exercises that follow it. Then, in the spaces provided, answer the following questions.

1. What will this reading selection cover? _____

2. What might you learn from reading this selection? _____

_____

_____

3. What do you already know about the topic? _____

_____

Vocabulary

Good comprehension of what you are about to read depends upon your understanding of the words below. The number following each word refers to the paragraph where it is used.

bustling urban centers (1) fast-growing, busy cities

the Old World (2) European countries, as contrasted with the New World, America

appalled (2) shocked, dismayed, horrified

prodigal (2) recklessly wasteful

ironically (3) oppositely or differently from what is expected

densely (3) thickly

prostrate (3) physically helpless

congregate (5) come together

fostered (7) helped cause to happen or occur

assimilation (7) a mixing or bringing together into one

Now read the essay.

Settling in the Cities

ALBERT ROBBINS

1   While most of the northern European immigrants who came to America prior to the Civil War were farmers, many city dwellers came to the new land as well. These newcomers were attracted to the bustling urban centers of the New World, and as a result, American cities expanded enormously. New York, for example, which had a population of only sixty thousand in 1800, grew to a city of more than one million people by 1860. As urban settlers moved west, they helped to change cities like St. Louis, Chicago, and Cincinnati from minor

frontier outposts to major metropolitan centers. For a time St. Louis doubled its population every nine years; Cincinnati every seven years.

2   As with immigrants who came to America to farm, urban immigrants were drawn to the rapidly growing cities by the promise. of economic improvement. The Old World looked on the New as a land of abundance, a magical place where "the streets were paved with gold." And to many northern European newcomers, America indeed lived up to that promise. Some, however, were appalled by what they saw as American wastefulness. Edward Bok, a Dutch immigrant who came to the United States as a boy of six and went on to become famous as the editor of the *Ladies' Home Journal*, described in his memoirs how different life in the New World was from life in his native Holland:

> I had been taught in my home across the sea that thrift was one of the fundamentals in a successful life. My family had come from a land (the Netherlands) noted for its thrift; but we had been in the United States only a few days before the realization came home strongly to my father and mother that they had brought their children to a land of waste.
>
> Where the Dutchman saved, the American wasted. There was waste, and the most prodigal waste, on every hand. In every street-car and on every ferry-boat the floors and seats were littered with newspapers that had been read and thrown away or left behind. If I went to a grocery store to buy a peck of potatoes, and a potato rolled off the heaping measure, the grocery-man, instead of picking it up, kicked it into the gutter for the wheels of his wagon to run over. The butcher's waste filled my mother's soul with dismay. If I bought a scuttle of coal at the corner grocery, the coal that missed the scuttle [a bucket], instead of being shovelled up and put back into the bin, was swept into the street. My young eyes quickly saw this; in the evening I gathered up the coal thus swept away, and during the course. of a week, I collected a scuttleful. . . .[1]

3   Bok's account, based on recollections of his boyhood in the 1870s, ignores another consequence of mass immigration to the cities—the growth of the urban slum, beginning in the 1840s. Municipal services we take for granted—a safe water supply, police and fire protection,

---

[1]*The Americanization of Edward Bok: The Autobiography of a Dutch Boy Fifty Years After* (New York: Charles Scribner's Sons, 1922), 434–435.

public transportation, and garbage collection—either were not provided or were primitive. With the extra demands made by expanding populations, these services often broke down. Housing was in short supply, and overcrowding was common—especially in poor immigrant neighborhoods. Ironically, the growth of the slums was viewed as a sign off material progress in the young industrial age because the increased population provided much of the labor for industry. The immigrants in the poor neighborhoods, however, often paid a high price:

> The . . . Ward was densely crowded with working classes . . . [and] showed a high rate of sickness and mortality, owing to the overcrowded and ill-ventilated dwellings. . . .
>
> The tenants are all Germans. . . . They are exceedingly filthy in person and their bedclothes are as dirty as the floors they walk on. Their food is of the poorest quality, and their feet and hands, doubtless their whole bodies are suffering from what they call rheumatism, but which in reality is a prostrate nervous system, the result of foul air and inadequate supply of nutritious food. . . . Not one decent sleeping apartment can be found on the entire premises and not one stove properly arranged. . . . The rooms are 6 by 10 feet. The inhabitants lead a miserable existence, and their children wilt and die in their infancy.[2]

4   Harsh as life could be in the cities, the immigrant's attitude toward the new country was generally not one of despair, but of accomplishment. The immigrants had made a hard and dangerous voyage to America. If poverty welcomed them on their arrival, at least it was no worse than the poverty they had left behind in Germany, Holland, or Scandinavia. And in America, unlike Europe, an immigrant could quickly improve his economic condition through hard work and diligence. . . .

5   To become in the majority, immigrants tended to congregate in neighborhoods where people from the Old World could create a little of what they had left behind. Their neighbors spoke their language, the stores sold the kind of goods they were used to, and traditional holidays could be observed with the same spirit and gusto. In Cincinnati in the nineteenth century, for example, almost fifty thousand Germans lived in a section of the city called "Over the Rhine." The

---

[2]Quoted in Isaac A. Hourwitch, *Immigration and Labor: The Economic Aspects of European Immigration to the U.S.* (New York: G. P. Putnam's Sons, 1912), 232–233.

same pattern was repeated in St. Louis, Milwaukee, almost every-where immigrants tended to settle. One visitor to New York City in the 1860s described its German section, then called *Kleindeutschland,* or Little Germany:

> New York has about 120,000 German-born inhabitants. Two-thirds of these live in Kleindeutschland. They come from every part of Germany. . . . Naturally the Germans were not forced by the authorities, or by law, to settle in this specific area. It just happened. . . . The Germans like to live together; this permits them to speak their own language and live according to their own customs.
>
> Life in Kleindeutschland is almost the same as in the Old Country. Bakers, butchers, druggists—all are Germans. There is not a single business which is not run by Germans. Not only the shoe-makers, tailors, barbers, physicians, grocers, and innkeepers are German, but the pastors and priests as well. There is even a German lending library where one can get all kinds of German books. The residents of Kleindeutsch-land need not even know English in order to make a living. . . .[3]

6   Immigrants tended to feel comfortable in neighborhoods like these. Their children, however, often felt different. They found them-selves torn between two worlds—an America that demanded con-formity to get ahead and the desires of their immigrant parents to pass on their European heritage. The result was often confusion and shame, as one college-educated daughter of a German immigrant expressed:

> My father made me learn German and always was wanting me to read it. I hated to have anything to do with it. It seemed to me something inferior. People in the West call a thing "Dutch" as a term of scorn. It was not till I was in college that I realized what German literature and philosophy have meant to the world, and that to be a German is not a thing to be ashamed of.[4]

7   Tensions like these, between generations, fostered the process of assimilation through which the children of immigrants could more

---

[3]Quoted in Howard B. Furer, ed., *The Germans in America, 1607–1970: A Chronology and Fact Book* (Dobbs Ferry, NY: Oceana Publications, 1973), 117–118.

[4]Quoted in Emily Balch, *Our Slavic Fellow Citizens* (New York: Arno Press and the *New York Times,* 1969), 414.

easily enter the American mainstream. Old habits die hard, however, and the immigrant neighborhoods, sitting like ever-shrinking ethnic islands in an American sea, survived to give comfort and shelter to new arrivals.

Understanding the Content

Feel free to reread all or parts of the selection to answer the following questions.

1. Why did European immigrants settle mostly in the cities rather than on farms during the 1800s?

2. What was city life like for most immigrants? Does it differ much from today?

3. Edward Bok, who was to become an editor for the *Ladies' Home Journal*, describes some differences he found between life in his native Holland and in "the New World." What differences surprised him?

4. Why did many immigrants tend to create neighborhoods of their own when they arrived in the cities? What was good and what was bad about this?

5. What problems existed for children of the first-generation immigrants?

6. What is Robbins's thesis? Is it stated or implied?

7. Can we infer that the author admires the immigrants of the 1800s?

8. Circle the letters of the statements from the essay that are factual or can be verified as fact:

    a. "New York, for example, which had a population of only sixty thousand in 1800, grew to a city of more than one million people by 1860." (1)

    b. "The Old World looked on the New as a land of abundance, a magical place where 'the streets were paved with gold.' " (2)

    c. "The immigrants had made a hard and dangerous voyage to America." (4)

Looking at Structure and Style

1. What is the topic sentence of the first paragraph? How is it supported?

2. Paragraph 2 uses a long quotation. (Notice how it is indented and clearly set off from the rest of the paragraph.) What is the purpose of the quotation? Why does it belong where it is?

3. How does the first sentence of paragraph 3 make a transition from the quotation in the previous paragraph? What becomes the point of the third paragraph?

4. Paragraph 3 uses another long quotation from another source. How does this help Robbins develop his topic sentence?

5. How effective are the quotations used in paragraphs 5 and 6?

6. Explain or rewrite the following passages from the reading selection:

   a. "Ironically, the growth of the slums was viewed as a sign of material progress in the young industrial age because the increased population provided much of the labor for industry." (3)

   b. "They found themselves torn between two worlds—an America that demanded conformity to get ahead and the desires of their immigrant parents to pass on their European heritage." (6)

   c. ". . . The immigrant neighborhoods, sitting like ever-shrinking ethnic islands in an American sea, survived to give comfort and shelter to new arrivals." (7)

7. Why does Robbins provide the sources of the quotations he uses in his essay?

Evaluating the Author's Viewpoints

1. Robbins states in his last paragraph that the tensions created between first- and second-generation immigrants "fostered the process of assimilation through which the children of immigrants could more easily enter the American mainstream." What does he mean? How would such tension help?

2. After discussing the life in a *Kleindeutschland* or Little Germany, Robbins says immigrants tended to feel comfortable in neighborhoods like these. What evidence does he have for this viewpoint?

3. The European immigrants of the mid-1800s experienced many hardships, but according to Robbins, their attitude was not one of despair. To what does he attribute their success?

Pursuing Possible Essay Topics

1. In paragraph 2, Edward Bok compares the thrift in his native homeland with the waste in America he observed in the 1870s. Write an essay that shows how waste does or does not exist in America today.

2. Look in the library for one of the works mentioned in the essay or read selections from Albert Robbins's book *Coming to America: Immigrants from Northern Europe* (one in a series of six books). Then write an essay on some aspect of the European immigrants' life: the emotional impact of leaving their homeland, the hard voyage, the shock of discovering America did not have "streets paved with gold," the difficulties with

language, getting through customs, or whatever strikes you as you read from one of the sources.

3. Interview someone who may be a recent immigrant to America. Ask that person to compare his/her experiences with those Robbins discusses.

4. Interview older members of your family who may have been or may have known others from the Old World. Write an essay that uses quotations from their stories and experiences.

5. Think of a country that you have always wanted to visit or live in for a while. Pretend you are willing to leave your home and family and emigrate to that country to start a new life. What hardships would you have to undergo? How would it feel to leave your roots?

6. By consulting family members or using the library, research your own heritage. How far back can you trace your roots? What blood lines have you inherited?

7. Discuss the differences and/or similarities between immigrants coming to America today and those who came in the 1800s. From what countries are most of today's immigrants?

8. Pretend you are an immigrant coming to America. Describe in an essay how you might feel as your ship sails into New York past the Statue of Liberty or under the Golden Gate Bridge in San Francisco.

9. Brainstorm or freewrite on one or more of the following:
   a. the Statue of Liberty
   b. the border patrol
   c. immigration hardships
   d. two different neighborhoods
   e. city culture
   f. starting a new life

10. If you don't like these, find your own topic on some aspect of cultural heritage.

📖 Preparing to Read

Take a minute or two to look over the following reading selection. Notice the title and author, read the opening paragraph, and check the length. Make certain you have the time now to read it carefully and to do the exercises that follow it. Then, in the spaces provided, answer the following questions.

1. What do you think the essay will say about Italians? _____

_____

2. What do you think is meant by "Hell's Kitchen"? _____

_____

_____

3. What might you learn from reading this essay? _____

_____

_____

Vocabulary

Good comprehension of what you are about to read depends upon your understanding of the words below. The number following each word refers to the paragraph where it is used.

Neapolitan ghetto (1) an Italian slum section (*Neapolitan* describes someone from Naples, Italy.)

clichés (1) trite, overused expressions

uncongenial (2) unfriendly

a grim lot (3) a stern, rigid, gloomy group of people

maligned (4) slandered, talked ill of

paranoiac (4) based on delusion

magnanimity (4) the quality of being generous in forgiving

contemptuous (5) scornful

condescending (5) treating as inferior, patronizing

omnisciently (6) as one with total knowledge

Dead End Kid flicks (7) several movies made in the 1930s starring a group of teenagers known as the Dead End Kids

John Garfield (7) a famous actor of the 1930s and 1940s who usually played a tough guy from the slums

tin lizzie (8) slang for a cheap or beat-up car (The Model T Ford was referred to as such.)

formidable (13) difficult to defeat or overcome

impunity (16) exemption from punishment or penalty

inevitable (17) unavoidable

forebears (18) ancestors

retrospective falsification (18) remembering the past as better than it was

comeuppance (20) a deserved punishment

patronizingly (20) condescendingly

Now read the essay.

Choosing a Dream: Italians in Hell's Kitchen

MARIO PUZO

1   As a child and in my adolescence, living in the heart of New York's Neapolitan ghetto, I never heard an Italian singing. None of the grown-ups I knew were charming or loving or understanding. Rather they seemed coarse, vulgar, and insulting. And so later in my life when I was exposed to all the clichés of lovable Italians, singing Italians, happy-go-lucky Italians, I wondered where the hell the moviemakers and story-writers got all their ideas from.

2   At a very early age I decided to escape these uncongenial folk by becoming an artist, a writer. It seemed then an impossible dream. My father and mother were illiterate, as were their parents before them. But practicing my art I tried to view the adults with a more charitable eye and so came to the conclusion that their only fault lay in their being foreigners; I was an American. This didn't really help because I was only half right. I was the foreigner. They were already more "American" than I could ever become.

3   But it did seem then that the Italian immigrants, all the fathers and mothers that I knew, were a grim lot; always shouting, always angry, quicker to quarrel than embrace. I did not understand that their lives were a long labor to earn their daily bread and that physical fatigue does not sweeten human natures.

4   And so even as a very small child I dreaded growing up to be like the adults around me. I heard them saying too many cruel things about their dearest friends, saw too many of their false embraces with those they had just maligned, observed with horror their paranoiac anger at some small slight or a fancied injury to their pride. They were, always, too unforgiving. In short, they did not have the careless magnanimity of children.

5   In my youth I was contemptuous of my elders, including a few under thirty. I thought my contempt special to their circumstances. Later when I wrote about these illiterate men and women, when I

thought I understood them, I felt a condescending pity. After all, they had suffered, they had labored all the days of their lives. They had never tasted luxury, knew little more economic security than those ancient Roman slaves who might have been their ancestors. And alas, I thought, with new-found artistic insight, they were cut off from their children because of the strange American tongue, alien to them, native to their sons and daughters.

6   Already an artist but not yet a husband or father, I pondered omnisciently on their tragedy, again thinking it special circumstance rather than a constant in the human condition. I did not yet understand why these men and women were willing to settle for less than they deserved in life and think that "less" quite a bargain. I did not understand that they simply could not afford to dream; I myself had a hundred dreams from which to choose. For I was already sure that I would make my escape, that I was one of the chosen. I would be rich, famous, happy. I would master my destiny. . . .

7   My family and I grew up together on Tenth Avenue, between Thirtieth and Thirty-first streets, part of the area called Hell's Kitchen. This particular neighborhood could have been a movie set for one of the Dead End Kid flicks or for the social drama of the East Side in which John Garfield played the hero. Our tenements were the western wall of the city. Beneath our windows were the vast black iron gardens of the New York Central Railroad, absolutely blooming with stinking boxcars freshly unloaded of cattle and pigs for the city slaughterhouse. Steers sometimes escaped and loped through the heart of the neighborhood followed by astonished young boys who had never seen a live cow.

8   The railroad yards stretched down to the Hudson River, beyond whose garbagey waters rose the rocky Palisades of New Jersey. There were railroad tracks running downtown on Tenth Avenue itself to another freight station called St. Johns Park. Because of this, because these trains cut off one side of the street from the other, there was a wooden bridge over Tenth Avenue, a romantic-looking bridge despite the fact that no sparkling water, no silver flying fish darted beneath it; only heavy dray carts drawn by tired horses, some flat-boarded trucks, tin lizzie automobiles and, of course, long strings of freight cars drawn by black, ugly engines. . . .

9   My father supported his wife and seven children by working as a trackman laborer for the New York Central Railroad. My oldest brother worked for the railroad as a brakeman, another brother was a railroad shipping clerk in the freight office. Eventually I spent some of the worst months of my life as the railroad's worst messenger boy.

10   My oldest sister was just as unhappy as a dressmaker in the garment industry. She wanted to be a school teacher. At one time or

another my other two brothers also worked for the railroad—it got all six males in the family. The two girls and my mother escaped, though my mother felt it her duty to send all our bosses a gallon of homemade wine on Christmas. But everybody hated their jobs except my oldest brother who had a night shift and spent most of his working hours sleeping in freight cars. My father finally got fired because the foreman told him to get a bucket of water for the crew and not to take all day. My father took the bucket and disappeared forever.

11   Nearly all the Italian men living on Tenth Avenue supported their large families by working on the railroad. Their children also earned pocket money by stealing ice from the refrigerator cars in summer and coal from the open stoking cars in the winter. Sometimes an older lad would break the seal of a freight car and take a look inside. But this usually brought down the "Bulls," the special railroad police. And usually the freight was "heavy" stuff, too much work to cart away and sell, something like fresh produce or boxes of cheap candy that nobody would buy.

12   The older boys, the ones just approaching voting age, made their easy money by hijacking silk trucks that loaded up at the garment factory on Thirty-first Street. They would then sell the expensive dresses door to door, at bargain prices no discount house could match. From this some graduated into organized crime, whose talent scouts alertly tapped young boys versed in strongarm. Yet despite all this, most of the kids grew up honest, content with fifty bucks a week as truck drivers, deliverymen, and white-collar clerks in the civil service.

13   I had every desire to go wrong but I never had a chance. The Italian family structure was too formidable.

14   I never came home to an empty house; there was always the smell of supper cooking. My mother was always there to greet me, sometimes with a policeman's club in her hand (nobody ever knew how she acquired it). But she was always there, or her authorized deputy, my older sister, who preferred throwing empty milk bottles at the heads of her little brothers when they got bad marks on their report cards. During the great Depression of the 1930s, though we were the poorest of the poor, I never remember not dining well. Many years later as a guest of a millionaire's club, I realized that our poor family on home relief ate better than some of the richest people in America.

15   My mother would never dream of using anything but the finest imported olive oil, the best Italian cheeses. My father had access to the fruits coming off ships, the produce from railroad cars, all before it went through the stale process of middlemen; and my mother, like most Italian women, was a fine cook in the peasant style. . . .

16   I had to help support my family by working on the railroad. After school hours of course. This was the same railroad that had supplied

free coal and free ice to the whole Tenth Avenue when I was young enough to steal with impunity. After school finished at 3 P.M. I went to work in the freight office as a messenger. I also worked Saturdays and Sundays when there was work available.

17   I hated it. One of my first short stories was about how I hated that job. But of course what I really hated was entering the adult world. To me the adult world was a dark enchantment, unnatural. As unnatural to the human dream as death. And as inevitable. . . .

18   Then why do I dream of those immigrant Italian peasants as having been happy? I remember how they spoke of their forebears, who spent all their lives farming the arid mountain slopes of Southern Italy. "He died in that house in which he was born," they say enviously. "He was never more than an hour from his village, not in all his life," they sigh. And what would they make of a phrase like "retrospective falsification"?

19   No, really, we are all happier now. It is a better life. And after all, as my mother always said, "Never mind about being happy. Be glad you're alive."

20   When I came to my "autobiographical novel," the one every writer does about himself, I planned to make myself the sensitive, misunderstood hero, much put upon by his mother and family. To my astonishment my mother took over the book and instead of my revenge I got another comeuppance. But it is, I think, my best book. And all those old-style grim conservative Italians whom I hated, then pitied so patronizingly, they also turned out to be heroes. Through no desire of mine. I was surprised. The thing that amazed me most was their courage. Where were their Congressional Medals of Honor? Their Distinguished Service Crosses? How did they ever have the balls to get married, have kids, go out to earn a living in a strange land, with no skills, not even knowing the language? They made it without tranquillizers, without sleeping pills, without psychiatrists, without even a dream. Heroes. Heroes all around me. I never saw them.

21   But how could I? They wore lumpy work clothes and handlebar moustaches, they blew their noses on their fingers and they were so short that their high-school children towered over them. They spoke a laughable broken English and the furthest limit of their horizon was their daily bread. Brave men, brave women, they fought to live their lives without dreams. Bent on survival, they narrowed their minds to the thinnest line of existence.

22   It is no wonder that in my youth I found them contemptible. And yet they had left Italy and sailed the ocean to come to a new land and leave their sweated bones in America. Illiterate Colombos, they dared to seek the promised land. And so they, too, dreamed a dream.

Understanding the Content

Feel free to reread all or parts of the selection to answer the following questions.

1. Puzo compares and contrasts his attitude about his Italian heritage when he was young with his present feelings. What are those feelings?

2. What is Puzo's thesis? Is it stated or implied?

3. Why do you think the area Puzo lived in was called Hell's Kitchen?

4. In paragraph 13 Puzo says, "I had every desire to go wrong but I never had a chance. The Italian family structure was too formidable." From this statement (and others), what can you infer about his family life?

5. Why does the author come to think that "the old-style grim conservative Italians" (20) whom he held in contempt now deserve to be called "heroes"?

6. In writing about his attitudes toward his neighborhood and early family life, Puzo reveals much of his own character. Describe what you learn about him through inference.

Looking at Structure and Style

1. What are some of the words Puzo selects to describe his feelings as a child toward Italian adults? What are some words he uses to refer to them when he speaks as an adult?

2. What is the basic function of the first five paragraphs? How do they establish attitude and tone?

3. In what paragraph does Puzo begin to shift from his negative comments to more positive ones regarding the Italians he knew? How effective is he?

4. Frequently Puzo seems to be writing negatively about others when he is really making fun of himself and his younger attitudes. In what paragraphs does he do this well?

5. In paragraph 21, Puzo says, ". . . They narrowed their minds to the thinnest line of existence." What does this mean?

Evaluating the Author's Viewpoints

1. In paragraph 2, Puzo, in describing his parents, says, "I was the foreigner. They were already more 'American' than I could ever become." Explain this viewpoint toward his parents. Do you agree?

2. Puzo says he was contemptuous of his elders because of the circumstances in which they lived, their illiteracy, their "grimness." Why did he feel

this way? Is it abnormal for children to experience such feelings about their parents?

3. When young, the author and other children stole coal and ice from the same railroad company that provided jobs for their parents. What do you think about this?

4. Now that he is older, Puzo's attitude toward his parents and other first-generation Italian immigrants has changed. He refers to them as "heroes." Do you think they are heroes? Explain.

Pursuing Possible Essay Topics

1. Write a descriptive essay based on a particular childhood memory. Beware of "retrospective falsification."

2. Ask your parents or other relatives for stories from their childhood. Write an account of their childhood dreams. Were they achieved?

3. Research the library for information on the contributions Italian immigrants have made to the United States. You may want to select one first-generation Italian immigrant who made a significant historical contribution. Begin by looking in the library's card catalogue under "immigrant," then for titles or references to Italian immigrants. If you have no luck, you might want to locate a copy of Gladys Nadler Rips's book *Coming to America: Immigrants from Southern Europe.*

4. Write an essay that compares/contrasts your neighborhood with Hell's Kitchen as Puzo describes it.

5. Research Mario Puzo, the author. Read other things he has written and evaluate his writing.

6. What advantages or disadvantages do you have that first-generation immigrants did not? What contributions have immigrants from other cultures brought here from which you now benefit?

7. Brainstorm or freewrite on one or more of the following:
   a. your heritage   d. Italian heritage
   b. childhood attitudes   e. childhood dreams
   c. foreigners   f. your neighborhood

8. Ignore these ideas and come up with your own on some aspect of cultural heritage.

📖 Preparing to Read

Take a minute or two to look over the following reading selection. Note the title and author, read the opening paragraph, and check the length. Make certain you have the time now to read it carefully and to do the exercises that follow it. Then, in the spaces provided, answer the following questions.

1. What do you think the author means by "black English"? _____

   _____

2. Do you think the essay will deal with what is "wrong" with black

   English? Explain. _____

   _____

3. What do you think the essay has to do with cultural heritage, the subject

   of this unit? _____

   _____

Vocabulary

Good comprehension of what you are about to read depends upon your understanding of the words below. The number following each word refers to the paragraph where it appears.

linguist (1) a specialist in the study of the nature and structure of human speech

patois (1) regional dialect, substandard speech

peers (2) equals

L. Frank Baum (3) author of *The Wizard of Oz*

Ray Bradbury (3) author of numerous science-fiction stories and novels, among them *Fahrenheit 451* and *The Martian Chronicles*

doggedly (4) stubbornly, relentlessly

Valley Girl jargon (5) slang and speech pattern attributed to teenage girls living in the San Fernando Valley

articulate (6) clear and expressive in speech

staples (6) major parts

academic abstractions (6) intellectual, theoretical discussions

Malcolm X, Martin Luther King, Jr. (7) black civil-rights leaders (Both were assassinated.)

Toni Morrison, Alice Walker, James Baldwin (7) famous contemporary black authors (Morrison, *Beloved;* Walker, *The Color Purple;* Baldwin, *Go Tell It on the Mountain*)

ethnic dialects (8) speech patterns of a particular cultural group

Now read the essay.

What's Wrong with Black English

RACHEL L. JONES

1   William Labov, a noted linguist, once said about the use of black English, "It is the goal of most black Americans to acquire full control of the standard language without giving up their own culture." He also suggested that there are certain advantages to having two ways to express one's feelings. I wonder if the good doctor might also consider the goals of those black Americans who have full control of standard English but who are every now and then troubled by that colorful, grammar-to-the-winds patois that is black English. Case in point—me.

2   I'm a 21-year-old black born to a family that would probably be considered lower-middle class—which in my mind is a polite way of describing a condition only slightly better than poverty. Let's just say we rarely if ever did the winter-vacation thing in the Caribbean. I've often had to defend my humble beginnings to a most unlikely group of people for an even less likely reason. Because of the way I talk, some of my black peers look at me sideways and ask, "Why do you talk like you're white?"

3   The first time it happened to me I was nine years old. Cornered in the school bathroom by the class bully and her sidekick, I was offered the opportunity to swallow a few of my teeth unless I satisfactorily explained why I always got good grades, why I talked "proper" or "white." I had no ready answer for her, save the fact that my mother had from the time I was old enough to talk stressed the importance of reading and learning, or that L. Frank Baum and Ray Bradbury were my closest companions. I read all my older brothers' and sisters' literature textbooks more faithfully than they did, and even lightweights like the Bobbsey Twins and Trixie Belden were allowed into my bookish inner circle. I don't remember exactly what I told those girls, but I somehow talked my way out of a beating.

4   I was reminded once again of my "white pipes" problem while apartment hunting in Evanston, Illinois, last winter. I doggedly made out lists of available places and called all around. I would immediately be invited over—and immediately turned down. The thinly concealed looks of shock when the front door opened clued me in, along

with the flustered instances of "just getting off the phone with the girl who was ahead of you and she wants the rooms." When I finally found a place to live, my roommate stirred up old memories when she remarked a few months later, "You know, I was surprised when I first saw you. You sounded white over the phone." Tell me another one, sister.

5   I should've asked her a question I've wanted an answer to for years: how does one "talk white"? The silly side of me pictures a rabid white foam spewing forth when I speak. I don't use Valley Girl jargon, so that's not what's meant in my case. Actually, I've pretty much deduced what people mean when they say that to me, and the implications are really frightening.

6   It means that I'm articulate and well-versed. It means that I can talk as freely about John Steinbeck as I can about Rick James. It means that "ain't" and "he be" are not staples of my vocabulary and are only used around family and friends. (It is almost Jekyll and Hyde-ish the way I can slip out of academic abstractions into a long, lean, double-negative–filled dialogue, but I've come to terms with that aspect of my personality.) As a child, I found it hard to believe that's what people meant by "talking proper"; that would've meant that good grades and standard English were equated with white skin, and that went against everything I'd ever been taught. Running into the same type of mentality as an adult has confirmed the depressing reality that for many blacks, standard English is not only unfamiliar, it is socially unacceptable.

7   James Baldwin once defended black English by saying it had added "vitality to the language," and even went so far as to label it a language in its own right, saying, "Language [i.e., black English] is a political instrument" and a "vivid and crucial key to identity." But did Malcolm X urge blacks to take power in this country "any way y'all can"? Did Martin Luther King, Jr. say to blacks, "I has been to the mountaintop, and I done seed the Promised Land"? Toni Morrison, Alice Walker and James Baldwin did not achieve their eloquence, grace and stature by using only black English in their writing. Andrew Young, Tom Bradley and Barbara Jordan did not acquire political power by saying, "Y'all crazy if you ain't gon vote for me." They all have full command of standard English, and I don't think that knowledge takes away from their blackness or commitment to black people.

8   I know from experience that it's important for black people, stripped of culture and heritage, to have something they can point to and say, "This is ours, *we* can comprehend it, *we* alone can speak it with a soulful flourish," I'd be lying if I said that the rhythms of my people caught up in "some serious rap" don't sound natural and

right to me sometimes. But how heartwarming is it for those same brothers when they hit the pavement searching for employment? Studies have proven that the use of ethnic dialects decreases power in the marketplace. "I be" is acceptable on the corner, but not with the boss.

9   Am I letting capitalistic, European-oriented thinking fog the issue? Am I selling out blacks to an ideal of assimilating, being as much like whites as possible? I have not formed a personal political ideology, but I do know this: it hurts me to hear black children use black English, knowing that they will be at yet another disadvantage in an educational system already full of stumbling blocks. It hurts me to sit in lecture halls and hear fellow black students complain that the professor "be tripping dem out using big words dey can't understand." And what hurts most is to be stripped of my own blackness simply because I know my way around the English language.

10   I would have to disagree with Labov in one respect. My goal is not so much to acquire full control of both standard and black English, but to one day see more black people less dependent on a dialect that excludes them from full participation in the world we live in. I don't think I talk white, I think I talk right.

Understanding the Content

Feel free to reread all or parts of the selection to answer the following questions.

1. What is Jones's position toward "black English"?

2. What reasons or support does Jones give for her argument? Are they valid reasons?

3. What do people mean when they accuse Jones of "talking white"?

4. What does Jones have to say about James Baldwin's defense of black English as being a "political instrument" and a "crucial key to identity"? (7)

5. Does Jones have anything good to say about black English?

6. Does Jones agree or disagree with the linguist Labov?

Looking at Structure and Style

1. Is the thesis stated or implied? If stated, where?

2. For what reasons does Jones begin and end her essay with a quote from and reference to William Labov, "a noted linguist"? Is this an effective writing method? Explain.

3. What is the importance of paragraph 2 to Jones's argument? Is it important that she provides this information? Why?

4. What is the function of paragraphs 3 and 4?

5. In paragraph 9, Jones asks two rhetorical questions. How well does she answer them?

6. For what reason does Jones begin paragraph 9 with questions? To what audience is she directing the questions?

7. Even if you were not familiar with the names Andrew Young, Tom Bradley, or Barbara Jordan mentioned in paragraph 7, what can you infer about them from the context?

8. Describe Jones's tone.

Evaluating the Author's Viewpoints

1. Jones says, "Studies have proven that the use of ethnic dialects decreases power in the marketplace." (8) Do you agree? Should Jones have provided the names of the studies to verify her position?

2. James Baldwin disagrees with Jones regarding black English. Do you agree more with Baldwin or Jones? Explain.

3. Jones asks in paragraph 9, "Am I letting capitalistic, European-oriented thinking fog the issue?" What does she mean? How do you answer her question?

4. Jones says her goal is "to one day see more black people less dependent on a dialect that excludes them from full participation in the world we live in." (10) Do you think that not knowing standard English excludes people from full participation in the world we live in? Does this apply only to blacks? Explain your views.

Pursuing Possible Essay Topics

1. Support or refute Jones's position.

2. Discuss the need for everyone in this country to know standard English, regardless of their cultural heritage. If you disagree, take the opposite viewpoint.

3. React to the idea that knowing one's ethnic language is a "vivid and crucial key to identity."

4. Because of the large numbers of Hispanic and Asian groups now in the United States, many states provide voter information, driver's license applications, and bus information in other languages. Argue for or against such practices. What effect will this have on our culture?

5. Should people who come to the United States seeking citizenship be required to learn English? Write an essay supporting your position.

6. It is predicted that large cities, such as Miami, New York, and Los Angeles will soon have more Spanish speakers than English speakers. Write an essay on what effects this will have or already is having in such areas.

7. Brainstorm or freewrite on one or more of the following:
   a. your cultural heritage
   b. ethnic dialects
   c. rapping
   d. language and culture
   e. what your speech says about you
   f. bilingualism

8. You may want to read one or more of the works written by the black authors mentioned in Jones's essay and write an evaluation of what you read. Here are some other suggested sources your school library may have:
   a. James A. Emanuel and Theodore L. Gross, *Dark Symphony: Negro Literature in America*
   b. Charles L. James, ed., *From the Roots: Short Stories by Black Americans*

9. If these lack appeal, find your own topic on some aspect of cultural heritage.

Preparing to Read

Take a minute or two to look over the following reading selection. Note the title and author, read the opening paragraph, and check the length. Make certain you have the time now to read it carefully and to do the exercises that follow it. Then, in the spaces provided, answer the following questions.

1. What will this essay be about? _____

_____

2. What does the title mean? _____

_____

3. What might you learn from reading this selection? _____

_____

Vocabulary

Good comprehension of what you are about to read depends upon your understanding of the words below. The number following each word refers to the paragraph where it is used.

mural (1) a painting applied directly on a wall

depicted (1) shown, represented

Latino (1) Spanish speakers from Mexico, Central America, or Caribbean countries

simmering (2) heating up slowly to a boiling point, seething

Chicano (3) Mexican-American

animated (3) lively

displacing (4) taking the place of

disparaging (5) insulting

wetbacks (5) derogatory term for Mexicans, especially those who entered the United States illegally

meager (8) small, scanty

los gringos y la raza (15) whites and Hispanics

ostensibly (15) outwardly in appearance, seemingly so

chinos (15) Chinese people (or Asians as a group)

barrio (17) a Spanish-speaking community within a U.S. city

enclave (17) an area within or surrounded by another group

Now read the essay.

Los Chinos Discover el Barrio

LUIS TORRES

1   There's a colorful mural on the asphalt playground of Hillside Elementary School, in the neighborhood called Lincoln Heights. Painted on the beige handball wall, the mural is of life-sized youngsters holding hands. Depicted are Asian and Latino kids with bright faces and ear-to-ear smiles.

2   The mural is a mirror of the makeup of the neighborhood today: Latinos living side-by-side with Asians. But it's not all smiles and happy faces in this Northeast Los Angeles community, located just a couple of miles up Broadway from City Hall. On the surface there's harmony between Latinos and Asians. But there are indications of simmering ethnic-based tensions.

3   That became clear to me recently when I took a walk through the old neighborhood—the one where I grew up. As I walked along North Broadway, I thought of a joke that comic Paul Rodriguez often tells on the stage. He paints the picture of a young Chicano walking down a street on L.A.'s Eastside. He comes upon two Asians having an animated conversation in what sounds like babble. "Hey, you guys," he says, "knock off that foreign talk. This is America—speak Spanish!"

4   When I was growing up in Lincoln Heights 30 years ago most of us spoke Spanish—and English. There was a sometimes uneasy co-existence in the neighborhood between brown and white. Back then we Latinos were moving in and essentially displacing the working-class Italians (to us, they were just *los gringos*) who had moved there and thrived after World War II.

5   Because I was an extremely fair-skinned Latino kid I would often overhear remarks by gringos in Lincoln Heights that were not intended for Latino ears, disparaging comments about "smelly wet-backs," and worse. The transition was, for the most part, a gradual process. And as I recall—except for the slurs that sometimes stung me directly—a process marked only occasionally by outright hostility.

6   A trend that began about 10 years ago in Lincoln Heights seems to have hit a critical point now. It's similar to the ethnic tug-of-war of yesteryear, but different colors, different words are involved. Today Chinese and Vietnamese are displacing the Latinos who, by choice or circumstance, had Lincoln Heights virtually to themselves for two solid generations.

7   Evidence of the transition is clear.

8   The bank where I opened my first meager savings account in the late 1950s has changed hands. It's now the East-West Federal Bank, an Asian-owned enterprise.

9   The public library on Workman Street, where I checked out *Charlotte's Web* with my first library card, abounds with signs of the new times: It's called "La Biblioteca del Pueblo de Lincoln Heights," and on the door there's a notice advising that the building is closed because of the Oct. 1 earthquake; it's written in Chinese.

10   The white, wood-frame house on Griffin Avenue that I once lived in is now owned by a Chinese family.

11   What used to be a Latino-run mortuary at the corner of Sichel Street and North Broadway is now the Chung Wah Funeral Home.

12   A block down the street from the funeral home is a *panaderia*, a bakery. As I would listen to radio reports of the U.S. war in faraway Indochina while walking from class at Lincoln High School, I often used to drop in the *panaderia* for a snack.

13   The word *panaderia*, now faded and chipped, is still painted on the shop window that fronts North Broadway. But another sign, a gleaming plastic one, hangs above the window. The sign proclaims that it is a Vietnamese-Chinese bakery. The proprietor, Sam Lee, bought the business less than a year ago. With a wave of his arm, he indicates that *La Opinion*, the Spanish-language daily newspaper, is still for sale on the counter. Two signs hang side-by-side behind the counter announcing in Spanish and in Chinese that cakes are made to order for all occasions.

14   Out on North Broadway, Fidel Farrillas sells *raspadas* (snow-cones) from his pushcart. He has lived and worked in Lincoln Heights "for 30 years and a pinch more," he says, his voice nearly whistling through two gold-framed teeth. He has seen the neighborhood change. Twice.

15   Like many older Latinos he remembers the tension felt between *los gringos y la raza* years ago—even though most people went about their business ostensibly coexisting politely. And others who have been around as long will tell an inquiring reporter scratching away in his notebook, "We're going out of our way to treat the *chinos* nice—better than the *gringos* sometimes treated us back then." But when the notebook is closed, they're likely to whisper, "But you know, the thing is, they smell funny, and they talk behind your back, and they are so arrogant—the way they're buying up everything in our neighborhood."

16   Neighborhood transitions can be tough to reconcile.

17   It isn't easy for the blue-collar Latinos of Lincoln Heights. They haven't possessed much. But they had the barrio, "a little chunk of the world where we belonged," as one described it. There may be some hard times and hard feelings ahead as *los chinos* continue to make inroads into what had been an exclusively Latino enclave. But there are hopeful signs as well.

18   On one recent Saturday afternoon a Latino fifth-grader, wearing the same type of hightop tennis shoes I wore as a 10-year-old on that same street corner, strode up to Senor Farrillas' snowcone pushcart. The kid pulled out a pocketful of dimes and bought two *raspadas*. One for himself, and one for his school chum—a Vietnamese kid. He was wearing hightops, too. They both ordered strawberry, as I recall.

Understanding the Content

Feel free to reread all or parts of the reading selection to answer the following questions.

1. Where do the events of this essay take place?

2. Who lived in the area before the Latinos? Now what group is moving in?

3. What changes are taking place that Torres mentions? How is the neighborhood responding to these changes?

4. What is Torres's attitude about the changes occurring in his old neighborhood?

5. What does the mural on the playground wall (described in the first paragraph) symbolize?

6. Can we infer that Torres is not a first-generation immigrant to the U.S.?

7. Can we infer that Torres no longer lives in Lincoln Heights?

8. What point of irony is being made in paragraph 15?

Looking at Structure and Style

1. How does Torres use his opening paragraph to establish his subject? Is it effective?

2. What is Torres's purpose in paragraphs 3–5? If we didn't know he was from this neighborhood would it change our reactions to what he says?

3. What function do paragraphs 7–13 serve? What paragraph patterns do they basically share?

4. How does the content of paragraphs 5 and 15 help us understand Torres's attitude toward the changes taking place?

5. What is the effectiveness of the last paragraph? How does it tie in with the opening paragraph?

6. Discuss your response to the author's style. What do you like/dislike about his writing?

Evaluating the Author's Viewpoints

1. What are Torres's feelings about the changes in his old neighborhood?

2. At the end of paragraph 2, Torres says, "But there are indications of simmering ethnic-based tensions." What evidence of this does he offer?

3. In paragraph 3, Torres recounts a joke told by the comic Paul Rodriguez. Is it possible that in a few years an Asian comic may be telling the same joke, changing the punch line to ". . . This is America—speak Chinese!"?

4. Reread the last paragraph. What message can we infer from this anecdote? Do you think these two boys can avoid growing up prejudiced against each other?

Pursuing Possible Essay Topics

1. Write an essay that shows how your neighborhood has changed since you were ten years old.

2. Pretend you are Fidel Farrillas, who has lived and worked selling *raspadas* in the same neighborhood for thirty years. Discuss how you feel about the changes occurring around your home.

3. Interview a recent Latino immigrant to the United States to learn what is it like for that person to be here. What difficulties has he or she had to face—from language barriers to prejudice?

4. Write an essay that deals with negative language used by people to hurt or make fun of other cultures. How does such language perpetuate prejudice?

5. Explore some stereotypes placed on various cultures. What effect do these stereotypes have on our attitudes toward people?

6. Go to your library to see if you can find more information on Hispanic or Asian immigrants that you might use in an essay. A place to start would be with one of the following books:
   a. Lillian Faderman and Barbara Bradshaw, *Speaking for Ourselves*, a collection of multi-ethnic writings
   b. Susan Garver and Paula McGuire, *Coming to America: From Mexico, Cuba and Puerto Rico*
   c. Linda Perrin, *Coming to America: Immigrants from the Far East*
   d. Dorothy B. Shimer, *Voices of Modern Asia*, translations of various Asian authors' works

   Read from one or more of these to acquaint yourself with another culture. Write an essay on what you learn from what you read.

7. Brainstorm or freewrite on one or more of the following:
   a. neighborhood changes
   b. transitions in life
   c. coexisting
   d. old vs. new generations
   e. what is a community
   f. ethnic differences in food

9. You don't like these? Come up with your own topic on cultural heritage.

Preparing to Read

Take a minute or two to look over the following reading selection. Note the title and author, read the opening paragraph, and check the length. Make certain you have the time now to read it carefully and to do the exercises that follow it. Then, in the spaces provided, answer the following questions.

1. What does the title imply? _____

_____

2. What is meant by the first sentence of the essay, "It is predictable"?

_____

_____

3. What do you think reading this essay will cause you to think about?

_____

_____

Vocabulary

Good comprehension of what you are about to read depends upon your understanding of the words below. The number following each word refers to the paragraph where it appears.

pseudo- (1) false

Anglo-featured (1) having the physical characteristics of white Americans

innocuous (3) harmless

trappings (3) ornamental clothing

social fabric (3) the various cultural groups that make up American society

per-capita (4) per person

ersatz (4) artificial

trivialize (6) to attribute little significance to

mayhem (6) willful, violent harm and destruction

impede (7) block, hold back

inadvertently (7) accidentally, unintentionally

denigrate (7) belittle, defame

deprivation (9) loss, the state of being needy

Now read the essay.

*It Is Time to Stop Playing Indians**

ARLENE B. HIRSCHFELDER

1   It is predictable. At Halloween, thousands of children trick-or-treat in Indian costumes. At Thanksgiving, thousands of children parade in school pageants wearing plastic headdresses and pseudo-buckskin clothing. Thousands of card shops stock Thanksgiving

---

* Editor's title

greeting cards with images of cartoon animals wearing feathered headbands. Thousands of teachers and librarians trim bulletin boards with Anglo-featured, feathered Indian boys and girls. Thousands of gift shops load their shelves with Indian figurines and jewelry.

2   Fall and winter are also the seasons when hundreds of thousands of sports fans root for professional, college and public school teams with names that summon up Indians—"Braves," "Redskins," "Chiefs." (In New York State, one out of eight junior and senior high school teams call themselves "Indians," "Tomahawks" and the like.) War-whooping team mascots are imprinted on school uniforms, post-cards, notebooks, tote bags and car floor mats.

3   All of this seems innocuous; why make a fuss about it? Because these trappings and holiday symbols offend tens of thousands of other Americans—the Native American people. Because these invented images prevent millions of us from understanding the authentic Indian America, both long ago and today. Because this image-making prevents Indians from being a relevant part of the nation's social fabric.

4   Halloween costumes mask the reality of high mortality rates, high diabetes rates, high unemployment rates. They hide low average life spans, low per-capita incomes and low educational levels. Plastic war bonnets and ersatz buckskin deprive people from knowing the complexity of Native American heritage—that Indians belong to hundreds of nations that have intricate social organizations, governments, languages, religions and sacred rituals, ancient stories, unique arts and music forms.

5   Thanksgiving school units and plays mask history. They do not tell how Europeans mistreated Wampanoags and other East Coast Indian peoples during the 17th Century. Social studies units don't mention that, to many Indians, Thanksgiving is a day of mourning, the beginning of broken promises, land theft, near extinction of their religions and languages at the hands of invading Europeans.

6   Athletic team nicknames and mascots disguise real people. War-painted, buckskin-clad, feathered characters keep the fictitious Indian circulating on decals, pennants and team clothing. Toy companies mask Indian identity and trivialize sacred beliefs by manufacturing Indian costumes and headdresses, peace pipes and trick-arrow-through-the-head gags that equate Indianness with playtime. Indian figures equipped with arrows, guns and tomahawks give youngsters the harmful message that Indians favor mayhem. Many Indian people can tell about children screaming in fear after being introduced to them.

7   It is time to consider how these images impede the efforts of Indian parents and communities to raise their children with positive information about their heritage. It is time to get rid of stereotypes

that, whether deliberately or inadvertently, denigrate Indian cultures and people.

8   It is time to bury the Halloween costumes, trick arrows, bulletin-board pin-ups, headdresses and mascots. It has been done before. In the 1970s, after student protests, Marquette University dropped its "Willie Wampum," Stanford University retired its mascot, "Prince Lightfoot," and Eastern Michigan University and Florida State modified their savage-looking mascots to reduce criticism.

9   It is time to stop playing Indians. It is time to abolish Indian images that sell merchandise. It is time to stop offending Indian people whose lives are all too often filled with economic deprivation, powerlessness, discrimination and gross injustice. This time next year, let's find more appropriate symbols for the holiday and sports seasons.

Understanding the Content

Feel free to reread all or parts of the selection to answer the following questions.

1. What is Hirschfelder arguing against? What does she mean when she says "it is time to stop playing Indians"?

2. Hirschfelder argues that Indian Halloween costumes "mask" the reality of the native American's problems and heritage. What examples of "the reality" does she provide?

3. Why, according to Hirschfelder, do some native Americans look at Thanksgiving as a day of mourning?

4. What Indian stereotypes does Hirschfelder claim are portrayed by certain manufacturers?

5. What evidence does the author provide to show that the issue has been dealt with before?

Looking at Structure and Style

1. In her opening paragraph, Hirschfelder repeats the phrase "Thousands of . . ." at or near the beginning of almost every sentence. Do you think this is an effective method for gaining a reader's attention? Explain.

2. How does the first sentence in paragraph 2 work as a transition from the opening paragraph? What transitional devices does she use?

3. Hirschfelder begins her third paragraph with a rhetorical question, almost anticipating what a reader might be thinking. How does she structure her answer to the question? Is this an effective technique?

4. In the first sentence of paragraphs 4, 5, and 6, the author uses the words "mask" and "disguise." Why are these words good choices considering what she is saying about costumes, plays, and names?

5. What is the point of paragraph 8?

6. Is the thesis stated or implied? If stated, where does it appear?

Evaluating the Author's Viewpoints

1. Does the author convince you that "it is time to stop playing Indians"? Why?

2. Do you think Hirschfelder is correct when she says that most people promote a stereotype of Indians and are unfamiliar with the complexity of the native American heritage? Did she point out any new information about native Americans of which you were unaware? Explain.

3. Hirschfelder says that we should "find more appropriate symbols for the holiday and sports season." (9) Do you agree? Can you think of some other symbols that wouldn't offend native Americans?

Pursuing Possible Essay Topics

1. Think about your image of someone from a culture different from yours. Where did you get this image? Is your image a stereotype? Write an essay about those things that influence our opinions of someone different from ourselves.

2. Write an essay about stereotypes people have of your own cultural heritage. Where do people get these impressions?

3. Select a particular custom or holiday ritual that your family practices. Describe it and discuss its value to you or your family.

4. Write about a time when you were in a school or church play or pageant and had to portray someone from another time or culture.

5. Think about a holiday tradition, custom, or ritual you practice somewhat regularly. Do you really understand its significance, or has it become a habit? Write an essay that re-examines the practice.

6. Go to the library and look in the card catalogue for one of the following titles:

   a. Dee Brown, *Bury My Heart at Wounded Knee*
   b. Vine Deloria, Jr., *Custer Died for Your Sins*
   c. Alvin M. Josephy, Jr., *The Indian Heritage of America*
   d. N. Scott Momaday, *House Made of Dawn*
   e. John G. Neihardt, *Black Elk Speaks*
   f. Dale Van Every, *Disinherited*

Read all or parts of one of these. Then write an essay on some aspect of native Americans that you never knew before.

7. Brainstorm or freewrite on one or more of the following:

   a. courting customs   d. marriage customs
   b. funeral customs   e. Halloween
   c. seasonal customs   f. Thanksgiving

8. Ignore these and find your own topic on some aspect of cultural heritage.

📖 *Preparing to Read*

Take a minute or two to look over the following reading selection. Note the title and author, read the opening paragraph, and check the length. Make certain you have the time now to read it carefully and to do the exercises that follow it. Then, in the spaces provided, answer the following questions.

1. What do you think is the point of this reading selection? _____

   _____

   _____

2. What do you already know about the topic? _____

   _____

3. What might you learn from reading this? _____

   _____

   _____

Vocabulary

Good comprehension of what you are about to read depends upon your understanding of the words below. The number following each word refers to the paragraph where it is used.

centennial (1) marking a 100-year anniversary

Indochinese boatperson (1) a refugee who fled by boat from the area of Southeast Asia that includes Vietnam, Cambodia, Thailand, Laos, Burma, and the Malay Peninsula

sham (2) something phony or fake

deposed (3) removed from office or power

upper-echelon (3) high-ranking

flourishing entrepreneurs (3) successful business people

precarious (4) dangerously unstable

bolster (4) support

traumas (4) severe shocks to the mind or body

Pol Pot's Cambodia (4) a 1970s period of ruthless government rule in Cambodia

". . . play well in Peoria" (5) satisfy the expectations of conservative, white, middle-class Americans

the dole (6) welfare, public assistance

shamans (8) priests, medicine men

sieges (10) prolonged periods

genocide (10) planned, systematic killing of a group or race

harrowing (11) extremely distressing, agonizing

atypical (11) unusual

exemplary (12) commendable, worthy of imitation

Now read the essay.

Trouble for America's "Model" Minority

DAVID WHITMAN

1   When 12-year-old Hue Cao shyly read her prize-winning essay at last year's nationally televised Statue of Liberty centennial celebration, she seemed the very model of a thriving Indochinese boat person. Only six years before, Hue, her mother, four brothers and two sisters fled Vietnam in a fishing boat, and now she was the center of national attention, having bested 2,000 other children in a highly competitive essay contest. "This nation has given my family a brand-new life," Hue recited proudly as tens of millions of equally proud Americans looked on.

2   Unfortunately, however, what they saw on their TV screens was something of a sham. Far from flourishing in the U.S., the Cao family turned out to be on welfare, unable even to accept the contest prize— a new automobile—because it would have meant surrendering their public-assistance benefits. "The girl's mother was in tears," recalls

Reg Schwenke of the Aloha Liberty Foundation, sponsor of the essay contest. "She was both anxious and ashamed."

3   The problems of Hue Cao and her family illustrate a major but long-hidden difference in social backgrounds between the two groups that make up the more than 800,000 Indochinese who sought refuge in the U.S. in the past 11 years. The first wave of 130,000 refugees— those who arrived in the immediate aftermath of the fall of Saigon in 1975—was largely an elite group. They were officials of the deposed South Vietnamese government, employees of the American military, dependents of U.S. servicemen and upper-echelon staffers of multi-national corporations. Given their experience and contacts, these refugees made a relatively easy transition to life in the U.S. and created a near mythic image of the Indochinese as brilliant students, flourishing entrepreneurs and altogether successful symbols of the American dream. After only four years in the U.S., the first wave of Indochinese refugees earned 18 percent more than the average American.

Behind the myth

4   The story, however, is far different for the second wave, the 640,000 who arrived in the U.S. following Vietnam's invasion of Cambodia in 1978. For many of them, life in America has been far less satisfying and considerably more precarious. In contrast to those who preceded them, the second wave of refugees had little education and few skills to bolster them in their new homes. Instead of sophisticated city dwellers, they were mostly rural people—farmers, fishers, small merchants and mountain tribespeople—many unable to speak English and illiterate in their own language. Half came from Laos and Cambodia, nations considerably poorer and socially less developed than Vietnam. And unlike the earlier refugees, those in the second wave often suffered brutal physical and psychological traumas before arriving in the United States. Many had been imprisoned in Vietnamese re-education camps, nearly starved and tortured in Pol Pot's Cambodia, or raped, beaten and robbed by the Thai pirates who preyed on the boat people in the Gulf of Thailand.

5   "This was the largest nonwhite, non-Western, non–English-speaking group of people ever to enter the country at one time," says Peter Rose, a Smith College professor who has written widely on the refugees. "The public assumed they succeeded just because the first wave did." Adds Ruben Rumbaut, director of the Indochinese Health and Adaptation Research Project at San Diego State University: "The Southeast Asian success stories play well in Peoria. Those of the losers don't."

6   Even when compared with depressed minorities in the U.S., "second wave" Indochinese fare poorly. A staggering 64 percent of the Indochinese households headed by refugees who arrived after 1980 are on public assistance—three times the rate of American blacks and four times that of Hispanics. And among refugee groups as a whole, the newly arrived Indochinese are by far the most dependent upon the dole.

7   *"In our old country, whatever we had was made or brought in by our hands," says Chong Sao Yang, 62, a former farmer and soldier who moved to San Diego from Laos. Yang and three family members have been on welfare for seven years. "We are not born on earth to have somebody give us food. Here, I'm sure we're going to starve, because since our arrival there is no penny I can get that is money I earn from work. I've been trying very hard to learn English, and at the same time look for a job. But no matter what kind of job—even a job to clean people's toilets—still people don't trust you or offer you such work. I'm not even worth as much as a dog's stool. Talking about this, I want to die right here so I won't see my future."*

8   Many in the newer wave of refugees grew up in Laos and Cambodia without electricity, running water, clocks or stoves—much less banks, savings accounts and credit cards. And Hmong tribesmen like Yang from the highlands of Laos feel even more isolated because of their illiteracy and traditional beliefs in witchcraft and shamans. "What we have here are 16th-century people suddenly thrust into 20th-century life," says Ernest Velasquez of the welfare department in Fresno, Calif., home for an estimated 18,000 Hmong. . . .

9   *Nao Chai Her was the respected head of a Hmong village of more than 500 people in Laos. Here, he is on welfare and shares a cramped three-bedroom apartment with 20 relatives. "We are just like the baby birds," says Nao, 61, "who stay in the nest opening their mouths, waiting only for the mother bird to bring the worms. When the government doesn't send the cash on time, we even fear we'll starve. I used to be a real man like any other man, but not any longer. The work I used to do, I can't do here. I feel like a thing which drops in the fire but won't burn and drops in the river but won't flow."*

10   Many Indochinese experience similar sieges of depression but manage to carefully disguise the condition behind a mask of hard work and traditional courtesy. In one standardized psychological test given in San Diego, 45 percent of the adult refugees showed distress symptoms serious enough to require clinical treatment, four times the proportion among the population at large. Cambodian women, many left husbandless by Pol Pot's genocide, are especially troubled. Lay Plok, 34, of Arlington, Va., lost her husband in 1977 when they fled the famine in Cambodia. "I'm down," she says quietly, "and yet I don't know what would make life feel better."

11   Like U.S. veterans with painful memories of Vietnam, some Indochinese refugees suffer repeated nightmares and evidence a variety of stress-related disorders. Indeed, emotional trauma among the new arrivals is so extensive and little understood that Dr. Richard Mollica and social worker James Lavelle of St. Elizabeth's Hospital set up the Indochinese Psychiatry Clinic in 1981 in Boston just to assist refugees. One woman treated at the clinic wandered from city to city in the U.S., fearful that her Communist jailers were out to recapture her. She told clinic doctors a harrowing but not atypical story of having been repeatedly raped, tortured and given mind-altering drugs while imprisoned.

12   For all their problems, however, the newer refugees don't fully fit the underclass stereotype. Most cherish hard work and stress the value of family and education. Divorce and out-of-wedlock pregnancy are still taboo. Drug and alcohol abuse is minimal. Studies of the refugee children, including those with illiterate Hmong parents, indicate they do quite well in school. And even where most of the family gets public-assistance payments, at least one member has a paying job, sometimes off the books. "The refugees make exemplary use of the welfare system," argues Nathan Caplan of the University of Michigan, an expert on the second wave of refugees. "They tend to have large families, so they pool resources to finance education and training. And they rely on welfare less as time goes by."

13   In the end, however, whatever their cultural liabilities, the refugees' greatest asset may be simply that they are survivors. Puthnear Mom, 22, also of Arlington, lost her husband while crossing the Cambodian border to Thailand. She can't read or write, and has been unemployed for two years. "I'm unhappy to receive welfare," she says through a translator, "but life is better now than in Cambodia or the refugee camp. I can learn anything here I want. Freedom does matter."

Understanding the Content

Feel free to reread all or parts of the selection to answer the following questions.

1. What was the difference between the first and second "wave" of Indochinese immigrants?

2. What were some of the hardships suffered by Indochinese immigrants?

3. Why are many of the "second wave" Indochinese in worse shape than most other minorities on public assistance?

4. What does Ernest Velasquez of the welfare department in Fresno, California, mean when he says that many of the 18,000 Hmongs living there are "16th-century people suddenly thrust into 20th-century life"? (8)

5. What percentage of adult refugees tested in San Diego showed distress symptoms serious enough to require clinical treatment? What types of experiences caused this distress to occur?

6. What are the reasons many of the "second wave" refugees are able to make "exemplary use of the welfare system"?

7. How well does the title reflect the point of the reading selection?

Looking at Structure and Style

1. How do paragraphs 1 and 2 work together? What is their function in relation to the main point of the reading selection?

2. How does the first sentence of the third paragraph work as a transition from paragraphs 1 and 2?

3. Is the essay mostly fact or opinion? What paragraphs can be verified as factual?

4. How do the quotations used in paragraphs 7 and 9 support the main point of the essay?

5. List the "troubles" for Indochinese mentioned in the essay. Are they presented in any particular order?

6. From paragraphs 12 and 13, list the positive attributes possessed by "the newer refugees." Why do you think Whitman waits until the end of the essay to mention these points?

Evaluating the Author's Viewpoints

1. In paragraphs 3 and 4, Whitman compares the first and second waves of Indochinese refugees, offering reasons for the second group's lack of success. Do these reasons make sense?

2. Look over the reading selection carefully for Whitman's sources. What are they? Are they reliable?

3. In paragraph 9, Nao Chai Her is quoted as saying, "I feel like a thing which drops in the fire but won't burn and drops in the river but won't flow." Explain what he means.

4. In paragraph 12, Whitman says, "For all their problems, however, the newer refugees don't fully fit the underclass stereotype." Based on his examples, what does he think the underclass stereotype is?

5. Whitman calls the refugees "survivors." Based on what you have read and know, do you agree with him?

Pursuing Possible Essay Topics

1. Compare/contrast the experiences of refugees coming from Europe in the 1800s (see Robbins's "Settling in the Cities") with those of Indochinese refugees in the 1980s.

2. Do some research on Indochinese immigrants, first or second wave, and write an essay on the differences between the two groups that strike you as interesting or important for native-born Americans to know. Refer to the library's card catalogue as well as the *Reader's Guide to Periodical Literature*, 1970s editions to the present.

3. Research Pol Pot's Cambodian regime to see what occurred that would cause so many refugees to flee to America. A good source is *Haing Ngor: A Cambodian Odyssey* by Haing Ngor, a Cambodian refugee. Your library's card catalogue will list other books and sources under "Cambodia" and "Pol Pot."

4. Interview an Indochinese refugee on your campus. Compare some aspect of that person's culture with your own, such as homelife, education, religion, marriage customs, holidays, etc.

5. Research one of the Indochinese countries. Find an interesting aspect of that culture to describe.

6. Pretend you are one of the "16th-century people suddenly thrust into 20th-century life." (8) What are some of the strange lifestyles to which you would have to become accustomed?

7. Discuss whether or not Indochinese refugees should be allowed to collect welfare, or discuss your feelings about the welfare system in general.

8. Ignore these ideas and come up with your own topic on the subject of cultural heritage.

Student Essay

Read the following narrative essay, written by a student who is in the process of learning English as a second language. As you read, look for answers to these questions:

1. Does the essay's subject fit the assignment to write about some aspect of cultural heritage?

2. How well does the narrative hold our interest?

3. Is the thesis clear and supported well?

Coming to America

Hieu Huynh

1   My coming to America in 1979 was not very pleasant. When I was twelve, my parents had to leave my homeland, Vietnam. We lived near My Tho all my years and I did not want to leave, but they said we must. My two sisters were younger, four and seven, and they did not know what it meant to leave. My mother said that we must not tell any of our friends, that our going was a secret. It was hard for me to think I would never see my home or some of my family again. Some of my story I tell here I remember well, but some is not clear and is from stories my family tells.

2   I was very sad the day we left my house. We could not take many things with us because we did not want the authorities to know we were trying to leave Vietnam. So we pretended that we were visiting my mother's sister and husband who lived in a fishing village in the Mekong Delta. Many times we were stopped by soldiers and officials who wanted to know where we were going. My sisters and I were afraid often. Finally, we reached their village.

3   We stayed there for several days. Our four cousins played with us and we did not really know what the family was planning. But after a few days, we were awakened one night and told to be quiet. My family, along with my uncle and aunt and cousins, all boarded a smelly fishing boat. The children were all told to go inside and sleep. There were already other people I did not know on the boat, but I found room for my sisters and they were tired and went to sleep. I couldn't because of all the hushed talking and I sensed fear.

4   Soon the boat started moving. It was still night and I wondered how anyone could see where the boat was going. Everyone was very quiet. I remember feeling sick from the smell of the boat and the smell of fear. When light broke, I felt the boat stop and many loud voices up above. Soon, my mother and two other women came down in the boat and went through our things, taking out gold and silver pieces. They whispered to be still and went

back up. Soon we were moving again. I learned later that my parents had to pay much gold and silver to the harbor authorities in order to let us continue.

5   I forget how many days we tossed about on the ocean. Almost everyone got sick. There was not much water so we had to drink sparingly. The boat leaked because it was old and the water was sometimes very rough. We could not always cook food. Sometimes we only ate uncooked rice. The younger children cried a lot. I wanted to but did not. My parents said I must be brave for my sisters.

6   The next part of the story I do not like to tell. A large boat with Thai men who had guns and knives stopped us and made us all go on their ship. They were very mean to everybody. They ripped at our clothes thinking that we might be hiding money and jewelry, which we were. When they found some gold in one woman's blouse, they made all of us take off our clothes. When my father and other men tried to stop them, they shot a man I didn't know. They hit my father with a gun and made us all get on our knees. The evil men were shouting and my sisters were screaming and crying for my mother, but she told us to do as the men say. I could not believe all this was happening. It was so terrible it did not seem real. But it was.

7   After they ripped up our clothes and took our valuables, they told all the men and children to go back to our boat. They threw the man they shot into the water and we never saw him again. They kept my mother and two other women on their boat. We could hear them weeping and we called to her, afraid we would never see her again. My father made all the children go down into the boat. He put his arms around us and he cried silently. Later, the women were put back on our boat and we were happy to see her alive. But she was never the same after that happened.

8   One or two days later one of the women died and it was decided to throw the body overboard. Her children cried and wanted to be thrown overboard too, but their father held them tight.

9   We all thought we would die soon on the ocean. But a Malaysian police boat found us. They were not nice, but they didn't

harm us. Of course we had nothing left to be taken, and I think my mother no longer cared what happened. But they took us to Bidong Island where thousands of other refugees like us had already been taken.

10   We spent many months there. It was not easy and food was scarce. There was not much water to go around. People were sick and dying. I got sick myself and often did not know what was happening.

11   Finally, our family was interviewed by authorities. Fortunately, my father's older brother was already in the United States. Somehow things worked out, and our family finally arrived in America. But getting here was not easy. We are all some happier, but there is a part of our lives we would like to never remember again.

Reaction

In the space below, write your reaction to the student essay. What would you tell this student about his essay?

Commentary

Hieu's essay stands as a good example of a first-person narrative. Originally, he was not certain he wanted to write about this experience, but he says he is now glad he did. This is his fourth draft and it could still use some more revision. However, because of the painful subject matter, Hieu was not required to do so at this point.

Hieu had spoken and written English only since his arrival in the United States eight years earlier, and so was provided tutorial help with some of his wording. Other than that, though, the essay is his own work. Writing in English is not easy for him, but he wants to put this draft away for a while and perhaps come back later to rewrite some of the sentences when he feels he has developed a more sophisticated vocabulary. Not happy with his opening, he wants to write in such a way that the reader "sees and feels" the difficulties his family underwent rather than his "just telling" us.

What holds the audience's attention is both the subject matter and the simple, straightforward way it is presented. It is written in a chronological fashion and his paragraphs move easily from one episode to the next. It was no doubt difficult for him to retell this part of his "coming to America" (his title), but he wrote about something he knew. As mentioned before, students too often attempt to write about something they really have not felt, experienced, or learned anything about. The results are usually uninteresting, boring, uninformative, and not worth the writer's or the reader's time.

Hieu shows in his essay that he understands the narrative form. Despite some of the simple sentences, the way he tells his story touches us. As time goes by and he continues to develop his understanding of the English language, Hieu should have little difficulty writing the way he wants. His sincere desire to learn to write better and his willingness to spend time revising are starting to show results.

Viewpoints on

Changing Social Values

"My proposal is for the revival or reassertion of personal responsibility in all human acts, good and bad."
Karl Menniger

BEIJING, CHINA A farmer who stole the head of a 3rd-century B.C. terra cotta warrior and tried to sell it for $81,000 has been sentenced to death, an official Chinese newspaper reported Saturday.

SAN FRANCISCO A man convicted and sentenced to prison for raping a young girl, then cutting off her arms and leaving her to die was released today after serving three years of a twenty-year sentence.

IN OUR SOCIETY most of us probably feel that a death sentence for stealing the head of a statue is too severe, while letting a man free after serving only a three-year term for rape and mutilation seems an outrage. But regardless of our reactions, the newspaper items reflect the social values of two different cultures.

As we live and grow, we learn the culture of the society in which we live. Sociologist Rodney Stark, in his book *Sociology*, tells us that the most significant elements of culture that we must learn are values, norms, and roles. Stark defines **values** thus: "The values of a culture identify its ideals—its ultimate aims and most general standards for assessing good and bad or desirable and undesirable. When we say people need self-respect, dignity, and freedom . . . we are invoking values." While values are rather general, **norms** are quite specific. "They are rules of governing behavior," Stark says. "Norms define what behavior is required, acceptable, or prohibited in particular circumstance. Norms indicate that a person should, ought, or must act (or not act) in a certain way." A collection of these norms connected with a particular position in a society is called a **role.** For instance, each of us has "a relatively clearly defined role to fulfill: student, friend, woman, husband, shopper, pedestrian, cop, nun, bartender, wife, and so on." Thus, values, norms, and roles are connected.

How we think and act in the various roles we play is based on our society's values and norms. For instance, we generally expect a minister's behavior to follow certain norms: no drinking alcoholic beverages, no smoking, no sexually deviant behavior, no using bad language, no wearing swim trunks while delivering a Sunday sermon. At the same time, your role while attending a church service is composed of certain norms: no playing your Walkman during the service, no shouting at friends across the way, no removing money from the collection plate.

History shows us that Americans have always been concerned with moral values. Chapters in textbooks are devoted to issues of right and wrong. Today we wonder how belief systems could ever have permitted the burning of people as witches in Salem, the once widespread acceptance of slavery, the disregard for the rights of the native American, the long lack of voting rights and working privileges for women, the overt discrimination toward Jews and other religious groups, the racial segregation from drinking fountains to schoolrooms, and the "blacklisting" and labeling as communists those who spoke out against government policies in the 1950s. Yet, at various times in our society such norms were considered acceptable social behavior.

More recently, our society has had to deal with the cultural clashes caused by our involvement in Vietnam, the Watergate and Iran-contra scandals, our presence in the Persian Gulf and Central America, attitudes toward gay rights, prayer in the public schools, and definitions of pornography and censorship, just to name a few. Disagreements over issues such as these create conflicts within our society which force us to re-examine our social values, norms, and roles. Doing so often brings about a change in attitudes and values from generation to generation. What was acceptable and valued in society yesterday may not be today. What is acceptable today may not be tomorrow.

The following reading selections reflect some viewpoints and reactions to changing social values, norms, and roles. Use them to practice your critical reading skills and to stimulate your own thinking regarding changes in social values.

📖 *Preparing to Read*

Take a minute or two to look over the following reading selection. Note the title and author, read the opening paragraph, and check the length. Make certain you have the time now to read it carefully and to do the exercises that follow it. Then, in the spaces provided, answer the following questions.

1. What do you think will be the author's viewpoint regarding the making

   of value judgments?_____

   _____

   _____

2. What might you learn from reading this selection?_____

   _____

   _____

Vocabulary

Good comprehension of what you are about to read depends upon your understanding of the words below. The number following each word refers to the paragraph where it is used.

   muddled (1) confused, jumbled

   ethics (1) the study of the nature of morals and specific moral choices

   accord (4) give or grant

   medieval (6) pertaining to a historical period known as the Middle Ages, from around 476 to 1453

   excommunicated (6) excluded or dropped from membership

   penetrate (6) to force a way into

reprehensible (6) worthy of blame

perspective (8) point of view, way of seeing things

condoned (8) forgave, overlooked

wanton (9) excessive

Now read the essay.

Debating Moral Questions

VINCENT RYAN RUGGIERO

1   Nowhere is modern thinking more muddled than over the question of whether it is proper to debate moral issues. Many argue it is not, saying it is wrong to make "value judgments." This view is shallow. If such judgments were wrong, then ethics, philosophy, and theology would be unacceptable in a college curriculum—an idea that is obviously silly. As the following cases illustrate, it is impossible to avoid making value judgments.

2   Raoul Wallenberg was a young Swedish aristocrat. In 1944 he left the safety of his country and entered Budapest. Over the next year he outwitted the Nazis and saved as many as 100,000 Jews (he was not himself Jewish) from the death camps. In 1945 he was arrested by the Russians, charged with spying, and imprisoned in a Russian labor camp. He may still be alive there.[1] Now, if we regard him as a hero—as there is excellent reason to do—we are making a value judgment. Yet if we regard him neutrally, as no different from anyone else, we are also making a value judgment. We are judging him to be neither hero nor villain, but average.

3   Consider another case. In late 1981 a 20-year-old mother left her three infant sons unattended in a garbage-strewn tenement in New York City.[2] Police found them there, starving, the youngest child lodged between a mattress and a wall, covered with flies and cockroaches, the eldest playing on the second-floor window ledge. The police judged the mother negligent, and the court agreed. Was it wrong for them to judge? And if we refuse to judge, won't that refusal itself be a judgment in the mother's favor?

4   No matter how difficult it may be to judge such moral issues, we *must* judge them. Value judgment is the basis not only of our social

---

[1] The story of Raoul Wallenberg is detailed in John Bierman, *Righteous Gentile* (New York: Viking, 1982).

[2] "Starving Children Saved by NYC Police," *Oneonta Star*, 13 October 1981, p. 13.

code, but of our legal system. The quality of our laws is directly affected by the quality of our moral judgments. A society that judges blacks inferior is not likely to accord blacks equal treatment. A society that believes a woman's place is in the home is not likely to guarantee women equal employment opportunity.

5   Other people accept value judgments as long as they are made *within* a culture, and not about other cultures. Right and wrong, they believe, vary from one culture to another. It is true that an act frowned upon in one culture may be tolerated in another, but the degree of difference has often been grossly exaggerated. When we first encounter an unfamiliar moral view, we are inclined to focus on the difference so much that we miss the similarity.

6   For example, in medieval Europe animals were tried for crimes and often formally executed. In fact, cockroaches and other bugs were sometimes excommunicated from the church.[3] Sounds absurd, doesn't it? But when we penetrate beneath the absurdity, we realize that the basic view—that some actions are reprehensible and ought to be punished—is not so strange. The core idea that a person bitten by, say, a dog, has been wronged and requires justice is very much the same. The only difference is our rejection of the idea that animals are responsible for their behavior.

7   Is it legitimate, then, for us to pass judgment on the moral standards of another culture? Yes, if we do so thoughtfully, and not just conclude that whatever differs from our view is necessarily wrong. We can judge, for example, a culture that treats women as property, or places less value on their lives than on the lives of men. Moreover, we can say a society is acting immorally by denying women their human rights. Consider the following cases.

8   In nineteenth-century Rio de Janeiro, Brazil, a theatrical producer shot and killed his wife because she insisted on taking a walk in the botanical gardens against his wishes. He was formally charged with her murder, but the judge dismissed the charge. The producer was carried through the streets in triumph. The moral perspective of his culture condoned the taking of a woman's life if she disobeyed her husband, even in a relatively small matter. A century later that perspective had changed little. In the same city, in 1976, a wealthy playboy, angry at his lover for flirting with others, fired four shots into her face at point-blank range, killing her. He was given a two-year suspended sentence in light of the fact that he had been "defending his honor."[4]

---

[3] Joseph Jastrow, *Effective Thinking* (New York: Simon and Schuster, 1931), p. 121.

[4] Warren Hoge, "Machismo 'Absolved' in Notorious Brazilian Trial," *New York Times*, 28 October 1979, p. 24.

9   Surely it is irresponsible for us to withhold judgment on the morality of these cases merely because they occurred in a different culture. It is obvious that in both cases the men's response, murder, was out of all proportion to the women's "offenses," and therefore demonstrated a wanton disregard for the women's human rights. Their response is thus properly judged immoral. And this judgment implies another—that the culture condoning such behavior is guilty of moral insensitivity.

Understanding the Content

Feel free to reread all or parts of the selection to answer the following questions.

1. What, according to Ruggiero, are value judgments?

2. How does Ruggiero feel about those people who accept value judgments as long as they are made *within* a culture, but not those made *about* other cultures?

3. What connection does the author make between the quality of our laws and the quality of our moral judgments?

4. Why does the author believe that it is important to debate moral issues?

5. Circle the letter of the following statements from the essay that are facts:
   a. "Many argue it is . . . wrong to make 'value judgments.' This view is shallow." (1)
   b. ". . . In medieval Europe animals were tried for crimes and often formally executed." (6)
   c. "In late 1981 a 20-year-old mother left her three infant sons unattended in a garbage-strewn tenement in New York City." (3)
   d. "Nowhere is modern thinking more muddled than over the question of whether it is proper to debate moral issues." (1)

6. Explain in your own words the meaning of the last two sentences in paragraph 9.

7. Can we infer from what the author says that he is against teaching or debating moral issues in schools?

8. Can we infer from what the author says that he feels our moral judgments and values should be based on what the majority of the people in the society believe?

Looking at Structure and Style

1. How does Ruggiero use paragraphs 2 and 3 to support paragraph 1? Is this a good method to use here? Why?

2. Where else in the essay does Ruggiero use this same method of development? Are they good examples?

3. Ruggiero documents four sources to help support his views. Are they good sources? What value is there in doing this?

4. Rewrite the following passages from the essay in your own words:
   a. "This view is shallow." (1)
   b. "... He outwitted the Nazis. ..." (2)
   c. "... not likely to accord blacks equal treatment." (4)
   d. "... penetrate beneath the absurdity ..." (6)
   e. "... His culture condoned the taking of a woman's life." (8)
   f. "... a wanton disregard for ..." (9)

5. What is Ruggiero's attitude toward his subject and the tone of his writing? To what audience is he probably writing?

6. Is this essay mostly written from an objective or subjective viewpoint? Explain.

7. Discuss your response to the writer's writing style. What techniques does he use that you like or dislike? What suggestions, if any, might you offer him for revision?

Evaluating the Author's Viewpoints

1. Explain why you agree or disagree with what the author says in paragraph 1. Is this his thesis? Explain.

2. In paragraph 4, Ruggiero says, "Value judgment is the basis not only of our social code, but of our legal system." Explain what he means and whether or not you agree.

3. Ruggiero feels that the examples in paragraph 8 reflect the thinking and actions of an immoral society. Explain why you agree or disagree.

4. In some societies, when a person is caught stealing, that person's hand is cut off. If caught stealing twice, the other hand is removed. What do you think Ruggiero might say about such a law? Why?

5. Has reading Ruggiero's essay caused you to think about issues you never thought about before? Explain.

Pursuing Possible Essay Topics

1. Make a list of Ruggiero's main points, then think of reasons to disagree with each of them, even if you really don't.

2. Brainstorm or freewrite on one or more of the following:
   a. morality
   b. social codes
   c. social values
   d. culture
   e. human rights
   f. immoral

3. Reread the opening question in paragraph 7. Write your own answer to it by supplying your own reasons and examples. Try to find examples from current events to support your views. If possible, document your sources as Ruggiero does. (See the Appendix for documentation information.)

4. Write about a custom or law in the United States which you feel reflects what Ruggiero calls "moral insensitivity" and which you feel should be changed.

5. Argue for or against Ruggiero's statement, "The quality of our laws is directly affected by the quality of our moral judgments." (4)

6. Write an essay that deals with a current social value that seems to be undergoing change. Show both the pros and cons of the issue but take a stand for one side.

7. Look for recent articles in the newspapers or magazines that would serve as examples Ruggiero could use to support his viewpoints (see examples in paragraph 3). Then use them to write your own essay patterned after Ruggiero's essay. Use recent issues of the *Reader's Guide to Periodical Literature* in your library.

8. Ignore all of these and come up with your own topic that deals with some aspect of changing social values.

Preparing to Read

Take a minute or two to look over the following reading selection. Note the title and author, read the opening paragraph, and check the length of the essay. Make certain you have the time now to read it carefully and to do the exercises that follow it. Then, in the spaces provided, answer the following questions.

1. What do you think the essay will be about? _____

_____

_____

2. What do you think the title means? _____

_____

_____

Vocabulary

Good comprehension of what you are about to read depends upon your understanding of the words below. The number following each word to the paragraph where it is used.

coming up (1) growing up

plight (1) difficult situation or condition

civics (2) the study of the rights/duties of a citizen

submissive (4) meek, tame, docile, subdued

segregated (4) separated, isolated

disillusionment (6) the experience of having your hopes shattered and learning the truth

endear (7) to make beloved, to cause a feeling of affection

boycott (9) a blocking or stopping of the use of something as a means of protest

awe (13) wonder, strong respect

Now read the essay.

A Long Way to Go

ROSA PARKS

1   When I was coming up, I went to a one-room country school in Pine Level, Ala., where all the pupils and the teachers were black. In the sixth grade, my mother sent me to Montgomery, where I went to the Montgomery Industrial School, which was run by Miss Alice White. She was a very proper older woman who ran the school with a group of Northern white ladies who were sympathetic to the plight of Negroes. That's what they called us back then.

2   In school, we learned all of the civics lessons that children were supposed to learn. We had to memorize Abraham Lincoln's Gettysburg Address and portions of the Constitution. We recited the Pledge of Allegiance. We studied all of the Presidents—Washington, Jefferson, Lincoln—and we knew about all the wars.

3   I guess for most of us children, the Statue of Liberty was just something we read about in a civics book. We learned that poem about the statue, but it was just another lesson we had to recite, just like the Civil War poem about the Blue and the Gray, or the Gettysburg Address.

4   The Africans who came over on the slave ships never saw the statue. Of course, they didn't mention that in the history books. The

studies we did in our books were based on freedom and equality and the pursuit of happiness and all. But in reality we had to face the fact that we were not as free as the books said. What they taught us in school didn't apply to us as a race. We were being told to be as submissive and as useful as possible to white people, to do their work and see to their comforts and be segregated from them when they saw fit for us not to be around.

5   Even Miss Alice White, who had all the best intentions in the world, was part of the system. In her lectures, she would tell us how horrible slavery was, but then she would say that at least it brought the Negro out of savagery in Africa. Of course, none of those slave traders ever asked the Africans whether they wanted to come to America. I imagine that if the Africans had come around after the statue was built, they would have had some terrible ideas about what it meant to them. I don't think they would have written any poems.

6   My family knew the brutality and disillusionment of not being treated like human beings. My grandfather was a slave. He was the son of the plantation owner, so he was very white in appearance. My grandfather used to say that the overseer took an instant dislike to him because he looked so white. He would always tell me how he had to dodge and hide to keep out of trouble with the overseer. Until the day he died, my grandfather had a fierce hatred of white people.

7   My mother had a mind of her own. She always held to the belief that none of us should be mistreated because of our race. She was pretty outspoken, and of course that didn't endear her to too many whites. It didn't endear her to too many blacks, either, because in those days the general attitude among our people was to go along in silence. If you differed with that, you had to stand pretty much alone.

8   I remember that one of the first books I read, back when I was 8 years old, was called *Is the Negro a Beast?* That was the kind of attitude that white people had in Alabama in those days. It was so different from what we were reading about in our American history and civics lessons, with all the positive messages about life in this country, and I could see that what we were being taught wasn't so, at least as far as black people were concerned.

9   It didn't change much when I was working. I encountered all kinds of discrimination. If you were black in the South, it was just something you lived with all the time. I would just meet it in silence, bite my lip, go on. I saw it a lot with the bus drivers. If they thought you were about to make trouble, they would just shut the door on you and drive on off. In fact, the same red-headed driver who arrested me in 1955 [starting the Montgomery bus boycott led by Martin Luther King] had evicted me from a bus in 1943. He didn't want me to walk through the white section of the bus to get to the section for

blacks, and I told him I wasn't going to get off the bus while I was already on. He took me by the sleeve of my winter coat and led me off. When I got on his bus again 12 years later, I remembered him very well, but I didn't expect him to disturb me a second time.

10   I didn't actually get to see the Statue of Liberty until about a year after the boycott. By that time, my attitude was a little different. I thought that saying—"Give me your tired, your poor . . ."—was impressive, that we should help people who come to the United States. This was a better place than where they had been.

11   I was invited to come to New York by Dr. Ralph Bunche and met him at the United Nations. I stayed with a Quaker couple, Mr. and Mrs. Stuart Meacham, who lived on Franklin D. Roosevelt Drive in Manhattan, right on the East River. Mr. Meacham asked me what was the first thing I wanted to do in New York. I told him, to see the Statue of Liberty. I had always been fascinated by tall buildings and monuments.

12   We went across the water by ferry about noon. It was just the way I thought it would be, that big arm waving the torch high above everything. We walked up all those stairs to the very top, right in the crown. We looked out from the windows in the crown, and we could see for miles. When we went back down, Mr. Meacham took my picture at the foot of the statue.

13   I guess the statue should be a symbol of freedom. I would not want our young people to be so disillusioned that they couldn't feel a sense of awe about it. But I can't find myself getting overwhelmed. We are supposed to be loyal and dedicated and committed to what America stands for. But we are still being denied complete equality. We have to struggle to gain a little bit, and as soon as it seems we make some gains for all our sacrifices, there are new obstacles, and people trying to take away what little we have.

14   Certainly there is a degree of freedom in America that we can celebrate, but as long as a difference in your complexion or your background can be used against you, we still have a long way to go.

Understanding the Content

Feel free to reread all or parts of the selection to answer the following questions.

1. Explain what the essay has to do with social values and roles.

2. Describe the type of education Rosa Parks received.

3. What can we infer about social values during Rosa Parks's childhood from the title of the book she read, *Is the Negro a Beast?*

4. What attitude toward the Statue of Liberty does the author feel Africans would have if it had been around when they were first brought to America? How is this contradictory to the symbolic meaning of the Statue of Liberty?

5. What can we infer was the historical significance of her arrest by a Montgomery, Alabama bus driver in 1955? (see paragraph 9)

6. How does she feel about the Statue of Liberty?

7. What does paragraph 6 say about "acceptable" social attitudes of whites during Parks's grandfather's time?

8. What attitude did the author's mother have that went against the social values held in that day by both whites and blacks?

9. What is the significance of her title, "A Long Way to Go"?

Looking at Structure and Style

1. In what paragraph is the thesis best stated? Is it implied or directly stated?

2. Select some passages that reveal the author's attitude and tone.

3. To what audience is Parks probably writing? What makes you think so?

4. The author spends the first several paragraphs narrating events of her early schooling. What is their purpose and function?

5. What is the point of paragraphs 6 and 7?

6. What is the value of the several references to the Statue of Liberty? How do they help support the author's point?

7. Discuss what you like or dislike about the author's style. What suggestions, if any, might you offer for revision?

Evaluating the Author's Viewpoints

1. Explain why you agree or disagree with the viewpoint expressed in the last paragraph.

2. What present social values do you think the author wants to see changed?

3. Mrs. Parks was arrested twice, once in 1943 and again in 1955, for not sitting in the section of the bus designated for blacks. In effect, she broke the law established by accepted social values of the time. What does this tell you about her? Should she have done this? Explain.

4. In paragraph 13, Parks says blacks are still being denied complete equality. Can you offer some examples to support this?

5. How has Parks's heritage, early education, and treatment by society influenced her viewpoints?

Pursuing Possible Essay Topics

1. Brainstorm or freewrite on one or more the following:
   a. civil rights
   b. civil disobedience
   c. racial prejudice
   d. Martin Luther King, Jr.
   e. boycott
   f. apartheid

2. Use the title "A Long Way to Go" and write an essay about social values that you feel need to change but have a long way to go.

3. Look for recent information that would support Rosa Parks's statement in paragraph 13 that blacks are still being denied complete equality, or look for support to show that gains by blacks are being made. Use the evidence as support for your own thesis.

4. Rosa Parks was willing to go to jail rather than give up her seat on a bus to a white man. Her trial was the beginning of the civil rights movement. For what cause would you be willing to go to jail? Explain the cause and support your viewpoints with reason.

5. In his book *Stride Toward Freedom*, Martin Luther King, Jr., considered by many the greatest leader in the history of the civil rights movement in America, wrote the following:

> There was to be much speculation about why Mrs. Parks did not obey the driver. Many people in the white community argued that she had been "planted" by the NAACP [National Association for the Advancement of Colored People] in order to lay the groundwork for a test case. . . . But the accusation was totally unwarranted, as the testimony of both Mrs. Parks and the officials of the NAACP revealed. Actually no one can understand the action of Mrs. Parks unless he realizes that eventually the cup of endurance runs over, and the human personality cries out, "I can take it no longer." Mrs. Parks's refusal to move back was her intrepid affirmation that she had had enough. It was an individual expression of a timeless longing for human dignity and freedom. She was not "planted" there by the NAACP, or any other organization; she was planted there by her personal sense of dignity and self-respect. She was anchored to that seat by the accumulated indignities of days gone by and by boundless aspirations of generations yet unborn.

   Use this and any other information you can discover through research and write an essay about your views of Mrs. Parks or about other people in history who have changed social values regarding race.

6. Write an essay that reflects various racist views. Show why these views are wrong.

7. Boycott these ideas and find your own topic on some aspect of changing social values.

Preparing to Read

Take a minute or two to look over the following reading selection. Note the title and authors, read the opening paragraph, and check the length. Make certain you have the time now to read it carefully and to do the exercises that follow it. Then, in the spaces provided, answer the following questions.

1. What do you think will be the authors' point? _____

_____

2. What is your definition of a baby boomer? _____

_____

3. What might you learn from reading this selection? _____

_____

_____

Vocabulary

Good comprehension of what you are about to read depends upon your understanding of the words below. The number following each word refers to the paragraph where it is used.

unprecedented (1) without previous occurrence

affluence (1) wealth, abundance

amassing (2) accumulating, gaining more

deferred (7) postponed

net (8) final, ultimate

fragmentation (8) the act of breaking up into pieces

libertarian (9) believing in freedom of thought and action

unbridled . . . license (9) permission to act with excessive freedom

the New Deal (9) the programs and policies for economic reform that were introduced by President Franklin Roosevelt in the 1930s

the Great Society (9) the programs and policies promised by President Lyndon Johnson in the 1960s

Oedipal rebellion (11) according to psychologist Sigmund Freud, the period during which a child (usually male) falls in love with his mother and feels hostile toward his father

self-actualization (12) achievement of one's full potential

ideologies (12) groups of ideas and beliefs belonging to an individual or a social group

Christopher Lasch and Richard Sennett (12) contemporary social/historical authors whose works examine cultural changes (see *The Culture of Narcissism* and *The Minimal Self* as examples)

narcissism (12) excessive admiration of oneself

tempered (14) moderated

Now read the essay.

What's a Baby Boomer?

JAY OLGILVY, ERIC UTNE, and BRAD EDMONDSON

1   The baby-boom generation was born between 1946 and 1964, a period of American history marked by unprecedented affluence and an unusually high birth rate. Today, the boomers number about 78 million people, or one-third of the total U.S. population. They have dominated America's cultural and economic life since their birth, and they will continue to dominate it as they move through the various stages of their life cycles.

2   When they were little, baby boomers filled the elementary schools and the suburbs. As they became teenagers, they built the record companies and the sporting goods and beauty aids industries. When they were old enough to drive cars, they fueled a golden age in Detroit. Now that they have reached maturity, America is becoming more of a middle-aged society, intent on amassing wealth and financial security.

3   The baby-boom generation is the most educated in American history. One boomer in four has a college degree, and half have gone to college. With education comes increasing income: Boomers with a high school degree had average household incomes of $19,200 in 1983, compared to $28,100 for college graduates and $32,300 for those who have gone to graduate school.

4   The lives and values of baby boomers are split in half by age. Most of the older boomers in their 30s live settled lives, while their younger siblings in their 20s are still looking for jobs, spouses, and

houses. More than one-quarter of the younger group still lives with their parents, which is a departure from earlier generations.

5   The older half has an enduring economic advantage: Many of them purchased housing during the 1970s, before prices skyrocketed. Sixty percent of people in their 30s own a home, compared to 31 percent of people in their 20s. The average monthly house payment of a person who bought before 1980 is less than $450; today, the average monthly house payment is $800. For this reason, older boomers who bought housing early have hundreds of dollars more to spend every month.

6   Understandably, the younger half of the baby boom is much more concerned with finances. Since 1967, UCLA has asked incoming students why they want to go to college; among the choices provided are "to become well off financially," or "to gain a meaningful life philosophy." In 1967, as the oldest boomers were entering college, nearly 85 percent said they were going to school for philosophical reasons, and less than half went to school to get rich. By 1985, as the youngest boomers were entering school, three-fourths said, "give me the money." Only 44 percent said they wanted to gain a meaningful life philosophy.

7   Education produces independent minds, and boomers are more willing than any previous generation to experiment with new values and new living arrangements. They are the main reason why deferred marriage, delayed childbearing, and divorce are becoming increasingly common. Before the boom was heard, the vast majority of men and women were married by their early 20s. But today, only 38 percent of men and 59 percent of women are married by their 25th birthday. Meanwhile, the number of divorces has tripled since 1960. Many boomers have decided not to have children, and the ones who do become parents are likely to delay childbearing until their 30th birthday or beyond. They are also likely to have fewer children. One or two is the norm, and larger families are increasingly rare. Boomers are also likely to be raising those children as single parents. The Census Bureau projects that among children born today, six out of 10 will spend some time in a single-parent family before they reach age 18.

8   The net effect of this social explosion is fragmentation. In the 1950s, American society was easy to understand: Dad made money while mom stayed home, raised kids, and went shopping. Today, the American household has been transformed. Married couples with children make up only 28 percent of all households. Childless married couples are another 30 percent, single persons are 26 percent, and single-parent families are 16 percent of the total picture. Each type of household has radically different needs. . . .

9   Today's liberals support inner-directed, libertarian moral values, such as the freedom of individuals to pursue religious and sexual preferences in the privacy of their own homes. Libertarians are supposed to be conservatives. But today's Republican Party conservatives attempt to legislate morality in the face of what they see as a dangerously unbridled individual license. They're using government every bit as much as the liberal Democrats did in the New Deal and the Great Society to advance their own social agendas.

10   Political definitions seem to be blurring as moral values replace ideological values as a political force. Most members of the so-called "Moral Majority," for example, come from Midwestern and Southern families that had voted Democratic since the New Deal. They are a largely downscale economic group that benefitted enormously from federal programs designed to redistribute income from rich to poor. As their lot improved, however, they became less interested in sharing the wealth and more interested in protecting their property, culture, and moral traditions. . . .

11   To a remarkable degree, the social history of the U.S. over the last several decades has been influenced by the maturing of baby boomers. The adult psychological development of the oldest baby boomers reads like a history of domestic affairs during the last 25 years. When they were teenagers, faced with the task of Oedipal rebellion and separation from their parents, they turned the campuses upside-down. During the '70s, when these boomers were in their 20s, their psychological task was to find a place in the world: The issue of the decade was work (and unemployment), and the hot spot was the singles bar. During the '80s, much of the baby boom entered its 30s. The 30s are what psychologist Daniel Levinson calls "the decade of achievement." . . .

12   Change, personal development, and self-actualization are core values for the baby-boom generation. Commentators who look for stable ideologies are confused by this root belief in change. Authors like Christopher Lasch and Richard Sennett see narcissism in this new individualism, but it's really just a stage of growth. And what change could seem more complete than the change from idealistic blue denim to selfish blue pinstripes?

13   But if change is the underlying value, then we can expect this generation to change yet again. The next decade, the 40s, is the time for the mid-life crisis. The fruits of economic achievement will be cast into question. Once they are past the pressing demands of rearing families, many of the baby boomers may return to the ideals that inspired their earlier protests. Fifty-six percent of the [more than 3000] respondents [of a 1986 *Utne Reader* survey] say that the 1960s were "an unfinished experiment," 18 percent say they were a "high

point for America," and 57 percent agree that "the 1960s will rise again." Almost three-quarters of the respondents feel that "a whole new way of life is growing in the cracks of the old order."

14   If the readers of *Utne Reader* are any indication, the liberals of the 1960s haven't given up. They're just taking time out for love and work—Freud's two essential ingredients for happiness. We can expect the baby boom to emerge from its decade of achievement sometime during the 1990s. As we enter the next decade, we may experience a national mid-life crisis of wrenching proportions. Perhaps the new garb will be blue velvet. But we expect to find an idealism tempered with age, and a commitment to social justice that comes from deep inside these ragged individuals.

Understanding the Content

Feel free to reread all or parts of the selection to answer the following questions.

1. Define what is meant by *baby boomer*. Are you one of them?

2. According to the authors, the reasons the older generation of baby boomers gave for attending college are different from the younger generation's. What are they?

3. The authors state that as the baby boomers became teenagers, "they built the record companies and the sporting goods and beauty aids industries." (2) What do they mean?

4. How has the baby-boom generation changed family lifestyle from that of the 1950s? What has caused some of this change?

5. Circle the letter of the following statements from the selection which probably are facts:
   a. "Today, the boomers number about 78 million people, or one-third of the total U.S. population." (1)
   b. "Meanwhile, the number of divorces has tripled since 1960." (7)
   c. "In the 1950s, American society was easy to understand." (8)
   d. "Change, personal development, and self-actualization are core values for the baby-boom generation." (12)
   e. "Authors like Christopher Lasch and Richard Sennett see narcissism in this new individualism, but it's really just a stage of growth." (12)

6. The authors say that once the baby boomers are finished raising their families, they may return to the "ideals that inspired their earlier protests." (13) What are some of these ideals that the authors seem to feel were lost?

7. Can we infer that the authors are disappointed in the baby-boom generation?

8. Can we infer that the authors believe that the young conservative Republicans of today are using legislature to make social changes in the same way the liberal Democrats did in the 1930s and the 1960s?

Looking at Structure and Style

1. From what source(s) did the authors get most of their information?

2. How do paragraphs 4 and 5 work together?

3. Which paragraphs in the essay use illustration/example as a way to support the topic sentence in each?

4. Which paragraphs use comparison/contrast as a way to support the topic sentence in each?

5. Rewrite or explain the following passages from the reading selection, using your own words where possible:
   a. "When they were old enough to drive cars, they fueled a golden age in Detroit." (2)
   b. ". . . before prices skyrocketed." (5)
   c. "The net effect of this social explosion is fragmentation." (8)
   d. "Today's liberals support inner-directed, libertarian moral values. . . ." (9)
   e. "As their lot improved . . ." (10)
   f. ". . . the change from idealistic blue denim to selfish blue pinstripes . . ." (12)
   g. " 'A whole new way of life is growing in the cracks of the old order.' " (13)

6. What audience do you think the authors had in mind as they wrote this essay? Explain.

7. What do you think is the basic intent of the authors in writing this piece. Are they successful? Why?

8. Discuss your response to the authors' style. What do you like or dislike? What suggestions, if any, might you offer them for revision? Why?

Evaluating the Authors' Viewpoints

1. The authors state that "Political definitions seem to be blurring as moral values replace ideological values as a political force." (10) What do they mean? Do you agree or disagree? Why?

2. State in your own words what you think is the thesis of this essay and why you do or do not agree with it.

3. Reread the last three sentences in the last paragraph. The authors mention two possibilities for the 1990s, but they seem to believe more in one. What do they expect to happen? Why do you agree or disagree? Are there other possibilities you see that they don't mention?

4. For which would you rather use your college education: "to become well off financially" or "to gain a meaningful life philosophy"? Explain.

5. Regardless of your age, what characteristics of the baby boomers do you have? Are you content with your values?

Pursuing Possible Essay Topics

1. Discuss the changes in personal development you hope to make during the next ten years.

2. Make up and distribute a questionnaire that asks students on your campus why they are going to college, what they hope to gain from an education, what their goals are, and where they hope to be in ten years. You might want to ask their age and sex as well. Use this information to write an essay similar to the one you just read.

3. Paragraph 12 mentions two authors who write commentaries on contemporary social values and problems. Research their works in the library and write an essay that presents some of their beliefs and your reaction to them.

4. Using the card catalogue in your library, look under the terms *New Deal* or *Great Society*. If you or a friend have an American history book, look for those terms in the index. Do some reading on one or both. In an essay, define the term and explain the merit or lack of merit in one or both.

5. Based on the information in "What's a Baby Boomer?", write an essay on what you think people will be most interested in by the year 2000: making money, nuclear destruction, global peace, space exploration, education. . . .

6. Paragraph 11 mentions psychologist Daniel Levinson, who is quoted as saying that the 30s age bracket is "the decade of achievement." Discuss what this means and whether or not it is true.

7. Brainstorm or freewrite on one or more of the following:
   a. the "me" generation   d. the generation gap
   b. my future   e. the need for welfare
   c. the number one value   f. a meaningful life

8. Ignore all these and come up with your own idea on some aspect of changing social values.

Preparing to Read

Take a minute or two to look over the following reading selection. Note the title and author, read the opening paragraph, and check the length. Make certain you have the time now to read it carefully and to do the exercises that follow it. Then, in the spaces provided, answer the following questions.

1. How do you define the American dream? _____

   _____

   _____

2. Guess what you think will be the author's attitude about the American

   dream. _____

   _____

   _____

Vocabulary

Good comprehension of what you are about to read depends upon your understanding of the words below. The number following each word refers to the paragraph where it is used.

lament (1) an expression of sorrow, wailing

"a Harvard" (2) used in quotes here to refer to any college that has the same high status as Harvard University

preamble (5) an introduction that explains the purpose of the main document or event (In this case the part of the Constitution that begins with "We, the people . . .")

elegy (6) a sad, mournful poem, sometimes put to music

free lunch (6) something for nothing

siren song (7) In Greek mythology, sea nymphs known as sirens lured sailors to their destruction with their beautiful songs.

Pied Piper (7) a fairy-tale character who rid a town of its rats by playing a flutelike pipe. When the town refused to pay him he led away the children of the town with his music.

Now read the essay.

The American Dream

BETTY ANNE YOUNGLOVE

1   The lament for the death of the American dream grows ever louder. And although the verses may vary, the chorus is the same: The American dream is out of reach, unattainable.

2   Some of the verses I hear most often:

- Young families cannot afford a three-bedroom house in the suburbs because the prices or interest rates or taxes are too high.

- The average family cannot afford to send its sons and daughters to "a Harvard" because the cost is equivalent to the total family income before taxes; moreover, there is not enough money to send the kids to a prep school to insure they can get into "a Harvard" even if they can come up with the money.

- Why, oh why, can't the young people of today be guaranteed the dreams their parents had?

3   First, let us get this dream business—and business it now seems to be—straight. The word *dream* is not a synonym for *reality* or *promise*. It is closer to *hope* or *possibility* or even *vision*. The original American dream had only a little to do with material possessions and a lot to do with choices, beginnings and opportunity. Many of the original American dreamers wanted a new beginning, a place to choose what they wanted and a place to work for it. They did not see it as a guarantee of success but an opportunity to try.

4   The dream represented possibilities: Get your own land and clear it and work it; if nature cooperates, the work might pay off in material blessings. Or the dream represented the idea that any citizen with the minimum qualifications of age and years of citizenship could run for President even if he were born in a humble log cabin. He had no guarantee he would win, of course, no more than the man clearing his land was guaranteed a good crop.

5   The preamble to the Constitution does not promise happiness, only the right to pursue it.

6   This new elegy, however, seems to define the American dream as possessions and to declare that material things, power and money are our rights; we not only deserve them but maybe a free lunch as well.

7   Whatever verse we have been listening to in this new song about the dream, we should recognize it as nothing more than a siren song leading us with Pied Piper promises. Let's go back to the original idea—a tune we can whistle while we work to achieve the goal of our choice.

Understanding the Content

Feel free to reread all or parts of the essay to answer the following questions.

1. How does Younglove define the "original" American dream?

2. How does she define the contemporary view of the American dream?

3. Which version of the American dream does the author prefer?

4. Circle the letter of the following statements from the essay that are facts:
    a. "Young families cannot afford a three-bedroom house in the suburbs because the prices or interest rates or taxes are too high." (2)
    b. "The word *dream* is not a synonym for *reality* or *promise*." (3)
    c. "The preamble to the Constitution does not promise happiness, only the right to pursue it." (5)

5. Explain the meaning of the last sentence in the essay.

6. What is the author's intent in writing this essay?

7. Based on what Younglove says, what can we infer about her sense of values? What values does she oppose?

Looking at Structure and Style

1. How does paragraph 2 relate to paragraph 1?

2. What do paragraphs 2 and 4 have in common structurally?

3. What is the purpose of paragraph 3?

4. Rewrite the following passages from the essay using your own words where possible:
    a. "The lament for the death of the American dream grows ever louder." (1)
    b. "This new elegy, however, seems to define the American dream as possessions. . . ." (6)
    c. ". . . We not only deserve them [possessions, power, money] but maybe a free lunch as well." (6)
    d. ". . . nothing more than a siren song leading us with Pied Piper promises." (7)
    e. "Let's go back to the original idea—a tune we can whistle while we work to achieve the goal of our choice." (7)

6. The author uses music-related vocabulary frequently throughout her essay (*lament, verses, chorus, song, tune, whistle*). Why does she do this? Is it effective?

7. Discuss your response to the author's style. What do you like or dislike? What suggestions, if any, do you have for revision? Why?

Evaluating the Author's Viewpoints

1. In paragraph 3, Younglove defines her view of the American dream. Do you agree with her? Explain? How does her definition fit yours?

2. Do you agree with her interpretation of the preamble to the Constitution (paragraph 5)? Explain. (You may need to read or reread the preamble yourself to answer this.)

3. Does Younglove deny that the "verses" she most often hears lamenting the death of the American dream (paragraph 2) are not true situations for many families? Explain why she feels they have nothing to do with the American dream. Do you agree?

4. Do you or others you know feel "the American dream is out of reach, unattainable"? Explain.

Pursuing Possible Essay Topics

1. Define the American dream.

2. Provide illustrations/examples of the "original" American dream.

3. Using more concrete examples than Younglove does, compare/contrast the values behind the "original" American dream with the "new" one.

4. Discuss your personal American dream and the values it reflects.

5. Do some research on the term *American dream*. Find out how and where the term originated. See if there is enough information for an essay on it.

6. Using the information provided in the essay "What's a Baby Boomer?", write an essay that shows the values of the baby-boomer generation as fitting either the "original" or "new" definition of the American dream.

7. Brainstorm or freewrite on one or more of the following:
   a. the American dream
   b. work ethic
   c. responsible citizenship
   d. beginnings and opportunities
   e. the unattainable dream
   f. the right to happiness

8. Ignore these and come up with your own topic on some aspect of changing social values.

Preparing to Read

Take a minute or two to look over the following reading selection. Note the title and author, read the opening paragraph, and check the length. Make certain you have the time now to read it carefully and to do the exercises that follow it. Then, in the spaces provided, answer the following questions.

1. Judging by the title, what do you think will be the subject of the essay?

2. Why do you think the author opens his essay with the incident he describes? _____

_____

3. What connection do you make between the title and the opening paragraph? _____

_____

Vocabulary

Good comprehension of what you are about to read depends upon your understanding of the words below. The number following each word refers to the paragraph where it appears.

severing (title) cutting, removing from

sullen (1) gloomy, showing no humor

skulk (1) creep around, move sneakily

striped overalls . . . pocket (1) prisoner's uniform

John Dillinger (3) bank robber declared by the FBI as one of the ten most wanted criminals, shot to death in 1934

deadbeat (3) a person who doesn't pay his or her debts

Mace (4) an irritating aerosol spray used to ward off an attacker

12-gauges (4) shotguns

Armageddon (4) in the Bible, the place where the end of the world will occur in a battle between good and evil

impenetrable (4) not capable of being entered or penetrated

depleting (4) using up

surveillance devices (4) equipment, such as closed circuit TV cameras and electronic sensors, that observes your actions while shopping

gas chiselers (4) those who drive away without paying for their gasoline

incorrigibly (5) in the manner of one who cannot be corrected or changed

integrity (5) personal honesty

collective paranoia (5) society's developing fear that no one can be trusted and "everyone is out to get me"

.38 (6) pistol

habitable (7) suitable for living in

punitive (7) punishing

Now read the essay.

Severing the Human Connection

H. BRUCE MILLER

1   Went down to the local self-serve gas station the other morning to fill up. The sullen cashier was sitting inside a dark, glassed-in, burglar-proof, bullet-proof, probably grenade-proof cubicle covered with cheerful notices. "NO CHECKS." "NO CREDIT." "NO BILLS OVER $50 ACCEPTED." "CASHIER HAS NO SMALL CHANGE." And the biggest one of all: "PAY BEFORE PUMPING GAS." A gleaming steel box slid out of the wall and gaped open. I dropped in a $20 bill. "Going to fill 'er up with no-lead on Number 6," I said. The cashier nodded. The steel box swallowed my money and retracted into the cubicle. I walked back to the car to pump the gas, trying not to slink or skulk. I felt like I ought to be wearing striped overalls with a number on the breast pocket.

2   The pay-before-you-pump gas station (those in the trade call it a "pre-pay") is a response to a real problem in these days of expensive gas and cut-rate ethics: people who fill their tanks and then tear out of the station without paying. Those in the business call them "drive-offs." The head of one area gasoline dealers' association says drive-offs cost some dealers $500 to $600 a month. With a profit margin of only about a nickel a gallon, a dealer has to sell a lot of gallons to make up that kind of loss. The police aren't much help. Even if the attendant manages to get a license plate number and description of the car, the cops have better things to do than tracking down a guy who stole $15 worth of gas. So the dealers adopt the pre-pay system.

3   Intellectually, I understand all of this, yet I am angry and resentful. Emotionally I cannot accept the situation. I understand the dealers' position, I understand the cops' position. But I cannot understand why I should be made to feel like John Dillinger every time I buy a tank of gasoline. It's the same story everywhere. You go to a department store and try to pay for a $10.99 item with a check and you have to pull out a driver's license, two or three credit cards and a character reference from the pope—and then stand around for 15 minutes to get the manager's approval. Try to pay with a credit card and you have to wait while the cashier phones the central computer bank to make sure you're not a deadbeat or the Son of Sam or something. It's not that we don't trust you, they smile. It's just that we have to protect ourselves.

4   Right. We all have to protect ourselves these days. Little old ladies with attack dogs and Mace and 12-gauges, shopkeepers with closed-circuit TVs and electronic sensors to nab shoplifters, survivalists storing up ammo and dehydrated foods in hope of riding out Armageddon, gas station owners with pay-before-you-pump signs and impenetrable cashiers' cages—all protecting themselves. From what? From each other. It strikes me that we are expending so much time, energy and anguish on protecting ourselves that we are depleting our stock of mental and emotional capital for living. It also strikes me that the harder we try to protect ourselves, the less we succeed. With all the home burglar alarms and guard dogs and heavy armament, the crime rate keeps going up. With all the electronic surveillance devices, the shoplifters' take keeps climbing. The gas chiselers haven't figured out a way to beat the pre-pay system yet, but they will.

5   Is it that the people are simply incorrigibly dishonest, that the glue of integrity and mutual respect that holds society together is finally dissolving? I don't know, but I suspect that if something like this really is going on, our collective paranoia contributes to the process. People, after all, tend to behave pretty much the way other people expect them to behave. If the prevailing assumption of a society is that people are honest, by and large they will be honest. If the prevailing assumption is that people are crooks, more and more of them will be crooks.

6   What kind of message does a kid get from an environment where uniformed guards stand at the entrance of every store, where every piece of merchandise has an anti-shoplifting tag stapled to it, where every house has a burglar alarm and a .38, where the gas station cashiers huddle in glass cages and pass your change out through a metal chute? What can he conclude but that thievery and violence are normal, common, expected behaviors?

7   A society which assumes its members are honest is humane, comfortable, habitable. A society which treats everyone like a criminal becomes harsh, unfeeling, punitive, paranoid. The human connection is severed; fear of detection and punishment becomes the only deterrent to crime, and it's a very ineffective one. Somehow, sometime—I don't know when, but it was within my lifetime—we changed from the first type of society to the second. Maybe it's too late to go back again, but the road we are now on is a dark and descending one.

Understanding the Content

Feel free to reread all or parts of the selection to answer the following questions.

1. What does Miller mean by his title, "Severing the Human Connection"? How does it relate to his thesis?

2. What is a "pre-pay" and why, according to the author, were they started?

3. Circle the letters of the following statements from the essay that are facts:
   a. ". . . The cops have better things to do than tracking down a guy who stole $15 worth of gas." (2)
   b. "The gas chiselers haven't figured out a way to beat the pre-pay system yet, but they will." (4)
   c. People, after all, tend to behave pretty much the way other people expect them to behave." (5)
   d. "The head of one area gasoline dealers' association says drive-offs cost some dealers $500 to $600 a month." (2)
   e. "A society which assumes its members are honest is humane, comfortable, habitable." (7)

4. In paragraph 3, Miller mentions the Son of Sam. Even if you don't know to whom this refers, what conclusions can you draw about the character of the Son of Sam, based on the way he uses this reference?

5. Can we infer that the author feels our society was more honest and humane when he was younger than it is today?

6. Can we infer that Miller believes that the more we surround ourselves with devices to protect us from crime, the more young people will assume that crime is a common way of life?

7. Do you think Miller himself has become a member of "our collective paranoia"?

8. Does Miller conclude his essay with any hope for a better society?

Looking at Structure and Style

1. What experience caused Miller to think about the subject of his essay? How does he use that experience to help him begin his essay?

2. What other examples besides the pre-pay gas station does the author use to help support his viewpoint?

3. What is the image the author wants us to see in the last sentence of paragraph 1?

4. Rewrite or explain the following passages from the essay in your own words:
   a. "The steel box swallowed my money and retracted into the cubicle." (1)
   b. "It strikes me that we are expending so much time, energy and anguish on protecting ourselves that we are depleting our stock of mental and emotional capital for living." (4)
   c. ". . . The road we are now on is a dark and descending one." (7)
   d. ". . . survivalists storing up ammo and dehydrated foods in hope of riding out Armageddon . . ." (4)

5. Reread the opening paragraph. How would you describe Miller's tone? What particular words or phrases help establish this tone?

6. Is this essay mostly written from an objective or subjective viewpoint? Explain.

7. Discuss your response to Miller's writing style. What techniques does he use that you like or dislike? Do you have any suggestions to offer him for revision?

Pursuing Possible Essay Topics

1. Agree or disagree with Miller's statement in question 4b above.

2. Write an essay describing a time in your life when you were treated or made to feel like a criminal.

3. Write an essay that answers the opening question in paragraph 5.

4. Do some research in the library on crime statistics over the last few years to see if Miller's statement that "... crime keeps going up" is true. Use the statistics to support or refute Miller. You might begin your research by using the *Reader's Guide to Periodical Literature* or the card catalogue. Look for current publication dates.

5. Miller suggests that the effect of seemingly everyone protecting themselves with "attack dogs and Mace and 12-gauges ... closed-circuit TVs ... enclosed cashier cages ... burglar alarms ... and shoplifting tags in stores" is causing young people to get the message that thievery and violence are normal behaviors. Argue for or against his viewpoint.

6. Look through your local newspapers for some stories that show not the severing of the human connection, but a "linking of the human connection."

7. Brainstorm or freewrite on one or more of the following:
   - a. crime
   - b. "pay before you pump"
   - c. mutual respect
   - d. collective paranoia
   - e. honesty is the best policy
   - f. expected social behaviors

8. Ignore these and come up with your own topic on some aspect of changing social values.

📖 Preparing to Read

Take a minute or two to look over the following reading selection. Note the title and author, read the opening paragraph, and check the length. Make certain you have the time now to read it carefully and to do the exercises that follow it. Then, in the spaces provided, answer the following questions.

1. What do you think the essay will discuss? _____

_____

_____

2. Do you think there will be a difference between this author's viewpoint on society and Bruce Miller's in "Severing the Human Connection"? Explain.

_____

_____

Vocabulary

Good comprehension of what you are about to read depends upon your understanding of the words below. The number following each word refers to the paragraph where it is used.

consolation (2) comfort

metaphor (2) a figure of speech that uses words in an imaginative, non-literal way to suggest a comparison of two unlike things; for instance, "We refuse to believe that the bank of justice is bankrupt . . . that there are insufficient funds in the great vaults of opportunity of this nation." (Martin Luther King, Jr.)

Mantovani (2) musician and orchestra conductor known for "easy listening" or Muzak-type music

the private sector (9) private business as opposed to public, federal, or tax-supported services

Kafka (9) an Austrian novelist whose works generally show man caught up in a nightmarish tangle of government red tape

ordeal (15) a difficult, painful experience

renovated (15) restored, repaired to look like new

Now read the essay.

America Isn't Falling Apart

RICHARD REEVES

1   Like a jerk, I lost my wallet in midtown Manhattan last Tuesday. I had trouble sleeping thinking about Wednesday and the agony of

waiting in long lines to prove I existed by getting a new driver's license, bank card, credit cards and all the rest.

2   My only consolation was that I could write this column using the hassle and the long lines as a metaphor to show that nothing works anymore in America. I composed whole paragraphs in bed: the confusion in airports with passengers and planes stacked up everywhere; the lousy service in stores that no longer seem to have clerks; the 800 numbers that never answer; being put on hold and being bombarded by Mantovani and little commercials until the dial tone suddenly returns.

3   Wednesday finally dawned as one of the worst days of my life. After screaming at the baby and turning her over to her older sister, I left for the lines at 10:40 a.m. I was on East 86th Street, and my first stop was five miles south at American Express' main office on lower Broadway.

4   "Mr. Reeves? We've been expecting you," the receptionist said, mentioning that the computer showed I had reported my credit card missing the night before. "I am sorry, but it will take us another 10 minutes to get your new card ready."

5   That one was easy.

6   At the Chemical Bank branch around the corner, the assistant manager said: "Your branch is in Sag Harbor? That's almost a hundred miles away. You'd better fill out this form."

7   That took 30 seconds. Name, address, account number. "OK," he said with a smile. "You'll get a new card in the mail within 10 days."

8   "Yeah," I said, "but how do I get money without a card to put in the cash machine?" He approved my check right there and I walked out with $200.

9   But all that was the private sector. Now it was Kafka time: the Department of Motor Vehicles.

10   "New or renewal?" said the lady at the information desk near City Hall, another couple of miles deeper in Manhattan.

11   "Well, I lost my license . . ." I said.

12   "Renewal," she barked. "Fill out Form 44 and then go to the yellow chain."

13   In five minutes, I was facing a woman wearing a tag that said "L. Blocker." She looked at my form and said, "Six-fifty." I paid and she said, "Go to the back and they'll take your photograph."

14   The photo-taker said: "Smile. OK. This is your temporary license. It's good for 45 days. The permanent one should arrive by mail within 10 days. Have a nice day."

15   It was exactly 11:38 a.m. My ordeal had taken all of 58 minutes. I went across to the Municipal Building and took the Lexington Avenue Local subway back uptown. The train was unmarked and spot-

less, inside and out, painted in a new color called Harvard Crimson. In a telephone call to the Transit Authority, I learned that the cars were actually 25 years old, originally built in St. Louis, and just renovated—graffiti were cleaned off at the end of each run, three times a day. Part of a new "clean car" program.

16   I got back to my office after lunch. The first call was from my union—AFTRA (American Federation of Television and Radio Artists). A lady named Marta Wagner had found my wallet in Central Park, seen my union card and delivered everything to AFTRA headquarters. Nothing was missing.

17   America may be falling apart. But you couldn't tell it by me today.

Understanding the Content

Feel free to reread all or parts of the selection to answer the following questions.

1. Near the beginning of his essay, Reeves mentions several things that annoy him as well as most of us. What are some of them?

2. Why does the loss of his wallet make him so irritable?

3. What are some of the pleasant surprises he receives?

4. Why does the author keep referring to how much time everything took?

5. What can we infer from the fact that Reeves was so surprised that the subway train he rode was "unmarked and spotless"?

6. Can we infer where the author lives? What are the clues?

7. Explain the last paragraph.

Looking at Structure and Style

1. Contrast the author's attitude in the first three paragraphs with that in the last paragraph.

2. Why, in paragraph 3, does the author mention that he screamed at the baby?

3. What is the basic function of paragraph 9?

4. Compare the way Reeves describes his conversations with those in the private sector with those in the Department of Motor Vehicles.

5. What is the point of paragraph 15? What does it have to do with the loss of his wallet?

6. After going through the ordeal of replacing his lost credit cards and driver's license, Reeves has his wallet returned with nothing missing. Rather than being angry or irritated that he went through all that for nothing, he ends on a happy note. How does doing so make this essay

more than just a description of a frustrating experience about the loss of his wallet? What is the author's basic intent? How does the last sentence of paragraph 16 reflect his intent?

7. What is your reaction to the author's style? What do you like or dislike about it? What suggestions, if any, would you offer for revision? Why?

Evaluating the Author's Viewpoints

1. Do you agree or disagree with Reeves's title statement? Explain.

2. Paragraph 2 contains several "gripes," or things that irritate the author. Have any of them ever happened to you? If so, how do you respond when you experience them?

3. Compare Reeves's attitude about society with Miller's attitude in "Severing the Human Connection." Which attitude do you mostly share?

Pursuing Possible Essay Topics

1. Write an essay using the title "America *Is* Falling Apart," in which you give examples that reflect the title.

2. Write about a time when you had to replace a lost credit card or driver's license. What were your experiences?

3. Discuss the pros and cons of using automated bank teller machines.

4. Reread paragraph 2. Pick one of the "irritants" mentioned and write about your experience with one of them.

5. Brainstorm or freewrite on one or more of the following:
   a. the human connection
   b. credit cards
   c. subway experiences
   d. pet peeves
   e. the need for identification
   f. being "just a number"

6. Ignore these and come up with your own topic on some aspect of changing social values.

Student Essay

Students were asked to write an essay on some aspect of changing social values that used and documented information from other sources but still contained their own thesis. They were cautioned not to write a report on what they read, but to use what information they found in their sources as a way of arguing for or against their own views on the subject. As you read the following student essay, look for answers to these questions:

1. Does the essay follow the assignment?

2. Does the student have a thesis? If so, what is it?

3. Is the source material used to support a thesis?

4. Is the documentation correctly done? (See "Documentation" in the Appendix.)

Has the Nation Lost Its Way?

Steve Brodie

1   Recently, the U.S. News and World Report* revealed the results of a survey done by them on the state of American values. In gathering their information, the magazine staff questioned experts in social behavior and a wide cross section of people around the country. One of the survey findings shows that the questions of morality are troubling ordinary people. Philosopher William Prior from the University of Colorado is quoted as saying, "Morality is more popular because of the attention the national media have given to such issues as abortion, euthanasia and the right of the elderly to health care. Things of that sort have caused the society to focus on ethics in a way people didn't 20 years ago. Ethics is very much in the public eye." And Michael Novak, a specialist in religion and public policy at the American Enterprise Institute, believes that today's problems date back to the 1930s. He states, "Many millions of American parents, born poor during the Depression, didn't know how to bring up their children during conditions of affluence. We knew how to bring them up under conditions of poverty because that's how we were brought up. But we didn't know what to do with affluence. As a result, the whole nation made many serious mistakes, and the whole nation has lost its way."

2   Whether or not the nation "has lost its way" is debatable, but it is interesting to note some of the changing moral positions on certain issues that are revealed in the U.S. News & World Report survey.

---

* All information and quotations were taken from Susanna McBee's "The State of American Values," U.S. News & World Report, December 9, 1985, pp. 54–58.

3   One of the most notable changes is with religious leaders themselves. Where once they spoke only to their congregations from the pulpit, today Catholic bishops, rabbis, and leaders of all religious denominations are growing more and more vocal publicly. Many have become activists against the nuclear-arms race and our involvement in Central America. The Christian Right speaks out strongly against homosexuality, abortion, and pornography forcing these issues into political debates. Dartmouth theologian Robert Brown believes that those persons grappling with such moral issues are "developing a much stiffer spine. Here and there, you see marvelous instances of personal integrity, of people standing up, taking risks."

4   Abortion is a major ethical and legal problem for Americans. Before 1973, abortion was illegal in most states. Today, it is legal in most states and widely practiced. Still, the issue of legal abortion is under strong attack by pro-life groups. Feelings run so high on the subject that several abortion clinics are constantly under harrassment, and several have been bombed.

5   When asked during the survey about the subject of adultery, the majority of people believe it to be wrong. But attitudes and behavior regarding adultery don't seem to fit. According to other studies done in the 1950s and 1960s, women were less likely to have extramarital affairs than men. But a recent Yale University study done for Psychology Today showed that 45 percent of women polled said they had cheated on their husbands or longtime lovers.

6   No one knows for certain whether or not people lie more than in the past; some think we do. Alexander Astin of UCLA reports that in his annual surveys of some 250,000 college freshman that young people are "less concerned with altruism, with helping society, and more concerned with making money and getting power status than they were in the past. When you put these ahead of everything else, it becomes easier to rationalize lying or cheating in pursuit of your goals."

7   Seymour Lipset, a sociologist at Stanford University, told U.S. News & World Report, "Everybody lies. But the question is, to

what extent do you consciously deceive others? Do you exaggerate to impress a girl or a guy? Do you fudge on your curriculum vitae to impress an employer? Do you twist the truth to succeed in your job?" In her book <u>Lying</u>, Sissela Bok claims that many people excuse dishonesty because "it does not matter whether or not we lie when we have a good reason for doing so."

8 Americans are obviously changing their minds on certain moral issues. At one time the drinking of alcohol was prohibited; today "nearly two-thirds of Americans drink at least occasionally," according to the survey. Gambling used to be fairly restricted to Nevada; now it is legal in Atlantic City with other cities thinking about it. Twenty-two states and the District of Columbia have lotteries, and more and more churches and charities use bingo as a way to raise money.

9 Despite these changes and confusion in social values, some critics find hope in the mere fact that morality is now a topic of concern. Though there are problems, there are also social programs that have benefited minorities, the poor, and the elderly from the debates. As Joseph Lee, an associate minister of the Chinese Presbyterian Church says, "Every time you think the place is falling apart, you see signs that people are concerned, that they still have their humanness. There is a greater acceptance of diversity and somewhere in that acceptance, morality comes in."

10 But the <u>U.S. News & World Report</u> article concludes:

> Where individuals should be cautious, warn social scientists and theologians, is in forcing their standards upon others. In the words of the Rev. McKinley Young of Big Bethal AME Church in Atlanta: "When you find somebody waving all those flags and banners, watch closely. Morality, if you're not careful, carries a sense of self-righteousness. Whenever you pat yourself on the back, it creates all kinds of cramps."

Reaction

In the space provided, write your reaction to the student's essay. What would you tell him about his essay?

Commentary

Steve says that he was having trouble coming up with a topic for an essay on changing social values. Then he happened to be waiting in a dentist's office, flipping through a copy of *U.S. News & World Report* when he noticed the article on American values. Since he had to use source material for his own essay, he asked if he could take the magazine home. As you can see from what you just read, it became the basic source for Steve's essay.

Normally, we don't recommend that you go to a dentist's office for your research material. In Steve's case, the article served as a useful beginning; but rather than use it as a guide to more sources, he limited his research to just one magazine article. Had Steve gone to the library and looked in the *Reader's Guide to Periodical Literature* under such headings as "values," "morality," or "ethics," he would have found not only the *U.S. News & World Report* article listed but other recent publications on the subject. Had he gone further and used the library card catalogue and looked under the same headings, he might have found listings for books and pamphlets on the topic. Steve even mentions two other sources in his own essay that he failed to check on: the *Psychology Today* survey and Sissela Bok's book, *Lying.* Part of Steve's problem, then, is that he limited his use of outside sources.

A major problem here is that Steve tries to cover too many issues. In attempting to say much, Steve says little about any of the subjects mentioned. He should have used the article from *U.S. News & World Report* merely as a starting point to pursue any one of the subjects the survey deals with: the change occurring in religious leaders, the ever-changing opinions on abortion, the conflict between opinions on adultery and people's actual behavior, the growing acceptance of lying, and so on. Steve's coverage is too broad. He needs to narrow his coverage to one issue on changing social values, such as lying, and then provide us with his viewpoints on the issue. Then, whatever sources he found on that issue could be used to support his thesis.

Another problem is that Steve doesn't have a thesis. The closest he comes to having one is in his second paragraph: "Whether or not the nation 'has lost its way' is debatable, but it is interesting to note some of the changing moral positions on certain issues that are revealed in the *U. S. News & World Report* survey." In fact, all Steve really does in his essay is to summarize what the article says about "changing moral positions on certain issues." He provides a paragraph each on religious leaders speaking out more publicly on moral issues, abortion as a major ethical problem, opinions and behavior regarding adultery, lying, and drinking and gambling.

On none of these issues does Steve let us know what he thinks, what his viewpoints are. We have no idea what Steve thinks about religious leaders speaking out, about abortion, about adultery, about lying, about drinking, or about gambling. For an essay he needs a thesis that starts with a statement as basic as, "I think religious leaders should stay out of political debates" or "I think those who are bombing abortion clinics are worse than those they are condemning" or whatever he truly believes. The fact that Steve does not take any position of his own puts this writing effort more in the category of a report than an essay. Notice, too, that he never answers the question in his title.

A final problem is Steve's incorrect documentation. See the "Documentation" section in the Appendix for the correct form.

Despite these problems, Steve shows some good writing techniques. His opening paragraph immediately lets his readers know his source and where his source got the survey information. The two quotes he uses in the introductory paragraph are good ones because they deal with the topic assigned—changing social values. The second quote is especially useful because it leads into Steve's second paragraph and uses the phrase from the quote ". . . has lost its way."

Steve lets his readers know that he will not say whether the nation has lost its way, but that it "is interesting to note . . . some of the changing moral values" reported in the magazine. If Steve had been writing a report rather than an essay, this would have been a good opening paragraph.

In paragraphs 3, 4 and 5, we can see the use of comparison/contrast. His use of transitional words and phrases such as "once" and "today," "before" and "today," and "but . . ." helps us follow the changes taking place.

Steve ends his paper with an interesting quote. This method for ending an essay is often useful. But because Steve has no thesis, the quote doesn't seem to support anything he himself has said. Quotations should only be used when you want to argue the author's point or when they lend support to your own viewpoints.

The essay was returned to Steve for revision based on these comments.

iewpoints on

Family and Relationships

*"Treat people as if they were what they ought to be
and you help them become what they are capable of being."*
Johann Goethe

*A*MERICA is made up of family groups of many diverse cultures: the Asian-American family, the Hispanic family, the black family, the European family, the Middle Eastern family, and so on. Still, despite this wide range of backgrounds, some recent research* suggests there are six major qualities shared by healthy families of all races:

1. a high degree of commitment to the family group and to promoting each other's happiness and welfare
2. an appreciation of one another; making each other feel good about himself or herself
3. good communication patterns developed through spending time talking with and listening to each other
4. a desire to spend time together in active interaction
5. a strong value system, such as that found in religious orientation
6. an ability to deal with crises and stress in a positive manner

Few families can live up to these ideals all of the time. Just as an individual must work to keep mentally and physically fit, so must family members work to keep the family mentally and physically fit. Like individuals, even strong families have problems. Sometimes families break up. And just as there are no perfect parents, there are no perfect children. But we have the option of changing our imperfect

---

* N. Stinnet and J. DeFrain, *Secrets of Strong Families* (Boston: Little, Brown, 1985).

family relationships by working to develop those six characteristics of a strong family.

The subject of family and relationships is one we all share no matter what our backgrounds. The following essays reveal some varied viewpoints on this broad subject, covering such aspects as romantic love, "house-fathering," gender differences, mother love, and the effects family breakups can have. Read them to understand how others feel about family and relationships, as well as to stimulate ideas for an essay of your own.

Preparing to Read

Take a minute or two to look over the following reading selection. Note the title and author, read the opening paragraph, and check the length. Make certain you have the time now to read it carefully and to do the exercises that follow it. Then, in the spaces provided, answer the following questions.

1. What do you think this selection will have to say about romantic love?

   _____

   _____

2. How do you define romantic love? _____

   _____

   _____

3. What might you learn from reading this selection? _____

   _____

Vocabulary

Good comprehension of what you are about to read depends upon your understanding of the words below. The number following each word refers to the paragraph where it is used.

intimacy (1) closeness or familiarity with someone

encompasses (1) includes, covers

idealized (1) considered perfect

marital (2) relating to marriage

repress (3) hold back

emerge (4) come out

premarital (4) occurring before marriage

pithy (5) precise, to the point

rose-colored glasses (7) overly optimistic view

Now read the essay.

Romantic Love

FRANK D. COX

1   For many Americans the idea of *romantic love* most influences their thoughts about attraction and intimacy. This concept of love encompasses such ideas as "love at first sight," "the one and only love," "lifelong commitment," "I can't live without him/her," "the perfect mate," and so forth.

2   In essence the concept of romantic love supplies a set of idealized images by which we can judge the object of our love as well as the quality of the relationship. Unfortunately, such romanticized images usually bear little relationship to the real world. Often we project our beliefs onto another person, exaggerating the characteristics that match the qualities we are looking for and masking those that do not. That is, we transform the other person into an unreal hero or heroine to fit our personal concept of a romantic marital partner. Thus we often fall in love with our own romantic ideas rather than with a real human being.

3   For example, the traditional romantic ideals dictate a strong, confident, protective role for a man and a charming, loving, dependent role for a woman. A woman accepting this stereotype will tend to overlook and deny dependent needs of her mate. She will tend to repress independent qualities in herself. Love for her means each correctly fulfilling the proper role. The same holds true for a man who has traditional romantic ideals.

4   Those who "fall in love with love" in this way will suffer disappointment when their partner's "real person" begins to emerge. Rather than meet this emerging person with joy and enthusiasm, partners who hold romanticized ideals may reject reality in favor of their stereotypical images. They may begin to search again for a love object, rejecting the real-life partner as unworthy or changed. Dating and broad premarital experience with the opposite sex can help correct much of this romantic idealism.

5   When people fall in love with their romanticized expectations rather than with their partner, they may either reject the partner or attempt to change the partner into the romantic ideal. John Robert Clark has a pithy description of the first action:

> In learning how to love a plain human being today, as during the romantic movement, what we usually want unconsciously is a fancy human being with no flaws. When the mental picture we have of someone we love is colored by wishes of childhood, we may love the picture rather than the real person behind it. Naturally, we are disappointed in the person we love if he does not conform to our picture. Since this kind of disappointment has no doubt happened to us before, one might suppose we would tear up the picture and start all over. On the contrary, we keep the picture and tear up the person. Small wonder that divorce courts are full of couples who never gave themselves a chance to know the real person behind the pictures in their lives.[1]

6   The second action, attempting to change one's spouse, also leads to trouble. Making changes is difficult, and the person being asked to do so may resent the demand or may not wish to change.

7   Generally, romantic love's rose-colored glasses tend to distort the real world, especially the mate, thereby creating a barrier to happiness. This is not to deny that romantic love can add to an intimate relationship. Romance will bring excitement, emotional highs, and color to one's relationship. From there one can move toward a more mature love relationship. As emotional, intellectual, social, and physical intimacy develops romance takes its place as one of several aspects of the relationship, not the only one.

---

[1] John Robert Clark, *The Importance of Being Imperfect.* (New York: McKay, 1961), p. 18.

Understanding the Content

Feel free to reread all or parts of the reading selection to answer the following questions.

1. How is the "traditional romantic ideal" defined? According to Cox, what is wrong with this ideal?

2. When people fall in love with their romanticized expectations rather than with their partner, what two actions commonly occur?

3. Should romantic love be totally discounted? Explain.

4. What other aspects of a relationship are mentioned besides the romantic one?

5. Is there a stated thesis? If so, where?

Looking at Structure and Style

1. What point is served by using all the phrases in quotation marks in paragraph 1?

2. What is the function of paragraph 3? How does it connect with paragraph 2?

3. Notice the long "block" quotation in paragraph 5. Why does the author use this quote? How does it help support his own views?

4. How well does the last paragraph work? Is it mostly a summary or does it draw a conclusion?

Evaluating the Author's Viewpoints

1. Cox says that romantic love "supplies a set of idealized images by which we can judge the object of our love as well as the quality of the relationship." (2) What does he mean? Do you agree? Why?

2. Do you agree with the definition of "the traditional romantic ideal" as defined in paragraph 3? Explain.

3. Cox uses the phrase "fall in love with love." What does it mean?

4. What is meant by the statement in paragraph 5, "We keep the picture and tear up the person." Do you think this is a valid reason some people divorce? Explain.

5. Based on the last paragraph, put together a definition of a good relationship as Cox might define it.

Pursuing Possible Essay Topics

1. Brainstorm or freewrite on one or more of the following:

   a. romance
   b. intimacy
   c. seeing life through
      rose-colored glasses

   d. the perfect mate
   e. marriage partners
   f. relationships

2. Write an essay that defines one of the following: true love, the ideal relationship, the perfect spouse, puppy love, brotherly love, maternal love.

3. Write about a time when you discovered that the someone you loved was not who you thought.

4. Explain where you think we get our concepts of romantic love: television? movies? advertisements? books? Are such concepts healthy? How do they affect real relationships?

5. Find a magazine or newspaper advertisement that portrays the concept of romantic love and write an essay that describes and evaluates it. What does the ad imply?

6. Write about a relationship that caused an "emotional high" you'll never forget.

7. In his book *The Art of Loving*, Eric Fromm states that the four basic elements necessary to any mature, intimate relationship are care, responsibility, respect, and knowledge. Defend or refute Fromm in an essay of your own.

8. You don't love any of these ideas? Ignore them and find a topic of your own that deals with some aspect of family and/or relationships.

Preparing to Read

Take a minute or two to look over the following reading selection. Note the title and author, read the first *four* paragraphs, and check the length. Make certain you have the time now to read it carefully and to do the exercises that follow it. Then, in the spaces provided, answer the following questions.

1. What do you think the essay is about? _____

   _____

2. How do you feel about fathers who stay home to watch the children

   while the mothers work? Why? _____

   _____

   _____

Vocabulary

Good comprehension of what you are about to read depends upon your understanding of the words below. The number following each word refers to the paragraph where it is used.

euphemism (4) a term used to replace one that might offend or upset someone (for example, *passed away* instead of *kicked the bucket* or *died*)

rhapsodized (4) expressed in an overly enthusiastic way

interminably (5) endlessly

ambivalent (7) having two conflicting feelings at the same time

treadmill (7) metaphor for a monotonous routine

lethargy (8) passiveness, indifference

taboo (9) something prohibited by social custom

mitigated (10) made less intense

therapeutic (11) having healing powers

chronic (11) constant, lingering

subside (11) lessen, decrease

obnoxious (11) highly disagreeable or offensive

heresy (11) a controversial, almost unacceptable opinion

benchmark (12) a standard by which others can be compared

typified (14) were typical examples of

proxy (14) authorization for another person to act on one's behalf

incredulously (17) disbelievingly

violated (18) broke (a law, for example), didn't follow

succumbing (18) yielding, giving in to

claustrophobics (22) people afraid of being in confined spaces

idyll (23) a carefree experience

apprehension (25) dread

tangible (25) real, concrete, touchable

contingent (26) a representative group

mundane (28) ordinary, common

anathema (28) something or someone shunned or avoided

resurrecting (28) bringing back to life, bringing back into practice

shtick (30) entertainment routine

Now read the essay.

Escaping the Daily Grind for Life as a House Father

RICK GREENBERG

1   "You on vacation?" my neighbor asked.

2   My 15-month-old son and I were passing her yard on our daily hike through the neighborhood. It was a weekday afternoon and I was the only working-age male in sight.

3   "I'm uh . . . working out of my house now," I told her.

4   Thus was born my favorite euphemism for house fatherhood, one of those new life-style occupations that is never merely mentioned. Explained, yes. Defended. Even rhapsodized about. I was tongue-tied then, but no longer. People are curious and I've learned to oblige.

5   I joined up earlier this year when I quit my job—a dead-end, ulcer-producing affair that had dragged on interminably. I left to be with my son until something better came along. And if nothing did, I'd be with him indefinitely.

6   This was no simple transition. I had never known a house father, never met one. I'd only read about them. They were another news magazine trend. Being a traditionalist, I never dreamed I'd take the plunge.

7   But as the job got worse, I gave it serious thought. And more thought. And in the end, I still felt ambivalent. This was a radical change that seemed to carry as many drawbacks as benefits. My dislike for work finally pushed me over the edge. That, and the fact that we had enough money to get by.

8   Escaping the treadmill was a bold stroke. I had shattered my lethargy and stopped whining, and for that I was proud.

9   Some friends said they were envious. Of course they weren't quitting one job without one waiting—the ultimate in middle-class taboos. That ran through my mind as I triumphantly, and without notice, tossed the letter of resignation on my boss' desk. Then I walked away wobbly-kneed.

10   The initial trauma of quitting, however, was mitigated by my eagerness to raise our son. Mine was the classic father's lament. I felt excluded. I had become "the man who got home after dark," that other person besides Mama. It hurt when I couldn't quiet his crying.

11   I sensed that staying home would be therapeutic. The chronic competitiveness and aggressiveness that had served me well as a daily journalist would subside. Something better would emerge, something less obnoxious. My ulcer would heal. Instead of beating deadlines, I'd be doing something important for a change. This was heresy coming from a newspaper gypsy, but it rang true.

12   There was unease, too. I'd be adrift, stripped of the home-office-home routine that had defined my existence for more than a decade. No more earning a living. No benchmarks. Time would be seamless. Would Friday afternoons feel the same?

13   The newness of it was scary.

14   Until my resignation, my wife and I typified today's baby-boomer couples, the want-it-all generation. We had two salaries, a full-time nanny and guilt pangs over practicing parenthood by proxy.

15   Now, my wife brings home the paychecks, the office problems and thanks for good work on the domestic front. With me at home,

her work hours are more flexible. Nanny-less, I change diapers, prepare meals and do all the rest. And I wonder what comes next.

16   What if I don't find another job? My field is tight. At 34, I'm not getting any more marketable and being out of work doesn't help.

17   As my father asked incredulously: "Is this going to be what you do?"

18   Perhaps. I don't know. I wonder myself. It's even more baffling to my father, the veteran of a long and traditional 9-to-5 career. For most of it, my mother stayed home. My father doesn't believe in trends. All he knows is that his only son—with whom he shares so many traits—has violated the natural order of men providing and women raising children. In his view, I've shown weakness and immaturity by succumbing to a bad job.

19   But he's trying to understand, and I think he will.

20   I'm trying to understand it myself. House fatherhood has been humbling, rewarding and unnerving.

21   "It's different," I tell friends. "Different."

22   Imagine never having to leave home for the office in the morning. That's how different. No dress-up, no commute. Just tumble out of bed and you're there. House fathering is not for claustrophobics.

23   I find myself enjoying early morning shopping. My son and I arrive right after the supermarket opens. The place is almost empty. For the next hour we glide dreamily, cruising the aisles to a Muzak accompaniment. This is my idyll. My son likes it, too; he's fascinated by the spectacle.

24   Housekeeping still doesn't seem like work, and that's by design. I've mastered the art of doing just enough chores to get by. This leaves me enough free time. Time to read and write and daydream. Time with my son. Time to think about the structure.

25   So much time, and so little traditional structure, that the days sometimes blur together. I remember on Sunday nights literally dreading the approaching work week, the grind. Today, the close of the weekend still triggers a shiver of apprehension; I now face the prospect of a week without tangible accomplishments, a void.

26   On our hikes to the playground, I can feel my old identity fading. All around are people with a mission, a sense of purpose. Workers. And then there's the rest of us—the stroller and backpack contingent. The moms, the nannies, and me. I wonder if I've crossed over a line never to return.

27   Still, the ulcer seems to be healing. I take pride in laying out a good dinner for the family and in pampering my wife after a tough day at the office. I love reading to my son. Running errands isn't even so bad. A lot of what had been drudgery or trivia is taking on new meaning; maybe I'm mellowing.

28   Which is ironic. To be a truly committed and effective at-home parent, there must be this change—a softening, a contentment with small pleasures, the outwardly mundane. This is a time of reduced demands and lowered expectations. Progress is gradual, often agonizingly so. Patience is essential. Ambition and competitiveness are anathema. Yet eliminating these last two qualities—losing the edge— could ruin my chances of resurrecting my career. I can't have it both ways.

29   The conflict has yet to be resolved. And it won't be unless I make a firm commitment and choose one life style over the other. I'm not yet ready for that decision.

30   In the meantime, a wonderful change is taking place in our home. Amid all the uncertainties, my son and I have gotten to know each other. He can't put a phrase together, but he confides in me. It can be nothing more than a grin or a devilish look. He tries new words on me, new shtick. We roll around a lot; we crack each other up. I'm no longer the third wheel, the man who gets home after dark. Now, I'm as much a part of his life as his mother is. I, too, can stop his crying. So far, that has made the experiment worthwhile.

Understanding the Content

Feel free to reread all or parts of the selection to answer the following questions.

1. What was Greenberg's job before he quit? What reasons does Greenberg give for quitting?

2. What are some of the things Greenberg mentions that were difficult to get used to as a house father? What advantages to his new role does he mention?

3. Being a traditionalist, how difficult was it for Greenberg's father to accept his son's new "job"? Why?

4. What does Greenberg believe a truly committed and effective at-home parent must be?

5. How would you describe Greenberg's attitude about being a house father?

6. What is Greenberg's thesis? Is it implied or stated?

Looking at Structure and Style

1. What function do paragraphs 1–4 serve?

2. What is the purpose of the first sentence in paragraph 6?

3. Why do paragraphs 7–9 work well in that order? What do they reveal about the author himself?

4. How do paragraphs 10 and 11 contrast with paragraphs 7–9?

5. Explain or rewrite the following passages from the essay:
   a. "I was tongue-tied then. . . ." (4)
   b. "Escaping the treadmill was a bold stroke." (8)
   c. "Time would be seamless." (12)
   d. "I'm not getting any more marketable. . . ." (16)
   e. "And then there's the rest of us—the stroller and backpack contingent." (26)

Evaluating the Author's Viewpoints

1. In paragraph 22, Greenberg says, "House fathering is not for claustrophobics." What does he mean? Do you agree?

2. Reread paragraph 28. Do you agree with his statement about what it takes to be an effective at-home parent? What does Greenberg mean when he says he can't have it both ways?

3. The author ends his essay by saying that what he has done so far has been worthwhile. Do you infer otherwise? Explain.

4. Do you think Greenberg will remain a house father? Why?

Pursuing Possible Essay Topics

1. Write an essay that tries to convince Greenberg to go back to work. Be sure to give counterarguments for some of his own.

2. Write an essay that supports the role of house father. Direct your arguments to those who feel as Greenberg's traditionalist father does.

3. Interview some older people to discover what a "traditional" family lifestyle was like forty years ago. Compare it to today's.

4. Talk to some recent immigrants to this country to discover what their traditional family lifestyle was like before and after coming to this country. How much, if any, has it changed?

5. Since many families now require both parents to work for economic reasons, what effect is that going to have on the way children of these families perceive family life, particularly parenting? Show how being a parent today is different from your grandparents' day.

6. What are some other things occurring in our society that are changing the traditional family unit as many people have known it? Write an essay on the forces in society that are changing the family unit.

7. Brainstorm or freewrite on one or more of the following:

a. family life
b. family traditions
c. the changing family

d. single parenting
e. house fathers
f. working mothers

8. Ignore these and come up with an idea of your own that deals with some aspect of family relationships.

Preparing to Read

Take a minute or two to look over the following reading selection. Note the title and author, read the first paragraph, and check the length. Make certain you have the time now to read it carefully and to do the exercises that follow it. Then, in the spaces provided, answer the following questions.

1. What do you think the title means? _____

_____

2. What do you think will be the subject of this selection? _____

_____

3. What do you expect to learn from this reading? _____

_____

_____

Vocabulary

Good comprehension of what you are about to read depends upon your understanding of the words below. The number following each word refers to the paragraph where it is used.

innate (1) possessed at birth, inborn

submission (1) the act of giving in (in this case, to men)

earnest (1) sincere and serious

unwittingly (1) unknowingly

saw (1) a familiar, often overused saying or phrase (Here she is referring to "Sugar and spice and everything nice/That's what little girls are made of. . . .")

the Celtics (6) the Boston basketball team

dissolution (1) disintegration

capsulize (7)n condense, summarize

Larry Bird (7) the star team member of the Celtics

Lucy and Ethel (7) gossipy housewives from the 1950s' television show "I Love Lucy"

muse (8) ponder, think about, consider

broached (8) brought up as a subject to discuss

quantum mechanics (10) a theory in physics that deals with small, indivisible units of energy

Now read the essay.

His Talk, Her Talk

JOYCE MAYNARD

1   It can be risky these days to suggest that there are any innate differences between men and women, other than those of anatomy. Out the window go the old notions about man and aggression, woman and submission (don't even say the word), man and intellect, woman and instinct. If I observe that my infant son prefers pushing a block along the floor while making car noises to cradling a doll in his arms and singing lullabies (and he does)—well, I can only conclude that, despite all our earnest attempts at nonsexist child-rearing, he has already suffered environmental contamination. Some of it, no doubt unwittingly, came from my husband and me, reared in the days when nobody winced if you recited that old saw about what little girls and boys are made of.

2   I do not believe, of course, that men are smarter, steadier, more high-minded than women. But one or two notions are harder to shake—such as the idea that there is such a thing as "men's talk" or "women's talk." And that it's a natural instinct to seek out, on occasion, the company of one's own sex, exclude members of the other sex and not feel guilty about it.

3   Oh, but we do. At a party I attended the other night, for instance, it suddenly became apparent that all the women were in one room and all the men were in the other. Immediately we redistributed ourselves, which was a shame. No one had suggested we segregate. The talk in the kitchen was simply, all the women felt, more interesting.

4   What was going on in the kitchen was a particular sort of conversation that I love and that most men I know would wash and wax

the car, change the oil filter and vacuum the upholstery to avoid. There is a way women talk with other women, and, I gather, a way that men talk when in the company of other men. They are not at all the same.

5   I think I know my husband very well, but I have no idea what goes on when he and his male friends get together. Neither can he picture what can keep a woman friend and me occupied for three hours over a single pot of coffee.

6   The other day, after a long day of work, my husband, Steve, and his friend Dave stopped at a bar for a few beers. When he got home, I asked what they had talked about. "Oh, the usual." Like what? "Firewood. Central America. Trucks. The Celtics. Religion. You know."

7   No, not really. I had only recently met with my friend Ann and her friend Sally at a coffee shop nearby, and what we talked about was the workshop Sally would be holding that weekend concerning women's attitudes toward their bodies, Ann's 11-year-old daughter's upcoming slumber party, how hard it is to buy jeans, and the recent dissolution of a friend's five-year marriage. Asked to capsulize our afternoon's discussion, in a form similar to my husband's outline of his night out, I would say we talked about life, love, happiness and heartbreak. Larry Bird's name never came up.

8   I don't want to reinforce old stereotypes of bubble-headed women (Lucy and Ethel), clinking their coffee cups over talk of clothes and diets while the men remove themselves to lean on mantels, puff on cigars and muse about world politics, machines and philosophy. A group of women talking, it seems to me, is likely to concern itself with matters just as pressing as those broached by my husband and his friends. It might be said, in fact, that we're really talking about the same eternal conflicts. Our styles are just different.

9   When Steve tells a story, the point is, as a rule, the ending, and getting there by the most direct route. It may be a good story, told with beautiful precision, but he tells it the way he eats a banana: in three efficient chews, while I cut mine up and savor it. He can (although this is rare) spend 20 minutes on the telephone with one of his brothers, tantalizing me with occasional exclamations of amazement or shock, and then after hanging up, reduce the whole conversation for me to a one-sentence summary. I, on the other hand, may take three quarters of an hour describing some figure from my past while he waits—with thinly veiled impatience—for the point to emerge. Did this fellow just get elected to the House of Representatives? Did he die and leave me his fortune?

10   In fairness to Steve, I must say that, for him, not talking about something doesn't necessarily mean not dealing with it. And he does

listen to what I have to say. He likes a good story, too. It's just that, given a choice, he'd rather hear about quantum mechanics or the history of the Ford Mustang. Better yet, he'd rather play ball.

Understanding the Content

Feel free to reread all or parts of the selection to answer the following questions.

1. What are some examples Maynard gives of what she calls "his talk"?
2. What examples does she give of "her talk"?
3. What is the difference between the way Maynard tells a story and the way her husband Steve tells it? What does this have to do with her thesis?
4. What is the thesis? Is it implied or stated? If stated, where does it appear?
5. Is Maynard defensive or biased about her subject? Explain.

Looking at Structure and Style

1. What is the point of paragraph 1? Why, for instance, does she use the words "risky" and "don't even say the word" in the first sentence? What function does the information about her son's preference for cars to dolls serve in that paragraph?
2. Maynard uses an anecdote in paragraphs 3 and 4. What viewpoint does the anecdote support?
3. What viewpoint of Maynard's do paragraphs 6 and 7 support?
4. Paragraph 9 draws an analogy between the way her husband eats a banana and the way she does. What does the eating of the banana metaphorically symbolize?
5. To whom is Maynard referring in paragraph 8 and "old stereotypes of bubble-headed women"? How does she use this example to help make her position on her topic clear?
6. To what audience do you think Maynard is writing? Why?

Evaluating the Author's Viewpoints

1. In paragraph 1, the author says, "It can be risky these days to suggest that there are any innate differences between men and women." Do you agree? Why?
2. Do you agree with Maynard's thesis? Explain.
3. Are the author's examples of "his talk" and "her talk" correct as far as you are concerned? Why do you say so?

4. Is it "a natural instinct" to seek out members of one's own sex to talk to on occasion? Is it being sexist to do so? Why?

5. If you look beyond the literal level of the essay, what might you infer about Maynard's views regarding sexism these days?

Pursuing Possible Essay Topics

1. Become Maynard's husband Steve. Write an essay called "Her Talk, His Talk" from his viewpoint.

2. Select another characteristic that you think is different in men and women and write an essay that supports your views.

3. Discuss stereotyped families or husbands and wives as they are portrayed on television programs. Is there any direct or indirect harm done from this?

4. Describe similarities and/or differences in the way your parents view things.

5. Brainstorm or freewrite on one or more of the following:
   a. men's work/women's work
   b. male/female relations
   c. sexist language
   d. kitchen talk
   e. office talk
   f. man's place/woman's place

6. Ignore these and find a topic of your own that deals with some aspect of family and relationships.

📖 Preparing to Read

Take a minute or two to look over the following reading selection. Note the title and author, read the first *two* paragraphs, and check the length. Make certain you have the time now to read it carefully and to do the exercises that follow it. Then, in the spaces provided, answer the following questions.

1. What do you think is the subject of this essay? _____

_____

2. What will the author probably say about mother love? _____

_____

_____

3. Do you think mother love is different from other types of love? Explain.

_____

_____

Vocabulary

Good comprehension of what you are about to read depends upon your understanding of the words below. The number following each word refers to the paragraph where it is used.

ambivalence (1) the state of having two conflicting feelings at the same time

infinite (3) endless

entrenches (3) fixes firmly and securely

stance (3) position

hailed (3) acclaimed, saluted

enigmatic (4) puzzling, confusing

articulate (4) express, make known

thwarted (4) prevented from taking place

matronly (7) motherly

invincible (8) not able to be conquered

inherent (8) existing as an essential characteristic

impaired (9) lessened the quality and intensity of

will-o'-the-wisp (9) a deceptive or misleading goal

touchstone (10) a test of value

pretense (10) a false appearance intended to deceive

Now read the essay.

Mother Love

NANCY FRIDAY

1   We are raised to believe that mother love is different from other kinds of love. It is not open to error, doubt, or the ambivalence of ordinary affections. This is an illusion.

2   Mothers may love their children, but they sometimes do not like them. The same woman who may be willing to put her body between

her child and a runaway truck will often resent the day-by-day sacrifice the child unknowingly demands of her time, sexuality, and self-development.

3   A woman without a daughter may try to explore life's infinite possibilities. Her own mother left out so much. But when a daughter is born, fears she thought she had conquered long ago are re-aroused. Now there is another person, not simply dependent on her, but *like* her, and therefore subject to all the dangers she has fought all her life. The mother's progress into a larger sexuality is halted. Ground gained that she could have held alone is abandoned. She retreats and entrenches herself in the cramped female stance of security and defense. The position is fondly hailed as mother protector. It is the position of fear. She may be only half alive but she is safe, and so is her daughter. She now defines herself not as a woman but primarily as a mother. Sex is left out, hidden from the girl who must never think of her mother in danger: in sex. It is only with the greatest effort that the girl will be able to think of herself that way.

4   When women's lives were more predictable, we could more easily afford this enigmatic picture of womanhood. When we had no alternative but to repeat our mother's life, our mistakes and disappointments were pretty much confined to her space, her margin of error and unhappiness. I do believe our grandmothers, even our mothers, were happier; not knowing as much as we do and not having our options, there was less to be unhappy about. A woman might give up her sexuality, hate being a housewife, not like children, but if every woman was doing it, how could she articulate her frustration? She could feel it certainly, but you can't want what you don't know about. Television, for instance, gave them no sense of thwarted expectations. Today women's lives are changing at a rate and by a necessity we couldn't control if we wanted to; we need all the energy that suppression consumes. If we are going to fill more than women's traditional role, we can't afford the exhaustion that goes with constant emotional denial. There are pressures on women other than the "maternal instinct." They are the new economic and social demands. Even if we decide to lead our mothers' lives, the fact is that our daughter may not. We may continue, through denial and repression, to keep alive the idealization of motherhood for another generation, but where will that leave her?

5   If women are going to be lawyers as well as mothers, they must differentiate between the two, and then differentiate once again about their sexuality. That is the third—and *not* mutually exclusive—option. As the world changes, and women's place in it, mothers must consciously present this choice to their daughters. A woman may incorporate all three choices within herself—and even more—but at

any given moment she must be able to say to herself and her daughter, "I chose to have you because I wanted to be a mother. I chose to work—to have a career, to be in politics, to play the piano—because that gives me a different feeling of value about myself, a value that is not greater nor lesser than motherhood, only different. Whether you choose to work or not, to be a mother or not, it will have nothing to do with your sexuality. Sexuality is the third option—as meaningful as either of the other two."

6   The truth is that the woman and the mother are often at war with one another—in the same body. Like so many women since the world began, my mother could not believe in this opposition of the two desires. Tradition, society, her parents, religion itself told her that there was no conflict; that motherhood was the logical and natural end product of sex. Instead of believing what every woman's body tells every woman's mind, that sexuality and eroticism are a fundamentally different and opposite drive to motherhood, my mother accepted the lie. She took as her act of faith the proposition that if she were a real woman, she would be a good mother and I would grow up the same. If I repeated her path and pattern of motherhood, it would justify and place the final stamp of value on what she had done. It would say her attitude, behavior, and deepest feelings were not split, but were in fact in harmony, a woman in unison with nature.

7   Some women do make this choice gladly. They may be the majority, but my mother was not one of them. As I am not—her daughter in this too. Even in a good marriage, many women resent the matronly, nonsexual role their children force them to play. My mother didn't even have a good marriage; she was a young widow.

8   Frightened as she was, as much in need of my father as my sister and I were of her, mother had no choice but to pretend that my sister and I were the most important part of her life; that neither fear, youth and inexperience, loss, loneliness or her own needs could shake the unqualified and invincible love she felt for us. My mother had no body of woman-to-woman honesty and shared experience to use in her fight against the folk wisdom that said just being a woman carried all the inherent wisdom needed to be a mother—that it was either "natural" to her, or she was a failure as a woman.

9   In all the years we lived together, it is a shame we never talked honestly about our feelings. What neither of us knew then was that I could have stood honesty, no matter how frightening. Her angers, disillusionments, fears of failure, rage—emotions I seldom saw—I could have come to terms with them if she had been able to speak to me. I would have grown used to the idea that while mother loved me, at times other emotions impaired that love, and developed trust that in time her love for me would always return. Instead, I was left

trying to believe in some perfect love she said she had for me, but in which I could not believe. I did not understand why I couldn't feel it no matter what her words said. I grew to believe that love itself, from her or anybody else, was a will-o'-the-wisp, coming or going for reasons I could not control. Never knowing when or why I was loved, I grew afraid to depend on it.

10   The older I get, the more of my mother I see in myself. The more opposite my life and my thinking grow from hers, the more of her I hear in my voice, see in my facial expression, feel in the emotional reactions I have come to recognize as my own. It is almost as if in extending myself, the circle closes in to completion. She was my first and most lasting model. To say her image is not still a touchstone in my life—and mine in hers—would be another lie. I am tired of lies. They have stood in the way of my understanding myself all my life. I have always known that what my husband loves most in me is that I have my own life. I have always felt that I had partially deceived him in this; I am very clever at pretense. My work, my marriage, and my new relationships with other women are beginning to make his assumptions about me true—that I am an independent, separate individual. They have allowed me to respect myself, and admire my own sex. What still stands between me and the person I would like to be is this illusion of perfect love between my mother and me. It is a lie I can no longer afford.

Understanding the Content

Feel free to reread all or parts off the selection to answer the following questions.

1. How does Friday define mother love? How is it different from or like other kinds of love?

2. What are the three options Friday says women have?

3. Friday says that "through denial and repression" women may "keep alive the idealization of motherhood." What is. this ideal she discusses? What is being denied and repressed?

4. What does Friday mean when she says that "the woman and the mother are often at war with one another—in the same body" (6)? What reasons for this does she give?

5. What "lie" does the author say she can no longer afford?

Looking at Structure and Style

1. How effective in getting your attention is Friday's opening paragraph? Why?

2. In paragraph 3, Friday discusses what often happens to a woman when she has a daughter. What is the function of paragraph 4?

3. Look carefully at paragraph 5. What writing method is used? Is it effective as structured?

4. Friday mentions her relationship with her own mother at times even though she is writing objectively about mother love. Are her subjective comments out of place or do they fit here? Explain.

5. What can you infer about the author's mother-daughter relationship?

6. Is Friday's intended audience only women? Explain.

Evaluating the Author's Viewpoints

1. Reread paragraph 1. Do you agree? Explain.

2. Friday discusses changes that women go through when they become mothers, changes that halt their growth as individuals. Which of these changes do you or don't you agree happen?

3. The author says that when women's lives were more predictable, a woman had "no alternative but to repeat [her] mother's life." (4). What does she mean? When were women's lives more predictable?

4. In paragraph 4, Friday says she believes "our grandmothers, even our mothers, were happier." What do you think?

5. How does Friday's view of mother love differ from that of her mother's?

Pursuing Possible Essay Topics

1. Use this line from Friday's essay to get you started: "The older I get, the more of my mother [father] I see in myself." (10)

2. Compare and contrast the way you and your mother might view mother love.

3. Write your own extended definition of mother love.

4. Write about a time in your life when you felt your mother or father didn't love you because he/she didn't live up to your image of what a parent should be. Were you right or wrong at the time? What did you learn from the incident?

5. Write about your relationship with your mother or father. How close are you? What have you experienced together? Can you be honest about your feelings and ideas with one another?

6. Have your feelings toward your mother [father] changed as you've gotten older? Why?

7. Brainstorm or freewrite on one or more of the following:
   a. motherhood/fatherhood
   b. the perfect mom/dad
   c. discussing sex with parents
   d. perfect love
   e. maternal instinct
   f. stereotyped parents

8. Forget these and come up with your own topic on some aspect of family and/or relationships.

Preparing to Read

Take a minute or two to look over the following reading selection. Note the title and author, read the opening paragraph, and check the length. Make certain you have the time now to read it carefully and to do the exercises that follow it. Then, in the spaces provided, answer the following questions.

1. What is your reaction to the title? _____

2. What do you think the subject of this essay is? _____

3. What do you think is going to happen? _____

Vocabulary

Good comprehension of what you are about to read depends upon your understanding of the words below. The number following each word refers to the paragraph where it is used.

ironically (2) oppositely or differently from what is expected

traumas (4) severe shocks to the mind or body

trounced (4) beaten, defeated

relinquishing (7) giving up to another, surrendering

quavering (8) quivering, trembling

taken aback (11) surprised, caught off guard

Now read the essay.

One Son, Three Fathers

STEVEN O'BRIEN

1   The first time I met him, he fell asleep in his spaghetti. It didn't matter. I was in love. Not with him, but with his mother. She had kept Sebastian from napping so that we wouldn't be interrupted after dinner. He was only 18 months old, a tiny little body topped off by a big head covered with blond hair.

2   His divorced mother and I, both 25, dated for a month, lived together nine more, and then married. It was Karen I wanted, not Sebastian, but they were a package deal. Ironically, he turned out to be the best part of the bargain.

3   Because my teaching schedule matched Sebastian's preschool schedule, I spent more time with him than his mother did. On the way home after school in the afternoon, he loved to sit on his Scooby-Doo lunch box in the back seat of my car and sing hit pop tunes like "Fly, Robin, Fly" and "SOS."

4   His biological father wasn't as available as I was to deal with the unscheduled traumas of childhood. I slowly began to fill his role. Seb turned to me for comfort the night before he had to face a bully who had promised to hurt him. At age 4, he didn't understand, and I couldn't explain, why the world needed bullies. I could only repeat what my father had said: fight back as best you can and don't let anyone know that he can push you around, or it will never end. He cried at breakfast, regained his composure before school, stood up for his rights and got thoroughly trounced. When he couldn't fall asleep that night, he asked to borrow my wool knit sailor cap. "To-morrow," he said, "with this on, I won't be afraid. I'll be 100 times stronger." The bully ignored him the next day, in order to torment someone else.

5   Brian, Sebastian's father, and I had been trained as teachers. Perhaps this was why both of us wanted to help the boy. Then, too, I had been raised with a stepsister and had seen the psychological damage that loss of contact with a parent could cause. In any case, Seb continued to spend time with me and with his father even after Brian remarried. Seb never had any problem distinguishing between the two of us, although other people were often confused because he referred to us as Daddy Steve and Daddy Brian. We all benefited from the arrangement. Sebastian shared things with Brian that I couldn't give him. For instance, I never followed sports, but Brian had studied to be a sports announcer.

6   After eight years of marriage, my wife and I separated. At first, Seb stayed with me and visited his mother, but after her remarriage, she missed him too much. He was moved to her new home nearby. Legally, of course, I had no rights. A child counselor I consulted suggested that I fade out of the picture as soon as possible. Instead, I maintained my home, with a bedroom for Seb, within walking distance of his. With his mother's consent, he started spending one night a week at my place. He loved to show off his second home to his friends by bringing them around, unannounced, for snacks.

7   Seb's grandparents had died years before. My place in his life gradually changed to resemble the role my favorite uncle and grandparents played in mine. It was hard at first, relinquishing my old relationship with him, but I grew to like the new one. I had the fun of seeing him without the frustration of trying to live with and discipline him.

8   Although we talked about it, and he understood after the divorce that we were no longer legally connected, Seb insisted on continuing to call me dad and using my last name as his own. I asked, "What's in a name, anyway?" He responded, "It says whose son I am." I told him that wasn't the issue. That I didn't have any choice. Neither biology nor law gave me the right to claim such a role; but he shattered my logic in a quavering voice with the question, "Don't you want to be my father anymore?" We hugged; I said: "Of course I want to. As long as you want me to be your father, I will be." That was five years ago.

9   Because Sebastian and I live in the same community, I often learn details about him I would otherwise miss. My neighbor, Sebastian's eighth-grade social-studies teacher, told me that he was going up and down the aisles asking each student at the end of the year if they had any brothers or sisters who would be going to the junior high the next fall. When he got to Seb, he said, "Oh, that's O.K. Seb, I used to live next door to you, and I know that you are an only child." Sebastian answered with a smile, "That's right, Mr. Tulley, there are so many parents in my family that there isn't room for any more kids."

10   After the laughter died down, several fellow students asked Seb how many parents he had. He said three fathers and two mothers. Another said, "Wow, Christmas must be great." Seb hesitated and then explained, "Christmas is about a 7, but birthdays are a definite 10."

11   Still, I wonder how he and his generation will view marriage. One night, we were talking about girls, the next-most-important issue on his mind, after driving. I said, "Well, someday, you'll find the right young woman and you won't be satisfied until you marry her." I

wasn't prepared for his reply: "No, dad, I don't think so. It never works for long, and divorce hurts too much." Taken aback, I assured him that marriage did work, and that just because his parents' marriages hadn't, it was no reason to give up on the institution. He looked at me patiently and said: "Dad, none of my friends' parents are still together. Everybody gets divorced sooner or later. Don't worry, I'm all right. I can take care of myself. Love 'em and leave 'em. Right?"

12   I don't think I had realized until that moment that, since my divorce from Sebastian's mother, "love 'em and leave 'em" exactly described the way I had been living and handling my own relationships with women. What could I say to Seb?

Understanding the Content

Feel free to reread all or parts of the selection to answer the following questions.

1. What is the exact relationship between O'Brien and Sebastian? Why does Sebastian have three fathers?

2. Why was O'Brien able to spend more time with Seb than Seb's mother was? What effect did this have on their relationship?

3. What advice did a child counselor give O'Brien when he and Seb's mother divorced? Did he follow this advice? Why?

4. What can you infer about the way O'Brien and Seb feel about each other now? Why do you think so?

5. What can you infer about the effects of divorce on Seb's views of marriage?

6. What revelation does O'Brien have at the end of the essay?

7. What is the point of this selection?

Looking at Structure and Style

1. How effective is the opening paragraph in getting your attention? Why?

2. What is the main idea of paragraph 2? What would be the effect if O'Brien had put his last sentence first?

3. What purpose does it serve for O'Brien to use dialogue in paragraphs 4, 8, 9, 10, and 11?

4. How much time is covered in this essay? How does O'Brien move us from one time period to the next?

5. While most of the essay deals with his relationship with Seb, the last paragraph shifts to O'Brien's relationships with women. Is this appropriate? Explain.

Evaluating the Author's Viewpoints

1. What are O'Brien's feelings about Seb's biological father, Brian? Seb's mother, Karen? Karen's third husband?

2. What does O'Brien mean in paragraph 4 when he refers to "the unscheduled traumas of childhood"? Why does he feel he was better prepared to help Sebastian deal with them than Brian was? Do you think he was?

3. In paragraph 5, O'Brien says that one of the reasons he may have wanted to help Seb after the divorce was because he was trained as a teacher, but he adds, "Then, too, I had been raised with a stepsister and had seen the psychological damage that loss of contact with a parent could cause." What can we infer from this statement about the author? Do you think O'Brien sees himself in Seb?

4. O'Brien says he had "the fun of seeing him [Seb] without the frustration of trying to live with and discipline him." (7) If you were one of Sebastian's biological parents living with and disciplining him, how would you feel about O'Brien's relationship with Seb? Why?

5. O'Brien chose not to take the child counselor's advice to "fade out of the picture as soon as possible." (6) Do you think he made the right choice? Why?

6. What do you think is O'Brien's attitude toward marriage? Why?

Pursuing Possible Essay Topics

1. Reread the last paragraph in the essay. Write an essay that answers the question, "What could I say to Seb?"

2. Assume that you have a four-year-old son and that he told you he had to face a bully at school tomorrow. Discuss how you might handle the situation. What would you do? What would you say to your son? Would you try to explain why there are bullies in the world? How?

3. Reread what Seb tells O'Brien in paragraph 11. Write an essay that argues against what Seb says.

4. Brainstorm or freewrite on one or more the following:

   a. divorce   d. stepparents
   b. marriage   e. "love 'em and leave 'em"
   c. stepchildren   f. loss of contact with a parent

5. Do some research on marriage and divorce. What are the latest trends? Is Seb right? (In addition to the card catalogue and the *Reader's Guide to Periodical Literature,* you might want to see what you can find in the latest *Facts on File* and the latest *World Almanac and Book of Facts.*)

6. Write about your views on marriage or divorce.

7. Divorce yourself from these and pick your own topic.

📖 Preparing to Read

The following selection is a little different from the rest of the readings in this unit. Make certain you have the time now to read it carefully and to do the exercises that follow it.

Vocabulary

Good comprehension of what you are about to read depends upon your understanding of the words below. The number following each word refers to the paragraph where it is used.

> **unicorn** (title) a mythical creature that looks like a horse with a spiraled horn coming out of its forehead
>
> **cropping** (1) cutting short
>
> **roused** (1) stirred from sleep, awakened
>
> **booby** (1) stupid person
>
> **booby-hatch** (1) slang for a hospital for the insane
>
> **gloat** (2) a look of evil pleasure
>
> **strait-jacket** (2) a jacket used to restrain the arms of a violent or uncontrollable person
>
> **solemn** (2) very earnest, seriously gloomy
>
> **subduing** (2) bringing under control

Now read the essay.

The Unicorn in the Garden

JAMES THURBER

1   Once upon a sunny morning a man who sat in a breakfast nook looked up from his scrambled eggs to see a white unicorn with a golden horn quietly cropping the roses in the garden. The man went up to the bedroom where his wife was still asleep and woke her. "There's a unicorn in the garden," he said. "Eating roses." She opened one unfriendly eye and looked at him. "The unicorn is a mythical beast," she said, and turned her back on him. The man walked slowly downstairs and out into the garden. The unicorn was still there; he was now browsing among the tulips. "Here, unicorn," said the man, and he pulled up a lily and gave it to him. The unicorn ate it gravely. With a high heart, because there was a unicorn in his garden, the man went upstairs and roused his wife again. "The unicorn," he said,

"ate a lily." His wife sat up in bed and looked at him, coldly. "You are a booby," she said, "and I am going to have you put in the booby-hatch." The man, who had never liked the words "booby" and "booby-hatch," and who liked them even less on a shining morning when there was a unicorn in the garden, thought for a moment. "We'll see about that," he said. He walked over to the door. "He has a golden horn in the middle of his forehead," he told her. Then he went back to the garden to watch the unicorn; but the unicorn had gone away. The man sat down among the roses and went to sleep.

2   As soon as the husband had gone out of the house, the wife got up and dressed as fast as she could. She was very excited and there was a gloat in her eye. She telephoned the police and she telephoned a psychiatrist; she told them to hurry to her house and bring a strait-jacket. When the police and the psychiatrist arrived they sat down in chairs and looked at her, with great interest. "My husband," she said, "saw a unicorn this morning." The police looked at the psychiatrist and the psychiatrist looked at the police. "He told me it ate a lily," she said. The psychiatrist looked at the police and the police looked at the psychiatrist. "He told me it had a golden horn in the middle of its forehead," she said. At a solemn signal from the psychiatrist, the police leaped from their chairs and seized the wife. They had a hard time subduing her, for she put up a terrific struggle, but they finally subdued her. Just as they got her into the strait-jacket, the husband came back into the house.

3   "Did you tell your wife you saw a unicorn?" asked the police. "Of course not," said the husband. "The unicorn is a mythical beast." "That's all I wanted to know," said the psychiatrist. "Take her away. I'm sorry, sir, but your wife is as crazy as a jay bird." So they took her away, cursing and screaming, and shut her up in an institution. The husband lived happily ever after.

4   *Moral: Don't count your boobies until they are hatched.*

Understanding the Content

Feel free to reread all or parts of the selection to answer the following questions.

1. What can be inferred about the married couple's relationship in this story?

2. With which character is Thurber most sympathetic? How do you know?

3. What unexpected events occur in this selection?

4. What is Thurber's purpose in writing this? What makes you think so?

Looking at Structure and Style

1. Thurber structures his story like an old-fashioned fable, a brief tale with a moral stated at the end. But the humor comes from his use of the unexpected reversal. What reversals does he use?

2. Thurber also uses understatement; that is, he states things with less completeness or truth for dramatic effect. What are some examples of his use of understatement? Why are they effective?

3. Most fables end with a serious moral or statement of instruction about what is good or evil. How does Thurber make a parody of the fable form?

4. Look carefully at the words or phrases Thurber uses to give his story the feeling of a fable. What are they?

5. Look carefully at the words Thurber uses to describe the man and his wife. How do these words establish the character of each? Why are these descriptions important to the story's effect on us?

6. How different would the story be if told from the point of view of the man? his wife?

Evaluating the Author's Viewpoint

1. What might you infer about Thurber's attitude regarding men and women?

2. On a literal level, Thurber makes the wife "the bad guy," yet it's the husband who has his wife unjustly committed. Comment on this.

3. Do you think the husband really saw a unicorn in the garden? Why?

4. Do you think Thurber was making an analogy between the existence of the mythical unicorn and the existence of an ideal relationship? Explain.

5. What do you think was Thurber's purpose in writing this parody? Explain.

Pursuing Possible Essay Topics

1. Use the fable structure to write your own views on the family or relationships.

2. Find a copy of Thurber's *Fables for Our Time*, the book from which this "fable" was taken. Read a few more of his pieces to see if they contain the same inferences about men and women. Then write an essay to support what you think Thurber's attitude about the sexes is.

3. From the viewpoint of a devout feminist, write an essay that reflects your reaction to Thurber's parody.

4. Defend Thurber from the viewpoint of someone calling him a sexist.

5. Brainstorm or freewrite on one or more of the following:

    a. the ideal relationship   d. the importance of the family
    b. gender role reversals   e. premarital cohabitation
    c. the family unit   f. living "happily ever after"

6. Ignore these and find a topic of your own on some aspect of relationships or family.

 Preparing to Read

Here's a short poem to read. Read it twice, once to yourself and once aloud. Then answer the questions that follow it.

My Papa's Waltz

THEODORE ROETHKE

The whiskey on your breath
Could make a small boy dizzy;
But I hung on like death:
Such waltzing was not easy.

We romped until the pans
Slid from the kitchen shelf;
My mothers countenance
Could not unfrown itself.

The hand that held my wrist
Was battered on one knuckle;
At every step you missed
My right ear scraped a buckle.

You beat time on my head
With a palm caked hard by dirt.
Then waltzed me off to bed
Still clinging to your shirt.

Understanding the Content

1. Explain what is happening in the poem.

2. What images does the poem provide?

3. What is the point of the poem?

4. What does the poem have to do with relationships and family, the theme of this unit?

Looking at Structure and Style

1. What is the tone of this poem? What words provide this tone?

2. This poem is made up of four stanzas of four lines each. What attention does Roethke give to rhyming words? Which ones rhyme? Is there a pattern? If so, what?

3. What image of the father does Roethke provide in the first stanza (first four lines)?

4. What image of the mother is given in the second stanza? What words create this image? (You may need to look up the word *countenance* in the dictionary or a thesaurus.)

5. What function does the third stanza serve?

6. What image are we left with in the last stanza?

7. Of what importance are Roethke's use of the words *dizzy, easy, waltz, waltzing, romped* and *still clinging?*

8. What does the line "You beat time on my head" mean? How does the line fit the waltzing going on?

Evaluating the Author's Viewpoints

1. How does the boy feel about his father? How do you know?

2. How does the father feel about the boy? Does he love him? Explain.

3. Roethke calls this poem, "My Papa's Waltz." Is this a good title? Explain.

4. Some readers feel that Roethke is expressing resentment and hatred toward a drunken brute who hurts his child while dancing about. Is this an acceptable interpretation? Why?

Pursuing Possible Essay Topics

1. Summarize the theme or point of the poem. See the student essay and commentary that deals with writing about a poem on pages 125–127.

2. Write about a time when one of your parents was feeling playful and did something that both frightened and delighted you. Why is the experience memorable? What did it reveal about your relationship with that parent?

3. Brainstorm or freewrite on one or more of the following:

   a. your father
   b. your mother
   c. your mother's anger
   d. your father's anger
   e. childhood memories of your parents

4. Ignore these and find a topic of your own on family or other relationships.

✍ Student Essay

As you read the following student essay, look for answers to these questions:

1. Does the essay fit the assignment to write on some aspect of family and relationships?

2. Is there a thesis? If so, is it well supported?

3. How well written is the essay? Does it hold your interest?

In Defense of Motherhood

Rosa Avolio

1   In Nancy Friday's essay "Mother Love," she states:

> We are raised to believe that mother love is different from other kinds of love. It is not open to error, doubt, or the ambivalence of ordinary affections. This is an illusion.

Perhaps this is what Ms. Friday was raised to believe, but I wasn't. While I agree with her that women should not have babies just because "women are supposed to," Friday seems to think that women in general give up a part of their individuality when they become mothers in order to become some standard of motherhood set by society. Her comments make me wonder if she is a mother herself.

2   As a daughter as well as a mother of two, I know that mother love is different from other kinds of love. Yes, I may have given up some things in expectation of others, but that happens to both men and women when certain life choices are made. We can't have it all in life. My choice to become a mother wasn't made because it was expected of me. My husband and I wanted to have a family. And our decision was worth it.

3   Certainly, motherhood sometimes has its down side. Staying up all night with a sick child is no fun. Preparing the meals and doing the dishes for a family of four is not always easy. Staying home with the kids instead of going out when you'd like sometimes feels confining. Worrying about finances for a decent house, clothes, and health care can be draining. But I expected those things when I decided to have a family.

4   What I've gained from being a mother far outweighs the negative. Motherhood is something very special. My pleasure comes from watching my children take the first steps or say "momma" for the first time with recognition. I enjoy watching them learn anything new. To see their eyes widen with excitement on Christmas morning or to hold them and help soothe the hurt from a fall is all part of the joy of being a mother.

5   No one can explain truly what it is like to get up twice a night to nurse a crying baby, but neither can they describe the wonderful feeling of holding that baby in your arms and nourishing it from your own body. Watching that baby grow and develop daily, I sometimes wanted to stop the clock to be able to savor a special time.

6   I have never felt that my children intruded on a happy marriage, rather, they enhanced it. We're a family now instead of a couple. I'm not saying all couples should have children. But if you decide to, don't feel that you have to be a super mom. You only have to enjoy your children and help them grow and develop.

Reaction

In the space below, write your reaction to the essay. What would you tell the student about her essay?

Commentary

Rosa's essay begins very well. She correctly identifies the author and the essay to which she is reacting. She also correctly uses a block quotation because of the length of the passage from Friday's essay. And while her sentence structure and paragraphing are acceptable, her thesis and support need some help.

Notice that Rosa's essay really has little to do with the passage she quotes. She says she agrees with Friday about not having children unless you want to, but disagrees that women give up part of their individuality in order to meet some social standard. Then she ends her paragraph by wondering if Friday is a mother herself. The problem here is that Rosa has drifted away from the content of the quote she cites. If you look at the quotation used, you will see that her comments have little to do with Friday's comments about the illusion of mother love.

In paragraph 2, Rosa starts to discuss mother love by disagreeing with Friday's quoted comment. But again Rosa drifts away with remarks that have nothing to do with mother love—at least not as she states them.

In paragraph 3, Rosa has a good, tight paragraph showing the examples of the "down side" of motherhood. Alone the paragraph is acceptable, but again she does not relate any of this to Friday's comments about mother love.

In paragraphs 4 and 5, we get examples of the positive side of having children. But what has this to do with the illusion of mother love that Nancy Friday discusses?

Rosa's last paragraph has three unrelated points: that her children have enhanced her marriage; that she doesn't recommend that all couples have children; and that if you do have children, don't feel you have to be a "super mom." (This last comment limits her audience to women.) In addition, each of these three points needs more development than she gives here. If Rosa wanted, she could write an essay based on those three points. But that would make it an entirely different essay, since none of the points have any direct bearing on the Friday quotation used in the opening. Also, her last sentence makes a difficult task sound rather simple.

Rosa no doubt disliked some of the things Nancy Friday has to say about mothers and mother love. Reacting to what she read was a good place to start. But Rosa never develops what she starts out to say and ends up writing about other things. We are left with an unclear thesis.

The essay was returned to Rosa for revision with the suggestion that she either clarify what she disagrees with in the Nancy Friday quote and then support her own position better, or that she use the three points in her last paragraph as a basis for a different essay altogether.

Viewpoints on

Work

"Every man's work, whether it be literature or music or picture or architecture or anything else, is always a portrait of himself."

Samuel Butler

*F*OR MANY PEOPLE the real reason for working is not the work itself but for the money or the status and power it may bring. Sociologists claim that the average person more or less puts up with a job because of private and family needs that are considered to be more important, such as food, clothing, and shelter.

The style of our lives is often based on the type of work we do. Some jobs allow for flexible schedules, which means we can take advantage of the time to meet personal or family needs; on the other hand, flexible schedules can be a disadvantage when we decide to take our work home with us. Other jobs are inflexible, even requiring us to punch time clocks. Such work means we cannot easily take time off to take care of personal or family needs, leaving only evenings and weekends. Yet, in those cases work can be left at the job site. The time that we have for ourselves and family, then, is determined by the type of job we have.

The work we do not only determines the quality of our lives by shaping our time, our leisure, our buying power, our ability to travel; it even shapes our identities. When we meet someone for the first time, we generally ask, "What do you do?" The meaning behind the question is understood: "What do you do for a living?" And when the answer is waitress, police officer, doctor, writer, sales clerk, or whatever, we generally categorize that person to fit our stereotype of the job.

As our economy changes, so do the jobs. Many of us find we must move from community to community to keep up with jobs that require our skills or to find new ones when laid off. Many of us attend college in preparation for a particular line of work only to discover that there are no positions available, or to realize that what we've prepared for is not what we really want to do for a living. Many of us who have been in the same job for years suddenly find we must go back to school to retrain in order to meet the advancements made in our field.

Changes in traditional family roles are also changing the work place. Some men are discovering they would rather stay home and raise their children while their wives go off to work. Many women are realizing they prefer a career to the traditional mother or house-wife role. Such changes are redefining the term *homemaker*.

The reading selections in this unit supply a wide range of viewpoints toward work, from how to go for a job interview to attempts at defining what "real work" is. Use them to discover and to stimulate your own viewpoints on work.

Preparing to Read

Take a minute or two to look over the following reading selection. Note the title and author, read the opening paragraph, and check the length. Make certain you have the time now to read it carefully and to do the exercises that follow it. Then, in the spaces provided, answer the following questions.

1. What is the subject of the essay? _____

_____

2. What do you think you will learn from reading this selection? _____

_____

_____

Vocabulary

Good comprehension of what you are about to read depends upon your understanding of the words below. The number following each word refer to the paragraph where it is used.

recruiter (1) a person who seeks out new employees (or members or students)

corporate headquarters (1) the main offices of a large corporation

cubicle (3) a small room or partitioned-off area

> **branch office** (3) a smaller office set up away from the main corporate headquarters, usually in another city or country
>
> **deteriorates** (10) declines, worsens
>
> **Laurel and Hardy** (10) a famous comedy team in the '30s and '40s
>
> **résumé** (13) a summary of work qualifications and experience
>
> **screening** (15) separating out unsuitable candidates
>
> **sidewinderlike** (21) like a rattlesnake, moving in sideways loops
>
> **strenuously** (30) forcefully, vigorously
>
> **adamant** (35) inflexible, firm of mind, unyielding

Now read the essay.

How to Take a Job Interview

KIRBY W. STANAT

1   To succeed in campus job interviews, you have to know where that recruiter is coming from. The simple answer is that he is coming from corporate headquarters.

2   That may sound obvious, but it is a significant point that too many students do not consider. The recruiter is not a free spirit as he flies from Berkeley to New Haven, from Chapel Hill to Boulder. He's on an invisible leash to the office, and if he is worth his salary, he is mentally in corporate headquarters all the time he's on the road.

3   If you can fix that in your mind—that when you walk into that bare-walled cubicle in the placement center you are walking into a branch office of Sears, Bendix or General Motors—you can avoid a lot of little mistakes and maybe some big ones.

4   If, for example, you assume that because the interview is on campus the recruiter expects you to look and act like a student, you're in for a shock. A student is somebody who drinks beer, wears blue jeans and throws a Frisbee. No recruiter has jobs for student Frisbee whizzes.

5   A cool spring day in late March, Sam Davis, a good recruiter who has been on the college circuit for years, is on my campus talking to candidates. He comes out to the waiting area to meet the student who signed up for an 11 o'clock interview. I'm standing in the doorway of my office taking in the scene.

6   Sam calls the candidate: "Sidney Student." There sits Sidney. He's at a 45 degree angle, his feet are in the aisle, and he's almost lying down. He's wearing well-polished brown shoes, a tasteful pair of brown pants, a light brown shirt, and a good looking tie. Unfor-

tunately, he tops off this well-coordinated outfit with his Joe's Tavern Class A Softball Championship jacket, which has a big woven emblem over the heart.

7   If that isn't bad enough, in his left hand is a cigarette and in his right hand is a half-eaten apple.

8   When Sam calls his name, the kid is caught off guard. He ditches the cigarette in an ashtray, struggles to his feet, and transfers the apple from the right to the left hand. Apple juice is everywhere, so Sid wipes his hand on the seat of his pants and shakes hands with Sam.

9   Sam, who by now is close to having a stroke, gives me that what-do-I-have-here look and has the young man follow him into the interviewing room.

10   The situation deteriorates even further—into pure Laurel and Hardy. The kid is stuck with the half-eaten apple, doesn't know what to do with it, and obviously is suffering some discomfort. He carries the apple into the interviewing room with him and places it in the ashtray on the desk—right on top of Sam's freshly lit cigarette.

11   The interview lasts five minutes. . . .

12   Let us move in for a closer look at how the campus recruiter operates.

13   Let's say you have a 10 o'clock appointment with the recruiter from the XYZ Corporation. The recruiter gets rid of the candidate in front of you at about 5 minutes to 10, jots down a few notes about what he is going to do with him or her, then picks up your résumé or data sheet (which you have submitted in advance). . . .

14   Although the recruiter is still in the interview room and you are still in the lobby, your interview is under way. You're on. The recruiter will look over your sheet pretty carefully before he goes out to call you. He develops a mental picture of you.

15   He thinks, "I'm going to enjoy talking with this kid," or "This one's going to be a turkey." The recruiter has already begun to make a screening decision about you.

16   His first impression of you, from reading the sheet, could come from your grade point. It could come from misspelled words. It could come from poor erasures or from the fact that necessary information is missing. By the time the recruiter has finished reading your sheet, you've already hit the plus or minus column.

17   Let's assume the recruiter got a fairly good impression from your sheet.

18   Now the recruiter goes out to the lobby to meet you. He almost shuffles along, and his mind is somewhere else. Then he calls your name, and at that instant he visibly clicks into gear. He just went to work.

19   As he calls your name he looks quickly around the room, waiting for somebody to move. If you are sitting on the middle of your back, with a book open and a cigarette going, and if you have to rebuild yourself to stand up, the interest will run right out of the recruiter's face. You, not the recruiter, made the appointment for 10 o'clock, and the recruiter expects to see a young professional come popping out of that chair like today is a good day and you're anxious to meet him.

20   At this point, the recruiter does something rude. He doesn't walk across the room to meet you halfway. He waits for you to come to him. Something very important is happening. He wants to see you move. He wants to get an impression about your posture, your stride, and your briskness.

21   If you slouch over him, sidewinderlike, he is not going to be impressed. He'll figure you would probably slouch your way through your workdays. He wants you to come at him with lots of good things going for you. If you watch the recruiter's eyes, you can see the inspection. He glances quickly at shoes, pants, coat, shirt; dress, blouse, hose—the whole works.

22   After introducing himself, the recruiter will probably say, "Okay, please follow me," and he'll lead you into his interviewing room.

23   When you get to the room, you may find that the recruiter will open the door and gesture you in—with him blocking part of the doorway. There's enough room for you to get past him, but it's a near thing.

24   As you scrape past, he gives you a closeup inspection. He looks at your hair; if it's greasy, that will bother him. He looks at your collar; if it's dirty, that will bother him. He looks at your shoulders; if they're covered with dandruff, that will bother him. If you're a man, he looks at your chin. If you didn't get a close shave, that will irritate him. If you're a woman, he checks your makeup. If it's too heavy, he won't like it.

25   Then he smells you. An amazing number of people smell bad. Occasionally a recruiter meets a student who smells like a canal horse. That student can expect an interview of about four or five minutes.

26   Next the recruiter inspects the back side of you. He checks your hair (is it combed in front but not in back?), he checks your heels (are they run down?), your pants (are they baggy?), your slip (is it showing?), your stockings (do they have runs?).

27   Then he invites you to sit down.

28   At this point, I submit, the recruiter's decision on you is 75 to 80 percent made.

29   Think about it. The recruiter has read your résumé. He knows who you are and where you are from. He knows your marital status,

your major and your grade point. And he knows what you have done with your summers. He has inspected you, exchanged greetings with you and smelled you. There is very little additional hard information that he must gather on you. From now on it's mostly body chemistry.

30   Many recruiters have argued strenuously with me that they don't make such hasty decisions. So I tried an experiment. I told several recruiters that I would hang around in the hall outside the interview room when they took candidates in.

31   I told them that as soon as they had definitely decided not to recommend (to department managers in their companies) the candidate they were interviewing, they should snap their fingers loud enough for me to hear. It went like this.

32   First candidate: 38 seconds after the candidate sat down: Snap!

33   Second candidate: 1 minute, 42 seconds: Snap!

34   Third candidate: 45 seconds: Snap!

35   One recruiter was particularly adamant, insisting that he didn't rush to judgment on candidates. I asked him to participate in the snapping experiment. He went out in the lobby, picked up his first candidate of the day, and headed for an interview room.

36   As he passed me in the hall, he glared at me. And his fingers went "Snap!"

Understanding the Content

Feel free to reread all or parts of the selection to answer the following questions.

1. According to Stanat, how should you dress for an interview on a college campus? Why?

2. Where and how do some recruiters technically begin the interview?

3. Why won't some interviewers walk across the waiting room to meet you halfway when it's your turn for an interview?

4. Why do some recruiters seem to block the doorway when you are called into the interviewing room?

5. According to Stanat, what percent of a recruiter's mind is made up by the time you sit down for an interview?

6. What is Stanat's thesis? Is is implied or stated?

Looking at Structure and Style

1. How do paragraphs 5–11 help Stanat develop his thesis? What advice regarding job interview techniques is being implied in these paragraphs?

2. What is the function of paragraph 12?

3. Paragraphs 13–28 reveal the way a recruiter works. What are each of the steps? Why do you think Stanat uses the point of view of the recruiter rather than the person being interviewed?

4. What transitional devices does Stanat use to move us smoothly through the essay?

5. The author uses short sentences and paragraphs on the whole. Is such writing effective in this case? Explain.

6. How would you describe Stanat's tone? What are some examples of words or phrases that establish his tone?

7. To what specific audience is Stanat writing? Does the tone fit?

Evaluating the Author's Viewpoints

1. Stanat states that college students often don't consider the way they dress when being interviewed. Do you feel that dress and appearance are important for job interviews? Explain.

2. Look at each of the steps you should have listed in question 3 above. Does Stanat exaggerate each step's importance? Explain.

3. Stanat says that by the time you are invited to sit down, a "recruiter's decision on you is 75 to 80 percent made." (28) Do you think this is true? Why?

4. The author implies that the actual interview itself may not be as important as your body language and chemistry. How do you react to this? Does Stanat provide enough evidence to make his implication factual?

Pursuing Possible Essay Topics

1. Think about a time when you wanted to make a good appearance but botched it up. Try writing an essay that uses some of the devices Stanat uses in paragraphs 5–11 to relate your experience comically. Try to imply your thesis rather than state it.

2. Write an essay that reflects all of the qualifications and experience you have for a job you are interested in. Your audience is your potential employer.

3. Using all the steps Stanat provides but with a more formal tone than Stanat uses, write an essay that deals with how to take a job interview.

4. Write about a time when you didn't get the job you applied for. Why do you think you didn't get it? How did you feel? What did you learn that will help you in the future?

5. If you are already working, write an essay directed to someone new on the job. Provide advice on how best to get the work done, how to get along with the boss and fellow employees, or how to do a specific task.

6. Write an essay that begins where Stanat stops: the interview itself. Provide practical advice for the actual interview. Try matching his tone and writing style.

7. Brainstorm or freewrite on one or more of the following:

   a. résumé   d. your dream job
   b. job interview   e. school vs. work
   c. job preparation   f. your first job

8. Ignore these and find your own topic that deals with some aspect of work.

 ## Preparing to Read

Take a minute or two to look over the following reading selection. Note the title and author, read the opening paragraph, and check the length. Make certain you have the time now to read it carefully and to do the exercises that follow it. Then, in the spaces provided, answer the following questions.

1. What does the title lead you to think is the subject of the essay? _____

   _____

2. To what audience do you think the essay is aimed? Why? _____

   _____

3. What might you learn from reading this selection? _____

   _____

Vocabulary

Good comprehension of what you are about to read depends upon your understanding of the words below. The number following each word refers to the paragraph where it is used.

   chuck (1) throw away, get rid of

   sector (4) a division of something (here, the service division of the workforce)

   encompasses (4) includes

   virtually (4) practically, for all intents and purposes

   kudzu (5) a vine native to Japan

   fellow (6) a member of a scholarly society

holographic inspector (7) one who examines products through the use of holography, a method for producing a three-dimensional image without a lens

lunar (7) pertaining to the moon

actuaries (8) those who compute insurance risks and premiums

gerontological (9) pertaining to the study of age and its problems

diverse (9) varied

optics (9) the scientific study of light and vision

entrepreneurial (11) referring to the undertaking of new businesses

abiding (11) long-lasting, enduring

tipped their hand (12) revealed their sources or intentions

dwindled (13) diminished, lessened

clamoring (16) demanding insistently

coupled (16) joined, linked

MBAs (17) Master's degrees in business administration

erosion (18) wearing away

constrained (18) held back, limited

endorsement (19) approval, support

canned (19) mechanical, uncreative, lacking thought and initiative

rigorous (20) strict, harsh

exploiting (24) using or utilizing fully

scenario (25) an outline of possible future events

flourish (27) thrive, grow well

inevitably (27) unavoidably

conspicuous (29) obvious

cushy (31) comfortable

Fortune 500 (31) the 500 wealthiest companies in the country

hallmark (32) a conspicuous feature or characteristic

Now read the essay.

Your Brilliant Career

JANET BODNAR

1   Whether you're 18 and thinking of a career, 38 and thinking of changing or 58 and looking for new challenges, it's high time to chuck a number of widely held beliefs about tomorrow's job market.

2   Most of tomorrow's brightest careers will *not* be in high-tech fields. If you don't have high-tech training, your career choices will *not* be limited to low-paying service jobs. And manufacturing jobs will *not* disappear.

3   It's true that high-tech jobs will grow rapidly, but by 1995 they'll still represent no more than one out of eight jobs and probably somewhat fewer.

4   It's true that most new jobs will be in service businesses, but that has been the case for three decades. And since the service sector encompasses hamburger flippers as well as neurosurgeons, it's a virtually useless starting point for discussing job possibilities.

5   It's also true that manufacturing jobs aren't exactly growing like kudzu, but measured by its contribution to the gross national product, the industrial sector is as big a part of the U.S. economy as it was a quarter-century ago.

6   Finally, there's no doubt that it takes specialized training to land a specialized job. But you'll be better prepared to launch or change careers in the future if you also possess a broadly based education gained at college or on your own. William Johnston, a senior research fellow at the Hudson Institute who directed *Workforce 2000*, a Labor Department study of future job-market needs, concluded that the jobs of tomorrow will belong to those "who can read, write and think."

Jobs Today and Tomorrow

7   Housing rehabilitation technician, holographic inspector, battery technician—though intriguing, the titles that appear in catalogs of tomorrow's jobs don't always provide a practical guide to what's available today. Neal Rosenthal, chief of the Labor Department's Division of Occupational Outlook, warns against a tendency to plan your future around fanciful forecasts of jobs that may or may not exist someday. "If someone asked me whether his son or daughter should train to be a lunar miner or a nurse, I'd say nurse," Rosenthal says.

8   In fact, nursing appears on the government's list of occupations that are expected to grow much faster than average between now and 1995. Others on the list are also jobs that exist already: accountants, engineers, actuaries, computer systems analysts, lawyers and legal assistants, occupational and physical therapists, public relations specialists, and financial services sales workers.

9   That list of occupations amounts to only a cross section of the fields offering the brightest career prospects.

- *Health services.* Demand will be especially great for primary-care workers such as nurse practitioners, nutrition counselors and gerontological social workers.

- *Hotel management and recreation.* This category includes restaurants, resorts and travel, as well as opportunities in conference planning.

- *Food service.* Managers and chefs will be in demand for all those restaurants and hotel kitchens, as well as for food-processing plants and labs.

- *Engineering.* In-demand specialties will be as diverse as robotics, aviation and aerospace, and waste management.

- *Basic science.* Look at molecular biology, chemistry and optics.

- *Computers.* Opportunities will continue strong in design, engineering, programming and maintenance.

- *Business services.* Accounting, statistical analysis and payroll management.

- *Human resources or personnel.* This includes job evaluation, hiring and firing, benefit planning, and training.

- *Financial services.* Financial planning and portfolio management.

- *Teaching.* Demand is growing in primary and elementary grades to serve the children of the baby-boom generation, and in certain specialties: math, sciences, engineering, computer operations and foreign languages, such as Russian and Japanese.

- *Maintenance and repair.* Somebody's got to take care of all the equipment that will keep tomorrow's world running.

10   That list of prospects contains plenty of encouragement for those who are technologically inclined, and for those who aren't. Futurist Marvin Cetron, president of Forecasting International Ltd., anticipates good opportunities for writers, sculptors and painters as well as for those with a technical bent.

11   Perhaps the best news for current and future job hunters is that the entrepreneurial spirit is alive and well in America. Between 1981 and 1985, start-up firms created 14.2 million new jobs in the U.S., according to David Birch, director of the Massachusetts Institute of Technology's Program on Neighborhood and Regional Change and head of his own consulting firm, Cognetics. Many of those were basement enterprises offering personal services to a fast-paced society that's short on time. But many were in traditional fields such as manufacturing, says Paul Reynolds, a University of Minnesota professor who has studied new business formations in Pennsylvania. And the drive behind the spirit is an abiding faith in the future of the economy. "People start new firms because they think they can sell something," says Reynolds.

Who Gets What

12   Corporate recruiters on college campuses have already tipped their hand regarding immediate job opportunities for new grads. The latest Endicott-Lindquist Report from Northwestern University shows companies offering 8% fewer jobs in engineering and a corresponding increase in such nontechnical fields as retailing, banking and insurance. Engineers still got the highest starting salaries, though—$28,932 for a bachelor's degree—followed by bachelor's graduates in chemistry ($27,048); computer science ($26,280); mathematics or statistics ($25,548); accounting ($22,512); economics or finance ($21,984); business administration ($21,972); liberal arts ($20,508); and sales and marketing ($20,232)....

13   The fact is that the percentage of workers employed in low-paying occupations has declined over roughly the last decade, while the percentage employed in middle-level and higher-paying jobs has increased. Reynolds' study of new businesses indicates that three-quarters of the jobs created required post–high-school training, and higher skills generally command higher wages. Secretary of Labor William Brock notes that since 1982, jobs paying $10 or more per hour have increased by more than 50%, while the number of workers earning the minimum wage or less has dwindled by 25%. "We aren't creating junk jobs," says David Birch.

14   Some job-market experts even view those low-paid service jobs as good training for better jobs later on. Bradley Schiller, an economics professor at American University, studied the early work experiences of 6,000 young men for the U.S. Small Business Administration. He discovered that two-thirds of them earned less than $5 an hour in their first out-of-school jobs. But most of the new-job holders reported that they were getting on-the-job training and had good promotion prospects, which led to better jobs and higher wages later. At McDonald's, at least 70% of the company's senior managers got their start—you guessed it—flipping burgers....

Hone Your Basic Skills

15   If you know exactly what you want, the best route to a job is to get specialized training. Michigan State's corporate-recruiting survey shows clearly that companies like graduates in such fields as business and health care who can go to work immediately with very little on-the-job training.

16   That's especially true of booming fields that are clamoring for workers. At Cornell University's School of Hotel Administration, for example, bachelor's degree graduates get an average of four or five job offers with salaries ranging from the high teens to the low 20s

and plenty of chances for rapid advancement. Large companies, especially, like a background of formal training coupled with work experience, says Fred Antil, director of career planning at Cornell's School of Hotel Administration.

17   But over the long run, too much specialization doesn't pay off. Business, which has been flooded with MBAs, no longer considers the degree an automatic stamp of approval, says Gary Silverman of Korn/ Ferry International, an executive-search firm. Companies are increasingly confining their job offers to candidates who have MBAs from top schools as well as job experience. And after several years it's the experience that counts, not the degree. "The MBA may open doors and may command a higher salary initially, but the impact of a degree washes out after five years," says Mary Anne Devanna, director of executive education at Columbia University's Graduate School of Business.

18   As further evidence of the erosion of corporate faith in specialized degrees, Michigan State's Scheetz cites a pattern in corporate hiring practices: Although companies tend to take on specialists as new hires, they tend to seek out generalists for middle- and upper-level management. "They want someone who isn't constrained by nuts and bolts to look at the big picture," says Scheetz.

19   This sounds suspiciously like an endorsement of the liberal-arts graduate. Time and again labor-market analysts cite a need for talents that liberal-arts majors are presumed to have: writing and communication skills, organizational skills, openmindedness and adaptability, and the ability to analyze and solve problems. David Birch claims he does not hire anybody with an MBA or an engineering degree. "I hire only liberal-arts people because they have a less-than-canned way of doing things," says Birch. Overall, says the College Placement Council, liberal-arts graduates got 29% more jobs last spring than in 1986.

20   Liberal arts means an academically rigorous program that includes literature, history, mathematics, economics, science, human behavior—plus a computer course or two. With that under your belt, you can feel free to specialize. "A liberal-arts degree coupled with an MBA or some other technical training is a very good combination in the marketplace," says Scheetz.

Keep Your Options Open

21   In the future it will be a rare bird who goes to school for four years and lands a job with a company from which he or she retires 40 years later. Workers should expect to return to school several times during their working lives just to keep up with developments in their

fields. To survive in this sort of environment, job-market experts advise, specialize if you must, but specialize as little as possible. Instead of training to be a laser engineer, for example, Scheetz suggests "training for a career in electronics with options A, B and C."

22   For career changers with a family to support and little time to spare, going back to school is often out of the question. Better to look for ways to adapt the skills you already have to new job opportunities. A broad view of the world is a valuable asset.

23   Nella Barkley, who with partner John Crystal runs the Crystal-Barkley Corp., a career-counseling service in New York City, says it's critical that those making a career change not repeat the mistake many of them made to begin with: getting into a field they didn't like just because a counselor said there would be a big demand for it. Rather than mold yourself to fit a certain job description, says Barkley, the trick is to identify your skills and transfer them to a job you're interested in doing. . . .

Where the Jobs Are

24   Workers will also have to become more mobile to take advantage of new job opportunities. David Birch believes the U.S. will have to do a better job of exploiting the chief competitive advantage it has over the rest of the world: brainpower. And that in turn will mean a competitive advantage for cities near universities or other research facilities.

25   Birch's scenario goes something like this: Universities will attract brains, which will generate ideas, which will give birth to new companies, which will create more jobs. Already, he says, all the growth in new jobs is coming from middle-sized and small companies. Among the cities on Birch's list of places most likely to succeed: Atlanta; Albuquerque; Austin, Tex.; Huntsville, Ala.; Manchester–Nashua, N.H.; Orlando, Fla.; Phoenix; Raleigh-Durham, N.C.; Tucson; and Washington, D.C.

26   As the entrepreneurial climate increasingly determines which regions are going to flourish, Sunbelt-Frostbelt distinctions will blur. Steven Malin, regional economist for the Conference Board, expects Texas to rebound from its oil slump and become an economic powerhouse by the end of the century. But Oklahoma and Louisiana will have a tougher time because their economies aren't as broad-based. In Malin's view, Florida has perhaps the brightest future of any of the 50 states. "If someone asked me where to go to find a good job in the next ten years, I'd send him to Florida and Florida," says Malin.

27   Meanwhile, areas like New England, New York and New Jersey, which have built a strong base of business and financial services, will

continue to flourish, but their growth rates will slow inevitably as they bump up against the limits of expansion: high land and labor costs and a shortage of workers, especially in New England.

28   A number of cities in the country's industrial heartland will get a new lease on life. "We've seen nice comebacks in Pittsburgh, Cincinnati and Columbus," says Malin. And cities like Omaha, Des Moines, Kansas City, Mo., and Chicago have the potential to become major financial centers.

29   Coastal areas will continue to be the most promising job markets, but with better times in the Oil Patch and agricultural and manufacturing areas in the Midwest, economic growth may well become more evenly spread. Still, Sunbelt cities are conspicuous by their presence on lists of fast-growing regions. Among the 25 metropolitan areas with the fastest-growing job markets identified by the National Planning Association, 14 are in Florida and California.

30   It's important to keep in mind the distinction between the rate of job growth and the number of new jobs expected to be created. The Los Angeles–Long Beach area doesn't even appear among the 25 fastest-growing job markets, yet in terms of sheer numbers it will provide more jobs than any other metropolitan area between now and the year 2010. Other metropolitan areas on the list: Chicago, Philadelphia, Minneapolis–St. Paul, Detroit and Baltimore.

31   The jobs that will be created in these and other cities won't be confined to opportunities to work for someone else. Shifting populations will open up innumerable chances to strike out on your own—as a consultant, or as a freelancer, or as an entrepreneur. "That's not as cushy as working for the Fortune 500," notes Richard Belous, a labor economist for the conference Board. "And you have to hustle more."

32   The ability to hustle will continue to be a hallmark of a successful career, as it has always been. The job market of tomorrow will provide somewhat less security than in the past but more opportunity for those who are willing to reach out and seize it.

Understanding the Content

Feel free to reread all or parts of the selection to answer the following questions.

   1. What four widely held beliefs about tomorrow's job market does Bodnar argue against?

   2. What are some of the jobs listed that are expected to grow much faster than average between now and 1995? Are most of these for the "technologically inclined"?

3. Why does Bodnar say, "Perhaps the best news for current and future job hunters is that the entrepreneurial spirit is alive and well in America"? (11)

4. Bodnar states that "corporate recruiters on college campuses have already tipped their hand regarding immediate job opportunities for new grads." (12) For what positions are they primarily recruiting?

5. What does Bodnar say is the best route to getting a job? In what fields might this not be the best route?

6. Why are more companies looking for people with a liberal arts background? What academic background does a liberal arts education involve?

7. Why in the near future will it be "a rare bird who goes to school for four years and lands a job with a company from which he or she retires 40 years later"? (21)

8. Why will workers have to become more mobile? Where will most of the future jobs be? Why?

Looking at Structure and Style

1. What does the opening paragraph imply regarding Bodnar's audience? Is it an effective opening? Why?

2. How do paragraphs 2–6 support the opening sentence? What transitional devices are used? What is the effect of repeating "It's true that . . . but . . . " in paragraphs 3, 4, and 5?

3. This is a rather long selection compared to most in this text. How does Bodnar break up her essay and help the reader move from one major point to the next? How do such devices help reading comprehension?

4. Bodnar frequently refers to many resources, such as those found in paragraphs 6, 7, 11, 12, 13, and so on. What function do they serve? What does this tell us about the author?

5. What is the tone of this selection? What words or phrases help establish tone?

6. Explain or rewrite the following passages from the selection:
   a. "And the drive behind the [entrepreneurial] spirit is an abiding faith in the future of the economy." (11)
   b. "Business, which has been flooded with MBAs, no longer considers the degree an automatic stamp of approval." (17)
   c. " 'They want someone who isn't constrained by nuts and bolts to look at the big picture.' " (18)
   d. "The ability to hustle will continue to be a hallmark of a successful career. . . . " (32)

Evaluating the Author's Viewpoints

1. Paragraphs 3–5 each take a belief about tomorrow's job market and state opposing views. Look again at each of the four predictions Bodnar makes. Do you think she is right? Does her essay provide support for each of these statements?

2. Bodnar predicts that future workers will have to return to school several times during their working lives just to keep up with developments in the field. Do you think this might be the case? If so, how do you feel about it?

3. "A broad view of the world is a valuable asset," says Bodnar (22). What does she mean? Do you agree? How does one get a broad view of the world?

4. Reread the last paragraph. Do you agree with the author? Why?

Pursuing Possible Essay Topics

1. Support or refute the notion that an academic education is important for _____ . [pick a career]

2. Explain why overspecialization for a job may be harmful in the future. Draw your support from the information in the Bodnar essay or elsewhere.

3. Discuss the advantages and disadvantages of a career in one of the armed services.

4. If you have decided on a career, write an essay that attempts to encourage someone to consider it as their career.

5. Pick a job you are interested in pursuing. Predict what skills will be necessary for that job in ten years.

6. See if your library has a copy of the *Occupational Outlook Handbook* or the *Dictionary of Occupational Titles*. Explain the usefulness of such publications when considering an occupation.

7. Brainstorm or freewrite on one or more of the following:
   a. sales promotion
   b. nursing
   c. liberal arts
   d. mortician
   e. architect
   f. bank clerk
   g. entrepreneur
   h. freelancer
   i. consultant

8. If none of these inspire you, work at finding your own topic on some aspect of work.

Preparing to Read

Take a minute or two to look over the following reading selection. Note the title and author, read the opening paragraph, and check the length. Make certain you have the time now to read it carefully and to do the exercises that follow it. Then, in the spaces provided, answer the following questions.

1. What does the title mean to you at this point? _____

_____

2. Do you agree with the opening sentence? Why? _____

_____

_____

3. What do you think will be the point of this essay? _____

_____

Vocabulary

Good comprehension of what you are about to read depends upon your understanding of the words below. The number following each word refers to the paragraph where it is used.

validate (1) verify, make acceptable

limbo (1) a place or condition of neglect and stagnation

cast in bronze (2) permanent or fixed (like a statue)

discounted (3) having undervalued significance

titled nobility (4) refers to such titles as Lord and Lady So-and-So, or the Duke and Duchess of Whatever

dynastic privilege (4) special favors to those powerful families or groups that have held their positions for several generations

deference (6) courteous respect, submission to others out of respect

entrepreneur (7) one who undertakes and assumes the risk of a new business venture

phenomenon (7) a perceivable, often unusual, occurrence or fact

fawn (7) to seek favor or attention by flattery

Now read the essay.

What You Do Is What You Are

NICKIE McWHIRTER

1   Americans, unlike people almost everywhere else in the world, tend to define and judge everybody in terms of the work they do, especially work performed for pay. Charlie is a doctor; Sam is a carpenter; Mary Ellen is a copywriter at a small ad agency. It is as if by defining how a person earns his or her rent money, we validate or reject that person's existence. Through the work and job title, we evaluate the worth of the life attached. Larry is a laid-off auto worker; Tony is a retired teacher; Sally is a former showgirl and blackjack dealer from Vegas. It is as if by learning that a person currently earns no money at a job—and maybe hasn't earned any money at a job for years—we assign that person to limbo, at least for the present. We define such non-employed persons in terms of their past job history.

2   This seems peculiar to me. People aren't cast in bronze because of the jobs they hold or once held. A retired teacher, for example, may spend a lot of volunteer time working with handicapped children or raising money for the Loyal Order of Hibernating Hibiscus. That apparently doesn't count. Who's Tony? A retired teacher. A laid-off auto worker may pump gas at his cousin's gas station or sell encyclopedias on weekends. But who's Larry? Until and unless he begins to work steadily again, he's a laid-off auto worker. This is the same as saying he's nothing now, but he used to be something: an auto worker.

3   There is a whole category of other people who are "just" something. To be "just" anything is the worst. It is not to be recognized by society as having much value at all, not now and probably not in the past either. To be "just" anything is to be totally discounted, at least for the present. There are lots of people who are "just" something. "Just" a housewife immediately and painfully comes to mind. We still hear it all the time. Sometimes women who have kept a house and reared six children refer to themselves as "'just' a housewife." "Just" a bum, "just" a kid, "just" a drunk, bag lady, old man, student, punk are some others. You can probably add to the list. The "just" category contains present non-earners, people who have no past job history highly valued by society and people whose present jobs are on the low-end of pay and prestige scales. A person can be "just" a cab driver, for example, or "just" a janitor. No one is ever "just" a vice-president, however.

4   We're supposed to be a classless society, but we are not. We don't recognize a titled nobility. We refuse to acknowledge dynastic priv-

ilege. But we certainly separate the valued from the valueless, and it has a lot do with jobs and the importance or prestige we attach to them.

5   It is no use arguing whether any of this is correct or proper. Rationally it is silly. That's our system, however, and we should not only keep it in mind we should teach our children how it works. It is perfectly swell to want to grow up to be a cowboy or a nurse. Kids should know, however, that quite apart from earnings potential, the cattle breeder is much more respected than the hired hand. The doctor gets a lot more respect and privilege than the nurse.

6   I think some anthropologist ought to study our uncataloged system of awarding respect and deference to each other based on jobs we hold. Where does a vice-president–product planning fit in? Is that better than vice-president–sales in the public consciousness, or unconsciousness? Writers earn diddly dot, but I suspect they are held in higher esteem than wealthy rock musicians—that is, if everybody older than 40 gets to vote.

7   How do we decide which jobs have great value and, therefore, the job-holders are wonderful people? Why is someone who builds shopping centers called an entrepreneur while someone who builds freeways is called a contractor? I have no answers to any of this, but we might think about the phenomenon the next time we are tempted to fawn over some stranger because we find out he happens to be a judge, or the next time we catch ourselves discounting the personal worth of the garbage collector.

Understanding the Content

Feel free to reread all or parts of the selection to answer the following questions.

1. How does McWhirter claim we define and judge others? Is it common worldwide or just an American trait?

2. According to McWhirter, how do we regard unemployed people?

3. The author states, "There is a whole category of other people who are 'just' something." (3) Who are some people who fit into this category? Who are some people never put in that category?

4. Does McWhirter think we are a classless society? Explain.

5. What does she say we should tell our children about certain occupations? Why?

6. What is the thesis of the essay? Is it stated or implied?

Looking at Structure and Style

1. How does McWhirter support her topic sentence in paragraph 1?

2. What is the function of paragraph 3? How does it relate to the thesis?

3. Explain or rewrite the following statements from the essay:
   a. "People aren't cast in bronze because of the jobs they hold or once held." (2)
   b. "But we certainly separate the valued from the valueless. . . ." (4)
   c. "Writers earn diddly dot, but I suspect they are held in higher esteem than wealthy rock musicians—that is, if everybody older than 40 gets to vote." (6)

4. What is McWhirter's tone? What words or phrases establish the tone?

5. To what audience is McWhirter writing? What makes you think so?

6. What advice, if any, would you give the author for revision?

Evaluating the Author's Viewpoints

1. McWhirter says we define and judge ourselves according to the jobs we do. Do you agree? Explain.

2. Is defining ourselves according to jobs an American trait as McWhirter says? How do you know?

3. Do we "separate the valued from the valueless"? Give some examples of your own if you agree with her.

4. In general, do people "fawn over some stranger because [they] find out he happens to be a judge" and discount "the personal worth of a garbage collector"? (7)

5. What can you infer about the author based on what she says here?

Pursuing Possible Essay Topics

1. Explain why you want to become a doctor, lawyer, teacher, mechanic, electrician, computer programmer, or whatever. How much of your desire has to do with what McWhirter discusses in her essay? How much of your desire has to do with earning money?

2. Compare/contrast a job with an occupation.

3. Write a rebuttal to McWhirter.

4. Write an essay that classifies our social structure as you see it. How much do job positions and money earned have to do with the way we classify people?

5. Write an essay that shows which of the following positions are most respected in our society and why:

a. police officer   f. lawyer
b. minister   g. elementary teacher
c. taxi driver   h. university professor
d. car salesman   i. writer
e. surgeon   j. garbage collector

Feel free to add job positions to the list.

6. Answer one of the questions McWhirter raises in her last paragraph. Turn the question into your thesis statement.

7. Brainstorm or freewrite on one or more of the following:

a. a job   d. nobility
b. housework   e. the TV show "Dynasty"
c. musician   f. "just a bum"

8. If you don't like these, try your own idea on some aspect of work.

Preparing to Read

Take a minute or two to look over the following reading selection. Note the title and author, read the opening paragraph, and check the length. Make certain you have the time now to read it carefully and to do the exercises that follow it. Then, in the spaces provided, answer the following questions.

1. What will be the subject of this essay? _____

_____

2. What policy for children do you think will be suggested? _____

_____

3. Is the author for or against day care for children? _____

_____

Vocabulary

Good comprehension of what you are about to read depends upon your understanding of the words below. The number following each word refers to the paragraph where it is used.

hearth (1) the fireside, used as a symbol of the family home

R, D (3) Republican, Democrat

monitoring (3) keeping track of

median (3) at the middle

vulnerable (4) easily harmed or hurt

spectrum (5) a broad range of related qualities

crazy quilt (5) a disorderly mix, hodgepodge

barrage (6) a rapid outpouring

shoddy (7) inferior, shabby

statutes (7) laws

abound (7) exist in great numbers

deployment (14) the act of being sent out

latchkey youngsters (16) children who must let themselves in when they get home from school because their parents are still at work

prenatal (18) before birth

piecemeal (18) piece by piece, gradually

perpetuate (18) prolong the existence of, cause to be remembered

utopian (19) perfect, so idealistic as to be impossible

entitlement (20) right, authorization

mandated (20) required by law

Now read the essay.

Needed: A Policy for Children When Parents Go to Work

MAXINE PHILLIPS

1   Opponents of day care still call for women to return to home and hearth, but the battle is really over. Now the question is: Will day care continue to be inadequately funded and poorly regulated, or will public policy begin to put into place a system that rightly treats children as our most valuable national resource?

2   More than 50% of the mothers of young children are in the work force before their child's first birthday. An estimated 9.5 million preschoolers have mothers who work outside the home. Most women, like most men, are working to put food on the table. Many are the sole support of their families. They are economically unable to stay at home, although many would prefer to do so.

3   Decent child care is now an issue that cuts across political and class lines. But this reality has not yet caught up with public policy. Conservative Sen. Orrin G. Hatch (R-Utah) is sponsoring a bill that would authorize $325 million in child-care costs for poor children. Liberal Sen. Christopher J. Dodd (D-Conn.) has just introduced a $2.5 billion bill for better child care, a far-reaching piece of legislation backed by 20 other senators and more than 100 members of the House. The Dodd measure would be a big improvement over current legislation, carrying provisions for information and referral, for standards and for monitoring that would have an impact on all children. But because eligible families could not earn more than 115% of a state's median income, the greatest impact would be on children of the working poor.

4   As long as public policy treats day care as a service for the poor, it will be vulnerable to . . . [having its] funds [cut]. . . .

5   Thus at one end of the spectrum we have far too few publicly funded day-care slots limited to poverty-level families. At the other are high-quality nonprofit centers available to the well-to-do. For the vast majority, in what *Business Week* calls the "the day-care crisis of the middle-class," there is a crazy quilt of arrangements with neighbors, relatives and poorly staffed centers.

6   A barrage of negative day-care information assaults the working mother, claiming that her children will not bond properly with her, will suffer emotionally and intellectually and will be exposed to deadly diseases.

7   True, many women rightly feel uncomfortable about leaving children in many situations available. Day-care workers' salaries are in the lowest 10%. Shoddy licensing statutes often allow one person to care for as many as six or eight infants. Unlicensed centers abound because working parents cannot pay the fees for the better ones. About 500,000 children are in scandalously unfit profit-making centers, which spend 45% less per child than federally funded nonprofit centers.

8   The average day-care cost is $60 per week—often as much as 30% of a working mother's salary. Quality day care costs about three times as much in urban situations, clearly beyond the reach of most families.

9   My family was among the lucky ones. When our daughter was 9 months old we enrolled her in a wonderful place where she has consistent, well-trained, loving caretakers, play equipment we could never afford at home and the intellectual stimulation that comes from being with other children overseen by concerned adults. Two years later, her verbal ability and social skills confirm the choice we made.

I sometimes worry that her days at home are not as rich as her days at the center.

10   Yet this kind of care, considered a societal responsibility in such countries as France or Sweden, is available here only to the lucky or the privileged few.

11   Today, when most Americans will need child care at sometime in their lives, day care should be a service universally available regardless of income. Then, as with public schools, parents can choose whether or not to use it.

12   This is what a national child-care policy would look like:

13   It would start with a family-leave law. If we seriously believe, as do most parents and other experts, that children should be with their parents in the early months when bonding is so important, why does society make it economically impossible? Unlike Canada, Italy, Sweden and many other nations, the United States has no national system of parental leave. Many women must return to work within a week or two of giving birth or risk losing their jobs. Yet a proposal in Congress this year to allow 16 weeks of unpaid parental leave met such resistance from the business community that it is almost dead.

14   Second, good policy would include neighborhood nonprofit daycare facilities open to everyone. These places would have parents involved, on the board and in the center. They would accommodate a variety of work schedules, with extra staff available for deployment to the homes of sick children whose parents could not make other arrangements.

15   Initial costs would be high (conservative estimates start at $30 billion) but must be measured against the lost tax revenues from people who would work—or work more productively—if reliable day care were available, not to mention the societal costs of children poorly cared for early in life.

16   Third, it would include after-school care for older children. Latchkey youngsters are a concern for all working parents; their lack of supervision poses a danger to them and to society.

17   These are the building blocks of a national system but the foundation must be a true commitment to the family unit.

18   This means prenatal care, nutrition, health care for both adults and children, decent welfare benefits to allow parents to feed, shelter and clothe their children—plus assurances that both mothers and fathers can find work at wages that allow them to live decent family lives. These programs are expensive but no more so than programs already in place to pick up the wreckage caused by their absence. As long as America approaches child care in piecemeal fashion—as part of a welfare package or as a service only for children at poverty

levels—we perpetuate the belief that this is an individual problem. We no longer believe that about education. In the current reality, why do we continue to believe it about child care?

19   Are these proposals utopian? No. Large parts are in place in every Western industrial society but our own.

20   We look most frequently to the public schools and Social Security as examples of entitlement accepted by the general society but I find added inspiration from a courageous group of parents who have already led the way in sensitizing the nation's conscience. Parents of developmentally disabled children, faced with a lifetime of caring for their youngsters and fears of what will happen after the parents die, organized to campaign for special funds and services. The results—including mandated education for all handicapped children—are far from perfect but demonstrate how parents can help society accept responsibility for some children. Now parents must help society accept responsibility for all of them.

Understanding the Content

Feel free to reread all or parts of the selection to answer the following questions.

1. What percent of mothers are in the work force before their child's first birthday? Why is this an important statistic in relation to day care?

2. What does Phillips consider wrong with the child-care bills that Senators Hatch and Dodd were proposing at the time this essay was written? What, according to Phillips, is the basic problem with the way public policy treats day-care service?

3. What are some of the arguments being used against day-care centers? How does Phillips respond to these?

4. How much is the average day-care cost?

5. How does the United States differ from such countries as Canada, Italy, France, and Sweden with regard to parental leave and day care?

6. What are the three elements of Phillips's proposal for a national child-care policy?

7. What is Phillips's thesis? Is it implied or stated?

Looking at Structure and Style

1. How does the phrasing of the question in paragraph 1 reveal the author's attitude toward day care?

2. What function do the statistics serve in paragraph 2?

3. How does Phillips use the negative assaults on day care mentioned in paragraphs 6 and 7 to make a positive case for child care?

4. What point is being made in paragraphs 9 and 10? Do you think Phillips makes her case for day-care credible by using her family as an example?

5. What transitional devices does Phillips use to help us recognize each of the three points in her child-care policy in paragraphs 12–16?

6. Explain or rewrite each of the following essay passages:
   a. "Opponents of day care still call for women to return to home and hearth, but the battle is really over." (1)
   b. " . . . a far-reaching piece of legislation . . . " (3)
   c. "For the vast majority . . . there is a crazy quilt of arrangements with neighbors, relatives and poorly staffed centers." (5)
   d. "These programs are expensive but no more so than programs already in place to pick up the wreckage caused by their absence." (18)

7. What paragraph, if any, comes closest to stating the author's thesis?

Evaluating the Author's Viewpoints

1. Re-examine each of the three points in Phillips's proposed policy for day care. How do you feel about each one? Are they necessary? Is she convincing?

2. Initial costs for the three-point policy for day care would be around $30 billion. Do you feel her program would be worth the costs? Why?

3. In her last paragraph, Phillips provides an example of how parents have led the way in raising society's consciousness regarding the needs of mentally disabled and handicapped children. She ends by calling upon parents to help do the same for all children. Do you think parents in general will be in favor of her proposal or something like it? Explain.

4. Phillips states, "As long as public policy treats day care as a service to the poor, it will be vulnerable to . . . [having its] funds [cut]." (4) What is the implication being made about our social attitude toward the poor in this country? Do you agree? Why?

Pursuing Possible Essay Topics

1. Defend or refute Phillips's thesis. Quote directly from her essay to help you support your own views.

2. Present your own views regarding day care.

3. Do some research on parental leave and day care in other countries. You might start by investigating those countries Phillips mentions. Ask the research librarian what sources would be most helpful in your search. React to the information you find.

4. Phillips says that her proposal is not "utopian". Write an essay that shows how her proposal could possibly be put into effect, or one that reveals why it is too idealistic.

5. Visit a local day-care center. Write your impressions of the type of care children are getting, or write about what job skills are needed to work in such a center.

6. Brainstorm or freewrite on one or more of the following:

   a. day care
   b. family leave
   c. the working mother/father

   d. working in a day-care center
   e. latchkey children
   f. why both parents must work

7. Forget these and find a topic of your own on some aspect of work.

Preparing to Read

Take a minute or two to look over the following reading selection. Note the title and author, read the opening paragraph, and check the length. Make certain you have the time now to read it carefully and to do the exercises that follow it. Then, in the spaces provided, answer the following questions.

1. What work-related subject will this essay discuss? _____

_____

2. What do you think will happen? _____

_____

_____

Vocabulary

Good comprehension of what you are about to read depends upon your understanding of the words below. The number following each word refers to the paragraph where it is used.

menial (1) servile, describing work regarded as lower class

skepticism (4) doubt, disbelief

tedious (5) boring, tiresome

ember (5) a piece of live coal from a fire

exotics (9) those from another part of the world; in this case, those new to his personal world

diversity (9) variety

aliens (10) unnaturalized residents of another country

debris (10) scattered remains of something destroyed

fatalistic (10) pertaining to the belief that all events are predetermined by fate

vulnerability (16) open to being taken advantage of

ludicrous (16) laughable, ridiculous

profoundly (18) deeply, absolutely

uncanny (19) inexplicable

compliance (19) an act of obeying a request or command

pathos (19) a quality in someone or something that arouses feelings of sympathy, sadness, sorrow, pity

Now read the essay.

Workers

RICHARD RODRIQUEZ

1   It was at Stanford, one day near the end of my senior year, that a friend told me about a summer construction job he knew was available. I was quickly alert. Desire uncoiled within me. My friend said that he knew I had been looking for summer employment. He knew I needed some money. Almost apologetically he explained: It was something I probably wouldn't be interested in, but a friend of his, a contractor, needed someone for the summer to do menial jobs. There would be lots of shoveling and raking and sweeping. Nothing too hard. But nothing more interesting either. Still, the pay would be good. Did I want it? Or did I know someone who did?

2   I did. Yes, I said, surprised to hear myself say it.

3   In the weeks following, friends cautioned that I had no idea how hard physical labor really is. ("You only *think* you know what it is like to shovel for eight hours straight.") Their objections seemed to me challenges. They resolved the issue. I became happy with my plan. I decided, however, not to tell my parents. I wouldn't tell my mother because I could guess her worried reaction. I would tell my father only after the summer was over, when I could announce that, after all, I did know what "real work" is like.

4   The day I met the contractor (a Princeton graduate, it turned out), he asked me whether I had done any physical labor before. "In high

school, during the summer," I lied. And although he seemed to regard me with skepticism, he decided to give me a try. Several days later, expectant, I arrived at my first construction site. I would take off my shirt to the sun. And at last grasp desired sensation. No longer afraid. At last become like a *bracero.* "We need those tree stumps out of here by tomorrow," the contractor said. I started to work.

5   I labored with excitement that first morning—and all the days after. The work was harder that I could have expected. But it was never as tedious as my friends had warned me it would be. There was too much physical pleasure in the labor. Especially early in the day, I would be most alert to the sensations of movement and straining. Beginning around seven each morning (when the air was still damp but the scent of weeds and dry earth anticipated the heat of the sun), I would feel my body resist the first thrusts of the shovel. My arms, tightened by sleep, would gradually loosen; after only several minutes, sweat would gather in beads on my forehead and then— a short while later—I would feel my chest silky with sweat in the breeze. I would return to my work. A nervous spark of pain would fly up my arm and settle to burn like an ember in the thick of my shoulder. An hour, two passed. Three. My whole body would assume regular movements. Even later in the day, my enthusiasm for primitive sensation would survive the heat and the dust and the insects pricking my back. I would strain wildly for sensation as the day came to a close. At three-thirty, quitting time, I would stand upright and slowly let my head fall back, luxuriating in the feeling of tightness relieved.

6   Some of the men working nearby would watch me and laugh. Two or three of the older men took the trouble to teach me the right way to use a pick, the correct way to shovel. "You're doing it wrong, too fucking hard," one man scolded. Then proceeded to show me— what persons who work with their bodies all their lives quickly learn—the most economical way to use one's body in labor.

7   "Don't make your back do so much work," he instructed. I stood impatiently listening, half listening, vaguely watching, then noticed his work-thickened fingers clutching the shovel. I was annoyed. I wanted to tell him that I enjoyed shoveling the wrong way. And I didn't want to learn the right way. I wasn't afraid of back pain. I liked the way my body felt sore at the end of the day.

8   I was about to, but, as it turned out, I didn't say a thing. Rather it was at that moment I realized that I was fooling myself if I expected a few weeks of labor to gain me admission to the world of the laborer. I would not learn in three months what my father had meant by "real work." I was not bound to this job; I could imagine its rapid conclu-

sion. For me the sensations of exertion and fatigue could be savored. For my father or uncle, working at comparable jobs when they were my age, such sensations were to be feared. Fatigue took a different toll on their bodies—and minds.

9   It was, I know, a simple insight. But it was with this realization that I took my first step that summer toward realizing something even more important about the "worker." In the company of carpenters, electricians, plumbers, and painters at lunch, I would often sit quietly, observant. I was not shy in such company. I felt easy, pleased by the knowledge that I was casually accepted, my presence taken for granted by men (exotics) who worked with their hands. Some days the younger men would talk and talk about sex, and they would howl at women who drove by in cars. Other days the talk at lunchtime was subdued; men gathered in separate groups. It depended on who was around. There were rough, good-natured workers. Others were quiet. The more I remember that summer, the more I realize that there was no single *type* of worker. I am embarrassed to say I had not expected such diversity. I certainly had not expected to meet, for example, a plumber who was an abstract painter in his off hours and admired the work of Mark Rothko. Nor did I expect to meet so many workers with college diplomas. (They were the ones who were not surprised that I intended to enter graduate school in the fall.) I suppose what I really want to say here is painfully obvious, but I must say it nevertheless: The men of that summer were middle-class Americans. They certainly didn't constitute an oppressed society. Carefully completing their work sheets; talking about the fortunes of local football teams; planning Las Vegas vacations; comparing the gas mileage of various makes of campers—they were not *los pobres* my mother had spoken about.

10   On two occasions, the contractor hired a group of Mexican aliens. They were employed to cut down some trees and haul off debris. In all, there were six men of varying age. The youngest in his late twenties; the oldest (his father?) perhaps sixty years old. They came and they left in a single old truck. Anonymous men. They were never introduced to the other men at the site. Immediately upon their arrival, they would follow the contractor's directions, start working—rarely resting—seemingly driven by a fatalistic sense that work which had to be done was best done as quickly as possible.

11   I watched them sometimes. Perhaps they watched me. The only time I saw them pay me much notice was one day at lunchtime when I was laughing with the other men. The Mexicans sat apart when they ate, just as they worked by themselves. Quiet. I rarely heard them say much to each other. All I could hear were their voices calling

our sharply to one another, giving directions. Otherwise, when they stood briefly resting, they talked among themselves in voices too hard to overhear.

12   The contractor knew enough Spanish, and the Mexicans—or at least the oldest of them, their spokesman—seemed to know enough English to communicate. But because I was around, the contractor decided one day to make me his translator. (He assumed I could speak Spanish.) I did what I was told. Shyly I went over to tell the Mexicans that the *patrón* wanted them to do something else before they left for the day. As I started to speak, I was afraid with my old fear that I would be unable to pronounce the Spanish words. But it was a simple instruction I had to convey. I could say it in phrases.

13   The dark sweating faces turned toward me as I spoke. They stopped their work to hear me. Each nodded in response. I stood there. I wanted to say something more. But what could I say in Spanish, even if I could have pronounced the words right? Perhaps I just wanted to engage in small talk, to be assured of their confidence, our familiarity. I thought for a moment to ask them where in Mexico they were from. Something like that. And maybe I wanted to tell them (a lie, if need be) that my parents were from the same part of Mexico.

14   I stood there.

15   Their faces watched me. The eyes of the man directly in front of me moved slowly over my shoulder, and I turned to follow his glance toward *el patrón* some distance away. For a moment I felt swept up by that glance into the Mexicans' company. But then I heard one of them returning to work. And then the others went back to work. I left them without saying anything more.

16   When they had finished, the contractor went over to pay them in cash. (He later told me that he paid them collectively—"for the job," though he wouldn't tell me their wages. He said something quickly about the good rate of exchange "in their own country.") I can still hear the loudly confident voice he used with the Mexicans. It was the sound of the *gringo* I had heard as a very young boy. And I can still hear the quiet, indistinct sounds of the Mexican, the oldest who replied. At hearing that voice I was sad for the Mexicans. Depressed by their vulnerability. Angry at myself. The adventure of the summer seemed suddenly ludicrous. I would not shorten the distance I felt from *los pobres* with a few weeks of physical labor. I would not become like them. They were different from me. . . .

17   In the end, my father was right—though perhaps he did not know how right or why—to say that I would never know what real work is. I will never know what he felt at his last factory job. If tomorrow I worked at some kind of factory, it would go differently for me. My long education would favor me. I could act as a public person—able

to defend my interests, to unionize, to petition, to speak up—to challenge and demand. (I will never know what real work is.) I will never know what the Mexicans knew, gathering their shovels and ladders and saws.

18   Their silence stays with me now. The wages those Mexicans received for their labor were only a measure of their disadvantaged condition. Their silence is more telling. They lack a public identity. They remain profoundly alien. Persons apart. People lacking a union obviously, people without grounds. They depend upon the relative good will or fairness of their employers each day. For such people, lacking a better alternative, it is not such an unreasonable risk.

19   Their silence stays with me. I have taken these many words to describe its impact. Only: the quiet. Something uncanny about it. Its compliance. Vulnerability. Pathos. As I heard their truck rumbling away, I shuddered, my face mirrored with sweat. I had finally come face to face with *los pobres.*

Understanding the Content

Feel free to reread all or parts of the essay in order to answer the following questions.

1. At what point in Rodriquez's life did the incidents in the essay occur?

2. For what reasons did Rodriquez take the summer job? Why didn't he want to tell his parents?

3. How did Rodriquez react to the work? Why was he reluctant to accept advice from the older workers?

4. What revelation about "real work" did Rodriquez have? How did this insight cause him to better understand the construction workers? What surprised him about the construction workers?

5. What did Rodriquez learn from the group of Mexican aliens hired by the construction boss? Why did his summer suddenly seem ludicrous after this encounter?

6. How does Rodriquez's definition of "real work" change over the course of the summer?

7. What is the point of the essay?

Looking at Structure and Style

1. Rodriquez compares/contrasts the American construction workers with the Mexican aliens. What is the advantage of discussing the alien group last? With which group does he mostly identify? How can you tell?

2. Much of the essay is told narratively. Which passages are not narrative? At what points in the essay do they occur? Why?

3. Rodriguez frequently uses Spanish words in a context that allows us to infer their meanings. Why does he use these words? How does their use add to the point he is making?

4. What is the effect of making paragraph 14 consist of only one sentence, when most of the other paragraphs are rather long?

5. Select some passages that reflect the author's ability to use descriptive language. What are some lifelike images he creates?

6. Explain or rewrite the following passages from the essay:
   a. "I would feel my body resist the first thrusts of the shovel." (5)
   b. "I was fooling myself if I expected a few weeks of labor to gain me admission to the world of the laborer." (8)
   c. "I felt easy, pleased by the knowledge that I was casually accepted, my presence taken for granted by men (exotics) who worked with their hands." (9)
   d. "My long education would favor me. I could act as a public person— able to defend my interests, to unionize, to petition, to speak up—to challenge and demand." (17)

Evaluating the Author's Viewpoints

1. What stereotyped attitude toward laborers did Rodriquez have before he took the summer job? Is your attitude similar?

2. Rodriquez did not want to accept advice on how to shovel correctly. At this point just before his insight, why is it important to him to feel the pain? How does this need connect Rodriquez to his father and uncle?

3. Do you agree with Rodriquez that he will probably never know what real work is? Is it because of his college education? Explain.

4. In paragraph 16, Rodriquez says he got angry with himself. Why? Should he have been?

5. In paragraphs 17 and 18, Rodriquez compares his advantages to those of *los pobres*. How does he view this group? What is he saying about cultural identity? about eduction?

Pursuing Possible Essay Topics

1. Describe vividly your first job experience. What did you expect? What insights did you gain?

2. Think about other jobs or occupations that are stereotyped. Pick one and show why the image is or isn't correct.

3. Describe the type of job one of your parents has. Analyze why you would or would not want to have that job.

4. Discuss a job you wouldn't take even if you were desperate.

5. Write your own definition of "real work." Depending upon your viewpoint regarding real work, you may want to begin your essay by reacting to the way Rodriquez defines it in his essay.

6. Reread paragraph 18. Write an essay that attempts to show how such conditions might be changed. Is is possible? What would have to be done?

7. Do some research on famous minority leaders involved in the labor problems of aliens, such as Cesar Chávez. See if anything you read triggers some ideas. Don't just write a report unless the assignment allows for it.

8. Brainstorm or freewrite on one or more of the following:

   a. menial jobs   d. blue-collar workers
   b. demeaning jobs   e. white-collar workers
   c. construction work   f. the perfect job

9. If these topics are too "menial" or not "real" enough, find your own topic on some aspect of work.

Preparing to Read

Take a minute or two to look over the following reading selection. Note the title and author, read the first *ten* paragraphs of dialogue and check the length. Make certain you have the time now to read it carefully and to do the exercises that follow it. Then, in the spaces provided, answer the following questions.

1. What do you think the essay is about? _____

_____

2. What do you think the social security worker will say when she gets back

   on the line? _____

_____

Vocabulary

Good comprehension of what you are about to read depends upon your understanding of the words below. The number following each word refers to the paragraph where it is used.

   dispensed (11) handed out, distributed

   wooed (11) sought to marry, courted

reciprocated (11) gave in return

capital (13) any form of material wealth

to set hens (13) to put hens on eggs in order to hatch them

scrounge (13) obtain by salvaging or foraging

shuck (13) remove the shell or husk

threshers (13) people who remove the grain from the plant

shock (13) gather into sheaves for drying

rutted (13) full of grooves made by wheels

reclaimed (14) made suitable for cultivation or habitation

Canadian thistles (14) prickly weeds

flax (14) a plant from which textile fibers are taken

spaded (14) dug

cholera (15) an infectious disease

sustenance (21) livelihood, that which provides nourishment and supports life

Now read the essay.

My Mother Never Worked

BONNIE SMITH-YACKEL

1 "Social Security Office." (The voice answering the telephone sounds very self-assured.)

2 "I'm calling about . . . I . . . my mother just died . . . I was told to call you and see about a . . . death-benefit check, I think they call it. . . ."

3 "I see. Was your mother on Social Security? How old was she?"

4 "Yes . . . she was seventy-eight. . . ."

5 "Do you know her number?"

6 "No . . . I ah . . . don't you have a record?"

7 "Certainly. I'll look it up. Her name?"

8 "Smith, Martha Smith. Or maybe she used Martha Ruth Smith. . . . Sometimes she used her maiden name . . . Martha Jerabeck Smith."

9 "If you'd care to hold on, I'll check our records—it'll be a few minutes."

10 "Yes. . . ."

11 Her love letters—to and from Daddy—were in an old box, tied with ribbons and stiff, rigid-with-age leather thongs: 1918 through 1920; hers written on stationery from the general store she had

worked in full-time and managed, single-handed, after her graduation from high school in 1913; and his, at first, on YMCA or Soldiers and Sailors Club stationery dispensed to the fighting men of World War I. He wooed her thoroughly and persistently by mail, and though she reciprocated all his feeling for her, she dreaded marriage. . . .

12 "It's so hard for me to decide when to have my wedding day— that's all I've thought about these last two days. I have told you dozens of times that I won't be afraid of married life, but when it comes down to setting the date and then picturing myself a married woman with half a dozen or more kids to look after, it just makes me sick. . . . I am weeping right now—I hope that some day I can look back and say how foolish I was to dread it all."

13 They married in February, 1921, and began farming. Their first baby, a daughter, was born in January, 1922, when my mother was 26 years old. The second baby, a son, was born in March, 1923. They were renting farms; my father, besides working his own fields, also was a hired man for two other farmers. They had no capital initially, and had to gain it slowly, working from dawn until midnight every day. My town-bred mother learned to set hens and raise chickens, feed pigs, milk cows, plant and harvest a garden, and can every fruit and vegetable she could scrounge. She carried water nearly a quarter of a mile from the well to fill her wash boilers in order to do her laundry on a scrub board. She learned to shuck grain, feed threshers, shock and husk corn, feed corn pickers. In September, 1925, the third baby came, and in June, 1927, the fourth child—both daughters. In 1930, my parents had enough money to buy their own farm, and that March they moved all their livestock and belongings themselves, 55 miles over rutted, muddy roads.

14 In the summer of 1930 my mother and her two eldest children reclaimed a 40-acre field from Canadian thistles, by chopping them all out with a hoe. In the other fields, when the oats and flax began to head out, the green and blue of the crops were hidden by the bright yellow of wild mustard. My mother walked the fields day after day, pulling each mustard plant. She raised a new flock of baby chicks— 500—and she spaded up, planted, hoed, and harvested a half-acre garden.

15 During the next spring their hogs caught cholera and died. No cash that fall.

16 And in the next year the drought hit. My mother and father trudged from the well to the chickens, the well to the calf pasture, the well to the barn, and from the well to the garden. The sun came out hot and bright, endlessly, day after day. The crops shriveled and died. They harvested half the corn, and ground the other half, stalks and all, and fed it to the cattle as fodder. With the price at four cents

a bushel for the harvested crop, they couldn't afford to haul it into town. They burned it in the furnace for fuel that winter.

17   In 1934, in February, when the dust was still so thick in the Minnesota air that my parents couldn't always see from the house to the barn, their fifth child—a fourth daughter—was born. My father hunted rabbits daily, and my mother stewed them, fried them, canned them, and wished out loud that she could taste hamburger once more. In the fall the shotgun brought prairie chickens, ducks, pheasant, and grouse. My mother plucked each bird, carefully reserving the breast feathers for pillows.

18   In the winter she sewed night after night, endlessly, begging cast-off clothing from relatives, ripping apart coats, dresses, blouses, and trousers to make them to fit her four daughters and son. Every morning and every evening she milked cows, fed pigs and calves, cared for chickens, picked eggs, cooked meals, washed dishes, scrubbed floors, and tended and loved her children. In the spring she planted a garden once more, dragging pails of water to nourish and sustain the vegetables for the family. In 1936 she lost a baby in her sixth month.

19   In 1937 her fifth daughter was born. She was 42 years old. In 1939 a second son, and in 1941 her eighth child—and third son.

20   But the war had come, and prosperity of a sort. The herd of cattle had grown to 30 head; she still milked morning and evening. Her garden was more than a half acre—the rains had come, and by now the Rural Electricity Administration and indoor plumbing. Still she sewed—dresses and jackets for the children, housedresses and aprons for herself, weekly patching of jeans, overalls, and denim shirts. She still made pillows, using the feathers she had plucked, and quilts every year—intricate patterns as well as patchwork, stitched as well as tied—all necessary bedding for her family. Every scrap of cloth too small to be used in quilts was carefully saved and painstakingly sewed together in strips to make rugs. She still went out in the fields to help with the haying whenever there was a threat of rain.

21   In 1959 my mother's last child graduated from high school. A year later the cows were sold. She still raised chickens and ducks, plucked feathers, made pillows, baked her own bread, and every year made a new quilt—now for a married child or for a grandchild. And her garden, that huge, undying symbol of sustenance, was as large and cared for as in all the years before. The canning, and now freezing, continued.

22   In 1969, on a June afternoon, mother and father started out for town so that she could buy sugar to make rhubarb jam for a daughter who lived in Texas. The car crashed into a ditch. She was paralyzed from the waist down.

23   In 1970 her husband, my father, died. My mother struggled to regain some competence and dignity and order in her life. At the

rehabilitation institute, where they gave her physical therapy and trained her to live usefully in a wheelchair, the therapist told me: "She did fifteen pushups today—fifteen! She's almost seventy-five years old! I've never known a woman so strong!"

24 From her wheelchair she canned pickles, baked bread, ironed clothes, wrote dozens of letters weekly to her friends and her "half dozen or more kids," and made three patchwork housecoats and one quilt. She made balls and balls of carpet rags—enough for five rugs. And kept all her love letters.

25 "I think I've found your mother's records—Martha Ruth Smith; married to Ben F. Smith?"

26 "Yes, that's right."

27 "Well, I see that she was getting a widow's pension. . . ."

28 "Yes, that's right."

29 "Well, your mother isn't entitled to our $255 death benefit."

30 "Not entitled? But why?"

31 The voice on the telephone explains patiently:

32 "Well, you see—your mother never worked."

Understanding the Content

Feel free to reread all or parts of the selection in order to answer the following questions.

1. Why was the author's mother afraid to marry, according to one of her letters? Were her fears realized?

2. How old was her mother when she had her last child? How many children did she have? How old was she when she died?

3. Describe the kind of life her mother led. Would you call what she did work? How does it differ from what the government defines as work?

4. Apparently the author's mother was eligible for a death benefit and Social Security pension when her husband died. Why wasn't the author's family eligible for a death-benefit check when her mother died?

5. What is the thesis? Is it implied or stated?

Looking at Structure and Style

1. How does Smith-Yackel use the narrative dialogue at the beginning and end of the essay to tell her story? How effective is this in creating our interests? Would the story have been as effective in making its point if we knew at the beginning that the family was not entitled to a death-benefit check?

2. What is the function of paragraph 12? Aside from being a bit ironic, what can we infer from the paragraph about the mother's character?

3. Smith-Yackel tells her story in a chronological fashion between paragraphs 11 through 25. What transitional devices does she use to help us follow along over so many years?

4. Why does the author spend so much time providing specific details, such as dates, number of farm animals, chores, the amount the death-benefit check would be, and so on? Do such details help the author make her point? Explain.

5. What attitude do you see revealed in the opening and closing dialogue passages with the voice from the Social Security office? Look carefully at the words used to describe the voice.

6. Look through the essay for words the author uses to help us feel and imagine the difficulties her mother experienced. How do such words and phrases help us understand the author's definition of work?

Evaluating the Author's Viewpoints

1. The author apparently felt the need to write this essay after being told that her mother "never worked." How would you describe Smith-Yackel's attitude toward this statement? toward the voice on the telephone?

2. Do you think the author has negative or positive feelings toward the Social Security system? Explain why you do or don't agree with her.

3. Does the author imply that families of people like her mother should receive a death-benefit check? If so, do you agree? If she doesn't imply this, then what is her point?

4. What adjectives do you think the author might use to describe her mother to us? Why?

5. Why do you think the author says so little about her father? Would a discussion of him help make her point stronger?

Pursuing Possible Essay Topics

1. Compare/contrast working conditions you have known with those your parents or grandparents have known. What changes have occurred? Would you want to have lived their work lives?

2. It is a fact that women in general receive less pay than men on most jobs, even when the same tasks are being done. Why does this policy seem to continue? Why did it begin?

3. Defend housework as "real work."

4. Research information on the Social Security system. Does it favor men over women? Are there inequities that need attention drawn to them? You might begin your research by asking the research librarian if the

library has any current government pamphlets on the Social Security system.

5. Define and classify "a man's job" and "a woman's job."

6. Brainstorm or freewrite on one or more of the following:
   a. a definition of work
   b. sexual harrassment at work
   c. "A woman's place is in the home."
   d. "A woman's work is never done."
   e. workaholics
   f. classifications of work

7. If none of these work for you, come up with your own topic on some aspect of work.

 Student Essay

Read the following student essay. As you read, look for the answers to these questions:

1. Does the essay fit the assignment to write on some aspect of work?

2. Does the essay have a thesis and adequate support?

3. Does the essay hold your interest?

"Oh, I'm Just a Housewife"

Roy Wilson

1   After watching my mother deal with our family of five, I can't understand why her answer to the question, "What do you do?" is always, "Oh, I'm just a housewife." JUST a housewife? Anyone who spends most of her time in meal preparation and cleanup, washing and drying clothes, keeping the house clean, attending PTA meetings, leading a cub scout troop, playing taxi driver to us kids when it's time for school, music lessons or the dentist, doing volunteer work for her favorite charity, and making sure that all our family needs are met is not JUST a housewife. She's the real Wonder Woman.

2   Why is it that so many mothers like mine think of themselves as second-class citizens or something similar? Where has this notion come from? Have we males made them feel this way? Has our society made "going to work" outside the home seem more important than what a housewife must face each day?

3   I would be very curious to see what would happen if a housewife went on strike. Dishes would pile up. Food in the house would run out. No meals would appear on the table. There would be no clean clothes when needed. Hobbed-nailed boots would be required just to make it through the cluttered house. Walking and bus riding would increase. Those scout troops would have to disband. Charities would suffer.

4   I doubt if the man of the house would be able to take over. Oh, he might start out with the attitude that he can do just as good a job, but how long would that last? Not long, once he had to come home each night after work to more chores. There would be no more coming home to a prepared meal; he'd have to fix it himself. The kids would all be screaming for something to eat, clean clothes and more bus fare money. Once he quieted the kids, he'd have to clean the house (yes, housewives do windows), go shopping (either take the kids or get a baby sitter), make sure that kids got a bath (after cleaning out all the dog hairs from the bathtub), and fix lunches for the next day. Once the kids were down for the night, he might be able to crawl into an unmade bed and try to read the morning newspaper.

5   No, I don't think many males are going to volunteer for the job. I know I don't want it. So, thanks, mom! I'll do what I can to create a national holiday for housewives. It could be appropriately called Wonder Woman Day.

Reaction

In the space below, write your reaction to the essay. What would you tell the student?

Commentary

Roy says the idea for his essay came from reading Bonnie Smith-Yackel's piece, "My Mother Never Worked." It made him take another look at his mother's typical day. While he had always appreciated everything his mother had done for him and his family, Roy says the Smith-Yackel essay caused him to get more in touch with his own mother and the work she does every day.

The short essay is a tribute of sorts to housewives like his mother. His title attracts our attention and his opening paragraph makes his viewpoint clear. His paragraphs are coherent and he supports them with specifics.

Some students, however, had trouble focusing on Roy's actual thesis statement when he shared his essay in class. Some students pointed out that the opening paragraph raises the question of why so many housewives think of themselves as "just" housewives. But the second paragraph, they said, raises a whole series of questions of "why"? Has the male caused this? Has society? Who is to blame for this?

In the next paragraph, a few students felt that Roy forgot his own questions as he began to wonder what would happen if housewives went on strike. They liked the way the paragraph describes what would happen, but felt that the questions in paragraph 2 still hadn't been addressed.

In paragraph 4, Roy shows us what would happen if the male tried to assume the housewife's role. While his descriptions of the chaos are clear and humorous, Roy's critics felt he still had not addressed his own questions.

Roy ends by saying he doesn't think males will take over, in essence because they couldn't handle the job. Then he calls for a national holiday for housewives.

While everything Roy says certainly centers around his subject, the essay seems loose and disjointed to some. They couldn't understand what specific point Roy wants to make. If his point is to develop the idea that housewives are "Wonder Women," then they felt he needs to provide more examples of why housewives deserve such praise and give less attention to the male's attempts at housework.

Other students in the class, however, felt that although Roy's essay was not tightly held together, he does imply that a housewife should be considered a Wonder Woman by showing the male's awareness that he wouldn't want the job. They felt his critics were being too picky for the type of essay Roy wrote.

What do you think? What advice did you give to Roy in the space above?

Viewpoints on the Media

"The only thing that counts is what comes out of the loudspeaker—and what we're trying to make come out is an honest, coherent account of events. It's not part of our job to please or entertain."
Edward R. Morrow

GETTING through a day without being touched by the media would be difficult. We have daily morning and evening newspapers. We have weekly news magazines to recap what we might have missed in the daily papers. We have digest magazines that gather articles and even books from a variety of sources and condense them for us so that we can keep up with what's new without straining ourselves. We have how-to books and magazines on everything from sex to bomb-making. We stand in line for hours to be among the first to see the latest Star Wars movie; we wouldn't think of owning a car without a radio (AM *and* FM, of course) and cassette player. We can't seem to get enough music as stores and elevators numb us with Muzak; the streets pulse with sounds from "boom boxes" on strollers' shoulders; parks fill up with runners wired to their headsets. More than 87 million homes in the United States alone have television sets, each one turned on for an average of more than seven hours a day. According to one study done by the Roper Organization, 64% of the American public turns to television for most of its news. And 53% rank TV as the most believable news source.

Collectively, the power the media have on us is worth examining. Both directly and indirectly, the media have a profound effect on our lives. What we eat, what we buy, what we do, even what we think is influenced by the media.

Recent concern for the direction the media are taking us has prompted such books as Marie Winn's *The Plug-In Drug* and *Unplugging the Plug-In Drug*, which deal with the negative effects of television; David Halberstam's *The Powers that Be*, an account of the people who create, control, and use the media to shape American policy and politics; Norman Corwin's *Trivializing America: The Triumph of Mediocrity,* a look at the way the media have contributed to a lowering of our cultural standards; Ben Bagdikian's *The Media Monopoly,* in which it is revealed that only 26 corporations control half or more of all media, including book publishers, television and radio stations, newspapers, and movie companies; and Mark Hertsgaard's *On Bended Knee: The Press and the Reagan Presidency,* which reveals how the press gets conned by the candidates and ignores election issues.

How believable, how revealing, how comprehensive, how good is what the media provide us? How much influence do advertising sponsors have on the media? Should we become more concerned with its effects than we are? Just what effects *do* the media have on our lives? These are questions that the reading selections in this unit may prompt you to ask. It is hoped that reading them will stimulate both your thinking and writing.

📖 *Preparing to Read*

Take a minute or two to look over the following reading selection. Note the title and author, read the opening paragraph, and check the length. Make certain you have the time now to read it carefully and to do the exercises that follow it. Then, in the spaces provided, answer the following questions.

1. What viewpoint about the media does the title indicate the essay will

   be about? _____

   _____

2. What do you think you will learn from reading this essay? _____

   _____

Vocabulary

Good comprehension of what you are about to read depends upon your understanding of the words below. The number following each word refers to the paragraph where it is used.

vulnerable (3) open to being harmed

petty (4) relatively insignificant

police blotter (6) a book with the records of the daily events at a police station

news binges (7) watching too much news on television

abated (7) lessened

ironically (8) oppositely or differently from what is expected

sporadic (9) occurring at irregular intervals

blitz (11) an intense campaign

affluent (12) wealthy, well-to-do

tout (13) recommend, advocate

panacea (13) cure-all

Now read the essay.

TV's Crime Coverage Is Too Scary and Misleading

GEORGETTE BENNETT

1   Joan, a 39-year-old lawyer living in Los Angeles, loves her home, her city and her work. But there's one thing that makes her constantly uneasy: crime. She says that her daily exposure to TV news makes her afraid to walk around her West Hollywood neighborhood at night.

2   "With what I hear, I'm afraid to go out. I always lock my car door when I'm driving. I always keep my eyes to the ground. I never make eye contact. I've always been careful—but now I'm careful and scared."

3   Like most people who are afraid of crime, Joan has never been a street-crime victim. The odds are she never will be, because she's white, female and no longer in the vulnerable 14-to-24-year-old age group. But media-manufactured myths about crime have robbed her of her sense of safety.

4   One myth is that most crimes are violent. Ten percent of network and 20 percent of local news time is devoted to crime stories, most of them violent. But in fact, only 10 percent of all crimes committed are violent. The majority are petty thefts, the kind in which a wallet or purse is stolen.

5   You'd never know that from watching TV news, where, according to a recent *Newsweek* poll conducted by Gallup, 62 percent of Americans get most of their news. At various times, Joan has turned on her TV and seen an account of a driver plowing his car into a crowd of people on Westwood Boulevard; or a mass murderer gunning down

the patrons of a McDonald's; or a mad rapist stalking women in the hills.

6   When TV talks crime, people listen. A recent study conducted by Michael J. Robinson, visiting scholar at the American Enterprise Institute, and Maura Clancey, at the University of Maryland, shows that "violent crimes are more memorable as news events than all but the most dramatic political occurrences." The crimes considered most newsworthy—children being molested in a Baltimore day-care center; a paroled mugger shooting a New York transit cop—have little in common with the routine petty crimes that dominate the police blotter.

7   Another common myth is that the crime rate is rising. Joan's morning and evening news binges have convinced her we're in the grip of a crime wave. Gallup polls, Harris polls and government research show she's not alone. There was a crime boom in the 1960s. The fear it generated has not abated, despite the fact that crime rates leveled off in the 1970s and (according to the National Crime Survey) have taken a nose dive in the 1980s.

8   Ironically, it's those least at risk who fear crime most. The little old lady next door is not the one most likely to be beaten or mugged. It's the young black dude on the other side of town.

9   Heavy TV viewers, according to the influential "Figgie Report on Fear of Crime" (conducted by Research and Forecasts, Inc., in 1980), are the ones most rattled by the myth of a crime explosion. Sporadic TV viewers tend to be less fearful. This is consistent with the findings of Dr. George Gerbner and historians at the Annenberg School of Communications.

10   Of course, we do have a massive crime problem in America. Even with the latest decreases, more than a quarter of all households were touched by crime last year. We can't blame TV for that. Nevertheless, the "body-count" approach to covering crime makes it harder for us to deal with the problem.

11   The day-care center media blitz would lead you to believe that schools and childcare facilities are where kids are in greatest danger of sexual abuse. Not so. According to estimates by the American Humane Association and the National Center on Child Abuse and Neglect, a high proportion of children are molested at the hands of their own families. But media-generated public outrage is leading legislators to give priority to day-care centers rather than the home.

12   Reports of doctors being robbed and murdered in their suburban homes might convince you that it's the affluent who are at greatest risk from crime. They're not. It's the poor. But fortunes are invested in security for upscale communities. The really vulnerable, low-income neighborhoods are left unprotected.

13   Most of our law-enforcement resources are devoted to street crime. Politicians tout the hiring of more police as a panacea. This, despite the Police Foundation's landmark research back in 1974 showing that larger numbers of police don't reduce crime.

14   All network and many local news shows employ specially trained reporters to cover health, science, economics and sports. Crime is at least as complex a subject. It should not be left to general-assignment or police-beat reporters who have no specialized knowledge of how to interpret crime statistics or what's behind them.

15   Aside from an occasional special report, such as ABC's 1983 crime series, TV's crime coverage is a public disservice. Viewers like Joan are doubly victimized. Not only are they assaulted by images of blood-spattered pavement, they're also panicked into supporting public policies that often make the problem worse.

Understanding the Content

Feel free to reread all or parts of the selection to answer the following questions.

1. According to a recent poll, what percent of Americans get most of their news from television?

2. Bennett presents four myths about crime that television perpetuates. What are they? What is the reality for each?

3. From what sources does Bennett get much of her information?

4. According to some research, would hiring more police help reduce crime?

5. What suggestion does Bennett offer the media regarding reporters who cover the news?

6. What is the thesis? Is it implied or stated?

Looking at Structure and Style

1. Bennett opens and closes her essay with the example of Joan. Of what is Joan an example? How does this example help develop Bennett's thesis? How does it help identify her audience? Is Joan a real person?

2. In order to disprove the myths about crime, Bennett needs proof. In what paragraphs does Bennett offer support that goes against the myths? Are her sources good?

3. What are some transitional devices Bennett uses to take us from the myths to her facts? Where do they appear?

4. What is the function of paragraph 10?

5. How do paragraphs 13–15 conclude the essay? What function does each paragraph serve? What is her answer to the problem?

6. Explain or rewrite the following passages from the essay:
   a. "When TV talks crime, people listen." (6)
   b. "Heavy TV viewers . . . are the ones most rattled by the myth of a crime explosion." (9)
   c. " . . . The 'body-count' approach to covering crime makes it harder for us to deal with the problem." (10)
   d. "Politicians tout the hiring of more police as a panacea." (13)
   e. "Viewers like Joan are doubly victimized." (15)

Evaluating the Author's Viewpoints

1. Bennett's title states her viewpoint on TV crime coverage. Do you agree with her? Why?

2. What do you think is Bennett's opinion of television viewers like Joan? What makes you think so?

3. Do you think that most of the author's sources that counter the myths about crime are reliable? Why?

4. In paragraph 13, Bennett says that despite the Police Foundation's landmark research showing that more police doesn't mean less crime, politicians continue to call for the hiring of more. Why do you think they ignore the research?

5. Do you agree with Bennett's suggestion for better television coverage of crime? Why? What other ideas might she suggest to her audience?

Pursuing Possible Essay Topics

1. Watch as much television news as you can for several days in a row, paying particular attention to the way crime is reported. How much time exposure does crime get? What crimes get featured most? Do any of them fit the four myths Bennett discusses? Write your own essay on how television covers the news.

2. Write an essay to the same audience as Bennett's. Instead of suggesting what the media can do, offer suggestions as to what the viewer can or should do to lose the fear of crime.

3. If 62 percent of Americans get their news from television, what does this suggest about our society? What's good and what's bad about it? If most frequent viewers are like Joan, what other misconceptions besides a fear of crime might they develop from watching so much television?

4. Write an essay about television's power to persuade.

5. Do some research on the negative influences of television viewing. Try Marie Winn's two books, *The Plug-In Drug* and *Unplugging the Plug-In Drug;* Jeffrey Schrank's *Snap, Crackle and Popular Taste in America;* Norman Corwin's *Trivializing America;* Mark Hertsgaard's *On Bended Knee;* or the reports mentioned in Bennett's essay. They should provide you with many ideas.

6. Brainstorm or freewrite on one or more of the following:

   a. TV crime shows
   b. local TV news
   c. network news (CBS, NBC, ABC)
   d. Televangelists
   e. TV addicts
   f. TV news vs. newspaper news

7. Ignore these and think of your own topic on some aspect of the media.

Preparing to Read

Take a minute or two to look over the following reading selection. Note the title and author, read the opening paragraph, and check the length. Make certain you have the time now to read it carefully and to do the exercises that follow it. Then, in the spaces below, answer the following questions.

1. In case you are not familiar with the *National Enquirer*, it is a weekly newspaper that deals with gossip about famous people and sensational, often misleading, stories. What does the title imply about the media?

   _____

   _____

2. With which of the media does the opening paragraph deal? _____

   _____

Vocabulary

Good comprehension of what you are about to read depends upon your understanding of the words below. The number following each word refers to the paragraph where it is used.

preserve (1) something considered restricted to the use of certain persons

slicksheet (2) the glossy paper used by magazines

preposterous (2) absurd

unverifiable (2) not able to be proven

tripe (3) rubbish, something of no value

warrant the prominence (5) deserve the wide exposure

query (6) inquiry, question

Angola (7) country in southwestern Africa

apparatchiks (8) part of the communist forces, presumably a play on the word apparatus with a Russian-type ending

reprehensible (9) worthy of blame

apartheid (9) an official policy of racial segregation in effect in the Republic in South Africa

sepsis (10) blood or tissue poisoning

inherent (11) existing as an essential characteristic of, intrinsic

guise (12) outward appearance

scam (12) fraud, swindle

breaches (13) violations

triviality (14) insignificance

herd instinct (14) people's tendency to go along with what everyone else does or thinks

Now read the essay.

The Media's Regrettable Imitation of the National Enquirer

BEN STEIN

1   How do the cover-story decisions of the major news magazines get made? When I was a child, *TIME* and *Newsweek* focused on major political and social events. Great political leaders, generals and thinkers graced their covers. Such subjects were their natural preserve.

2   Today, magazine journalism looks more like the *National Enquirer* on slicksheet. Take the Oct. 12 *TIME* cover story "Are Women Fed Up?" If you looked inside, you found a story as preposterous as its title: a marginally qualified woman talking about her latest (unverifiable) "study" on American women and their relationships. They are, according to her report, whining and griping about men.

3   *TIME*'s story will no doubt preoccupy the minds of the beauty-parlor set. But more important is the fact that this intellectual tripe ended up on *TIME*'s cover. That says volumes. Add to it the recent

Life cover on what it's like to be 17, mix in gossipy stories about politicians' love lives, then stir in "business" magazine "coverage" of who are the richest, and what do you have?

4   You have stories absolutely without relevance to anything in the tide of man's affairs. What can it possibly matter to the future of man whether or not the sultan of Brunei is richer than Laurence Tisch? What is the possible significance of whether or not Donna Rice had her breasts done and how much it cost?

5   I'm not saying that these stories are undeserving of coverage. Quite the contrary. The question is whether or not these stories warrant the prominence they receive, possibly at the expense of real stories.

6   Which brings me to an even more important query: Who decides what stories will go uncovered in the mass media? There are truly important stories going on in the world today that are virtually ignored by the world press:

7   *Item:* There is a brutal war taking place in Angola. Cuban, Soviet and East German soldiers have murdered thousands of black Africans seeking freedom from Soviet domination. With virtually no outside help, Jonas Savimbi's pro-Western UNITA movement has fought and sometimes defeated the communist storm troopers. This is a major story, yet it is seldom reported by our major news organizations. It is important because it tells us about the nature of our world in basic, essential terms. The war in Angola tells us about the real aims and morals of the Soviet Union.

8   Every year in Angola, several thousand black African children are taken against their will by Cuban soldiers to the Isle of Pines. There, they are trained to be little apparatchiks. This is slavery in every meaningful sense of the term. In many respects, it is the Africa-West Indies slave trade reconstructed. Only this time it is being done by the communists.

9   Stories about what's really going on in Angola typically appear only in the "right-wing" press. They reveal brutality toward blacks at least as bad, and probably far worse, than the reprehensible acts of the apartheid regime of South Africa. Yet they largely go unreported. Why?

10   *Item:* In the Soviet Union, there is a full-scale health crisis. Life expectancy is declining. The average middle-aged woman there has had 10 abortions. There is widespread death from sepsis in hospitals. Decent medical care is hard to come by, unless you're a high party official. Yet the Soviet government will not use "defense" money to heal its people.

11   This is big news. It tells us something about the inherent cruelty of the Marxist-Leninist state. Yet it is seldom emphasized. Why?

12   *Item:* There is widespread looting going on in America under the guise of "going private." In this scam, managers of publicly held companies buy the company's stock at low prices, own the business for a while, then sell it off for many times what they paid the original shareholders. In the process, they realize huge profits. Some of those billionaires on the magazines' richest lists got there by simply looting their own stockholders through "going private."

13   This story, too, is only occasionally reported in the financial press, and never in the general press. Great crimes are taking place, great breaches of trust, and no ink gets spilled to speak of.

14   My point is that the news media of this country choose its subjects on the basis of triviality, gossip, herd instinct, ignorance, pro-Soviet feelings and still more ignorance. This is not a small matter. We cannot act on threats of which we are kept unaware. We cannot defend ourselves against dangers we are not told of. If this is just coincidence, it is an unfortunate coincidence indeed. We have a great media apparatus, and basically, it is putting us to sleep. I wonder why.

Understanding the Content

Feel free to reread all or parts of the selection to answer the following questions.

1. Stein sees a difference in the cover stories of magazines such as *TIME* and *Newsweek* today from when he was a boy. What is the difference?

2. What are some examples of recent cover stories that Stein feels are not worth the prominence given them?

3. What are some examples of stories *not* given the prominence that the author feels they deserve?

4. Based on Stein's comments in paragraphs 7, 8, and 11, what can you infer about his feelings toward the Soviet Union and communism?

5. Why is Stein concerned with what he calls magazine journalism that "looks more like the *National Enquirer*"?

6. What is Stein's thesis? Is it stated or implied?

Looking at Structure and Style

1. How well do the comparisons made in paragraphs 1 and 2 work? Is the use of the *National Enquirer* effective in making his point?

2. Stein uses questions frequently throughout his essay. Where do they appear? Are they effective?

3. What is Stein's point in using the word *Item* to begin paragraphs 7, 10, and 12?

4. Stein is straightforward in his views. What are some words that he uses throughout that reflect his opinions (for example, "a story as preposterous as its title")?

5. Why does Stein place quotation marks around the words "business" and "coverage" in paragraph 3 and in other places?

6. Explain or rewrite the following passages from the essay:
   a. " . . . a marginally qualified woman talking about her latest (unverifiable) 'study' . . . " (2)
   b. "*TIME*'s story will no doubt preoccupy the minds of the beauty-parlor set." (3)
   c. "There is widespread looting going on in America under the guise of 'going private.' " (12)
   d. "We have a great media apparatus, and basically, it is putting us to sleep." (14)

7. What advice, if any, would you offer the author for revision?

Evaluating the Author's Viewpoints

1. Stein feels that the news media of this country are choosing their coverage on the basis of "triviality, gossip, herd instinct, ignorance, pro-Soviet feelings and still more ignorance." (14) Do you agree? Do you read the magazines he mentions often enough to make a thoughtful reply?

2. Stein supports his views in part by mentioning events in Angola, South Africa, and the Soviet Union that he claims go relatively unreported. Are they worthy of cover stories on major news magazines? Explain.

3. Stein implies that reports on the Soviet Union are too "pro-Soviet." Is he right? Do you share his concerns?

4. Have any of the events Stein mentions as newsworthy received more prominence in the news since his essay was written? Explain.

5. Is our "great media apparatus . . . putting us to sleep"? (14) Explain why you agree or disagree.

Pursuing Possible Essay Topics

1. Agree/disagree with Stein's thesis. Use your own examples from some recent news magazine cover stories to support your viewpoint.

2. Discuss what obligation, if any, news magazines have to report the type of stories Stein claims they are ignoring. Is it the business of a news magazine to report such stories or to make a profit by providing stories it feels its readers want?

3. Do some research and compare the cover stories in a major news magazine, such as *TIME* or *Newsweek*, from twenty years ago with one from

today. The library should have copies on file or on microfilm. Check with your librarian.

4. Read a few issues of the *National Enquirer, Star,* or *Globe* and write your opinion of one of them. Who reads it? What news is given most space? What of importance can be learned from reading it?

5. If Stein is correct in saying that news magazines are getting more like the *National Enquirer,* why do you suppose it is happening? What does this say about our society's values?

6. When *TIME* magazine discovered that one of its favorite features among readers was its "People" section, it started a spinoff magazine, *People.* Examine an issue or two of *People* and evaluate it and/or its readers. Does it look "more like the *National Enquirer* on slicksheet"?

7. Discuss why it is important for a democratic society to keep its people well-informed. Are we a well-informed people? Do we have access to the kind of news with which Stein says we should be familiar? Do most people really care or want to know about what's happening in the rest of the world?

8. Ignore these and find your own topic on some aspect of the media.

📖 *Preparing to Read*

Take a minute or two to look over the following reading selection. Note the title and author, read the opening paragraph, and check the length. Make certain you have the time now to read it carefully and to do the exercises that follow it. Then, in the spaces provided, answer the following questions.

1. What do you think the essay will be about? _____

_____

_____

2. What can you tell about the author's attitude and tone from the title and

first paragraph? _____

_____

3. What do you think you will learn from reading this essay? _____

_____

_____

Vocabulary

Good comprehension of what you are about to read depends upon your understanding of the words below. The number following each word refers to the paragraph where it is used.

striding (1) walking in big steps

burly (3) heavy and strong

inducement (5) an incentive or persuasion

upsurge (7) a rapid rise

saturated (7) thoroughly soaked, filled

Mary Lou Retton (7) Olympic goldmedal gymnast

Now read the essay.

Red, White, and Beer

DAVE BARRY

1   Lately I've been feeling very patriotic, especially during commercials. Like, when I see those strongly pro-American Chrysler commercials, the ones where the winner of the Bruce Springsteen Sound-Alike Contest sings about how The Pride Is Back, the ones where Lee Iacocca himself comes striding out and practically challenges the president of Toyota to a knife fight, I get this warm, proud feeling inside, the same kind of feeling I get whenever we hold routine naval maneuvers off the coast of Libya.

2   But if you want to talk about *real* patriotism, of course, you have to talk about beer commercials. I would have to say that Miller is the most patriotic brand of beer. I grant you it tastes like rat saliva, but we are not talking about taste here. What we are talking about, according to the commercials, is that Miller is by God an *American* beer, "born and brewed in the U.S.A.," and the men who drink it are American men, the kind of men who aren't afraid to perspire freely and shake a man's hand. That's mainly what happens in Miller commercials: Burly American men go around, drenched in perspiration, shaking each other's hands in a violent and patriotic fashion.

3   You never find out exactly why these men spend so much time shaking hands. Maybe shaking hands is just their simple straightforward burly masculine American patriotic way of saying to each other: "Floyd, I am truly sorry I drank all that Miller beer last night and went to the bathroom in your glove compartment." Another possible

explanation is that, since there are never any women in the part of America where beer commercials are made, the burly men have become lonesome and desperate for any form of physical contact. I have noticed that sometimes, in addition to shaking hands, they hug each other. Maybe very late at night, after the David Letterman show, there are Miller commercials in which the burly men engage in slow dancing. I don't know.

4   I do know that in one beer commercial, I think this is for Miller—although it could be for Budweiser, which is also a very patriotic beer—the burly men build a house. You see them all getting together and pushing up a brand-new wall. Me, I worry some about a house built by men drinking beer. In my experience, you run into trouble when you ask a group of beer-drinking men to perform any task more complex than remembering not to light the filter ends of cigarettes.

5   For example, in my younger days, whenever anybody in my circle of friends wanted to move, he'd get the rest of us to help, and, as an inducement, he'd buy a couple of cases of beer. This almost always produced unfortunate results, such as the time we were trying to move Dick "The Wretch" Curry from a horrible fourth-floor walk-up apartment in Manhattan's Lower East Side to another horrible fourth-floor walkup apartment in Manhattan's Lower East Side, and we hit upon the labor-saving concept of, instead of carrying The Wretch's possessions manually down the stairs, simply dropping them out the window, down onto the street, where The Wretch was racing around, gathering up the broken pieces of his life and shrieking at us to stop helping him move, his emotions reaching a fever pitch when his bed, which had been swinging wildly from a rope, entered the apartment two floors below his through what had until seconds earlier been a window.

6   This is the kind of thinking you get, with beer. So I figure what happens, in the beer commercial where the burly men are building the house, is they push the wall up so it's vertical, and then, after the camera stops filming them, they just keep pushing, and the wall crashes down on the other side, possibly onto somebody's pickup truck. And then they all shake hands.

7   But other than that, I'm in favor of the upsurge in retail patriotism, which is lucky for me because the airwaves are saturated with pro-American commercials. Especially popular are commercials in which the newly restored Statue of Liberty—and by the way, I say Lee Iacocca should get some kind of medal for that, or at least be elected president—appears to be endorsing various products, as if she were Mary Lou Retton or somebody. I saw one commercial strongly suggesting that the Statue of Liberty uses Sure brand underarm deodorant.

8   I have yet to see a patriotic laxative commercial, but I imagine it's only a matter of time. They'll show some actors dressed up as hardworking country folk, maybe at a church picnic, smiling at each other and eating pieces of pie. At least one of them will be a black person. The Statue of Liberty will appear in the background. Then you'll hear a country-style singer singing:

> *"Folks 'round here they love this land;*
> *They stand by their beliefs;*
> *An' when they git themselves stopped up;*
> *They want some quick relief."*

9   Well, what do you think? Pretty good commercial concept, huh?

10   Nah, you're right. They'd never try to pull something like that. They'd put the statue in the *foreground*.

Understanding the Content

Feel free to reread all or parts of the selection to answer the following questions.

1. What, according to Barry, has been the theme of recent commercials?

2. What product does Barry feel reflects *"real patriotism"* in its commercials? What brand does he call the most patriotic?

3. What do the men in beer commercials seem to spend most of their time doing? How does Barry explain it?

4. Why is Barry in favor of the "upsurge in retail patriotism"? (7)

5. What product does Barry foresee being advertised in the near future?

6. What is the thesis? Is it implied or stated?

Looking at Structure and Style

1. How would you describe the tone of the essay? What words and phrases help establish this tone?

2. What is Barry's attitude toward his subject? How can you tell?

3. What is the function of the first sentence in paragraph 2?

4. How do paragraphs 4–6 work as a unit? What inferences do you draw from his treatment of the subject?

5. What is the function of paragraph 8?

6. Why do you think Barry uses Lee Iacocca, Bruce Springsteen, Mary Lou Retton, and the Statue of Liberty as references?

7. Explain the following passages from the essay:

    a. "... the ones where Lee Iacocca himself comes striding out and practically challenges the president of Toyota to a knife fight..." (1)

    b. "... the same kind of feeling I get whenever we hold routine maneuvers off the coast of Libya." (1)

    c. "... Miller is by God an *American* beer, 'born and brewed in the U.S.A.'..." (2)

    d. "... his bed, which had been swinging wildly from a rope, entered the apartment two floors below his through what had until seconds earlier been a window." (5)

    e. "Nah, you're right. They'd never try to pull something like that. They'd put the statue in the *foreground*." (10)

Evaluating the Author's Viewpoints

1. How well does Barry's title fit his point?

2. What do you think is Barry's opinion of commercials? Do you agree with his views? Explain.

3. To what audience do you think Barry is writing? Why do you think so?

4. In paragraph 5, Barry portrays an account of his "younger days." Do you think this really happened? What is the purpose of the paragraph?

Pursuing Possible Essay Topics

1. Watch as much television news as you can for several days in a row paying particular attention to beer commercials. How close do they come to Barry's account of them? Write your own essay on beer commercials.

2. Write an essay to the same audience as Barry. Instead of being humorous and sarcastic, write a serious account of the effects beer advertising has on a younger audience.

3. Think about other television commercials you have seen. How realistically do they portray male-female relationships? What do they suggest? Are stereotypes portrayed? Write an evaluation of such commercials.

4. Analyze some television commercials, looking carefully at what is being sold besides the product. What suggestions are being made or implied regarding the use of the product? At whom are they aimed? What values, if any, are implied that have nothing to do with the product itself?

5. Brainstorm or freewrite on one or more of the following:

    a. TV automobile commercials   d. TV beer commercials

    b. TV soap commercials   e. humor in TV ads

    c. frequency of TV ads   f. the use of sex in TV ads

6. Ignore these and think of your own topic on some aspect of the media.

📖 *Preparing to Read*

Take a minute or two to look over the following reading selection. Note the title and author, read the opening paragraph, and check the length. Make certain you have the time now to read it carefully and to do the exercises that follow it. Then, in the spaces provided, answer the following questions.

1. What do you think the title means? _____

_____

2. What subject does the essay discuss? _____

_____

3. What do you think is the author's viewpoint on the subject? _____

_____

Vocabulary

Good comprehension of what you are about to read depends upon your understanding of the words below. The number following each word refers to the paragraph where it is used.

grisly (1) gruesome, horrible

allegedly (2) supposedly

Mrs. Grundy (3) an extremely conservative, prudish person

garroting (3) strangulating

desecrating (4) abusing something sacred

prestigious (5) highly respected

denunciations (5) formal condemnations or accusations

advocates (7) recommends, supports

purveyors (7) distributors

lepers (7) outcasts

proffers (7) offers

Walter Cronkite (8) a popular TV news announcer, now retired

sanction (9) authorize, approve

trivial (10) insignificant

cerebral (10) intellectual, theoretical

propagandists (11) advocates, those who spread their doctrines and beliefs

rampant (13) widespread
endemic (14) prevalent, common in our society
forum (15) a medium for open discussion
bluenoses (15) puritanical people

Now read the essay.

The Issue Isn't Sex, It's Violence

CARYL RIVERS

1   After a grisly series of murders in California, possibly inspired by the lyrics of a rock song, we are hearing a familiar chorus: Don't blame rock and roll. Kids will be kids. They love to rebel, and the more shocking the stuff, the better they like it.

2   There's some truth in this, of course. I loved to watch Elvis shake his torso when I was a teen-ager, and it was even more fun when Ed Sullivan wouldn't let the cameras show him below the waist. I snickered at the forbidden "Rock with Me, Annie" lyrics by a black Rhythm and Blues group, which were deliciously naughty. But I am sorry, rock fans, that is not the same thing as hearing lyrics about how a man is going to force a woman to perform oral sex on him at gunpoint in a little number called "Eat Me Alive." It is not in the same league with a song about the delights of slipping into a woman's room while she is sleeping and murdering her, the theme of an AC/DC ballad that allegedly inspired the California slayer.

3   Make no mistake, it is not sex we are talking about here, but violence. Violence against women. Most rock songs are not violent—they are funky, sexy, rebellious, and sometimes witty. Please do not mistake me for a Mrs. Grundy. If Prince wants to leap about wearing only a purple jock strap, fine. Let Mick Jagger unzip his fly as he gyrates, if he wants to. But when either one of them starts garroting, beating, or sodomizing a woman in their number, that is another story.

4   I always find myself annoyed when "intellectual" men dismiss violence against women with a yawn, as if it were beneath their dignity to notice. I wonder if the reaction would be the same if the violence were directed against someone other than women. How many people would yawn and say, "Oh, kids will be kids," if a rock group did a nifty little number called "Lynchin'," in which stringing

up and stomping on black people were set to music? Who would chuckle and say, "Oh, just a little adolescent rebellion" if a group of rockers went on MTV. dressed as Nazis, desecrating synagogues and beating up Jews to the beat of twanging guitars?

5   I'll tell you what would happen. Prestigious dailies would thunder on editorial pages; senators would fall over each other to get denunciations into the Congressional Record. The president would appoint a commission to clean up the music business.

6   But violence against women is greeted by silence. It shouldn't be.

7   This does not mean censorship, or book (or record) burning. In a society that protects free expression, we understand a lot of stuff will float up out of the sewer. Usually, we recognize the ugly stuff that advocates violence against any group as the garbage it is, and we consider its purveyors as moral lepers. We hold our nose and tolerate it, but we speak out against the values it proffers.

8   But images of violence against women are not staying on the fringes of society. No longer are they found only in tattered, paper-covered books or in movie houses where winos snooze and the scent of urine fills the air. They are entering the mainstream at a rapid rate. This is happening at a time when the media, more and more, set the agenda for the public debate. It is a powerful legitimizing force—especially television. Many people regard what they see on TV as the truth; Walter Cronkite once topped a poll as the most trusted man in America.

9   Now, with the advent of rock videos and all-music channels, rock music has grabbed a big chunk of legitimacy. American teen-agers have instant access, in their living rooms, to the messages of rock, on the same vehicle that brought them Sesame Street. Who can blame them if they believe that the images they see are accurate reflections of adult reality, approved by adults? After all, Big Bird used to give them lessons on the same little box. Adults, by their silence, sanction the images. Do we really want our kids to think that rape and violence are what sexuality is all about?

10   This is not a trivial issue. Violence against women is a major social problem, one that's more than a cerebral issue to me. I teach at Boston University, and one of my most promising young journalism students was raped and murdered. Two others told me of being raped. Recently, one female student was assaulted and beaten so badly she had $5,000 worth of medical bills and permanent damage to her back and eyes.

11   It's nearly impossible, of course, to make a cause-and-effect link between lyrics and images and acts of violence. But images have a tremendous power to create an atmosphere in which violence against certain people is sanctioned. Nazi propagandists knew that full well when they portrayed Jews as ugly, greedy, and powerful.

12   The outcry over violence against women, particularly in a sexual context, is being legitimized in two ways: by the increasing movement of these images into the mainstream of the media in TV, films, magazines, albums, videos, and by the silence about it.

13   Violence, of course, is rampant in the media. But it is usually set in some kind of moral context. It's usually only the bad guys who commit violent acts against the innocent. When the good guys get violent, it's against those who deserve it. Dirty Harry blows away the scum, he doesn't walk up to a toddler and say, "Make my day." The A Team does not shoot up suburban shopping malls.

14   But in some rock songs, it's the "heroes" who commit the acts. The people we are programmed to identify with are the ones being violent, with women on the receiving end. In a society where rape and assaults on women are endemic, this is no small problem, with millions of young boys watching on their TV screens and listening on their Walkmans.

15   I think something needs to be done. I'd like to see people in the industry respond to the problem. I'd love to see some women rock stars speak out against violence against women. I would like to see disc jockeys refuse air play to records and videos that contain such violence. At the very least, I want to see the end of the silence. I want journalists and parents and critics and performing artists to keep this issue alive in the public forum. I don't want people who are concerned about this issue labeled as bluenoses and bookburners and ignored.

16   And I wish it wasn't always just women who were speaking out. Men have as large a stake in the quality of our civilization as women do in the long run. Violence is a contagion that infects at random. Let's hear something, please, from the men.

Understanding the Content

Feel free to reread all or parts of the selection to answer the following questions.

1. What does Rivers mean by her title, "The Issue Isn't Sex, It's Violence"? Violence against whom?

2. Why is Rivers concerned that teenagers who were raised on Sesame Street might be mislead by some rock videos and all-music channels?

3. Rivers says that violence is rampant in the media, mentioning the Dirty Harry movies and the now cancelled show on television, "The A Team." Why does she consider this type of violence less harmful than some of the rock lyrics and rock videos? How do the heroes in these shows differ from the "heroes" in the rock videos?

4. What examples from her personal life does Rivers offer to support her view that violence against women " is not a trivial issue"? Are they good examples?

5. What are the suggestions Rivers offers to people in the music industry as a way to combat violence against women? Who else does she wish would speak out? Why?

Looking at Structure and Style

1. In paragraph 2, Rivers mentions that she "loved to watch Elvis shake his torso," and "snickered" at certain rock lyrics that were "deliciously naughty." What function does this serve?

2. What function does paragraph 3 serve?

3. How do paragraphs 4–6 work together to make her point? Why does she make paragraph 6 a single sentence?

4. How do paragraphs 7 and 8 work together? Why does she make it clear she is not talking about censoring rock lyrics or videos?

5. What is the function of paragraphs 13 and 14? How do they work together to help support her thesis?

6. Concluding paragraphs 15 and 16 present Rivers's suggestions for curtailing the problem. Would it make much difference if she reversed the order of the two paragraphs? Explain.

7. Explain or rewrite the following passages from the essay:
   a. "I always find myself annoyed when 'intellectual' men dismiss violence against women with a yawn, as if it were beneath their dignity to notice." (4)
   b. "Usually, we recognize the ugly stuff that advocates violence against any group as the garbage it is, and we consider its purveyors as moral lepers." (7)
   c. "It [the media] is a powerful legitimizing force. . . ." (8)
   d. "I don't want people who are concerned about this issue labeled as bluenoses and bookburners and ignored." (15)

Evaluating the Author's Viewpoints

1. Rivers believes that some rock lyrics and music videos express a violence toward women, frequently a sexual violence. Do you agree? Have you listened to enough rock lyrics or seen enough MTV to speak from knowledge?

2. Look at each of the suggestions Rivers offers in paragraph 15. Do you think each suggestion is worth considering? Would the implementation of her suggestions be better than applying censorship laws? Explain.

3. In paragraphs 4 and 16, Rivers implies that men are not doing enough, that they are too silent about the problem. Do you agree? On what do you base your answer?

4. What is your response to paragraph 12? Is this a fairly good statement of her thesis?

Pursuing Possible Essay Topics

1. If you are not familiar with some recent rock lyrics or music videos, turn on the radio or MTV. Do you see or hear any violence toward women? Write an essay that agrees or disagrees with Rivers's thesis.

2. Analyze the lyrics of a "top-ten" rock song. What is being said? What is being implied? Do the words have any merit?

3. Write an essay that describes a rock video that appears on MTV (or some other all-music channel). What is happening? Do the images fit the lyrics? Are the images suggestive? What values are being portrayed that young people might accept because they admire the musician or singer?

4. Defend or refute the need for some type of censorship in the music industry as a way to protect young children and teenagers from exposure to sexual looseness or violence in songs and videos.

5. Brainstorm or freewrite on one or more of the following:
   a. MTV
   b. punk rock
   c. the Top Forty
   d. rock-and-roll
   e. your favorite music group
   f. influence of music

6. Come up with your own topic on some aspect of the media.

Preparing to Read

Take a minute or two to look over the following reading selection. Note the title and author, read the opening paragraph, and check the length. Make certain you have the time now to read it carefully and to do the exercises that follow it. Then, in the spaces provided, answer the following questions.

1. What will you be reading about? _____

_____

2. Why do some controversial books not get published? _____

_____

3. What might you learn from reading this selection? _____

_____

Vocabulary

Good comprehension of what you are about to read depends upon your understanding of the words below. The number following each word refers to the paragraph where it is used.

Catcher in the Rye (1) a J. D. Salinger novel that appears frequently on banned book lists in many school districts

timidity (1) reluctance, shyness

pervasive (1) widespread

credibility (2) believability

jeopardized (2) exposed to harm

Andrea Dworkin (2) a feminist writer

disseminated (4) distributed, handed out

touted (4) praised highly

incurring (4) bringing upon oneself, subjecting oneself to

wrath (4) rage, fury

detrimental (5) causing damage or harm

prevailing (6) triumphing

subsidiaries (6) companies owned by another larger company

chronicled (7) recorded

moguls (7) powerfully rich persons

diversity (7) variety

overheads (8) companies' operating expenses

megacorporations (9) huge companies with many subsidiaries

paramount (9) highest, greatest

integrity (9) honesty, honor, worthiness

CEO (9) chief executive officer of a corporation

number crunchers (9) computers

via (10) by way of

Now read the essay.

Censorship in Publishing

LYNETTE LAMB

1   Book censorship is not confined to small-town bonfires of *Catcher in the Rye*, nor does it necessarily begin only after a book is published. Many controversial books today never make it past the editor's desk. Critics contend that the current structure of the industry—with huge corporations pushing blockbuster bestsellers—has increasingly led to timidity among publishers and pervasive self-censorship among writers and editors.

2   Books written by marketable name authors have a better chance of being published today than do good books, claims Louise Armstrong in *The Women's Review of Books* (March 1987). She believes feminist writers have toned down their former "passion and intensity" in order to be accepted by female editors who fear their own credibility will be jeopardized should they appear too feminist. Women writers thus have difficulty finding publishers for their more radical work. Says agent Ellen Markson, who represents Andrea Dworkin, among others, "It is women who are censoring women and you can quote me on that."

3   A book that does make it off the press can still be censored— usually by a publisher who decides at the last minute that its business interests are threatened by the book's content. A prime example of this brand of censorship, writes Michael Moore in *Multinational Monitor* (Sept. 1987), was the destruction of all 20,000 copies of the first printing of *Katharine the Great: Katharine Graham and the Washington Post*.

4   In her 1980 book (which finally hit the bookstores in 1986 when it was republished by the National Press), author Deborah Davis contended that the *Washington Post* disseminated information helpful to certain U.S. administrations and had maintained close ties with the CIA. Although the book had already been chosen as a Literary Guild selection and touted by publisher Harcourt Brace Jovanovich (HBJ) as a top nonfiction selection (and with the entire first printing already sold to eager bookstores), HBJ chose to yank it when *Washington Post* editor Ben Bradlee implied that its publication would put HBJ in the *Post's* bad graces. Like most publishers, HBJ relies on favorable reviews in powerful newspapers to help sell its books, so rather than risk incurring the *Post's* permanent wrath, HBJ chose to destroy the books.

5   Frightening as it is when two supposed upholders of the First Amendment conspire, as Moore put it, "to kill a book that one of them

found embarrassing and the other found detrimental to his business interests," the *Washington Post* example is by no means unique.

6   Indeed, cases of business interests prevailing over freedom of the press are only likely to become more common in the U.S. as the book publishing industry becomes increasingly concentrated in the hands of a few owners. Ten large companies own the majority of the 2,500 publishing houses in this country, Moore points out, and most of these corporations also own banking, insurance, industrial, and defense-related subsidiaries.

7   In *Extra! The Newsletter of FAIR* (Fairness and Accuracy in Reporting, June 1987), Ben Bagdikian points out that just 26 corporations control half or more of *all* media (including book publishers, TV, radio, newspapers, and movie production companies)—down from 50 corporations in 1982. (This situation is chronicled in a new updated version of his important book, *The Media Monopoly*, Beacon Press.) Although this will undoubtedly prove profitable for the shrinking number of media moguls, it is highly dangerous to freedom of the press, says Bagdikian, adding, "The safest way to ensure diversity of opinion is diverse ownership."

8   Publishing's increasingly corporate mentality has changed the whole nature of the profession, says Ted Solotaroff in *The New Republic* (June 8, 1987). Once a world of small, privately owned houses supported by the classic books on their backlists, the publishing business today must rely on blockbuster bestsellers to support their fat ad budgets and high overheads.

9   As the old publishing companies are swallowed up by megacorporations and move further and further from their proud roots, says Solotaroff, publishing " . . . works, thinks, and wills like any other big business. Its paramount concern is not the integrity of its product but the value of its share. . . . " The result, says the author (who is a senior editor at Harper & Row), is an exploding number of self-help, cooking, romance, fad, celebrity, and other big mall-selling books and a dwindling number of riskier serious fiction and non-fiction books, especially those written by unknown authors. "As the CEO and his number crunchers exert themselves, publishing decisions become more reckless and short-sighted," concludes Solotaroff.

10   The one piece of good news, says Solotaroff, is that serious books are still finding their way into print via alternative and university-based publishers still willing to take a chance on them.

Understanding the Content

Feel free to reread all or parts of the selection to answer the following questions.

1. What kind of censorship in publishing does Lamb discuss?

2. According to Lamb, why do some publishers decide not to publish a book that may deserve to be published?

3. Why did the publishers of *Katherine the Great: Katherine Graham and the Washington Post* destroy 20,000 copies of the book after it had been published?

4. How many companies own the majority of the 2,500 book publishing firms in this country? How many corporations controlled half of more of *all* media in this country as of June 1987?

5. What kind of books are being published at the expense of "riskier serious fiction"?

6. What is the danger in making profit the first priority in the book publishing field?

7. What is the thesis? Is it implied or stated?

Looking at Structure and Style

1. How does Lamb use her reference to *Catcher in the Rye* as a lead in to her subject and thesis? Is the use of that novel a good choice? Explain.

2. Lamb uses four other sources to help support her thesis. What are they? Are they reliable sources? What points are made with each source? Is this more of a report than an essay? Explain.

3. For what reasons does Lamb use parentheses in paragraphs 4, 7, and 9? (These are called parenthetical comments.) Are they necessary?

4. Explain or rewrite the following passages from the essay:
   a. "Book censorship is not confined to small-town bonfires. . . ." (1)
   b. " . . . HBJ chose to yank it when *Washington Post* editor Ben Bradlee implied that its publication would put HBJ in the *Post's* bad graces." (4)
   c. " . . . two supposed upholders of the First Amendment . . ." (5)
   d. " . . . an exploding number of self-help, cooking, romance, fad, celebrity, and other big mall-selling books and a dwindling number of riskier serious fiction and non-fiction books, especially those written by unknown authors." (9)
   e. " 'As the CEO and his number crunchers exert themselves . . . ' " (9)

5. What advice for revision, if any, would you offer the author?

Evaluating the Author's Viewpoints

1. Lamb states that "critics contend that the current structure of the [book publishing] industry . . . has increasingly led to timidity among publishers and pervasive self-censorship among writers and editors." (1) How

well does she support this criticism? Does she convince you that this is happening? Do you know of any other examples?

2. It is suggested that because large corporations own most of the publishing houses, an interest in making a profit is more important than publishing good, "riskier" books. If this is true, what effect does it have on you? Is it something you should be concerned about? Explain.

3. Does it matter that there is a "media monopoly" on all media in this country? Does the author suggest a danger in this?

4. What is the one piece of "good news"? Is it really good news?

Pursuing Possible Essay Topics

1. Brainstorm or freewrite on one or more of the following:
   a. censorship
   b. influence of the media
   c. media monopoly
   d. the power of the press
   e. freedom of the press
   f. responsibility of the press

2. Frequently, local newspapers will omit materials from their pages when they think it is offensive. For instance, Gary Trudeau's cartoon strip "Doonesbury" (see page 88) has frequently been "pulled" when editors found particular segments not to their liking. Is this a form of censorship? Should editors have the right to decide what you should and shouldn't read? (In a sense they do every day by deciding what news to print.) What responsibilities do newspapers have to the public? To their owners?

3. Write an essay explaining why you like to read a particular column in the newspaper. What do you gain from it? What is its appeal?

4. Examine closely the way two newspapers in your area report the news. How much are they alike, how much different? Does one paper seem to be biased on any subject? What are the sources for their news reporting?

5. In January 1988, the U.S. Supreme Court ruled that school administrators have the right to censor school newspapers, stating that the freedom of speech mentioned in the First Amendment does not apply. Argue for or against this ruling.

6. Read for yourself one of the publications mentioned in Lamb's essay, such as *The Women's Review of Books, Multinational Monitor,* or *The New Republic,* and write an evaluation of it.

7. Write a reaction to this quote from Lamb's essay: "The safest way to ensure diversity of opinion is diverse ownership [of the media]." (7)

8. Censor these and find your own topic on some aspect of the media.

📖 *Preparing to Read*

Take a minute or two to look over the following reading selection. Note the title and author, read the opening paragraph, and check the length. Make certain you have the time now to read it carefully and to do the exercises that follow it. Then, in the spaces provided, answer the following questions.

1. What do you think is the good news about black college students? ____

_____

2. What does the author feel the media are doing that is wrong? _____

_____

Vocabulary

Good comprehension of what you are about to read depends upon your understanding of the words below. The number following each word refers to the paragraph where it is used.

clamor (1) a loud outcry, hubbub

plight (1) difficult situation or condition

amiss (2) out of proper order

handicaps (2) causes to be at a disadvantage, hinders

harping on (3) continually discussing something to the point of boredom and annoyance

attrition (3) a gradual lessening of numbers; here, the student drop-out rate

engenders (4) causes, gives rise to

implicity (5) implied by indirect expression

exacerbate (6) make worse

alleviate (6) make better, lessen

white-sheeted cross burners (7) a reference to the Ku Klux Klan, a racist group that believes in white supremacy

abounds (8) exists in great number or amount

demographic (9) pertaining to the statistical study of human population

coveted (11) greatly desired or wanted

realm (12) sphere, field

pitfalls (14) dangers or difficulties that are hard to anticipate or avoid

perseverance (14) persistence

coincide (15) meet, occupy the same position

Now read the essay.

Presenting the Good News About Black College Students

R. RICHARD BANKS

1   I wish that I could put an end to the clamor that the media have made recently about racism on college campuses and about the plight of black college students.

2   Though factually accurate, there's something amiss in the media coverage, an element of distortion. Every headline, every story that highlights the supposed rise in racism and the plight of black college students handicaps more black students than it helps.

3   In harping on the gloom and doom themes, the media give us only the bad news, and make it seem much worse than it is. Last year's stories give the impression that the few black students who make it to college spend all their time battling campus racism or failing their classes and adding to the attrition statistics. Such is not the case.

4   What is the case is that hearing only bad news engenders self-defeating attitudes in black high-school and college students who wonder, "How can I possibly succeed when the campus is so racist and all the other black students are failing anyway?"

5   The media preoccupation with the difficulties and drawbacks of college implicitly tells students, "Maybe this isn't for you."

6   In giving students such a message, the media exacerbate rather than alleviate the plight of black students.

7   The alternative is not to ignore racist incidents on college campuses—the white-sheeted cross burners at the Citadel Military Academy in South Carolina deserved to be dealt with harshly—or to overlook the substantial decline in college attendance among black students. Rather, the media should *add* a theme to the coverage. Tell what's good on the college campuses and among the black students there.

8   Good news abounds:

9   —Colleges are as eager as ever to enroll qualified black students, a new emphasis that's reflected in college recruiting drives that are aimed at those who might not enroll in college without encouragement. Far from being unwanted, black students are in great demand as colleges have begun to realize that demographic trends will force

them to depend more and more on minority students to maintain their enrollment levels.

10 —Student support structures once scarce at predominantly white colleges—black fraternities and sororities, black professional and pre-professional organizations, black student unions—have become so commonplace and so successful that we take them for granted, forgetting the tremendous progress that they represent.

11 —Many black students are excelling. There were many news stories about racial conflict at Stanford, but how many people know that 3 of the last 10 Stanford students to receive the coveted Rhodes scholarship were black? Blacks make up only about 6% of the student body, yet nearly 30% of Stanford's Rhodes scholars over the past four years. Such accomplishments say more than an isolated racist incident does about the experience and roles of black students on white college campuses.

12 —Career opportunities for educated blacks are better than ever. For example, a black woman who just received her Ph.D. in English from Stanford received 19 job offers. That's right, 19. The fields to which so many of my peers have flocked—investment banking, consulting, advertising, engineering—were beyond the realm of possibility for most black students a generation ago.

13 —The GRE and SAT scores of black students, although still significantly lower than for white students, have been rising at a much faster rate than white students' scores during the past several years. While the average verbal and math SAT scores of black students increased by 4.2% and 6.2% respectively between 1976 and 1985, the average scores of white students actually declined slightly, by 0.4% and 0.6%, during the same period.

14 Those are newsworthy facts, but they are not nearly as well publicized as isolated racist incidents. By including the good news, the media would present the entire picture and thereby give students an image of college that shows them how they can and why they should succeed—as well as the obstacles that lie in their path. Only when we equip black students with a knowledge of both the rewards and the possible pitfalls of college life will they develop the motivation and perseverance necessary to fulfill the promise that higher education embodies.

15 As the challenges of international competition push us to advance our nation's educational and technological expertise, and as minority students make up an ever-increasing proportion of the young minds to whom we must look to meet the challenges, the fate of our country will coincide more and more with the fate of these students.

16 My wish that black students hear the good news about college expresses my hope not only for their success but for the success of our nation as well. If they too do not succeed, neither will we.

Understanding the Content

Feel free to reread all or parts of the selection to answer the following questions.

1. What "element of distortion" does Banks say exists in the media coverage of black college students? Does he want to do away with reporting bad news?

2. Can you infer what "gloom and doom themes" regarding black students were being widely reported by the media at the time this essay was written? What example does Banks provide?

3. According to Banks, what effect does reporting only the negative news about the plight of black students have?

4. Banks offers five examples of good news regarding black students that he feels needs reporting. What are they?

5. According to Banks, how would the reporting of both good and bad news regarding racial issues on campus help black students?

Looking at Structure and Style

1. Banks opens his essay with a direct statement of his viewpoints on media coverage of black college students. Paragraph 2 reflects a cause and effect viewpoint. What is the cause and the effect?

2. How do paragraphs 3 and 4 function together? What transitional device is used?

3. Banks's answer to what he sees as wrong is contained in paragraph 7. Why does he italicize the word *add?*

4. Paragraphs 9–13 are technically part of paragraph 8. What do they all have in common? What is their function?

5. How does paragraph 14 reinforce what Banks has already said? Is it redundant? Explain.

6. How does Banks use the last two paragraphs to show that his concern goes beyond a call for balanced news coverage of black students?

Evaluating the Author's Viewpoints

1. Banks claims that during the time he wrote his essay, a balanced coverage of news regarding black students did not exist. Is that still the case? Is it the case with the reporting of racial issues in general? Explain.

2. Does Banks make a convincing argument for the type of coverage he feels would be more appropriate? Do you agree with him?

3. Banks mentions in paragraph 7 that there has been a decline in college attendance of black students. Do you think part of the reason may be

that the media tend to be preoccupied with reporting only the racial tensions and difficulties of minority students? Why?

4. What does Banks mean when he says that "the fate of our country will coincide more and more with the fate of these [black] students"? (15)

Pursuing Possible Essay Topics

1. Argue for more balanced media coverage on an area you feel is neglected by the press. Provide examples for your argument, just as Banks does in paragraphs 8–13.

2. Frequently we hear people complaining that the media seem to report only "bad news," such as airplane crashes, freeway accidents, murders, riots, wars, and so on. What "good news" should be emphasized instead? What if only "good news" were reported? Describe the difference in the way the news might affect us.

3. Write an extended definition of journalism. What makes good journalism? What is its importance in our society?

4. Compare/contrast television reporting with newspaper reporting.

5. Compare/contrast two news magazines, such as *TIME* and *Newsweek*. How are they alike (not in physical appearance)? Do they both emphasize the same news stories each week? What news do they consider more/less important? Is the news balanced?

6. Is your local newspaper really a *news*paper? How much of it contains advertisements, horoscope predictions, advice columns, comics, and the like? How do you rate it in fairness and balanced coverage?

7. Write an essay prompted by the statement, "It's as dead as yesterday's news."

8. What would your day be like without any news?

9. Use your own newsworthy topic on some aspect of the media.

📖 *Preparing to Read*

Read the following poem at least twice, once to yourself and once aloud. Then answer the questions that follow.

Vocabulary

Good comprehension of the poem depends upon your understanding of the words below.

matching pearls   straight, pearly-white teeth

sets   sets of teeth

hybrid   of mixed origin, different in variety or species

clergy   people ordained for religious service

M.C.s   masters of ceremonies (sometimes written **emcees**)

crooner   singer

teem   abound, swarm, are full

orthodontist   dentist who specializes in straightening crooked teeth

miser   one who hoards, a cheapskate

incisors   the sharp teeth used for tearing

Reflections Dental

PHYLLIS McGINLEY

How pure, how beautiful, how fine
Do teeth on television shine!
No flutist flutes, no dancer twirls,
But comes equipped with matching pearls.
Gleeful announcers all are born
With sets like rows of hybrid corn.
Clowns, critics, clergy, commentators,
Ventriloquists and roller skaters,
M.C.s who beat their palms together,
The girl who diagrams the weather,
The crooner crooning for his supper—
All flash white treasures, lower and upper.
With miles of smiles the airwaves teem,
And each an orthodontist's dream.

'Twould please my eye as gold a miser's—
One charmer with uncapped incisors.

Understanding the Content

Feel free to refer to the poem for the answers to the following questions.

1. What is the point of the poem?

2. What type of television entertainers does McGinley mention?

3. Does the title "Reflections Dental" fit? Explain.

Looking at Structure and Style

1. What words in the poem rhyme? Do they form a pattern?

2. Why does McGinley separate the last two lines from the rest of the poem? Does this serve a function? What do they mean?

3. Explain the following passages from the poem:
   a. "M.C.s who beat their palms together"
   b. "The girl who diagrams the weather"
   c. "With miles of smiles the airwaves teem"
   d. " 'Twould please my eye as gold a miser's"

4. What is the tone of the poem? Explain why you think so.

Evaluating the Author's Viewpoints

1. What is McGinley's view of people on television?

2. Is what she claims true? Why?

3. Why is it important to understand the tone of the poem in order to understand the author?

Pursuing Possible Essay Topics

1. Write an essay that evaluates the poem. See the student essay and commentary on pages 125–127.

2. Write an essay that says what the poem says. Provide more support than the poem does.

3. Watch some television with the intent to evaluate the appearance of key personalities, such as news anchors, weather presenters, masters of ceremonies, and so on. Do their appearances have anything in common? Are they alike in any particular way?

4. Brainstorm on one or more of the following:
   a. popular TV personalities
   b. how commercials portray us
   c. the media's portrayal of age
   d. glitz, glitter, and glamour on television

5. Ignore these and come up with your own topic on some aspect of the media.

✍ Student Essay

Read the following student essay, looking for answers to the following questions:

1. Does the essay fit the assignment to write on some aspect of the media?

2. Does the essay have a clear thesis and good support?

3. Does the essay follow the writing guidelines suggested in Unit 2, "Viewpoints on Writing Essays"?

TV News: Journalism or Propaganda?

Jim Stone

1   Not all television news organizations report the news fairly or completely. They all may begin covering stories with the basic idea of truthfulness in reporting, but by air time this has fallen by the wayside. All news organizations face pressures from many different angles. Each sponsor has its wishes, special interest groups have theirs, the network and local station executives have theirs, and finally, the censors and "old man time" limit what can be shown. These pressures, as well as manipulation on the part of government, can all act on a news story and, in many cases, slant it by the time we get it.

2   Here's how it typically works. A news crew, usually consisting of a reporter and a cameraman, is sent to the scene of an incident or press conference. Today's story is about a leaking toxic waste dump. A state spokesman is holding a press conference at the site of the dump. The conference is attended by most major newspapers, the major wire services (AP, UPI, etc.), and the local TV networks. The state spokesman presents the problem to the press in a prepared statement, and then our illustrious reporter faces the camera and paraphrases what the state spokesman just said. The crew then gets some camera shots of leaking chemical drums and proceeds to tour the neighborhood.

3   They are, of course, looking for "the man in the street" for a "salt of the earth" impression of this latest item of gloom and

doom. The first person being interviewed, someone who wants the dump removed from his neighborhood anyway, begins to see some fairly lucrative lawsuits on the horizon. When asked to describe any recurrent or frequent health problems, the interviewee rattles off a lengthy list including but not limited to gout, ulcers, arthritis, hemorrhoids and many other common ailments that he feels sure are caused by the leaking dump next door. The news crew repeats this scene two or three times with other disgruntled neighbors and gets almost identical answers from each respondent. The news crew then returns to the studio and proceeds to review the fruits of their labors in the video editing room.

4   The editor then begins to "make" the story. This is where the potential for propaganda comes in; the editor is the person who bears the brunt of the pressures from special interest groups. At this point he can downplay the story by stressing the state's official assertion that they do not know the extent of the hazard, while dropping the spokesman's later comment that damage appears extensive. Or, at the request of another interest group, such as an environmental one, the editor can stress that damage is believed to be extensive and may even be irreversible. He drops the spokesman's comment that damage assessments cannot be made at this time. Or, the editor can stress the cost of the cleanup in order to help the state environmental protection agency secure a larger budget by the use of public furor that will no doubt occur from an incident of this sort. In this instance, he would probably tie in footage of all the other leaking waste dumps around the state as well as total cleanup costs. To add the human element, he can put in some of the footage of the neighborhood people with their assorted illnesses, or just the portion of the interview in which the people express their shock and outrage over the dump spill.

5   In most cases, if not all, the editor is trying to do us, the viewer, a favor. He is creating a news story that is digestible in the short time allotted for each news story. If time allows, and the story is really important, the network can do an in-depth story

which might include history, background, further ramifications, and future dump site plans. Most of us would not want to sit and sift through the daily deluge of news items. This would quickly become a full-time job and is best left to the professionals.

6   But in a few instances, the editor does the viewing public a disservice by slanting the story in order to influence public opinion. This can be done either through omission or through emphasis of key points, as is often done in political campaigns. The editor favoring a candidate can downplay or ignore negative items while stressing the good ones. In contrast, if the editor dislikes a candidate, he can emphasize the negative items and downplay the positive ones.

7   In today's political world, television plays a huge role in who will get elected. Most of us don't take the time to really deal with the issues. A 1988 TV Guide poll shows that most of us vote for the candidate who makes the most favorable impression on us. The politician knows this as well as news editors.

8   All of this leads to the conclusion that we still can't believe everything we see in print or on television. That old warning about buyer beware, caveat emptor, should be changed to include television news.

Reaction

In the space below, write your reaction to the essay. What would you tell the student about his essay?

Commentary

This final revision of Jim's essay shows his attention to some basic composition guidelines: a clear thesis, strong support, good paragraph control, sentence variety, helpful transitions, and attention to word choices. Let's look at some of these elements.

Notice in the first paragraph that Jim makes it clear what his subject and thesis are. Although television stations may begin with the intention of truthfully covering news stories, pressures from various sources, including time itself, may all serve to slant a story by the time we see in on television.

His second paragraph begins, "Here's how it typically works." From there through paragraph 4, Jim takes us from the step-by-step process of reporters covering a news story to the editorial room where the selection of what will be finally shown is decided. As he describes the process, he is also supporting his thesis by showing how and why a story may become slanted by the time we view it on television.

Paragraphs 5 and 6 deal with the editor. Paragraph 5 gives the editor credit for the job he must perform. It recognizes the service the editor provides for us and lets us know that Jim is not accusing all editors of slanting news stories. Paragraph 6, in contrast, shows the disservice an editor can perform when his biases interfere with a story.

It could be argued that paragraph 7 is not needed because it begins to raise a different issue. Jim's topic sentence (that television plays a huge role in who will get elected) is certainly true, but that in itself seems a thesis of its own needing further development and discussion. The previous paragraph (6) ends with a commentary on how editors may slant stories to favor or downplay a political candidate. No doubt that statement brought up the ideas Jim expresses in paragraph 7. But as written, the paragraph takes us away from the process involved in developing a television news story. It doesn't support Jim's thesis.

The last paragraph draws a good conclusion: we shouldn't believe everything we see and hear on television news. The body of his essay shows us why.

Despite the question of the appropriateness of paragraph 7, Jim's essay shows he applied what he has learned about composition. Jim began writing with the idea he would compare/contrast the way newspapers report a story with the way television does. As you can see, he narrowed the topic down to something more manageable. After several false starts and many revisions, Jim finished with an acceptable essay that fits the assignment.

*V*iewpoints on
Controversial
Issues

"When a thing ceases to be a subject of controversy,
it ceases to be a subject of interest."
William Hazlitt

SOMEONE once said that there are three sides to every questionable issue: your side, my side, and the "right" side. In truth, there may be many sides, depending upon the issue itself. For instance, the reactions to the issue of abortion are usually divided into two basic viewpoints: for or against. But the issue is not that simple. Other questions begin to surface. For instance, do women have the right to decide for themselves whether or not they wish to remain pregnant? Does the government have the right to involve itself in such an issue, or is it meddling in private lives? Are abortion laws, whether pro or con, constitutional? Is abortion really a legal question or a moral and religious one? When should a fetus be considered a "person"? Are a potential mother's rights and a fetus's rights equal? Can aborting a fetus be considered murder, as some say? Are there times when an abortion is more humane than the alternative? What if an abortion under certain circumstances would save an endangered mother's life? Is it better to have an unwanted child who can't or won't be cared for than to have an abortion? Should pregnant junior and senior high schoolers be forced to have unwanted children? Are those who call abortion murder, yet proudly let their sons go to war, holding a double standard? These are just a few of the kinds of questions that create controversy on touchy issues, making it difficult for any thinking person to make quick decisions.

According to psychologists, numerous studies have been done that show the urge to conform to group thinking is too powerful for most people to resist. Unknowingly, we become conditioned to ways of thinking. This usually happens because we are molded at an early age by our parents, relatives, teachers, and friends. We tend to honor their value systems because we love them and trust their judgments. If our families vote Republican, we usually vote Republican. If our families go to a particular church, we tend to continue in that church. If our parents and church leaders speak out against abortion, we tend to accept such views as "right." Their beliefs become our beliefs without much questioning or thought.

As we mature, our beliefs are also molded both directly and indirectly by the media. What we wear, what we eat, what music we accept, even what media we enjoy become tied in with our desire to be accepted as part of a group. Even when we think we are acting as individuals by rejecting the ideas of one group, we are often just accepting the ideas of another. We become self-deceptive. Our thinking process becomes overruled by others' opinions that we think are truly our own thoughtful reactions because we have heard them for so long. We become biased and forget to weigh our opinions by looking at facts or reasoning that goes against our belief system. And even when we do try to see "facts," we often don't have the experience needed to evaluate the information. In such cases, it is better to suspend our decision on which "side" to take until we do some more investigating.

This unit contains essays on only three of many controversial subjects: the need and worth of bilingual education, capital punishment (the death penalty), and handgun control. Two opposing essays on the three controversial subjects are provided. As you read, try to avoid letting your own biases come out. Read first to understand the author's views, suspending your own viewpoints. Then look at the strengths or weaknesses of the arguments being made. Ask yourself what facts are being used, what emotions, what judgments. Is the author playing on your biases? Is the evidence convincing? Is the problem being expressed too simplistically? Try letting go of your own feelings long enough to understand the author's position, especially if it is different from your own.

It is possible that even after reading the selections you will discover you need more information than is provided here in order to take your own stand. That's a healthy sign. You will probably want to read more or discuss these subjects with others. That, of course, is the idea behind these reading selections.

One final word. New information on controversial issues continues to come out. What you may think today, you may not think tomorrow. That's healthy, too, as long as you are truly making judgments and weighing the evidence critically on your own.

📖 *Preparing to Read*

Take a minute or two to look over the following reading selection. Note the title and author, read the opening paragraph, and check the length. Make certain you have the time now to read it carefully and to do the exercises that follow it. Then, in the spaces provided, answer the following questions.

1. What is the subject of this essay? _____

_____

2. What are the author's feelings about his subject? _____

_____

3. What are your feelings, if any, about the subject? _____

_____

Vocabulary

Good comprehension of what you are about to read depends upon your understanding of the words below. The number following each word refers to the paragraph where it is used.

Bilingual Education (1) any program in which non-English-speaking students study basic subjects in their native language while also being taught English

innovation (1) something new

compromising (1) giving in to certain demands

ethnolinguistic (1) having various ethnic languages

crucial (2) of extreme importance

vehicles (2) means, conveyances, media

spurred (2) urged, prompted

leverage (2) power to act effectively

cultural deficit approaches (2) past (unsuccessful) programs set up to help minorities

anglicizing of Hispanic surnames (3) changing people's Spanish-sounding last names to English-sounding ones (for example, changing Rivera to Rivers)

etched (3) engraved, scratched

delve (4) search carefully

equitable (4) fair, equal

curricular (4) referring to the courses of study

at first blush (5) at first glance

implementers (5) those who put into effect

justify projected cutbacks (5) provide reasons for proposing to decrease the money requested for programs

explicitly (6) clearly

federal intervention (6) the stepping in of the U.S. government (a reference to the fact that the federal government had to force some states to confront the needs of minorities through laws and grants)

redress (6) correction of wrong done

embark (6) set out on a venture, commence

deliberations (6) formal discussions and debates on all sides of the issue

upheaval (7) a sudden and violent disruption

barrios (7) Spanish-speaking communities within U.S. cities

Watts riots (7) the violent response to racial unrest in the 1960s in Watts, a black community in Los Angeles

coupled (7) joined, linked

barometer (8) indicator, something that shows fluctuations

rhetorical (8) high-sounding

Title VII programs (9) federally funded programs aiding minority students

Now read the essay.

Bilingual Programs: Crucial Vehicles*

TOMAS A. ARCINIEGA

1   Billingual Education is the most important educational innovation ever launched in this country on behalf of Hispanics. Hispanics are quick to point out that there can be no qualifying or compromising

---

* Editor's title

on this. As a concept as well as a program, Bilingual Education has served ethnolinguistic people well.

2   Across the nation, bilingual programs have proved to be crucial vehicles whereby Hispanics may press for language rights and these programs have spurred the parents of Hispanic students to action. It is heartwarming to see Hispanic parents fight for the right to have a say-so about the education their children receive. At all levels of the educational system, Bilingual Education has provided needed leverage in moving districts away from those cultural deficit approaches in which minorities have labored and suffered for so long.

3   In California, for example, the issue of language rights has tremendous symbolic value for Mexican Americans. It wasn't very long ago that Mexican Americans were openly barred from white schools. In the southwest prior to 1940, less than 5% of Mexican American children of school age were allowed to go to school. Even as late as the 1950s, this country still had school systems with the good "American" and the inferior "Mexican" schools. And we all know too well the cases of Mexican kids being spanked for speaking Spanish and about the forced anglicizing of Hispanic surnames. That history is deeply etched in the minds and souls of Chicanos. This is too often overlooked and seldom fully appreciated by those who persist in the use of the catch phrase: I just can't understand why Chicanos get so worked up about Bilingual Education.

4   It is not appropriate to delve any deeper into the specifics of how to change the public schools. But obviously meaningful reform has to begin with the need to effect changes which bring about equitable representation of Hispanics, yield necessary curricular adaptations and insure a meaningful involvement of the Hispanic community.

5   How best to push for these needed reforms in the face of decreased special program funding is the central issue for the eighties. The nature of that problem for U.S. society is a bit more complex than might appear at first blush. Although many of the implementers of national and state policies have tended to justify projected cutbacks by pointing to perceived problems with existing special programs, the issue is a much broader one. What is really at stake is this country's expressed commitment to act on the needs of the neediest first.

6   During the last two decades, this country made clear to the world and to future generations its intent to equalize educational opportunities for all Americans. It explicitly recognized the black, brown, red, and yellow peoples of this nation as the most disadvantaged of its citizens. The nation recognized also that only through federal intervention could meaningful redress of past injustices be brought about. Although often overlooked today, it is important to recall that the decision to embark on that national strategy was made only after long and serious deliberations regarding the difficulties involved.

7   What remains to be seen in the eighties is how true the new administration holds to that national commitment. If all that is ahead is a change in tactics—in how best to achieve educational equity for ethnic minorities—rather than a pullback from that national commitment, then I foresee only minor adjustment problems. But if what lies ahead is really a decision to abandon that ideal, then this country may well be headed toward the biggest internal civil rights upheaval yet. The social dynamite in the ghettos and barrios of this land, which we heard so much about after the Watts riots, is certainly still there. It would be a serious mistake to think that it is not—an even more serious mistake to underestimate the explosive potential of that social fact. If anything, what should be apparent is that the rise in expectations coupled with the worsening of economic conditions will intensify that explosive potential in the barrios and ghettos of this land.

8   The Federal Bilingual Education Program, although in dollar terms not the largest of the special federal programs, should prove a very accurate and clear barometer in determining early on what is in store for minorities in the eighties. Hispanics and other ethnolinguistic minorities across the country are watching with intense interest how bilingual education fares under the new administration. Having only recently won the right to construct a national delivery system for bilingual education, Hispanics will not be easily convinced by those rhetorical arguments that maintain the English Only approaches represent a *better solution.*

9   On the contrary, from the Hispanics' perspective, the involvement of their children in Title VII programs during the past decade has convinced these parents and supporters of the educational worth of bilingual education. They know bilingual programs work for these children and understand also the key role played by the federal government in the establishment of such programs. Thus, it should surprise none that Hispanics tend to view any and all attempts to cut back or to discontinue bilingual education as anti-Hispanic actions. Early actions by the current administration would seem to indicate a very serious lack of appreciation of that fact.

Understanding the Content

Feel free to reread all or parts of the selection to answer the following questions.

1. Why does Arciniega see bilingual programs as "crucial vehicles" for Hispanics? What good does he feel has come from them?

2. What disadvantages have school age Mexican-American children faced in the past?

3. What is the author's concern about future Hispanic education?

4. How does Arciniega think minorities may react if the federal government doesn't support the bilingual education program?

5. According to the author, how do Hispanic parents feel about bilingual education?

6. What is Arciniega's thesis? Is it implied or stated?

Looking at Structure and Style

1. How well does the first paragraph establish the subject and thesis of the essay?

2. How do paragraphs 2 and 3 function as a unit? What point is being made?

3. How do paragraphs 4 and 5 function as a unit? What point is being made?

4. How do paragraphs 6 and 7 function as a unit? How do they support the thesis?

5. How do paragraphs 8 and 9 function as a unit? What point is being made?

6. To what audience is the author writing? Explain.

7. Explain or rewrite the following passages from the essay:
   a. " . . . Bilingual programs have proved to be crucial vehicles whereby Hispanics may press for language rights. . . . " (2)
   b. " . . . These programs have spurred the parents . . . into action." (2)
   c. "That history is deeply etched in the minds and souls of Chicanos." (3)
   d. "The social dynamite in the ghettos and barrios of this land . . . is certainly still there." (7)

Evaluating the Author's Viewpoints

1. Arciniega views bilingual education as "the most important educational innovation ever launched in this country on behalf of Hispanics." (1) Does he convince you of this in his essay? Do you know enough about the programs to agree or disagree?

2. The author states that what is really at stake when governmental administrators try to justify cutbacks in the bilingual education programs is "this country's expressed commitment to act on the needs of the neediest first." (5) Do you think that bilingual programs act "on the needs of the neediest"? Explain.

3. Arciniega predicts that if there is no national commitment shown toward minorities' educational needs, "this country may well be headed toward the biggest internal civil rights upheaval yet." (7) Does he convince you of this? How do you react to this statement?

4. Hispanics' past involvement in bilingual programs, says the author, "has convinced these parents and supporters of the educational worth of bilingual education." (9) Does he offer any proof of this statement? Do you think there may be parents who are not in favor of the program? Explain.

Pursuing Possible Essay Topics

Unless reading the essay above stimulated some ideas for an essay that you want to pursue, you should read the next essay, which also deals with bilingual education, and use the list of possible topics that follows it.

⬚ *Preparing to Read*

Take a minute or two to look over the following reading selection. Note the title and author, read the opening paragraph, and check the length. Make certain you have the time now to read it carefully and to do the exercises that follow it. Then, in the spaces provided, answer the following questions.

1. How do you think the author defines "bilingualism's goal"? _____

_____

2. What do you think the author will say about the role of the school system?

_____

_____

Vocabulary

Good comprehension of what you are about to read depends upon your understanding of the words below. The number following each word refers to the paragraph where it is used.

instilling (1) introducing gradually, teaching bit by bit

inculcate (2) instill, teach

advocate (3) speak in favor of, recommend

alienated (3) excluded

simulated (4) imitated, reproduced

encompasses (6) includes

curricula (6) courses of study offered by schools (plural of **curriculum**)

notoriously (8) famously, but unfavorably so

median (8) at the middle

menial (9) appropriate to a servant

vulnerable (9) capable of being harmed

exploitation (9) the act of being taken advantage of

Now read the essay.

Bilingualism's Goal

BARBARA MUJICA

1   Mine is a Spanish-speaking household. We use Spanish exclusively. I have made an effort not only to encourage use of the language but also to familiarize my children with Hispanic culture. I use books from Latin America to teach them to read and write, and I try to maintain close contacts with Spanish-speaking relatives. Instilling in my children a sense of family and ethnic identity is my role; it is not the role of the school system.

2   The public schools, supported by public funds, have the responsibility to teach skills needed in public life—among them the use of the English language. They also must inculcate an appreciation of all the cultures that have contributed to this country's complex social weave. To set one ethnic group apart as more worthy of attention than others is unjust, and might breed resentment against that group.

3   I differ with educators who advocate bilingual education programs whose goal is to preserve the Spanish language and culture among children of Hispanic families. These professionals argue that in an English-speaking environment, Spanish-speaking children often feel alienated and that this causes them to become withdrawn and hostile. To prevent this reaction, they say, the home environment must be simulated at school.

4   Imagine how much more alienated these youngsters will feel, however, if they are kept in special bilingual programs separate from the general student body, semester after semester. How much more uncomfortable they will feel if they are maintained in ghettos in the school. Youngsters feel a need to conform. They imitate each other in dress and in habit. To isolate Spanish-speaking children from their English-speaking peers may prove more psychologically damaging than hurling them into an English-speaking environment with no transition courses at all.

5   The purpose of bilingual education must be to teach English to non-English-speaking youngsters so that they will be able to function in regular classes.

6   The term "bilingual education" encompasses a huge variety of programs ranging from total immersion to special classes for foreigners to curricula that offer courses in mathematics and history in the child's native language. The most effective bilingual education programs have as their goal the gradual incorporation of non-English-speaking students into regular programs in which English is used.

7   Not all children of Spanish-speaking parents need bilingual education. Many Spanish-speaking parents oppose the placement of their children in special programs; the wishes of these parents should be respected. Furthermore, very young children are able to learn a foreign language rapidly; bilingual programs for the nursery, kindergarten and early primary years should be kept to a minimum. Older children who have done part of their schooling in a foreign country often need to be eased into an English-speaking curriculum more gently. For them, it is helpful to offer certain subjects in their native tongues until they have learned English; otherwise, they may feel so lost and frustrated that they will drop out of school. High school dropouts have less chance than others of finding satisfying careers and are more likely to find themselves in trouble and unemployed.

8   Hispanics are now the fastest-growing minority in the United States. According to the Population Reference Bureau, a private organization, Hispanics, counted at 14.6 million in the 1980 census, may well number 47 million by the year 2020. Yet, they are notoriously underrepresented in the arts, sciences, professions and politics. Economically, as a group, they tend to lag behind non-Hispanics. According to March 1983 Federal figures, the median income for Hispanics is $16,227; for non-Hispanics, $23,907. Certainly, part of the remedy is educational programs that give young people the preparation and confidence necessary to pursue satisfying careers.

9   To get better jobs, young people must be fluent in English. Without English, they will be stuck in menial positions. Without English, they will be unable to acquire advanced degrees. Without English, they will be unable to protest to the proper authorities if they are abused. Non-English-speaking individuals are vulnerable to not only economic but also political exploitation. Too often, politicians who speak their language claim unjustly to represent their interests.

10   The primary goal of bilingual education must be mainstreaming of non-English-speaking children through the teaching of English. But while the schools teach my children English, I will continue to teach them Spanish at home, because Spanish is part of their heritage. Ethnic identity, like religion, is a family matter.

Understanding the Content

Feel free to reread all or parts of the selection to answer the following questions.

1. What is Mujica's view of bilingual education? How does it differ from Arciniega's views as expressed in the previous essay? Is Mujica opposed to bilingual education?

2. How does Mujica view the difference between responsibilities of the school and the home in education?

3. How does the author define bilingual education? Is her definition different from Arciniega's? Explain.

4. What arguments or support does Mujica provide for her position on bilingual education?

5. Mujica refers to a 1980 census that shows Hispanics are the fastest-growing minority in the United States. What might the Hispanic population be by 2020?

Looking at Structure and Style

1. What is the function of paragraph 1? Why does Mujica place so much emphasis on her Spanish-speaking household? Does this help her argument? Why?

2. How do paragraphs 1 and 2 function as a unit?

3. How do paragraphs 3 and 4 function as a unit?

4. In paragraphs 5 and 6, Mujica states her definition of bilingual education. What other educational goal does she think the schools should have? Where does she state it? Is this an appropriate place? Explain.

5. What are Mujica's arguments in paragraphs 8 and 9? What are causes and what are effects?

6. How do Mujica's opening and closing paragraphs make her position clear? Describe her tone and attitude in these paragraphs.

7. To what audience is the author writing? Explain.

8. Is Mujica's essay mostly fact or opinion? Explain.

Evaluating the Author's Viewpoints

1. Mujica makes it clear that she feels that developing a sense of ethnic identity should occur in the home, not in the school. Is her argument convincing? Explain why you do or do not agree with her.

2. One of Mujica's arguments is that placement of Spanish-speaking children in bilingual classes actually makes them feel as if they are "in ghettos in school." (4) What does she mean? Is this a possibility?

3. Reread paragraph 5. Is this a good definition of bilingual education? Should it include more? Explain.

4. Do you agree with Mujica's last line? Can ethnic identity and religion be made analogous (treated the same) in this case? Explain.

5. Do Mujica's views in paragraphs 7 and 10 differ from Arciniega's in his last paragraph? Explain.

Pursuing Possible Essay Topics

1. Write a rebuttal to Arciniega or Mujica or both.

2. Write an essay that reflects the points regarding bilingual education on which Arciniega and Mujica might agree/disagree. Use quotations from the essays.

3. Write a description of bilingual education as you think it should be presented in the school systems.

4. Write an argument against/for bilingual education.

5. If you have experienced instruction in a bilingual program, write about your views of that program. Was it a profitable experience? Was it taught correctly? Would you support more programs like it?

6. Research the present governmental support for bilingual education. Write your views of the program. Would Arciniega be happy with the present federal funds for bilingual education or other programs that are supposed to help minority groups? In addition to the card catalogue and the *Reader's Guide to Periodical Literature,* you might want to use the *Monthly Catalog of United States Government Publications* and the *New York Times Index* for more current sources on bilingual education.

7. Arciniega says that "Hispanics will not be easily convinced by those rhetorical arguments that maintain English Only approaches represent a *better solution*" to bilingual education (paragraph 8, previous essay). Write an essay that argues for or against his statement.

8. What if the Hispanic population got so large that English became a second language in the United States? Write about the possible changes that might take place. How would it affect your life?

9. If you don't like these ideas, write an essay that deals with another controversial subject.

Preparing to Read

Take a minute or two to look over the following reading selection. Note the title and author, read the first *two* paragraphs, and check the length. Make certain you have the time now to read it carefully and to do the exercises that follow it. Then, in the spaces provided, answer the following questions.

1. What is the subject of the essay? ————————————

————————————————————————————————

2. What is the author's viewpoint on the subject? ———————

————————————————————————————————

3. Do you already have views on the death penalty that might make you

   biased as you read this essay? Explain. ———————————

————————————————————————————————

Vocabulary

Good comprehension of what you are about to read depends upon your understanding of the words below. The number following each word refers to the paragraph where it is used.

dispatching (2) killing

abundance (6) great number or amount

retribution (7) punishment, something demanded in return for harm having been done

Cook County (8) the county in Illinois that includes the city of Chicago

delegate (9) authorize, entrust someone

deter (10) prevent, discourage

decomposed (12) rotted, falling apart

befriended (18) was friendly toward

Now read the essay.

Death to the Killers

MIKE ROYKO

1   Some recent columns on the death penalty have brought some interesting responses from readers all over the country.

2   There were, of course, expressions of horror and disgust that I would favor the quick dispatching of convicted murderers.

3   I really don't like to make fun of people who oppose the death penalty because they are so sincere. But I wish they would come up with some new arguments to replace the worn-out ones.

4   For example, many said something like this: "Wouldn't it be better to keep the killers alive so psychiatrists can study them in order to find out what makes them the way they are?"

5   It takes the average psychiatrist about five years to figure why a guy wants to stop for two drinks after work and won't quit smoking. So how long do you think it will take him to determine why somebody with an IQ of 92 decided to rape and murder the little old lady who lives next door?

6   Besides, we have an abundance of killers in our prisons—more than enough to keep all the nation's shrinks busy for the next 20 years. But shrinks aren't stupid. Why would they want to spend all that time listening to Willie the Wolfman describe his ax murders when they can get $75 an hour for listening to an executive's fantasies about the secretarial pool?

7   Another standard is: "The purpose of the law should be to protect society, not to inflict cruel retribution, such as the death penalty."

8   In that case, we should tear down all the prisons and let all the criminals go because most people would consider a long imprisonment to be cruel retribution—especially those who are locked up. Even 30 days in the Cook County Jail is no picnic.

9   And: "What gives society the right to take a life if an individual can't?" The individuals who make up society give it that right. Societies perform many functions that individuals can't. We can't carry guns and shoot people, but we delegate that right to police.

10   Finally: "The death penalty doesn't deter crime." I heard from a number of people who have a less detached view of the death penalty than many of the sensitive souls who oppose it.

11   For instance, Doris Porch wrote me about a man on Death Row in Tennessee. He hired men to murder his wife. One threw in a rape, free of charge.

12   Porch wrote: "My family had the misfortune of knowing this man [the husband] intimately. The victim was my niece. After her decomposed body was found in the trunk of her car, I made the trip to homicide with my sister."

13   Sharon Rosenfeldt of Canada wrote: "We know exactly what you are talking about because our son was brutally murdered and sexually abused by mass murderer Clifford Olson in Vancouver.

14   "Words can't explain the suffering the families of murder victims are left to live with. After two years, we're still trying to piece our lives back together mentally and spiritually."

15   Eleanor Lulenski of Cleveland said: "I'm the mother of one of the innocent victims. My son was a registered nurse on duty in an emergency room. A man walked in demanding a shot of penicillin. When he was told he would have to be evaluated by a physician, he stomped out, went to his car, came back with a shotgun and killed my son.

16   "He was sentenced to life, but after several years the sentence was reversed on a technicality—it being that at the time of his trial it was mentioned that this was his second murder."

17   And Susie James of Greenville, Miss.: "My tax dollars are putting bread into the mouth of at least one murderer from Mississippi who showed no mercy to his innocent victim.

18   "He caught a ride with her one cold February night. She was returning to her home from her job in a nursing home. She was a widow. The murderer, whom she had befriended, struck her on the head with a can of oil. Ignoring her pleas, he forced her through a barbed-wire fence into the woods at knifepoint. He stabbed her repeatedly, raped her and left her for dead.

19   "When the victim's son walked down the stairs to leave the courthouse after the guilty sentence had been uttered, he happened to look at the killer's mother.

20   "She said: 'You buzzard, watching me.'

21   "The murder victim was my mother."

22   There are many others. The mother of the boy who angered some drunken street thugs. They shot him and then ran him over repeatedly with a car. The mother whose son and daughter were beaten to death. The brother who remembers how his little sister would laugh as they played—until she was butchered.

23   They have many things in common. They suffered a terrible loss, and they live with terrible memories.

24   One other thing they share: The knowledge that the killers are alive and will probably remain alive and cared for by society.

25   Opponents of the death penalty should try explaining to these people just how cruel it is to kill someone.

Understanding the Content

Feel free to reread all or parts of the selection to answer the following questions.

  1. What is Royko's viewpoint on the death penalty?

  2. Royko says that he wishes people who oppose his views would come up with some new arguments. What are the "worn-out" ones he cites? What are his responses to each one?

3. Royko quotes from several letters of people who wrote in favor of his views. What does he say they all have in common?

4. What is the thesis? Is it implied or stated?

Looking at Structure and Style

1. Royko's essay originally appeared as a newspaper column, which is why there are so many short paragraphs. Are there any sentences you would combine into one paragraph if you were to edit this essay? Which ones? Why?

2. How would you describe the tone of this selection? What words or phrases contribute to this tone?

3. What is Royko's attitude toward people who oppose capital punishment? toward psychiatrists? How can you tell?

4. What is the basic writing method Royko uses in paragraphs 11–21? Is this effective?

5. Explain or rewrite the following passages from the essay:
   a. "... the quick dispatching of convicted murderers." (2)
   b. "Why would they ["shrinks"] want to spend all that time listening to Willie the Wolfman describe his ax murders when they can get $75 an hour for listening to an executive's fantasies about the secretarial pool?" (6)
   c. "Even 30 days in the Cook County Jail is no picnic." (8)
   d. "I heard from a number of people who have a less detached view of the death penalty than many of the sensitive souls who oppose it." (10)

6. To what audience is Royko writing? Explain.

Evaluating the Author's Viewpoints

1. Does Royko convince you that there should be laws for "the quick dispatching of convicted murderers"? Why?

2. In paragraphs 4, 7, 9, and 10, Royko provides four "worn-out" arguments of those who oppose the death penalty. Are they worn-out? Comment on the reasoning he uses to disagree with them. Are they logical rebuttals? Is he convincing in his counterarguments for each one?

3. How effective is Royko's use of quotes from letters in paragraphs 11–21? Do they gain your sympathy? Is this "stacking the deck" in favor of his views?

4. What is the function of paragraph 22?

5. Do you agree with Royko's conclusion? Explain.

Pursuing Possible Essay Topics

Unless reading Royko's column stimulated some ideas for an essay that you want to pursue, you should read the next essay, which also deals with capital punishment, and use the list of possible topics that follows it.

📖 *Preparing to Read*

Take a minute or two to look over the following reading selection. Note the title and author, read the first *two* paragraphs, and check the length. Make certain you have the time now to read it carefully and to do the exercises that follow it. Then, in the spaces provided, answer the following questions.

1. What do the title and the opening paragraph tell you about the subject

   of the essay? _____

   _____

2. What is King's view of capital punishment? _____

   _____

3. After reading Royko's views in the previous essay, what should you look

   for in this essay? _____

   _____

   _____

4. Have you heard of the author? What do you know about her? _____

   _____

   _____

Vocabulary

Good comprehension of what you are about to read depends upon your understanding of the words below. The number following each refers to the paragraph where it is used.

   backlash (3) angry reaction

abhor (3) strongly hate

sanctioned (3) permitted

deterrent (3) prevention, discouraging force

unequivocally (4) clearly, without doubt

capital offenses (4) crimes involving death

redeemed (5) made up for

retaliation (5) revenge, paying back evil with evil

irrevocable (7) irreversible

miscarriage (7) mismanagement, bad administration

specter (7) haunting possibility

unwarranted (8) not supported by facts

inequitable (9) unfair

credibility (10) believability

proponents (11) supporters, those in favor of

defies (11) challenges

Now read the essay.

The Death Penalty
Is a Step Back

CORETTA SCOTT KING

1   When Steven Judy was executed in Indiana [in 1981] America took another step backwards towards legitimizing murder as a way of dealing with evil in our society.

2   Although Judy was convicted of four of the most horrible and brutal murders imaginable, and his case is probably the worst in recent memory for opponents of the death penalty, we still have to face the real issue squarely: Can we expect a decent society if the state is allowed to kill its own people?

3   In recent years, an increase of violence in America, both individual and political, has prompted a backlash of public opinion on capital punishment. But however much we abhor violence, legally sanctioned executions are no deterrent and are, in fact, immoral and unconstitutional.

4   Although I have suffered the loss of two family members by assassination, I remain firmly and unequivocally opposed to the death penalty for those convicted of capital offenses.

5   An evil deed is not redeemed by an evil deed of retaliation. Justice is never advanced in the taking of a human life.

6   Morality is never upheld by legalized murder. Morality apart, there are a number of practical reasons which form a powerful argument against capital punishment.

7   First, capital punishment makes irrevocable any possible miscarriage of justice. Time and again we have witnessed the specter of mistakenly convicted people being put to death in the name of American criminal justice. To those who say that, after all, this doesn't occur too often, I can only reply that if it happens just once, that is too often. And it has occurred many times.

8   Second, the death penalty reflects an unwarranted assumption that the wrongdoer is beyond rehabilitation. Perhaps some individuals cannot be rehabilitated; but who shall make that determination? Is any amount of academic training sufficient to entitle one person to judge another incapable of rehabilitation?

9   Third, the death penalty is inequitable. Approximately half of the 711 persons now on death row are black. From 1930 through 1968, 53.5% of those executed were black Americans, all too many of whom were represented by court-appointed attorneys and convicted after hasty trials.

10   The argument that this may be an accurate reflection of guilt, and homicide trends, instead of a racist application of laws lacks credibility in light of a recent Florida survey which showed that persons convicted of killing whites were four times more likely to receive a death sentence than those convicted of killing blacks.

11   Proponents of capital punishment often cite a "deterrent effect" as the main benefit of the death penalty. Not only is there no hard evidence that murdering murderers will deter other potential killers, but even the "logic" of this argument defies comprehension.

12   Numerous studies show that the majority of homicides committed in this country are the acts of the victim's relatives, friends and acquaintances in the "heat of passion."

13   What this strongly suggests is that rational consideration of future consequences are seldom a part of the killer's attitude at the time he commits a crime.

14   The only way to break the chain of violent reaction is to practice nonviolence as individuals and collectively through our laws and institutions.

Understanding the Content

Feel free to reread all or parts of the selection in order to answer the following questions.

1. What is King's viewpoint toward the death penalty?

2. Aside from her feeling that capital punishment is immoral, what are the "practical reasons" she presents as arguments against it?

3. King says that proponents of the death penalty often cite it as a "deterrent effect." What argument does she present against this?

4. King cites a recent Florida survey which showed that persons convicted of killing whites were four times more likely to receive a death sentence than those convicted of killing blacks. How does she interpret this?

5. Does King suggest an alternative to the death penalty? Explain.

Looking at Structure and Style

1. What is the function of the first two paragraphs?

2. In paragraph 4, King refers to the assassination of two family members, including her husband, Martin Luther King, Jr. What effect might this have on her credibility to discuss capital punishment?

3. What transitional devices does King use in paragraphs 6–9?

4. Paragraphs 7–9 state what King calls "practical reasons which form a powerful argument against capital punishment." What is the function of paragraphs 10–11? What arguments in favor of the death penalty does King dispute?

5. What is the point being made in paragraphs 12–13? How do they relate to her thesis?

6. How effective is her concluding paragraph?

7. Explain or rewrite the following passages from the essay:
   a. "An evil deed is not redeemed by an evil deed of retaliation." (5)
   b. ". . . Capital punishment makes irrevocable any possible miscarriage of justice." (7)
   c. "Time and again we have witnessed the specter of mistakenly convicted people being put to death in the name of . . . justice." (7)
   d. "The only way to break the chain of violent reaction is to practice nonviolence as individuals and collectively through our laws and institutions." (14)

Evaluating the Author's Viewpoints

1. Reread the rhetorical question King asks in paragraph 2. Based on what Royko says in the previous essay, how would he answer the question? (See Royko's paragraph 9.) What is your response?

2. One of King's arguments against the death penalty is that it "makes irrevocable any possible miscarriage of justice." What does she mean? Do you agree that even if it only happens once it is too often? Why? What do you think Royko's response would be?

3. Another of her arguments is that no one can say whether or not a person can be rehabilitated, implying that efforts toward rehabilitation should

be made. Reread paragraphs 4–6 in Royko's essay. How does his discussion of rehabilitation differ from King's? Which one presents the better argument? Why?

4. King says that the death penalty does not deter crime (paragraphs 3 and 11); Royko implies it does (paragraphs 10 +). Who provides the best argument? How and why?

5. King calls the death penalty "inequitable." What does she mean? Is her support valid?

6. Reread paragraph 14. Is King correct? Explain.

Pursuing Possible Essay Topics

1. Write an argument against Royko's viewpoint. Show the fallacies (examples of false or incorrect reasoning) you find in his statements. Or, agree with Royko, but provide your own arguments. Use quotations from his essay.

2. Write an argument against King's viewpoint. Show the fallacies you find in her statements. Or, agree with King, but provide your own arguments. Use quotations from her essay.

3. Research any information on the death penalty that has been published since 1981. Use the sources to take a stand on capital punishment. In addition to the library's card catalogue and the *Reader's Guide to Periodical Literature*, you might want to look in the *Criminology and Penology Abstracts*.

4. King claims that the death penalty is "unconstitutional." Read the Constitution and its Amendments (found in the appendix of most U.S. history books) and write an essay that supports or refutes King's position.

5. In a 1986 Gallup Poll, 70% of the people polled were in favor of the death penalty. Between 1977 and 1987, 37 states passed new death-penalty laws. Twenty years earlier, a slight majority opposed the death penalty. Should laws regarding the death penalty change based on popular opinion? Are most people well informed enough to make intelligent decisions on the subject? How important are emotions in making such a decision?

6. Write an essay that outlines when the death penalty is and when it isn't appropriate.

7. Between 1930–67, 3,859 people were legally executed. Of this number a slight majority were blacks, a proportion that is far above blacks' share of the population. This supports King's statistics in paragraph 9. But what do current statistics show? Do some research on the number of legal executions since 1977. Does King's implication that there is racial discrimination when applying the death penalty seem plausible? See item 3 above for possible sources.

8. Brainstorm or freewrite on one or more of the following:
   a. death row
   b. degrees of murder
   c. death penalty as deterrent
   d. "an eye for an eye"
   e. punishment for crimes
   f. legal loopholes

9. If you don't like any of these ideas, write an essay on some other controversial issue.

📖 *Preparing to Read*

Take a minute or two to look over the following reading selection. Note the title and author, read the opening paragraph, and check the length. Make certain you have the time now to read it carefully and to do the exercises that follow it. Then, in the spaces provided, answer the following questions.

1. What is the subject of the essay? _____

_____

2. What is the author's attitude toward the subject? _____

_____

3. What is the author's attitude toward those who disagree? _____

_____

Vocabulary

Good comprehension of what you are about to read depends upon your understanding of the words below. The number following each word refers to the paragraph where it is used.

reputable (1) honorable, having a good reputation

maligned (1) spoken of harmfully, slandered

sensational (1) intended to arouse strong reaction by exaggerated details

vehement diatribes (1) violent, abusive verbal attacks

reek (1) stink (used figuratively)

bigotry (1) strong prejudice, intolerance of others who are different

parochial (1) narrowly restricted, shortsighted

affiliated (2) associated

premise (3) the idea upon which an argument is based

sanctions (3) authorizes, approves

tangible (4) real, concrete

notwithstanding (5) despite

libelous (5) slanderous, meant to harm another's character

Now read the essay.

United We Stand

EDITOR, *THE AMERICAN RIFLEMAN*

1   Members of the National Rifle Association of America and other reputable gun owners are being maligned by sensational reporting on the part of some writers. By means of cleverly written articles, these authors are presenting vehement diatribes against firearms of all description, against NRA, and against gun owners in general. Some reek of bigotry and parochial thinking, while others appear to be a deliberate attempt to divide and conquer.

2   The time has come to make a positive effort to overcome the ignorance and misunderstanding about firearms and the people who use them. Those who appreciate and enjoy guns and shooting must share their knowledge and their beliefs with others in their home communities. They must emphasize to public officials and people in general the importance of firearms in America; the positive values of shooting and hunting; the necessity for firearms safety programs and marksmanship training activities of the National Rifle Association, and the contribution of these programs to the American way of life. Those who have most to gain, and most to lose, must convince their friends and associates that guns and shooting are an essential part of our priceless heritage which must be cherished and encouraged. They must make known the true facts about the NRA, its affiliated shooting organizations, and its members in every state of the Union.

3   The NRA, more than any other organization, promotes the best interests of gun owners and shooters. As a public service, it is dedicated to firearms safety education, marksmanship training, and shooting for recreation. It stands squarely behind the premise that the lawful ownership of firearms must not be denied American citizens of good repute so long as they continue to use them for lawful purposes. The NRA is recognized as the leading authority in the field of firearms safety education and marksmanship training because of its nationwide programs for the youth of America. It has demonstrated the soundness of the theory that the educational approach is

the most effective method of avoiding gun accidents in the home and in the field. It has developed shooting activities for young people which bring out the qualities of sportsmanship, fair play, self-control, and cooperation so essential to responsible citizenship and to success in life. Its instruction guides and training courses have been prepared as aids for teaching proper gun handling in local communities. The program is conducted on a volunteer basis by thousands of NRA certified instructors in schools, summer camps, shooting clubs and other youth groups, in cooperation with state agencies and local organizations. The NRA is the governing body of competitive rifle and pistol shooting in the United States and, in this capacity, establishes rules and regulations, sanctions tournaments, recognizes national champions, and maintains official records. It represents the shooters of America in the United States Olympic Committee and the International Shooting Union.

4   The strength of the NRA and therefore the ability to accomplish its objects and purposes, depends entirely upon the support of loyal Americans who believe in the right to "keep and bear arms." Every reputable citizen who owns a gun or who shoots a gun should be a member. The small investment for dues will return to each individual member valuable dividends in tangible benefits and in the personal satisfaction derived from being a part of a great patriotic organization.

5   Notwithstanding libelous statements and false information appearing in a few publications, the National Rifle Association of America is composed of loyal, law-abiding American citizens. Anyone who has an affection for guns and shooting, and anyone who believes in the right to keep and bear arms, belongs in the NRA, because *united we stand.*

Understanding the Content

Feel free to reread all or parts of the selection in order to answer the following questions.

1. What caused the editor of NRA to write this essay?

2. What does the editor call upon NRA members to do? Why?

3. What is the purpose of the NRA? What are some of the services the NRA performs?

4. According to the editor, what type of people are members of the NRA? Who should belong? Why?

5. What is the thesis? Is it stated or implied?

Looking at Structure and Style

1. What is the function of the first paragraph? Describe the attitude expressed. What are some words or phrases that help reveal that attitude?

2. Paragraph 2 calls upon the people who use guns to "overcome the ignorance and misunderstanding about firearms." Make a list of the points the author wants the public to know in order to overcome this ignorance and misunderstanding. Are the points good support?

3. Paragraph 3 discusses what the NRA does to promote "the best interests of gun owners and shooters." Sort through the paragraph and list each supporting point used.

4. What is the function of paragraph 4? How would you describe the tone of the paragraph? What words or phrases give it its tone?

5. How effective is the last paragraph? Why is the phrase *united we stand* italicized?

6. To what audience is this selection written?

Evaluating the Author's Viewpoints

1. Does the editorial convince you that the NRA is a worthy organization? Explain your reaction to it.

2. Paragraph 2 asserts that some of the NRA activities contribute to "the American way of life." What do the authors mean by this? Exactly what is the American way of life?

3. The editor states that those who enjoy guns and shooting "must emphasize to public officials and people in general the importance of firearms in America." (2) What does this mean? Do you agree that firearms are important in America? Explain.

4. The phrase "to keep and bear arms" used in paragraph 4 is taken from the Second Amendment to the Constitution of the United States, which states, "A well-regulated Militia, being necessary to the security of a free State, the right of the people to bear Arms, shall not be infringed." The NRA believes that the Constitution supports the people's right to own guns. Do you agree that the Constitution grants this right? How do you interpret the passage?

5. The authors say that "guns and shooting are an essential part of our priceless heritage which must be cherished and encouraged." (2) How do you interpret this statement? Do you agree? Explain.

6. In the last line of paragraph 4, the NRA is referred to as "a great patriotic organization." Do you see it as such? Explain.

Pursuing Possible Essay Topics

Unless reading the NRA editorial above stimulated some ideas for an essay that you want to pursue, you should read the next essay, which also deals with guns, and use the list of possible topics that follows it.

📖 Preparing to Read

Take a minute or two to look over the following reading selection. Note the title and author, read the opening paragraph, and check the length. Make certain you have the time now to read it carefully and to do the exercises that follow it. Then, in the spaces provided, answer the following questions.

1. Why does the title have a question mark in parentheses after the word

   Right? _____

   _____

2. What is the author's attitude about guns? _____

   _____

3. How will this essay differ from the NRA editorial in its attitude toward

   guns? _____

   _____

Vocabulary

Good comprehension of what you are about to read depends upon your understanding of the words below. The number following each word refers to the paragraph where it is used.

advocate (1) someone in favor of

lobbies (1) individuals or private groups seeking to influence lawmaking in their favor

stance (2) position

propagandize (3) actively spread an opinion

infringed (3) violated, abused

collective (4) referring to a group acting as one

prominent (5) famous, distinguished

Now read the essay.

The Right (?) to Bear Arms

ADAM RIBB

1   An obvious advocate of gun ownership, the National Rifle Association has done much in the way of promoting gun safety and competitive shooting events. It is not difficult to understand why large numbers of men and women around this country who love to hunt and shoot for sport belong to the NRA. The legitimate ownership and use of rifles and shotguns goes without question. What does come in question, however, is the need to own and use handguns. Why *do* people own handguns? And why does the NRA, now one of the most powerful lobbies in Washington, D.C., spend so much and fight so hard to stop handgun control measures that have nothing to do with taking away people's rifles and shotguns?

2   The very name of the organization, National *Rifle* Association, is misleading. The name of the NRA publication, "The American *Rifleman*," is misleading. There's nothing in either of these names to indicate their peculiar stance on handguns. Yet, every time a new bill is introduced in Washington that even hints at some measure of handgun-control legislation, the NRA goes to work and successfully stops it.

3   The NRA chooses to propagandize to its members that the United States Constitution gives us the "right to bear arms." But they fail to tell its members that this phrase is taken out of context. The full statement in the Second Amendment to the Constitution reads: "A well-regulated Militia, being necessary to the security of a free State, the right of the people to keep and bear Arms, shall not be infringed." The NRA conveniently leaves off the first part of the wording. That "well-regulated Militia" is known today as the National Guard. The framers of the Constitution were worried that a newly formed federal government might try to disarm members of each state's militia. It was never intended to be interpreted the way the NRA does.

4   In his book *Guns Don't Die—People Do*, Pete Shields reveals that on five separate occasions, the Supreme Court has ruled against the NRA's interpretation. In addition, Shields points out that the American Bar Association, at its annual convention in 1975, stated that "every federal court decision involving the [Second] amendment has given the amendment a collective, militia interpretation . . ." (Shields 168). Yet, the NRA continues to use the phrase to its own advantage.

5   Why all the fuss over handguns? The FBI claims that handguns are used annually to murder at least 15,000 Americans, accidentally cause the deaths of another 3,000 people, and wound 100,000. More than 60 percent of all murders are caused by guns, and handguns account for more than 70 percent of these (*Uniform Crime* 24). An estimated 100,000 handguns are stolen by criminals from law-abiding citizens during home burglaries each year (Shields 81). About 40 percent of the handguns used in crimes are stolen (Wright, Rossi and Daly 181). Yet, we hear from people as prominent as ex-Senator Barry Goldwater who claims, "We have a crime problem in this country, not a gun problem" (Goldwater 186).

6   Handguns are convenient for committing crimes. They can be hidden; rifles and shotguns are hard to hide. The handgun is the number one choice of weapon used by criminals. Their main use is to kill at close range. True hunters and sportsmen rely more on rifles and shotguns than handguns. Why, then, do NRA-types oppose laws that would restrict the sale of handguns?

7   A frequent argument for owning a handgun is "I need one to protect my home." Yet police reports show that the home handgun is far more likely to kill or injure members of the family than serve as a protective device. Since 90 percent of all burglaries take place when no one is at home, the handgun usually ends up being stolen. In some cases it is the homeowner who ends up getting shot because he warns the thief he has a gun (Shields 189).

8   Let's be honest. There is no *real* need for handguns. The harm they cause far outweighs the need to shoot holes in a paper target, the only legitimate use handguns may have. The National Rifle Association would do a great service to this country if it spent its lobbying money to educate its members to the truth about handguns. But considering the number of guns already out there, it may be too late.

Bibliography

Goldwater, Barry. "Why Gun Control Laws Don't Work." *Reader's Digest.* Dec. 1975: 183–188.

Halbrook, Steven P. *That Every Man Should Be Armed: The Evolution of A Constitutional Right.* University of New Mexico Press, 1985.

Shields, Pete. *Guns Don't Die—People Do.* Arbor House, 1981.

Uniform Crime Reports for the United States. U.S. Department of Justice, 1985.

Wright, J. D., P. H. Rossi, and K. Daly. *Under the Gun.* Aldine, 1983.

Understanding the Content

Feel free to reread all or parts of the selection to answer the following questions.

1. What is Ribb's position toward firearms? toward handguns?

2. What is his attitude toward the National Rifle Association? Why does he feel this way? What does he want the organization to do?

3. How does Ribb interpret the phrase "the right to bear arms"? Upon what does he base this interpretation?

4. Why is Ribb opposed to handguns?

5. What is the thesis? Is it implied or stated?

Looking at Structure and Style

1. Why does Ribb open his essay with positive comments about the NRA and then attack the organization's position on handguns?

2. What is the function of paragraph 2? What point is being made?

3. What is the function of paragraphs 3 and 4? How do they work as a unit?

4. Paragraphs 4 and 5 both rely on other sources for information. Does this help or hinder Ribb's thesis? Explain.

5. How do paragraphs 6 and 7 work as a unit? What is their purpose?

6. Is the closing paragraph a strong conclusion? Explain.

Evaluating the Author's Viewpoints

1. Does Ribb convince you that handguns should be outlawed? Why?

2. Why does Ribb feel the NRA should stop lobbying against stricter handgun control laws? Do you agree with his arguments?

3. Ribb claims that the NRA is misrepresenting to its membership and others the meaning of the phrase "the right to bear arms." Based on its use in the editorial "United We Stand," and based on the information in Ribb's essay (paragraph 3), what is your opinion?

4. Look at the information Ribb presents to argue against handgun ownership. Is the support valid? Are these good reasons to have stricter handgun laws? Explain.

5. Ribb ends his essay by saying that other than for law enforcement there is no real need for handguns. Do you agree? Why?

Pursuing Possible Essay Topics

1. Defend or refute the NRA's position against strict gun control legislation.

2. Argue for or against Ribb's position on handguns.

3. Research the references listed in Ribb's bibliography or any others that you can find. Take a stand on gun control and use your sources to support your viewpoint. Include a bibliography.

4. Compare/contrast "United We Stand" and "The Right (?) To Bear Arms" by examining the writing styles, structure, and support. Which one is more convincingly written, regardless of your views on the subject? Explain.

5. Write an essay that classifies people according to the reasons they want to own handguns, such as protection, target practice, to commit crime, and so on. Evaluate each of these reasons.

6. Brainstorm or freewrite on one or more of the following:
   a. "Guns don't kill; people do."
   b. "Guns don't kill people; criminals do."
   c. "Defend your right to arm bears."
   d. "We have a crime problem in this country, not a gun problem."
   e. "Use a gun; go to jail."
   f. "If guns are outlawed, only outlaws will have guns."

7. If you've shot down all of these, then find a topic of your own on some other controversial issue.

🔊 Student Essay

As you read the following student essay, look for answers to these questions:

1. Does the essay fit the assignment to write about some aspect of a controversial issue?

2. Is the thesis clear? Is good support provided?

3. Does the essay cause you to think about the subject?

4. Is the essay well-written?

Ignorant to What Is Sacred

Benjamin Little

1   It is quite conceivable and quite possible that you could wake up, expect to start a typical day and instead face a world that has been destroyed as the result of a nuclear disaster. A fetid stench

will permeate your surroundings, as the result of the charred, smoldering corpses, which lie everywhere in a hellish atmosphere. All your loved ones are dead. Only a few of you are left because you survived the initial blast. Your suffering and mourning will be brief, however, because you too will be dead in a couple of weeks from the exposure of the deadly radiation.

2   Before you die, you wonder why you, along with those you had known, had never realized that the morbid destruction surrounding you was always hovering over your heads as a possibility for the future. Your realization of a lifeless world to come was a consideration which was not considered.

3   The issue of nuclear war is a popular one, but rarely discussed in such graphic terms. It is continuously in the news, but always mentioned as if it were just another current event. People regard nuclear arms in terms of how its reductions or build up affect our leverage over the rest of the world. More concern needs to be put into the fundamental consequences of existing and future nuclear weapons; we need to realize the possibility of total world destruction. It is up to each individual to contemplate, analyze, and visualize the disturbing aftermath of a nuclear disaster. We must break through our political and social attachments which lead us to believe that sustaining nuclear weapons is an explanation for preserving our freedom.

4   What aspects of your life do you hold in highest value? Is it your life? Or is it the life of a loved one? Maybe your achievements, aspirations, or life-long dreams are the parts of your life that you most treasure. All the things that you cherish will be gone forever, if the nuclear holocaust, which many of us fear, were to happen. It is a very troublesome thought, that no matter how you lead your life, and no matter what you think and do, it can all be taken away. True, you could die tomorrow; but your experiences and ideas will still live with the many people you have known. Perhaps it is most distressing for the individual who understands that the natural process that allows mankind to flourish throughout time could be destroyed. It is only when one is able to view man's existence as sacred that one comes to realize the insanity of maintaining nuclear weapons.

5   With this country's shift to the political right in recent years,
it has become clearer than ever that the leaders of this country
have disregarded the enormous threat that nuclear arms have
over mankind. They have condensed the whole issue into an apparent simple belief, that what is right for this country is all that
matters. President Reagan's motto of "peace in strength," only
adds to the deviated rationale of nuclear arms. This is especially
true after he has already indoctrinated many Americans with his
simplistically grotesque remarks. These remarks include refering
to the Soviet Union as the "evil empire," or promoting his position on defense by declaring that the United States is building
nuclear bombs in the name of God. It is quite clear that this irra-
tional kind of thinking is the result of a fearful narrowminded-
ness, which is being instilled in the minds of too many people.

6   Our continuous desire to conform to the social standards is a
conditioning factor that allows people to accept the belief that our
support of nuclear weapons is reasonable. This, again, is a representation of how people surmise this matter at a level which
clearly disregards the indication that mankind is at the threshold
of nonexistence. Unfortunately, the public is more sensitive to the
social pressure, which forces each individual into an "either-or"
conception in regards to this problem. This, in turn, compels people to separate into groups to help soothe their one-sided viewpoint. People, then, become trapped into a continuous belief, as
the result of group pressure; and individual reasoning is seen as a
threat of alienation. And a universal agreement that preserving
humanity is the most essential concern is now needed more than
ever.

7   The nuclear age has brought with it the need for everyone to
conceive of the implicit outcome that this world is heading toward. It must be realized that total obliteration of the human race
is certainly a possibility for our coming time. It must also be
understood that jeopardizing humanity is a chance that we
should not be taking. It is true that there are no simple answers
to reducing nuclear arms; but, if everyone can comprehend that
no ideology, religious belief, or human event is as sacred as the

existence of mankind, this objective may be possible. People have to take the time to realize, or else....

Reaction

In the space below, write your reaction to the essay. What would you tell the student about his essay?

Commentary

Ben's essay appears here for two reasons: one, it serves as an example of how long and how hard writers often must work to reach a final draft; and two, it reflects an honesty and an earnestness toward a controversial topic of a student's choice.

This version of Ben's essay is the result of an entire semester's work. The nuclear arms issue is a controversial issue for which Ben obviously has strong feelings. But despite his desire to express himself on the subject, Ben was never satisfied with any of his other drafts that he worked on earlier in the semester. He says he wrote one version after another, but never felt he was saying what he wanted to say. He frequently wondered if he really knew enough about the subject to use it as a topic. But he continued to try, working at it on and off between other writing assignments. When he finally turned this draft in, he still felt it might not be "good enough."

At the beginning of the semester, Ben's writing was far from the quality revealed here. As a matter of fact, Ben almost dropped the class because his first essay attempts were "unacceptable." But Ben's problem was not that he couldn't write or didn't have anything to say. His problem was that he was writing for the instructor rather than himself. He would quickly turn out a composition that contained what he thought the teacher wanted to hear. Ben hadn't found his own voice yet. After a few conferences with his instructor and an awareness that good writing comes from thoughtful revision of his true feelings, Ben began to write acceptable papers.

Ben's final idea for his essay came from hearing a debate on the nuclear arms race. Because of his interest in the subject, he read a few of the books recommended during the debate, one of which was Jonathan Schell's *The Fate of the Earth*. Ben's opening paragraph was prompted by Schell's vivid description of what New York City would be like if subjected to a nuclear bomb. Feeling that most people are ignoring or hiding from the nuclear arms issue, Ben opens with his own vivid description of a nuclear aftermath to grab his reader's attention. And since he was no expert on nuclear problems, he felt his best approach was to try to wake up his readers to what he feels may be destruction of life as we know it. Rather than dealing with the numbers of nuclear arms in existence, Ben wants his audience to see life as sacred. He calls for us to stop conforming to social standards that lead to destruction, to quit allowing ourselves to be conditioned by the fear of those in power. Instead, he calls for us to "conceive of the implicit outcome that this world is heading toward."

Once Ben felt he had expressed his feelings, he worked and reworked his sentence structure and vocabulary, frequently seeking advice through conferences with his instructor. You may not agree with Ben's thesis, but you'll probably agree that this is certainly an acceptable essay with no doubt as to where the author stands on the nuclear arms controversy.

Appendix

Essay Format and Proofreading Guide

Essay Format

If your instructor does not tell you what form your final essay draft should take, follow these standard rules.

If you type or use a word processor

1. Use standard 8½" × 11" bond typing paper. Don't use erasable paper because it smears too easily. Make certain that your typewriter or computer printer ribbon makes a clear, dark imprint. Don't use script or unusual type, especially if you print out your paper on a dot matrix printer. Make certain all letters are distinguishable (for instance, some printers don't make clear p's or d's).

2. Double-space your paper to provide room for your instructor to make comments and corrections. This also leaves enough space for you to correct any typing, spelling, or punctuation errors you notice when proofreading your typed copy. (See proofreading correction symbols on page 420.) If your paper is very messy, retype it.

3. Leave at least 1" margins all around your page.

4. Your name, your instructor's name, the course number, and the date should appear in the upper left- or right-hand corner on the first page. Double-space, then center your title, capitalizing the first letter of each word unless it is an article, conjunction, or preposition. Don't underline or place quotation marks around your title. (If other writers refer to your essay by title in their writing, then they should place quotation marks around your title to identify it as such.)

5. Indent the first line of each paragraph five spaces.

6. Leave two spaces after every period, question mark, or exclamation mark; use only one space after commas, semicolons, or colons.

7. Use quotation marks around short quotations that run less than five lines of your own manuscript. If the quote runs longer, then

417

First Page of Manuscript Without a Title Page

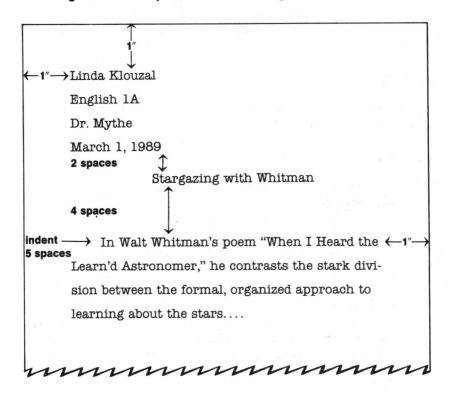

Numbering Subsequent Pages

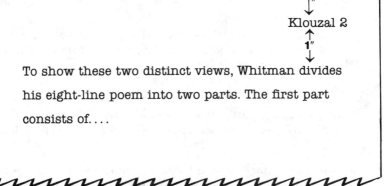

indent ten spaces from the left to set it off from your own writing; no quotation marks are needed, but the quote should be followed by the source cited in parentheses (see Appendix C, "Quoting and Documenting Sources"). When the quote is completed, return to your regular margins.

8. Number all pages consecutively in the upper right-hand corner about ½" from the top. You may want to place your last name next to the page number. No page number is needed for the first page unless your instructor wants a title page. In that case, ask the instructor for more details on format. Title pages are generally used for lengthy research papers, which require outlines and footnote and bibliography pages.

9. Staple your pages together in order at the upper left-hand corner only. Don't use paper clips; they fall off or get caught in other students' essays when stacked in a pile. Don't bend the corners together with a little tear—it doesn't work.

10. Don't use binders or folders unless your instructor requests them.

11. Make a copy in case something happens to the original. If you use a word processor, be sure to save it on disk.

If your essay is handwritten

It's generally not a good idea to submit handwritten papers. If your instructor does permit it, you should follow the rules above for typed papers, with these differences:

1. Use white, wide-lined paper, no smaller than 8½" × 11".

2. If you write on paper from a spiral notebook, cut off the ragged edges before you submit it.

3. Write on every other line, using only one side of a page.

4. Use only black or dark blue ink.

5. If your handwriting is poor, print. If you can't write or print neatly, pay a typist. An instructor has many papers to grade and has little patience with papers that are difficult to read.

Following these essay format rules is fairly safe, but it is always a good idea to ask any instructors who require written essays what format they want you to use.

Proofreading Guide

Correction Symbols

Once you have finished typing your paper, be certain that you or someone else carefully proofreads it. Read it aloud or have it read aloud to you. If you notice many mistakes, you should type it over. If there are only a few errors, you can correct them by hand using the following symbols. Just be neat and use dark ink.

a. to insert an apostrophe or double quotation marks

ᵛIs this the professoɾ̆s book?ᵛ

b. to insert a word, letter, or comma

insert‸word, let‸er‸or comma

c. to insert a period

Insert a period⊙

d. to delete

del⫽ete

e. to indicate a new paragraph

... end of a sentence. The next sentence ...

f. to indicate no new paragraph

... end of a sentence.⟩
no⁋ ⊂The next sentence ...

g. to insert space

insert#space

h. to close up space

close up sp‿ace

i. to transpose (reverse) letters or words

rev⁀ese

j. to indicate a capital letter

september
‗

k. to indicate a lower-case letter

⫽mall ⫽etters

Proofreading for Mechanics

The following brief summary of some mechanical rules may be of help before you finalize your paper.

Underlining

In typing, underlining is reserved for the following:

a. to identify books, magazines, newspapers, films, or record albums

Herman Melville's <u>Moby Dick</u>

<u>TIME</u> magazine   (Notice that *magazine* is not underlined.)

<u>Los Angeles Times</u>   (Quotation marks are used around titles of chapters, articles, essays, or poems that appear in books, magazines, or newspapers.)

Woody Allen's <u>The Purple Rose of Cairo</u>

The Beatles' <u>Sergeant Pepper's Lonely Hearts Club Band</u>   (Quotation marks are used around titles of songs in an album.)

b. to identify foreign words not in everyday use

The Welsh call themselves <u>cymry</u>.

c. to call attention to a particular word

The word <u>run</u> has over twenty definitions.

The student used <u>affect</u> when she meant <u>effect</u>.

d. to denote sounds

With a <u>plunk</u>, the penny slowly dropped to the bottom of the well.

Numbers

In general, these rules apply to writing numbers and figures:

a. Spell out numbers that can be written in one or two words.

twenty

twenty-two   (hyphenated numbers are considered one word)

twenty-two thousand

b. Use numerals for numbers that require more than two words.

275   (two hundred seventy-five)

22,645   (twenty-two thousand, six hundred forty-five)

c. Numerals are almost always used for money: $35; occasionally they're written out: one dollar. There are times when the use of figures is more impressive looking. For instance, *one trillion* doesn't have the visual snap that seeing the figure *$1,000,000,000,000* has.

d. When starting a sentence, it's better to use words.

Forty-three people attended the lecture.

e. When referring to page numbers, prices, or scores, use figures.

From page 16 of Newsweek, he learned that the tickets were $15.

The Giants beat the Cardinals 10-4.

Capital Letters

Use capital letters:

a. to refer to persons, places, and brand names

Albert Einstein

Yellowstone National Park

Porsche

Harvard University

b. to refer to title or rank

Mayor Koch

Bishop Tutu

Prince Charles

c. to refer to names of religions and members of them

Buddhism, Unitarians, Jewish

d. to refer to titles of written works

Bloom's <u>The Lexington Reader</u> (book)

Smith's "What Will Become of the Latchkey Kids?" (essay)

Frost's "Stopping by the Woods" (poem)

Notice that the phrases "of the" and "by the" in the titles are not capitalized. Unless they begin the title, **articles** (a, an, the), **prepositions** (of, on, by, in to, etc.), and **conjunctions** (and, or) are not capitalized.

e. for the names of the days and months

There are four Sundays in March this year.

Manuscript style manuals vary, but unless your instructor wants you to follow a particular style manual, these rules should be acceptable.

APPENDIX B
Library Research Sources

There are two types of library sources, primary and secondary. Primary sources are original sources, such as literary works (novels, poems, stories), autobiographies, journals, diaries, letters, or first-hand accounts of events. Secondary sources are works that explain or interpret primary sources, such as a literary critic's explanation of a literary work, a biography, an interpretation of a Supreme Court decision, or an analysis of data based on a scientific study or survey. Secondary sources are often helpful in research because they pull together other information on your topic. However, they are generally opinions or interpretations of others. Primary sources, on the other hand, require your own analysis and interpretation.

Let's say you are assigned to do research on what critics have said about John Updike's novel *The Witches of Eastwick*. In such a case secondary sources will be called for in your paper. If, on the other hand, the assignment calls for *your* analysis of the novel, you will need to stick to the primary source, the novel. Reading secondary sources on the novel, however, may provide you with ideas and arguments that could be useful in supporting your own analysis of the book. The assignment itself will determine which sources are the most useful.

In addition to the usual starting places—the library card catalogue, which catalogues works in the library under subject and title, and the *Reader's Guide to Periodical Literature*, which indexes current articles from popular magazines such as *TIME, Newsweek, Harper's,* and *Ladies Home Journal*—here are some other sources. Look over the list now to get an idea of what is available in various subject areas.

Encyclopedias

General:

Encyclopedia Americana
Encyclopaedia Britannica
Collier's Encyclopedia
New Columbia Encyclopedia
Random House Encyclopedia

Specialized:

Bibliography of the Negro in Africa and America
Encyclopedia of World Art
Encyclopedia of the Biological Sciences
Encyclopedia of Management
Encyclopedia of Chemistry
Encyclopedia of Education
Engineering Encyclopedia
Dictionary of American History
Oxford Companion to American History
Oxford Companion to American Literature
Oxford Companion to English Literature
Oxford Companion to the Theatre
Literary History of the United States
Grove's Dictionary of Music and Musicians
Encyclopedia of Pop, Rock, and Soul
World's Encyclopedia of Recorded Music
American Political Dictionary
Encyclopedia of Modern World Politics
Encyclopedia of Psychology
Encyclopedia of Philosophy
Concise Encyclopedia of Western Philosophy
Dictionary of Anthropology
Encyclopedia of Science Fiction and Fantasy
Encyclopedia of the Social Sciences
Encyclopedia of Social Work
Complete Encyclopedia of Television Programs, 1947–1979
New York Times Encyclopedia of Television
Oxford Companion to Sports and Games

Biographical References

Current Biography
Contemporary Authors
Dictionary of American Biography
Twentieth-Century Authors
Who's Who in America
Who's Who Among Black Americans

Who's Who and Where in Women's Studies
Who's Who in Education
Who's Who in American Politics
Who's Who in Rock

Indexes

Social Science and Humanities Index
Humanities Index
Social Sciences Index
Essay and General Literature Index
Art Index
Music Index
Book Review Index
Business Periodical Index
Education Index
American Statistics Index
Applied Science and Technology Index
Biological and Agricultural Index
Computer Literature Index
Engineering Index

Your Librarian

Most librarians enjoy showing students what materials are available on a subject and where to locate them in the library. Of course they won't do your research for you, but they can save you time when you need to find something. Don't overlook this vital resource, especially if you're unfamiliar with library usage.

APPENDIX C
Quoting and Documenting Sources

Quoting Sources

Quotations from other sources are basically used for one of three reasons: (1) they contain authoritative information or ideas that support or help explain your thesis, (2) they contain ideas you want to argue against or prove wrong, or (3) they are so well-written that they make your point better than your own explanation could. However, before you use any quotations, ask yourself what purpose they serve. The use of too many quotations can be confusing and distracting to a reader. Quotations should not be used as a substitute for your own writing.

There are several ways of quoting your source material. One way is to quote an entire sentence, such as:

> In her article, "The State of American Values," Susanna McBee claims, "The recent <u>U.S. News & World Report</u> survey findings show that the questions of morality are troubling ordinary people."

Notice that the title and author of the quotation are provided before the quotation is given. Never use a quotation without providing a lead into it. Usually, verbs such as "says," "explains," "states," and "writes," are used to lead into a quotation. In this case, it is "claims." Notice, too, the placement of punctuation marks, especially the comma after "claims" and the closing quotation marks after the period.

Another way to quote sources is to incorporate part of a quotation into your own writing:

> In her article, "The State of American Values," Susanna McBee claims that a recent survey conducted by <u>U.S. News & World Report</u> shows that "the questions of morality are troubling ordinary people."

Quotation marks are only placed around the exact words of McBee. Since her words are used as part of the writer's sentence, the first word from McBee's quotation is not capitalized. Notice the way the quotation marks are placed at the beginning and end of the quotation being used.

At times, you may want to make an indirect quotation. Indirect quotations do not require the use of quotation marks because you are paraphrasing, that is, rewriting the information using your own words. Notice how the McBee quotation is paraphrased here:

> In her article, "The State of American Values," Susanna McBee states that according to a recent survey conducted by U.S. News & World Report, the average person is bothered by what is and isn't moral.

When the exact wording of a quotation is not vital, it is better to paraphrase the quotation. However, be sure not to change the meaning of the quotation or to imply something not stated there. When paraphrasing, you must still provide the reader with the source of the information you paraphrase.

When quotations run more than five lines, don't use quotation marks. Instead, indent the quoted material ten spaces from your own margin and skip a line. This is called a **block quote** and it shows that the quotation is not part of your own writing:

> In her article, "The State of American Values," Susanna McBee concludes by stating:
>
>> Where individuals should be cautious, warn social scientists and theologians, is in forcing their standards upon others. In the words of the Rev. McKinley Young of Big Bethal AME Church of Atlanta: "When you find somebody waving all those flags and banners, watch closely. Morality, if you're not careful, carries a sense of self-righteousness. Whenever you pat yourself on the back, it creates all kinds of cramps."

Here, quotation marks are not needed for the McBee quotation. But because McBee's quoted statement contains a quotation by someone else, her quotation marks must be included in the block quote. This is a quotation within a quotation.

Try to avoid quotations within a quotation that is shorter than five lines. They are awkward to follow. But if you do need to, here is the way:

McBee concludes by saying, "In the words of Rev. McKinley Young of Big Bethal AME Church of Atlanta: 'Morality . . . carries a sense of self-righteousness. Whenever you pat yourself on the back, it creates all kinds of cramps.' "

Notice the position of the first set of quotation marks (")—just before the beginning of the McBee quotation. Then, when McBee begins quoting Young's words, a single quotation mark (') is used. Since the entire quotation ends with a quote with in a quote, a single quotation mark must be used to show the end of Young's words, plus regular quotation marks must be used to show the end of McBee's words. You can see why it's best to avoid this structure if possible.

Look in the example above at the use of what looks like three periods (. . .) between the words "Morality and "carries." This is called an **ellipsis.** An ellipsis is used to indicate that part of the quotation is left out. When part of a quote is not important to your point, you may use an ellipsis to shorten the quoted material. Be sure, however, that you haven't changed the meaning of the original quotation. Furthermore, always make certain that the remaining quoted material reads like a complete thought or sentence, as in the example.

Documenting Sources

Most English instructors require that you document your sources by following the guidelines of the Modern Language Association. The following examples show how to document most of the sources you would probably use. However, it is not complete, so you may want to consult the *MLA Handbook for Writers of Research Papers* for further information.

When you use quotations in your paper, you are required to identify your sources. Documenting your sources lets your readers know that the information and ideas of others is not your own. It also lets readers know where more information on your subject can be found in case they choose to read your sources for themselves. You cite your sources in two places: in your paper after the quotation, and at the end of your paper under a heading entitled "Works Cited."

Citing within the paper

Here's how you would show where the examples above came from.

> In her article, "The State of American Values," Susanna
>
> McBee claims, "The recent U.S. News & World Report sur-
>
> vey findings show that the questions of morality are trou-
>
> bling ordinary people" (54).

The number in parentheses (54) refers to the page number in the McBee article where the quotation can be found. Since the author and article title are provided in the lead-in to the quote, only the page number is needed at the end. Readers can consult the "Works Cited" page at the end of your paper to learn where and when the article appeared. Notice that when the source ends with a quotation the parentheses and page number go *after* the quotation marks and *before* the period.

When paraphrasing a quotation, use the following citation form:

> In her article, "The State of American Values," Susanna
>
> McBee states that according to a recent survey conducted
>
> by U.S. News & World Report, the average person is both-
>
> ered by what is and isn't moral (54).

Here the parentheses and page number go after the last word and before the period.

If the quote is not identified by author, the author's name and page number should be included in the parentheses.

> A recent survey shows that the average person is bothered
>
> by what should be considered moral (McBee 54).

By including the author's name and page number, you let the reader know where to look on the "Works Cited" page for the complete documentation information.

The "Works Cited" Page

All the sources you used for writing your paper should be listed alphabetically by the author's last name on the "Works Cited" page. If there is no author's name on the work, then alphabetize it using the first letter of the first word of the title, unless it begins with an article (*a, an, the*). Here are the proper forms for the more basic sources. Note especially the punctuation and spacing.

For books by one author:

> Bloom, Alan. <u>The Closing of the American Mind</u>. New York:
>
> Simon, 1987.

As usual, two spaces are used after periods; single spacing is used elsewhere. A colon is used after the name of the city where the publisher is located, followed by the publisher's name. Book publisher's names can be shortened to conserve space. For instance, the full name of the publisher in the example above is Simon and Schuster. A comma is used before the date and a period after it.

If two or more books are listed by the same author, you do not need to provide the name again. Use three hyphens instead. For example:

> ---. <u>Shakespeare's Politics</u>. Chicago: U of Chicago P, 1972.

For books by two or three authors:

> Jones, Judy, and William Wilson. <u>An Incomplete Educa-</u>
>
> <u>tion</u>. New York: Ballantine, 1987.

The same punctuation and spacing are used, but only the name of the first author listed on the book's title page is inverted. The authors' names are separated by a comma.

For books by more than three authors:

> Gundersen, Joan R., et al. <u>America Changing Times</u>. 2nd
>
> ed. New York: Wiley, 1982.

The Latin phrase *et al.*, which means *and others*, is used in place of all but the name of the first author listed on the book's title page. Notice its placement and the use of punctuation before and after.

For books that are edited:

> Dupuis, Mary M., ed. <u>Reading in the Content Areas</u>. New-
>
> ark: Int. Reading Assoc., 1984.

The citing is the same as for authored books except for the insertion of *ed.* to signify that it is edited rather than authored by the person named. If there is more than one editor, you follow the same form as for authors, inserting *eds.* after the last editor's name.

For magazine articles:

> McBee, Susanna. "The State of American Values." <u>U.S. News</u>
>
> <u>& World Report</u> 9 Dec. 1985: 54–58

When citing magazine articles, use abbreviations for the month. The order of the listing is (1) author, (2) article title, (2) magazine title, (3) date, and (4) page number(s) of the article. Note carefully how and where the punctuation is used.

For newspaper articles:

> Reeves, Richard. "America Isn't Falling Apart." <u>San Fran-</u>
>
> <u>cisco Chronicle</u> 24 June 1987: C2.

The citing is basically the same as that for a magazine article. The difference here is that you include the letter of the newspaper section with the page number ("C2" in the sample).

For scholarly journal articles:

> Kellman, Stephen G. "The Cinematic Novel: Tracking a
>
> Concept." <u>Modern Fiction Studies</u> 33 (1987): 467–77.

The citing for a scholarly journal article begin the same as for a magazine article except that the journal volume number (33 in the example) and the date (only the year in parentheses) are cited differently. Volume numbers for journals can usually be found on the cover or on the table of contents page.

For an encyclopedia article:

> "Television." <u>Encyclopedia Americana</u>. 1985 ed.

Since encyclopedias are written by many staff authors, no author can be cited. Begin with the title of the section you read, then the name of the encyclopedia, and the date of the edition you used. No page numbers are needed. Notice the position of the punctuation marks.

For an interview that you conducted yourself:

> Stone, James. Personal interview. 9 Jan. 1988.

For a lecture:

> Dunn, Harold. "Poverty of the Arts in an Affluent Society."
>
> Santa Barbara City College. 3 May 1985.

If a lecture has no title, substitute the word *Lecture*.

For movies:

> <u>Jules and Jim</u>. Dir. Francois Truffaut. With Jeanne Mo-
>
> reau, Oscar Werner, and Henri Serre. Carrose Films,
>
> 1962.

The listing order is title, director, actors, distributor, and year the film was made.

For television shows:

> <u>ABC Nightly News</u>. With Peter Jennings. KABC, Los Ange-
>
> les. 2 May 1988.

APPENDIX D
Sample Research Paper

The following student research paper can be used as a model if you are required to write a documented essay. If you look closely, you will notice that it follows the guidelines for quoting and documenting provided in Appendix C.

Steve Brodie

English 1A

Dr. Wilson

3 March 1988

Television News as Show Business

Television has become the most powerful force in America. Anyone who doubts it need only look at some recent statistics:

—98% of all American homes have at least one television set;

—51% of all homes have two or more television sets;

—an average American family watches television over 7 hours a day;

—at that rate, the average family views over 22,000 commercials in one year alone;

—by the time you are eighteen you will have watched over 15,000 hours of television (you will have spent only 11,000 in school);

—every 3.5 seconds you are shown a different image (every 2.5 seconds for commercials);

—watching soap operas is a daily habit for over 30 million people (Bill 38–39).

Because television can provide immediate access to what is going on in the world, it might appear that these long hours of viewing keep Americans well-informed at a fast pace. This is not the case. Most of those viewing hours are spent watching mindless programs that have little to do with reality, programs either so void of thought that laugh tracks are provided to let us know when something is funny, or present life as so crime-filled that some people are afraid to go outside.

A bigger problem, however, is the way television treats the news. Grown used to being "entertained" from so many hours of viewing TV, we have unwittingly allowed television producers to present the news as "live" entertainment.

Even worse, Americans are relying too much on television as a source of their information and accepting on faith what they see and hear (Corwin 18). Forgetting that television's primary reason for existing is to gain our attention so that stations can sell time to sponsors, so that sponsors in turn can sell us a need for their products, Americans have become willing "boobs of the tube." One of the many sad side effects of America's love affair with television is that it has placed the need for entertainment high on our cultural priorities. "And the problem that results is that television, because of its entertainment format—its visual nature—turns all forms of discourse into entertainment packages," says Neil Postman in his article, "TV Has Culture by the Throat" (58).

Look at the way television news is presented. Television news gives us the illusion that we are informed. Because we are taken around the world with "live coverage" visuals, we think we know what is going on. We don't. What we see is selected for its visual entertainment value and then controlled in its presentation. Robert MacNeil, executive editor and coanchor of the "Mac-

Neil-Lehrer Newshour," says that the idea behind major network television news broadcasting "is to keep everything brief, not to strain the attention of anyone, . . . to provide constant stimulation through variety, novelty, action, and movement, . . . to pay attention to no concept, no character, and no problem for more than a few seconds at a time" (2). To further soothe us and to add to our enjoyment, all television news broadcasts begin and end with dramatic music. In his book Amusing Ourselves to Death, Neil Postman asks why; his answer: ". . . for the same reason music is used in the theatre and films . . . entertainment" (102).

In addition to packaging the presentation of the news for our entertainment, television producers are careful about who they select to present the news. Norman Corwin, in his book Trivializing America: The Triumph of Mediocrity, calls TV news "a kind of succotash" served by people who "had better be good-looking, sparkling or cute—weathermen with party charm, anchorladies with good teeth and smart coiffures, sportscasters with macho charisma" (33). In her book And So It Goes, Linda Ellerbee, a television journalist and reporter, refers to most news-anchor persons as "twinkies," selected for their smiles, not their journalism ability (12). In turn for making bad news seem trivial and merely a lead into a commercial, some of them earn a million dollars or more a year.

It is even possible to be fired from your job as news anchor if you aren't considered pretty enough to make the news seem pleasing. In 1985, Christine Craft, an anchorwoman at KMBC-TV

in Kansas City, Missouri, was fired because she was thought "too
old, too unattractive, and not deferential to men," even though
she was described as having "wholesome, outdoorsy good looks"
(Corwin 34). Even though Craft sued and was awarded damages
by a jury, a higher court overturned the award. That's entertainment.

Television news broadcasts have also gone Hollywood in
their settings. While the camera focuses on the news commenta-
tor, we see in the background what looks like busy editors at
computers and TV monitors keeping up with the latest news
breaks. We are made to feel that we are a part of the news making itself. In his book Talking Tombstones & Other Tales of the
Media Age, Gary Gumpert writes:

> It is therefore surprising to discover that the CBS newscast
> is taped at 6:30 P.M. (Eastern Standard Time) and, while it
> is broadcast live to a limited number of stations on the
> East Coast, most of the East Coast receives the broadcast at
> 7:00 P.M. via videotape. The rest of the nation receives a
> taped version later, depending on the time zone. If late
> items do develop, the videotape is interrupted with a live
> insert.... To some extent, the "aura" of "immediacy" which
> pervades the newscast is a facade manufactured for au-
> thenticity (49).

The harm in all this is that entertainment becomes more important than substance. "Television makes Americans know of a
lot of things, but about very little. Knowing about implies a historical dimension, an inkling of the implications," declares Post-

man ("TV Culture" 58). In his informal study conducted during the Iranian hostage crisis, Postman found that while people closely watched each news-breaking report, most of the people he asked could not answer questions that dealt with where Iran was, what language Iranians spoke, who the Ayatollah was, or why the hostages were taken. Those who could answer the questions gained the information from reading newspapers and magazines (58). Television, it would seem, was more interested in entertaining us with the latest visuals than really informing us about the situation.

Because television news coverage is more concerned with images than content, it can make or break political candidates, ignore less sensational issues that should be brought to our attention, and even give us a false sense of security. Some historians, as well as Nixon himself, feel that Kennedy won the presidential campaign because he looked better than Nixon on television (Gumpert 40). Certainly Reagan's ability to perform aided his television image. And frequently, issues of greater importance than the fact that Coca-Cola is changing its formula (a lead story when it happened) frequently go unnoticed. For example, in his book The Whole World Is Watching, Todd Gitlin shows how television usually narrows an important issue down to just another story. He cites as an example the way television news coverage can take the idea of "social activism" and make it look like a street crime. Reporters will be sent to cover a protest movement. The story will focus on several 3.5-second scenes of street arrests and property damage rather than on the serious issues behind the protesting. Those involved then appear as criminals rather than social activists protesting acid rain or a company dumping pollutants in our drinking water (46).

Television news coverage seems mostly concerned with giving us quick-paced images, the sensational, the odd. Only twenty-two minutes of news reporting is devoted to a thirty-minute time slot. In that twenty-two minutes, we are given international news, national news, business news, sports news, the weather around the country, entertainment news, and usually a personal interest story at the end of the broadcast that will make us forget the "heavy" news. If it is true that most people get their news from television, it is easy to understand Postman's remark that "most Americans know of rather than about" anything of significance. America is now more concerned with image than substance. We want movie stars for presidents, not intellectuals; we want entertainment tonight, not news; we want to watch the world on television, not communicate with it.

But television news is, after all, only a business, right? We are only being given what we want, right? If that's true, let us hope those in charge never realize that our craving for entertainment and their ability to provide it have us completely in their control. Right?

At any rate, we can rest assured that if and when there is a "second coming," television crews will be right there to cover it "live" so we can see it at 6:30 P.M. Eastern Standard time on a limited number of stations, 7:00 P.M. via videotape for most other Eastern stations, and a taped version for those in other time zones.

Works Cited

Bill, Brent, Jr. Stay Tuned. Old Tappan, N.J.: Revell, 1986.

Corwin, Norman. Trivializing America: The Triumph of Mediocrity. Secaucus, N.J.: Stuart, 1986.

Ellerbee, Linda. And So It Goes: Adventures in Television. New
York: Putnam's, 1986.

Gitlin, Todd. The Whole World Is Watching. Berkeley: U of Calif. P,
1980.

Gumpert, Gary. "The Ambiguity of Perception." Talking Tombstones & Other Tales of the Media Age. New York: Oxford,
1987. 38–53.

MacNeil, Robert. "Is Television Shortening Our Attention Span?"
New York University Education Quarterly 14.2 (1983): 2–5.

Postman, Neil. Amusing Ourselves to Death. New York: Viking,
1985.

---. "TV Has Culture by the Throat." U.S. News & World Report
Dec. 1985: 58–59.

Index

Instructor's Guide for

VIEWPOINTS

*Readings Worth Thinking
and Writing About*

Instructor's Guide for

V iewpoints:

Readings Worth
Thinking and
Writing About

W. ROYCE ADAMS
Santa Barbara City College

D. C. Heath and Company
Lexington, Massachusetts   Toronto

Published simultaneously in Canada.

Printed in the United States of America.

International Standard Book Number: 0-669-16130-6

INTRODUCTION

The purpose of this *Instructor's Guide* is to offer some suggestions for users of *Viewpoints: Readings Worth Thinking and Writing About.* The first suggestion is to quickly read it through to familiarize yourself with the contents of the anthology itself. The commentaries on each of the ten units and individual reading selections may help you decide which ones you wish to assign during the course and in which order. Suggestions are offered for assigning and helping students get the most from Part I, "Viewpoints on Reading and Writing Essays." Information on rhetorical modes used, direction to those questions following the readings in Part II that will bring about the most lively class discussions, and guidance on the teaching compatibility of some reading selections with others are included in the individual commentaries for each reading selection.

The readability level of all reading selections is provided. Depending on the level of the class you are teaching, this information may or may not be useful. Reading levels are not provided as indicators that some selections are too easy or too difficult for your students. They are there to identify which ones may require more class time or teaching effort on your part. As you probably know, readability levels are merely averages and don't necessarily reflect true comprehension difficulty. What may seem easy reading could contain difficult concepts, inferences, and unfamiliar innuendoes. And what may seem difficult reading is often overcome through reader interest in the content.

Frequent suggestions are provided throughout that call for small group or class discussions. While it may seem strange that such emphasis is given in a book dealing with composition, I can only say that in my experience lively class discussions and a controlled exchange of viewpoints stimulate student thinking and bring out better student composition content by the end of the term.

For those teaching the research paper, you will find that in addition to the information and model research paper provided in the text's appendix, frequent references are made throughout this guide to particular units or individual essays and questions that can serve as research subjects and sources. I selfishly prefer that students, with my approval, select research subjects of interest to them, saving me from reading so many papers on the same subject.

As you read through this guide you may notice some redundant comments. It seems unavoidable. Remarks made for one selection or unit may also apply to another, and since instructors will no doubt skip around in the text or omit certain readings from their course syllabus, repetition of some suggestions has to occur.

All the approaches presented here have worked for me, but they are by no means the only ways you can use the book. My hope is that the design of *Viewpoints* will make it compatible with the individual teaching styles of all users.

RATIONALE FOR PART I

Many years of teaching freshman composition have led me to believe that most students lack the analytical skills required to read and react to assigned readings as instructors would like. In addition, many students have little or no understanding of the writing process or of what good writing entails. Since one of the goals of *Viewpoints* is to teach the interrelationship of reading and writing skills, Part I is divided into two units for this purpose. Unit 1 teaches students how to read essays; Unit 2 teaches them how to write them. Every effort has been made to show how these two basic skills complement one another.

For some students, Unit 1 serves as an introduction and for others a review of such fundamentals as the essay structure, the difference between a topic and a thesis, paragraph patterns or modes used for developing topic sentences, and transitional devices required of certain patterns. The same fundamentals presented when teaching composition are presented here as tools for better reading comprehension. In addition, Unit 1 shows students how to separate main ideas from supporting details, how to distinguish fact from opinion, and how to draw inferences. These reading skills are, of course, the same skills a writer must consider when composing. Finally, ways to retain comprehension through note taking, textbook marking, and journal keeping are explained and encouraged. In effect, Unit 1 is a minicourse on how to read analytically with frequent references to the writing connection.

Unit 2 builds on the content of Unit 1 by showing how the methods and qualities of good essay reading can be applied to essay writing. The unit provides the student with what is generally accepted as the three basic writing stages: prewriting, writing, and rewriting. Again, this unit serves as an introduction or a review of the writing process, continually reminding students that writing is a recursive process.

My experience has been that freshman students need a sense of direction, a model to follow in order to get started on safe ground. Unit 2 does this by taking students through the entire process, showing them how someone might begin an essay and work through several revisions before arriving at a final draft. In so doing, students are provided a model of the writing process from prewriting techniques (such as using questions or reactions from their reading journals, brainstorming, clustering, and freewriting), writing techniques (such as discovering a working thesis, developing and organizing support, and writing a first draft), to revising techniques, including editing and proofreading. The text points out, as you will no doubt wish to do, that there are as many ways to approach writing as there are

1

writers, and that students must discover what works best for themselves.

Part I, then, provides a background and a useful resource for students to establish a sense of direction and an understanding of what is expected of them when they are assigned the readings in Part II and full-length compositions.

Using Unit 1: Reading Essays

Unit 1 supplies students with the analytical reading skills necessary for reading the essays in this book (as well as other sources) by teaching them what an essay is and how it is structured, how to read with greater comprehension, and how to retain and use an essay's content. For this reason, I recommend that Unit 1 be assigned the first week of class.

The Writing Exercises   At certain points during the discussion of reading to understand topic, thesis, supporting evidence, paragraph patterns, and order of support, students are asked to interact by responding to questions that test their understanding. Because these questions are followed by explanatory answers, it is possible to assign all or parts of Unit 1 for out-of-class reading. However, in order to monitor students' comprehension of this information, three brief one-paragraph writing exercises have been provided at appropriate breaking points. Rather than assigning the entire unit at once, you may prefer using the writing exercises as a breaking point for three separate assignments. This depends on the ability of the class and how thoroughly you want to cover this unit.

The writing exercises can be used in several ways. One way is to have students return all three for grading, as an assurance that the material has been understood before moving on. The results of the paragraph writings may reveal a need to go over all or parts of the unit in class, or they may reflect that the class is ready for Unit 2. Another approach is to use the exercises as "pop" quizzes, surprising the students to see if they did read the assignment. Still another approach is to have students write the three exercises as they come to them in their reading journals. You then can read them during a later journal check.

The Reading Journal   You'll notice that keeping a reading journal is stressed, emphasizing why and how to write summaries of assigned readings, the need for recording any personal reflections after reading, and the maintenance of a vocabulary list for study. Keeping a reading journal may not be an approach you wish your students to take; if so, mention it as something they may want to do on their own if they feel it will help them. However, it *will* help them, and I strongly recommend that students be required to maintain a reading journal, at least in part. If journal keeping is done correctly, students become more actively involved in the reading process. You can modify the journal assignments by selecting certain readings for which you want entries, rather than requiring entries for all assigned readings. The reading journal can also be used for other items for which you wish a student response, such as writing answers to any of the questions that follow the reading selections, freewriting, or in-class writing practices.

Marking Notes in the Text   Another reason for assigning Unit 1 first is that the unit illustrates for students how to separate main ideas from supporting details, how to separate facts from opinions, and how to draw inferences. Students are also shown how to read with pen in hand, to make thoughtful notations, and to have a dialogue with the author as they read. This information lays the groundwork for careful reading of all the assigned selections in Unit 2.

Even though students are provided with practice in marking up Pete Hamill's essay, "The Wet Drug" (page 32), it might be efficacious during the first or second week to select one or two essays from any unit in Part II for additional practice of the skills taught in Unit 1. Since the units do not have to be read in any order, you could, for example, assign Phil Donahue's "Beauty and the Beast" (page 134) and Jean Shepherd's "The Endless Streetcar Ride into the Night . . ." (page 159). They are distinctly different in structure, tone, and language. Donahue's piece has a clear thesis and a standard organizational pattern, using comparison-contrast, illustrations, description, and cause-effect passages that can be easily pointed out in class. Shepherd's first-person narrative reflects a different tone and attitude, uses many short, one-sentence paragraphs, dialogue, and on the surface may seem to reflect no thesis. Pointing out these differences, discussing thesis and location, main ideas and supporting details, implied statements, facts versus opinion, and so on, would aid students when called upon to read on their own. Such an approach would reveal some of the range and diversity of authors and focus on the need for analytical reading comprehension.

Initially, students need to be shown how to read and mark assigned reading selections. I've found it's helpful and fun to read aloud frequently many of the passages from the readings, providing the necessary tone and attitude students must learn to provide themselves when reading silently. It is wrong to assume that students can initially read the way we want them to read; thus, we must show them. Only then can we begin to use the readings as examples and models for writing compositions, as well as a means for exposing them to humanistic ideas.

Some students show a reluctance to mark up their textbooks. But I show them how one of my books looks after I've read and reacted to an author. I try to convince them, as Mortimer Adler does so well in his classic "How to Mark a Book," that the benefits of marking up a book far outweigh any price they may receive during the campus bookstore buy-back period. I share with them the Herman Ebbinghaus "curve of forgetting" that appears in most freshman psychology textbooks, which reveals how quickly we forget what we learn if we don't reinforce our memory (over 40 percent within twenty minutes, over 55 percent in one hour, and around 70 percent after nine hours).

If you have students keep a reading journal, you may want them to share their entries either in small groups or with the entire class. Students will see that not everyone responds to a selection the same way, nor comprehends the same meaning. This serves to make clear that some reading selections require more than one reading, and that through exchange of thoughtful discussions, most everyone can eventually come to an agreement on what an author's thesis is, without necessarily agreeing with the viewpoint.

I contend that the time spent dealing with the reading skills taught in Unit 1 will result in better student compositions. My recommendation is that you don't assign any full-length essays until after you have covered both Units 1 and 2.

Using Unit 2: Writing Essays

I'd suggest that you not assign Unit 2 until at least a week has been spent on Unit 1 and after close examination of two or three selected essays in Part II has taken place. Rather than leaving them on their own, it seems best to make certain students have some guided practice applying the skills taught in Unit 1. Then, at least the same amount of time should be given to Unit 2, depending upon the level of your students, of course. Some classes may require more time, some less.

There are four writing exercises, similar to those in Unit 1, appearing periodically after specific information on composition has been presented. The exercises call for a written application or a summary of the material read. You may want to use these exercises as a way to divide the unit into four separate assignments, each one followed by the completion of the writing exercise. As in Unit 1, these exercises can either be graded or used as quizzes or journal assignments. I favor collecting them so that student comprehension can be monitored, using them as a gauge for the amount of time needed to be spent on the unit. These exercises also serve as an indicator of which students are keeping up with the assignments.

The Prewriting Activities   While many prewriting heuristics exist, three rather universally accepted ones are presented for students in *Viewpoints:* reacting to questions and statements from the readings recorded in their journals, brainstorming (both listing and clustering), and freewriting. [If you are unfamiliar with freewriting and clustering as prewriting activities, Peter Elbow's *Writing with Power* (Oxford Press, 1978) and Gabriele Lusser Rico's *Writing the Natural Way* (J.P. Tarcher, 1983) are highly recommended.] Once presented with various prewriting methods, students seem to favor one of these three approaches. It's been my experience that students need practice in prewriting beyond what they get in the text.

Take the time to do some prewriting board work in class. For instance, I ask students to give me a topic, any topic, which I then write on the board. Next, I ask them to provide some possible working theses based on the topic. This activity helps clarify the difference between a topic and a thesis, and reveals for them the wide range of directions one can take on any given subject. Then I ask students to provide some ideas or supporting evidence that can be used to support one of the thesis statements we formulate together. Sometimes we brainstorm, sometimes we cluster. When thoughts are exhausted or time infringes, we look over our list or clusters, erasing those points that fail to relate to the thesis. I never know what the results will be any more than the students do. Together we discover what will work and what won't. The students thus take part in the prewriting stage and learn what is expected of them when given their first full-length essay writing assignment.

This type of board work can be followed with the next phase, organizing those ideas left on the board that relate to the thesis. Students learn that there is a variety of ways to organize supporting evidence for an essay and that it may take several drafts to figure out which approach reads best. After such a class activity, I call their attention to pages 53–67 to show the parallel of what we've done on the board with the example in the text itself.

Whatever way it is done, the teaching of prewriting activities is an important one. Practice in one or more of these prewriting exercises before assigning full-length essays benefits both the student and you when the full-length composition is finally assigned.

The Nutshell Statement   You may not want to require students to complete a nutshell statement as described on pages 59–61 in the text. However, I find it helpful to them and to me when I require that one be attached to every essay, at least during the early stage of the course. When I have individual conferences with students, I use the nutshell statements to point out where their strengths and weaknesses are in relation to their purpose (thesis), support (organization and logic), and audience (tone and style). Once students are writing well enough, I no longer require the nutshell statement unless they find it helpful.

If you do want to use nutshells, you will probably find that students need some help in writing ones that are not vague or hurriedly written. Sometimes I distribute handouts with examples of nutshell statements from previous students' work. I usually share in class both good and bad student examples without identifying the authors.

I frequently ask students to write a nutshell statement for one of the reading selections in the text as a writing assignment. Sharing their written statements in class leads to interesting discussions of the assigned reading, often revealing biases and discrepancies in their comprehension of the reading selection. It is also revealing to have students exchange their own essays, requesting that classmates write a nutshell statement for comparison with the student author's, showing the students how others perceive their work and making them aware that the instructor is not the only audience for whom they are writing.

Paragraph Patterns   The information on rhetorical modes on pages 61–65 should be compared with that on pages 8–18 in Unit 1. It serves as a reinforcement of the reading-writing connection.

I find it rather artificial to ask students to write using a particular rhetorical mode. It seems to place the pattern before thought and content. Still, there may be a place for requesting students to use a particular paragraph pattern as a drill or an exercise in understanding that pattern. You may want to select examples of various modes reflected in paragraphs from essays in Part II as models to share in class. See the Rhetorical Table of Contents for a classification of essays by modes.

Viewpoints approaches the use of paragraph patterns as a way to develop information based on the way a topic sentence is written. The text itself says all that need be said here.

The Student Model Essay   It's worth class time to look carefully at the various drafts of the model student essay on pages 65–82 as a way to discuss recursive writing. Point out the various changes from draft to draft, stressing the importance of revision. While the text visually illustrates these changes, it is recommended that you ascertain through class discussion that students see and understand the changes and additions that were made. Many students will not actually notice some of the changes unless they are pointed out.

The student model essay offers an opportunity to emphasize the need for revision, but it also provides you with a tool for discussing how you would respond to and grade the essay, and provides students with a better understanding of your own particular demands and expectations.

In addition to the model student essay in this unit, there is one at the end of every unit in Part II. Some are well written, some flawed. They are followed by commentaries explaining my reaction to them. Certainly you should provide your own commentary as well.

The Revision and Editing Checklists   You will probably want to discuss in class the checklists provided to help clarify any terminology or points students don't understand. The checklists are of little value if the students can't interpret what they are meant to check.

A brief version of the longer revision and editing checklists are provided at the end of Unit 2 for the convenience of the student. You can request that the students apply these checklists to each of their essays before submitting them to you.

RATIONALE FOR PART II

The eight units that compose **Part II** fulfill several of this book's objectives. They provide a variety of thematically arranged viewpoints on contemporary issues; they contain readings and follow-up questions that stimulate or suggest to students ideas for their own essays; they contain models of professional and student writing; and they directly or indirectly offer possibilities for research projects. The units can be read in any order, and, if you wish, you can skip around through the units ignoring the themes altogether. Having more essays in the book than you will have time to cover during the course allows you to choose only the selections you want to assign or use in class.

Each unit is devoted to a theme broad enough for which all students can feel some familiarity. The photos, quotes, and prefaces that precede each unit reveal the scope of the unit's theme. You can use them to prepare students for the unit readings. When assigning essays from any unit, I suggest some class time and attention be spent on the short prefatory comments. For instance, Unit 4, which deals with human behavior, begins with a husband's letter to Ann Landers describing his wife's strange habits. Discussing it might provoke some thinking for an essay on human behavior. Unit 4's prefatory comments also explain how social scientists, sociologists, psychologists, and economists define human behavior. You can remind students that their textbooks from these classes might contain a wealth of stimulation for an essay or possible research paper. Students will begin to see that ideas for essays don't have to come from those suggested in the book, that there is a connection between the English course they are taking and the "real world."

Many students often have difficulty concentrating on assigned readings unless the subject truly interests them. As a way to prepare students for a reading assignment, prereading questions require a brief survey of the selection and a prediction about the content. The questions are based on two well-known reading techniques, the DRTA (Directed Reading-Thinking Activity) and the first steps of the SQ3R (Survey, Question, Read, Recite, Review). Requiring students to answer these prereading questions forces them to concentrate on what they are about to read. Just as a camera must be focused before taking a picture, the reader must focus on what is about to be read. Remind students that the prereading questions are part of each reading assignment. In fact, you may want to go over the prereading questions with the students at the time you assign the reading selection, a sort of preview of coming attractions.

A list of key vocabulary words provided before the selection itself permits students to preview the definitions and the paragraph where the words appear in the reading. Some instructors like to discuss these words with the students at the time the reading assignment is given. Others prefer to deal with vocabulary after students have read the assignment. Still others leave the learning of vocabulary up to the individual student.

The four sets of questions that follow each reading selection reinforce the skills presented in Part I. The first set, "Understanding the Content," deals with basic comprehension elements: recognizing thesis, main ideas, supporting evidence, fact and opinion, and so on. They are questions for which answers can usually be agreed upon. The next set, "Looking at Structure and Style," focuses on the author's organization, paragraph patterns, language usage, transitional techniques, and the like; in effect, most of the composition fundamentals taught in Unit 2. The third set of questions, "Evaluating the Author's Viewpoints," calls for personal reactions, critical thinking, and evaluation of what was read. "Pursuing Possible Essay Topics," the last set, offers a variety of ideas or starting points for student essays or research projects dealing with the unit's theme.

The first three sets of questions can be used in several ways. Some can be selected for reading journal entries, some for class discussion, others for "pop" quizzes. Some instructors like to break the class into small groups, making each group responsible for providing answers to specific questions, or to assign individuals specific questions to answer orally in class. More ways to use the questions are mentioned later in this guide when individual essays are discussed.

For those instructors introducing their students to the research project, the fourth set of questions frequently contains suggestions that require more reading. Some of the items offer specific book titles or library sources for students to pursue.

Part II provides more than enough reading selections for a one-term course. The abundance and diversity of style and difficulty is intentional, allowing you to choose the readings most appropriate for the level of your class and the length of the course. The Fry Readability Formula [Edward Fry, "Graph for Estimating Readability—Extended," *Journal of Reading* (December, 1977)] was applied to each of the essays. The readability grade level appears with the comments on each reading selection that follows. While some of the reading selections may seem a bit formidable for students considered weak in English skills, none has proven out of reach if the instructor takes the time to help students through the more difficult sections. I have found that if interested in the subject, students can often read above their expected level. Don't let a high readability level for a selection deter you from assigning it. If they are to develop their skills, students need the challenge of more difficult reading. The intent is to provide instructors with interesting material that will be useful in teaching students how to read and write at a higher level than when they entered the class. Good instruction can help them meet that challenge.

Using Unit 3: Learning

While it is not necessary to begin with this unit after finishing Part I, to do so can be useful because most students at this point in the course are experiencing a new kind of learning: adaptation to college life. If you are assigning essay topics on themes, learning is an appropriate starting place. Discussing in class the photo, quotation, and prefatory materials can be useful for stimulating ideas for essays and in helping students focus on the broad theme of learning.

When assigning a reading selection, periodically remind students of the reading skills taught in Unit 1. Go over the prereading questions and vocabulary words with the students. You may want to look at some of the words in context as part of a prereading activity. Although it may not be practical to do this with every reading assignment, it helps with the more difficult reading selections.

Following are some comments and suggestions for using the essays in this unit.

"School vs. Education" by Russell Baker

Reading level: 9th–10th grade

To help students recognize Baker's sarcastic and cynical tone, read it orally in class. Because of its brevity, there is time to discuss most of the questions that follow it. Particularly important under the content questions are items 3, 5, and 6, dealing with thesis and tone. All the questions under "Looking at Structure and Style" are important if the selection is used at an early stage in the course.

One way to facilitate coverage of all the questions is to divide the class into small groups, assigning each one those questions you wish to emphasize. Then have each group report its findings to the entire class. Ask some students to research more about Russell Baker, then report back to class with some other examples of his work.

You may wish to assign a student composition at this point by asking students to use the list of possible essay topics as thought provokers. I prefer to wait until we have discussed all the essays in a given unit so that students can choose from all of the "Pursuing Possible Essay Topics" lists. These lists of suggestions can also be used for in-class writing exercises or journal writings. If you want a more controlled essay-writing assignment, pick the item yourself. Personally, I find this too stifling for the student and usually results in student writing that reflects what they think I want to hear.

"The Practicality of the Liberal Arts Major" by Debra Sikes and Barbara Murray

Reading level: 12th grade

Even though the authors intended this essay for college teachers, students will find this essay interesting because it reflects what research has discovered about the practicality of the liberal arts degree. Paragraph 5 discusses where and what the research project was about. Paragraph 7 shows the skills, in order of importance, that a college student should acquire for future jobs. Paragraph 8 provides the authors' recommendations to students based on their findings.

It can be a useful essay for getting students to rethink their college goals. You might want to call their attention to the key points in paragraphs 7 and 8. Ask them if they are presently taking or planning to take the courses that will benefit them the most. Do they believe it is possible to be "overeducated"? Such questions get students to see that the reading selection can and does relate to them personally.

Good follow-up writing drills and/or essay topics are numbers 2, 4, 5, and 6, as they direct the students to consider their reasons for attending college, their learning skills, and the benefits derived from a college education.

Calling attention to the stylistic differences between this and the Baker essay may prove valuable. Structure, as well as tone and attitude, are quite different.

"To Err Is Wrong" by Roger von Oech

Reading level: 9th grade

If you can't assign all of the essays in this unit, this is *not* one to skip. The subject of failure and success is on the minds of most students; indeed, most all of us. The idea that failure can bring success is important, especially to student writers who struggle with the fear of failure or live with their failure from the past. I recommend at least reading paragraph 26 aloud and discussing the four tips in class.

In paragraph 8, von Oech quotes the baseball player Yaz, "If you want hits, be prepared for misses," and equates this to the way the game of life goes. Remind students that that's also the way writing an essay goes—lots of false starts, lots of errors, lots of revisions before that successful final draft. Errors can be stepping stones to success.

Because of the variety of paragraph patterns used—cause/effect, comparison/contrast, examples, use of anecdote—the selection can be used to discuss and reinforce rhetorical modes. The questions under "Looking at Structure and Style" provide for such an approach. As an aside, you might want to point out the difference in handling a lengthy quotation (the block quote in paragraph 17) and the way quotations are used in paragraphs 11 and 19.

Students who respond favorably to this selection may want to read *A Whack on the Side of the Head* (Warner Books, 1983), the book from which this was taken.

"Salvation" by Langston Hughes

Reading level: 6th grade

A classic of sorts, appearing in many other reading anthologies, it's a touching story, a type of initiation rite into adulthood that most of us go through. Although it is a simple story on the surface, other deeper implications and analogies can be made from the story. Discussing content questions 5 and 6 are especially important in teaching this selection.

The narrative is well done; consequently, assigning or discussing all the questions under "Looking at Structure and Style" may be called for. None of the other readings in this unit deals quite as effectively with description (note paragraphs 3 and 4 especially) and dialogue (paragraphs 8–10) in the way Hughes does here.

"Students' Love Affair with Anne Frank" by Sharon Whitley

Reading level: 9th grade

Unlike Hughes in "Salvation," whose narrative implies and suggests through a story, Whitley uses narrative up to paragraph 11 then switches in the last paragraphs to statements of others to back up her argumentative thesis that *The Diary of Anne Frank* is a useful teaching tool and must not be censored. The Hughes essay and this one serve to show the differences in the way "I" can be used.

You may want to read a passage or two from Anne Frank's diary, particularly passages that some might find objectionable (although I don't know what they would be). You may also want to discuss journals or diaries and their possible importance to the future, perhaps not at a global level, but certainly at a personal or family history level.

Because this essay deals with censorship as well as learning, it makes for a healthy class discussion of the subject of censorship. Is censorship ever warranted? If so, when and by whom? What do we mean by censorship? Who should be the censors? If students are stimulated to write about censorship rather than learning, why not let them?

"Seeing Freshly" by Robert M. Pirsig

Reading level: 8th grade

A passage from *Zen and the Art of Motorcycle Maintenance*, it too works well when read orally in class. I've put it in the text because many students often say, "I don't know what to write about." It reflects both teacher and student frustration. Sharing it with students frequently helps them "see freshly."

I have had good success with item 4 under "Pursuing Possible Essay Topics" by using it as a writing practice. I encourage students to capture as best they can their senses, using language that reflects sound, sight, touch, taste and smell. While most of the results of the assignment are not essays in the true sense of the word, they show an attempt to write descriptively and imaginatively. It also makes a good writing practice or journal assignment.

"When I Heard the Learn'd Astronomer" by Walt Whitman

A poem or two in an anthology never hurts. After students—especially those who feel that poetry is beyond them—read this poem three or four times, they feel they have made a breakthrough. Not only do they come to see that it is an easy poem to grasp, but they realize what it takes to read a poem. They also understand what Whitman is feeling. (How many lectures have you walked out on, or wished you had?) There's a sharing between student and poet that takes place.

I feel poetry should be heard, so I read it aloud or ask for volunteers. It's interesting to get three or four different students to try their hand at reading it. As the timidity begins to melt, more feeling enters as the oral readings become more liquid. Better comprehension of the poem itself occurs.

Items 2 and 3 under "Pursuing Possible Essay Topics" make good discussion questions in class.

STUDENT ESSAY: **"Stargazing with Whitman"** by Linda Klouzal

Reading level: 7th grade

Be certain that you assign the student essay, requiring students to write their reactions where it is called for. A class session could easily be spent looking carefully at the three prereading questions, having students share their written responses, and sharing your own comments as well as reacting to the text commentary. Grading varies from instructor to instructor. My criteria may not be yours. But in order for students to understand yours, discuss the grade you would give the student essay. If you disagree with my commentary, explain why to your students. I wouldn't mind hearing from you, either.

Linda's essay is certainly not an example of the type of writing I usually get at the beginning of a course. I point that out, reminding students that some of the qualities found here are those for which students should strive. This also may be an appropriate place to discuss the form you wish students to follow when turning in full-length essays. You may want something different from the model explained on pages 417–419.

Using Unit 4: Human Behavior

The theme of human behavior appears after the one on learning simply because it too is broad and familiar enough for all students to relate to without much strain. Should you use the topic for a full-length essay assignment, the unit's introductory comments help reflect the wide explanations for human behavior frequently given in textbooks. You might remind students that if they are taking courses in psychology, sociology, or anthropology that they are studying human behavior and may find ideas and sources for essay topics from their other textbooks and lectures as well as from this book.

"Beauty and the Beast" by Phil Donahue

Reading level: 10th–11th grade

If you like to teach rhetorical modes, use this selection as an excellent example of the use of comparison and contrast. Man and animal, beauty and beast, Chartres and the Crusades, individual achievements and group achievements, past and present are a few of the comparisons drawn. But even more interesting to me are Donahue's questions and comments in paragraphs 12–13. The questions are thought-provoking ones, ones that educational institutions should spend more time asking and trying to answer. Some of our students may never take another course in which such humanistic questions might be raised. Take every opportunity to expose students to a bit of humanism.

Because some students lack much in the way of historical background, a first reading may seem a bit difficult. But by assigning and discussing some of the questions listed under the "Looking at Structure and Style," students will see that the selection is rather well done and easier to follow than they thought.

Some possible library research interest may be piqued here: the cause of the Crusades, the history of Chartres cathedral, the Muslims, the IRA in Belfast today, the most important inventions of man, and so on.

"Superstitious Minds" by Letty Cottin Pogrebin

Reading level: 8th grade

An essay to read and understand, Pogrebin's piece makes a nice model for students who wish to write a first-person narrative about a family member. It can also be used to stimulate some library research on topics such as black magic, voodoo, the occult, astrology, ESP, Shirley MacLaine's other lives, and those beings from outer space the *National Enquirer* always reminds us are out there.

"Night Walker" by Brent Staples

Reading level: 11th grade

Staples's opening paragraph is very well-done. So well-done, in fact, that after reading the first sentence, one of the early reviewers of the *Viewpoints* manuscript said that she would not read or teach this essay. Staples, of course, deliberately leads us to think he is some sinister person, probably a rapist or murderer. But as we read on, we learn as he did about "his unwieldy inheritance, the ability to alter public space" by just being a black man among fearful whites.

Have students deal especially with questions 2–6 under "Looking at Structure and Style." Some readers may find it overly descriptive, a good discussion point. All the questions under "Evaluating the Author's Viewpoints" create some lively discussions, especially item 3.

You might, if you have time, get students to do some non-library research. Have them keep track for a week or two of the number of street violence episodes being reported on national and local television news, in daily papers, and in national news magazines. Is such news frequent? Can it create more fear than it deserves? Does it seem biased in presentation as Staples suggests?

"Slow Descent into Hell" by Jon D. Hull

Reading level: 7th grade

Taken from a longer essay in *TIME* magazine (February 2, 1987), this portion illustrates good use of descriptive techniques as well as a way to discuss the growing homeless situation. You or your students may want to research the article and share more of it in class.

For those of you teaching rhetorical modes, Hull provides a fine example of descriptive writing. You may want students to look through it for examples of passages that utilize our five senses.

At the time of this printing, the problems of the homeless were receiving much publicity, thus providing some possible sources for research projects.

"Fun. Oh, Boy. Fun. You Could Die from It." by Suzanne Britt Jordan

Reading level: 6th grade

Despite the essay's brevity and ease of reading, some students may not really grasp Jordan's point because of her tone. (They wonder what the grouch is complaining about. People *should* have fun, right?) It helps to combat such reactions by pointing out paragraphs 4, 5, and 13 to help clarify her thesis. Have them think back for other examples of "fun" that bombard us daily by elaborating more specifically on paragraph 10.

Ask students how Jordan defines fun in paragraph 14. This is a good springboard for dealing with essays that define if you're interested in teaching modes.

"The Endless Streetcar Ride into the Night..." by Jean Shepherd

Reading level: 8th grade

Students have fun with this one, even though there are some vocabulary difficulties. Use it to discuss tone, attitude, narration, description, and story entertainment. The subject is one that most all of us have experienced or might someday.

If there is time, try to read aloud parts of the essay that require proper intonations and pacing. Doing so helps students see what they need to bring to such a reading selection if they are to get full appreciation of it.

Most of the students will probably find that the suggestions for "Pursuing Possible Essay Topics" are more than enough to tap ideas for an essay on human behavior.

STUDENT ESSAY: **"Man and Woman: A Soap Opera with Real Soap"** by Cindy Evans

Reading level: 9th grade

As mentioned before, it is important to have students carefully read the student essay and for you to provide class time for them to share their written reactions called for in the text. The student model essays reflect what other students have done with the topic, revealing their strengths and their weaknesses.

The commentary following Cindy's essay points out three strengths: making a topic one's own, appropriate use of the comparison/contrast pattern, and attention given to word choice. You may want to discuss how Cindy does this by going over the essay with your class.

Using Unit 5: Cultural Heritage

If the make-up of your class is culturally diverse, consider using this unit early in the course. As the unit's introduction states, a great immigrational surge to this country has occurred since the 1970s, both legal and illegal. The U.S. is the fifth largest Spanish speaking country in the world. Soon major cities, such as Los Angeles and Miami, will have more Spanish speakers than English. Over twelve million Asians will have immigrated here by the year 2000. A great change in the cultural make-up of our country is in process and makes for a current theme of interest to many students.

The diversity of cultural heritage is reflected in this unit's reading selections: one deals with the history of the German and Dutch influx of immigrants in the mid-1800s; one deals with growing up in an Italian "ghetto" in New York; another focuses on "black English"; another reflects on the gradual change of a Spanish barrio into a Chinese neighborhood; one defends the American Indian from false image making, and still another presents the problems some Indochinese immigrants are having adjusting to America. The student essay, written by a Vietnamese, describes the hardships of his flight to this country.

Cultural heritage makes a good topic for research projects. You might want to call for some non-library research, suggesting that students interview family members for more information about their own culture, or interview students on campus from a culture different from their own.

"Settling in the Cities" by Albert Robbins
Reading level: 13th grade

Since this work is based on research, it can be used for historical background, for making comparisons with the reactions of today's immigrants to this country with earlier ones, and for introducing students to the way quoted information is presented.

If you prefer the MLA style of citing, which is what appears in the Appendix, show students how the MLA citing would be done as opposed to the way it is done here. Examples of other documentation uses appear in paragraph 2 (working a quotation into part of a statement as well as how to block quote longer passages), paragraph 3 (the use of ellipsis and insertion brackets, as well as block quoting), and the footnotes, which can be rewritten on the chalkboard to explain the MLA style, both for footnoting citing and bibliographical listings.

Item 2 under "Pursuing Possible Essay Topics" provides some sources for a possible library research project. Of course, items 3 and 4 could also be a different type of research project, using people instead of printed material.

"Choosing a Dream: Italians in Hell's Kitchen" by Mario Puzo
Reading level: 8th grade

If you permit or teach autobiographical essays, Puzo's is a good model to use. He reflects two tones and attitudes here: contempt and seeming disdain, but in reality admiration and love. As he compares his youthful appraisal of his family and background with his adult appraisal, we learn much about his family as well as about Puzo himself. Students see that writing an autobiographical account is more than just retelling what happened; it should have a point or a thesis.

It surprises some students when they make the connection between this essay and the author of *The Godfather*, which sold more than 15 million copies in the U.S. alone. That awareness often creates an interest in Puzo's autobiographical reflections. This selection was taken from *The Immigrant Experience*, edited by Thomas Wheeler

(Dial Press, 1971). Some students may want to read other autobiographical selections from it.

Students of Italian descent may want to pursue item 3 under possible essay topics.

"What's Wrong with Black English" by Rachel L. Jones

Reading level: 9.5th grade

Some students may have to be shown why this essay is presented in a cultural heritage section, thinking it belongs better in a section on language. They have a point, but for a large number of people, black English is a living example of one aspect of cultural heritage. The subject prompts some great discussions, especially if you have some vocal blacks in class. Ask: Is there such a thing as black English? Is speaking black English speaking incorrectly? Is speaking black English similar to speaking both Spanish and English? Should black English be preserved? Why is there such a thing as "black English"?

A counterargument to Jones can be found in James Baldwin's "If Black English Isn't Language, Then Tell Me What Is?" which appears in many other anthologies. It's worthwhile to read portions of Baldwin's viewpoints to compare with Jones's.

"Los Chinos Discover el Barrio" by Luis Torres

Reading level: 9th–10th grade

In addition to a discussion on cultural heritage, this essay, as does Puzo's, raises such issues as "then and now," prejudicial feelings, and stereotypes we place on foreign people. Like the neighborhood changes Torres describes, many students may be experiencing the same thing in their neighborhoods, prompting some written experiences of their own. Class discussions or individual essays that deal with what Torres calls "hopeful signs" are worth it in these changing times.

This piece makes good use of comparison and contrast, as well as description. Torres dwells on the changes that are occurring now, but refers to the fact that the Spanish community of which he writes was once an Italian one that apparently underwent the same type of changes.

For interested Latino students, item 6 under "Pursuing Possible Essay Topics" can be of particular help on research projects.

"It Is Time to Stop Playing Indians" by Arlene B. Hirschfelder

Reading level: 13th grade

Hirschfelder's essay is a useful example of argumentation. Most students are familiar with "playing Indian" or with what Hirschfelder calls "war-whooping team mascots . . . imprinted on school uniforms, postcards, notebooks, tote bags and car floor mats." As most people are oblivious to much of the negative aspects of this, Hirschfelder does a credible job in calling our attention to it.

An examination of Hirschfelder's arguments would be appropriate. Many students may feel she is making too much of a small thing. Unless students are aware of the abuse American Indians have taken, her comments in her last paragraph regarding economic deprivation, powerlessness, discrimination, and gross injustice will not mean much. However, she seems to base much of her argument on the belief that her audience is aware of certain historical facts.

For those students who become interested in the injustice, culture, or literature of the American Indian, a list of a few resources is provided in item 6, "Pursuing Possible Essay Topics." These, of course, can be useful for research projects as well.

An education consultant with the Association on American Indian Affairs and the author of numerous texts on the Indian plight, Hirschfelder's book, *Happily May I Walk* (Scribner's 1986), won the 1987 Woodson award from the National Council for Social Studies.

"Trouble for America's 'Model' Minority" by David Whitman

Reading level: 12th–13th grade

Based on interviews with Indochinese, much of this selection contains quotations, with long passages in italics. It might be necessary to distinguish for students how a magazine handles these long quotations compared with the way students are expected to do it in their own writing. If students are conducting personal interviews as a form of research, they can be shown how the author paraphrases as well as quotes directly.

More important, however, might be the discussion of the plight of these people, both past and present, and the courage involved in beginning a new life in a country so foreign to them in language and culture. Many students of mine seem woefully ignorant of the effects the Vietnam war has had and continues to have on the U.S. today. An excellent book from which you might read passages, or at least recommend to students, is *Haing Ngor: A Cambodian Odyssey* by Haing Ngor. The author was the subject of the movie, "The Killing Fields."

STUDENT ESSAY: **"Coming to America"** by Hieu Huynh

Reading Level: 5th grade

When we have foreign students in our classes, we should take every opportunity to make use of their experiences as a way of broadening both our students' and our own awareness of other cultures. I have found that most Asians are a bit shy about talking in class or discussing anything about themselves, but once made to feel comfortable, they open up and add much to a class.

The student essay in this unit may not stand as an example of college-level writing, but it reflects much worth discussing: the struggle some immigrants suffer to get to this country, the struggle to survive in a new country, and the struggle to learn a new language. Many of our students have never experienced what this young man has had to deal with. The essay speaks for itself.

Using Unit 6: Changing Social Values

Like the former unit, this one can be used as a basis for research projects. Ruggiero's essay, "Debating Moral Questions," uses citations from other sources that can be used for modeling. Rosa Parks's "A Long Way to Go" brings up the entire civil rights issue, past and present. The New Deal, the Great Society, and the Me Generation are a few of the possible research areas brought up in "What's a Baby Boomer?" Younglove's essay on the American dream, past and present, can be tied in with the unit on cultural heritage. And the student documented essay, although flawed, can be useful in teaching the research paper.

This is not to say that the unit has to be used as such. The apparatus following the reading selections continues to build upon the reading and writing skills taught in Part I.

"Debating Moral Questions" by Vincent Ryan Ruggiero

Reading level: 9th grade

It generally doesn't matter with what essay you begin in any given unit, but in this case it seems most appropriate to start with Ruggiero's. Once students have been exposed to the question of morals through this essay, they tend to let the concept filter into the other essays in this unit. In this selection from his book *The Art of Thinking* (Harper & Row, 1984), Ruggiero raises the question: Is it legitimate for us to pass judgment on the morals of another culture? Quite provocative, the subject of moral issues can be extended into such topics as the morality of abortion, capital punishment (see Unit 10), apartheid, selling arms to warring countries, business ethics, morality in politics, and on and on. For instance, you might ask your class whether or not the U.S. has a right to tell other countries what form of government they should have. Another way to phrase the question is to ask whether or not we have a moral obligation to bring democracy to underdeveloped countries. Lively class or small group discussions on morality often lead to some thoughtful student essays.

Ruggiero cites four sources in his essay. You might want students to research these in the library, or as a practice you might have students convert them to the MLA style found in the Appendix.

"A Long Way to Go" by Rosa Parks

Reading level: 7.5th grade

Here is an excellent piece raising the issue of civil disobedience. Thoreau's viewpoints and his famous night in jail can be used for historical perspective.

Rosa Parks was arrested in Montgomery, Alabama on the evening of December 1, 1955 for refusing to give up her bus seat to a white man. The seamstress's act of defiance touched off a boycott of the city's buses, led by Martin Luther King, Jr. Some say that Parks's refusal to give up her bus seat was the beginning of the civil rights movement. Now 76, Parks lives in Detroit, working as an assistant to a Michigan congressman.

Her essay provides a rather succinct three-generation history of blacks in the south, especially eye-opening for those students unaware of the reasons behind the 1960s civil rights movement. The essay can lead to many thought-provoking areas: racial prejudice, black history, the Statue of Liberty, the NAACP, Martin Luther King, Jr, and apartheid, to name a few.

"What's a Baby Boomer?" by Jay Olgilvy, Eric Utne, and Brad Edmondson

Reading level: 9th grade

Three major rhetorical modes can be illustrated through this selection: definition (of a baby boomer), comparison/contrast (of older and younger baby boomers), and illustration/example (used to support the comparisons). How the authors use data from the *Utne Reader* survey should also be pointed out.

A close look at the values attributed to the baby boomers can also be useful for getting into a discussion of the differences in political, ideological, and moral values. Some questions you may want to ask are: In what circumstances are these values in harmony? When are they at odds? When is one more important than the other? Try to get students to examine their own values in these areas.

Item 2 under "Pursuing Possible Essay Topics" interests many students. Ask the class to create a questionnaire for which they must ask students on campus to answer. The students then write up the results and submit their findings to the campus or local newspaper for possible publication.

"The American Dream" by Betty Anne Younglove

Reading level: 10th grade

Short and argumentative, Younglove's essay can be read aloud in class and examined closely for structure and style. It's helpful to point out the music-related vocabulary Younglove uses. It provides an opportunity to discuss analogy, metaphor, and simile. See question 6 under "Looking at Structure and Style."

I'd suggest you first assign the essay as outside reading, then go over it in class. Doing so will help substantiate what the students discover for themselves and show them what they may have missed when reading on their own.

To back up a bit, if you plan to have students read a few essays after they have read Unit 1 in order to practice the skills taught on reading and textbook marking, consider using this short piece. It's short enough to allow students time to read it, mark it, and discuss it in one class period.

"Severing the Human Connection" by H. Bruce Miller

Reading level: 6th grade

Miller's essay raises the issue of honesty and integrity. "Is it that the people are simply incorrigibly dishonest," he asks, "that the glue of integrity and mutual respect that holds society together is finally dissolving?" A good question for us to consider.

I find it interesting to mention to my classes that in my youth we never locked our house or car doors. It was safe for a youngster to ride the city bus alone or walk the streets at night. Storekeepers trusted you to pay the next time if you happened to be short on a purchase. Then I ask why it has changed, and in what direction we seem to be going. I get some interesting answers.

This selection works well when taught with the following one by Richard Reeves, because the difference in tone, attitude, and style are distinctly evident to students. Point out that in both cases, the authors were prompted to write by reacting to ordinary events in life. Students often overlook such personal incidents and perspectives as possibilities for interesting compositions.

"America Isn't Falling Apart" by Richard Reeves

Reading level: 9th grade

Very informal stylistically, this is a good companion piece for the previous essay. Miller has a negative look at society; Reeves has a positive one. Both touch on honesty. We have all probably shared the way both men feel at various times, which makes these essays examples of writing that is generated by a new awareness of something familiar.

Another area to which Reeves's essay may lead is that of our growing personal identification as numbers: driver's license, social security, bank cards, credit cards, union cards, magazine and book subscriptions, and so on. Can we exist today without having proof of who we are?

If your students are experiencing difficulty with punctuation, especially quotation marks, use this essay to show examples of correct usage.

STUDENT ESSAY: **"Has the Nation Lost Its Way?"**
by Steve Brodie

Reading level: 11th–12th grade

Rather than provide an example of the "perfect" student research paper, I have included a flawed one. (A good student model appears in the Appendix.) The example reflects what to me seems more typical of student submissions. By showing its good qualities along with its errors, students see better what is expected of them as well as things to avoid. The commentary that follows the student effort explains why I rejected it. Based on your expectation of students, you will probably want to add to or modify my remarks.

Using Unit 7: Family and Relationships

As with the other reading selections, this unit's theme is broad and significantly familiar to most students. It contains an assortment of writing styles and viewpoints on family and personal relationships. The Cox selection is from his textbook, *Human Intimacy: Marriage, Family and Its Meaning* (West, 1987) and illustrates the use of definition as a rhetorical pattern. Rick Greenberg's first-person narrative presents the emotional struggle of a father who quits work to stay home with his son while his wife works. Joyce Maynard argues for the difference in the male-female style of talking. Nancy Friday defines mother-love as she has experienced it, arguing that "the woman and the mother are often at war with one another." Steven O'Brien relates for us his personal discovery of the effect several divorces can have on a child. Less serious, James Thurber's humorous fable, "The Unicorn in the Garden," deals with the battle of the sexes. Last, Theodore Roethke's "My Papa's Waltz" changes the reading pace, but fits well into the unit's theme.

The introductory comments to the unit discuss six major qualities shared by healthy families of all races. One way to get students interested in the unit's theme would be to discuss these in class or to have students react to them in a writing exercise as a warm-up before assigning the readings.

"Romantic Love" by Frank D. Cox
Reading level: 11th grade

Use this selection to teach or reinforce student understanding of paragraph patterns. While the point of the passage is to define romantic love, paragraph 1 uses examples, paragraph 2 combines cause-effect with comparison-contrast, paragraph 3 uses examples, paragraph 4 uses cause-effect, paragraph 5 uses a descriptive example, and paragraph 7 uses cause-effect. Since the selection is taken from a college textbook, you might mention the usefulness of the patterns as an aid to comprehending textbooks. Assigning or discussing the four questions under "Looking at Structure and Style" should help students see how Cox organizes and supports his points.

Even though Cox defines romantic love, the passage can bring about a discussion of all types of love. The suggestions under "Pursuing Possible Essay Topics" also work well as class or group discussion starting points.

"Escaping the Daily Grind for Life as a Housefather" by Rick Greenberg
Reading level: 6th grade

Despite the fact that we hear more and more men are staying home while the women work, many of my male students rebel against the concept. Thus, Greenberg's essay often creates a stir among male students. The traditional roles still abound: a woman's place is in the home and the man "brings home the bacon," something's wrong when a woman has to support a man, and so on. Consequently, the essay sometimes leads into discussion of changing values as well as changing roles in relationships.

Greenberg's use of the first-person provides a narrative model. You can also use the essay to teach more mundane skills: punctuation within quotations (paragraphs 1, 3, 17, 21), punctuation of dialogue (paragraphs 4, 7, 18, 27, 30), the use and effectiveness of one-sentence paragraphs (paragraphs 13 and 19), and transitions (paragraphs 4, 7, 18, 27, 30).

If you or your students are so inclined, some of the suggestions under "Pursuing Possible Essay Topics," such as 3, 4 and 6, can be used as research assignments.

"His Talk, Her Talk" by Joyce Maynard

Reading level: 10th grade

As the title implies, the essay can be used to show the use of comparison and contrast. Paragraph 9 is an especially good example, drawing an analogy between the way she and her husband tell a story with the way they eat bananas.

Maynard's piece can also be used for getting into a discussion on sexism and stereotypes. Ask, "What is sexism? What is sexist? Can the sexes be equal? Why do we stereotype people?" Students usually take it from there, with many of them not able to answer the questions clearly.

You may need to explain or elaborate a bit on some of the comments Maynard makes in paragraph 8, especially if you have some English-as-a-second-language students in class. (Difficult to believe, but there are people who have never heard of "I Love Lucy.") It's also interesting to get students from other countries to discuss the differences in male-female roles in their homelands.

Some people may recognize Joyce Maynard as the author of *Baby Love* (Knopf, 1981), a best-selling novel a few years ago about young mothers and would-be mothers trying to live out America's T.V. and Top-40 fantasies.

"Mother Love" by Nancy Friday

Reading level: 8th grade

Some instructors may want to skip Friday's essay, feeling that it is too difficult for the level of their students. I disagree; students need to be challenged, to be faced with the type of reading they must do in their other classes. Some misreading of certain statements may occur, with students concluding that Friday hates her mother, or blames her mother for failing her in some way. But a closer look at some of her statements, especially the last paragraph, is in order. It seems to me it is not her mother, but the illusion of some type of perfect love between mother and daughter that Friday comes to realize has kept her from clearly seeing the true relationship with her mother.

The "Understanding the Content" questions, if looked at carefully, can put students on safe ground. Her definition of mother love is more what it is *not* than what it is. Her comparison of a woman's traditional roles—her grandmother, her mother, herself—are used to help define mother love. And her implications call for drawing inferences. It is, then, a good reading teaching tool.

"One Son, Three Fathers" by Steven O'Brien

Reading level: 7th grade

Many students can relate to O'Brien's essay. While it reflects a warm relationship between stepson and stepfather, the selection deals with some of the emotional traumas and effects of divorce on both child and adult. O'Brien doesn't solve any issues or take any stands here, but rather leaves us with a revelation of his own lifestyle and its effect on his stepson. It's interesting that O'Brien never uses the word stepson or stepfather.

It's suggested that you deal with all of the questions listed under "Looking at Structure and Style," as well as those under "Evaluating the Author's Viewpoints."

"The Unicorn in the Garden" by James Thurber

Reading level: 6th grade

Thurber's parody on fables delights students when read in class. A discussion of fables and their moral statements may be necessary for students to understand what a parody is. Particularly important for students are the answers to those questions dealing with structure and style. The suggestions under "Evaluating the Author's Viewpoints" are designed mostly for group or class discussion, especially questions 2 and 4, which deal with the possible analogy Thurber is making between the existence of the mythical unicorn and the existence of an ideal relationship. Discussing the fable from such a perspective will cause students to look at it anew.

If your students are not familiar with fables, read one or two in class so that they have a better grasp of Thurber's parody. If your class responds well to Thurber, read some more to them from his book, *Fables of Our Times.*

"My Papa's Waltz" by Theodore Roethke

Easy to read, Roethke's poem nevertheless often creates controversy over the father-son relationship. Some students see the father as a drunken childbeater, while others see him as just a rough man displaying love and affection to his son. I prefer the latter interpretation once the key words are examined and we realize we are seeing this from the viewpoint of a young boy. The poem also has a waltz-like tempo which can be illustrated by reading the poem aloud. Ask if a waltz theme would be a proper form for describing an abusive father.

If you want students to write an evaluation or explication of the poem, you can refer them to Linda Klouzal's student essay in response to "When I Heard the Learn'd Astronomer" in Unit 1.

STUDENT ESSAY: "In Defense of Motherhood" by Rosa Avolio

Reading level: 8th grade

The commentary following Rosa's essay explains what I find is a common problem in many student essays—a lack of development and a tendency to drift away from a clearly stated thesis. As an exercise, you can ask students to outline the essay. The difficulty involved would leave them with an understanding of the need for organizational control.

Don't, however, overlook the plus side to Rosa's paper, which admittedly is more on the mechanical side.

Using Unit 8: Work

The reading selections deal with process ("How to Take a Job Interview"), illustration and example ("Your Brilliant Career"), classification ("What You Do Is What You Are"), argumentation ("Needed: A Policy for Children Whose Parents Go to Work"), comparison-contrast ("Workers"), and narration ("My Mother Never Worked"), thus supplying a variety for those who like to teach rhetorical modes. Of course, paragraph examples of other patterns appear within these selections.

Since many students have worked, are presently working, or are in college preparing for some type of employment, familiarity with and interest in the work theme is built in. However, if you've been teaching long, you know that many students don't know what type of career for which to prepare, or they have grandiose expectations for future professions they probably will never fulfill. This unit offers students an opportunity to reflect on their work goals.

"How to Take a Job Interview" by Kirby W. Stanat

Reading level: 6th grade

The "How to . . ." of the title leads one to believe that the author will provide a step-by-step procedure for taking a job interview, but it isn't quite that straightforward. Stanat uses first-person, establishing himself in a position to watch and relate how a job recruiter does interviewing on a college campus. He then presents his "how to . . ." or rather "how *not* to . . ." by describing the recruiter's reactions to "Sidney Student" and then "you," the reader, before and during the interview process. In so doing, Stanat makes his point that most recruiters have made up their minds about an interviewee before the actual interview begins. The essay takes a rather interesting twist on the use of process analysis.

Whether you assign it as an essay or a writing practice of some sort, item 2 under "Pursuing Possible Essay Topics" is a good one for students to think about.

"Your Brilliant Career" by Janet Bodnar

Reading level: 10th grade

A longer than usual selection in the text, Bodnar's essay is more an example of a report than an essay. It's useful for students to see the distinction. Probably of more interest to your students than to you, this selection may be one you assign for outside reading rather than for class discussion. However, if discussed in class, this piece can be used to illustrate mechanics and organizational patterns, as it contains examples of most rhetorical modes, many forms of punctuation, and a variety of transitional devices.

"What You Do Is What You Are" by Nickie McWhirter

Reading level: 7th grade

After reading this essay, students can be asked to do a little introspection. Why do they want to get into a particular profession or job? Money? Status? Power? What do their answers say about their values? Does it appear from what Bodnar says in the previous selection that the jobs they want will still be necessary or available?

Paragraphs 3 and 7 make good springboards for a discussion of stereotyping people based on our sense of values and class system.

The selection can also be useful if you wish to deal with argumentation and classification. Because it is short, you can go over the entire essay in class, pointing out rhetorical and stylistic devices McWhirter uses.

"Needed: A Policy for Children When Parents Go to Work" by Maxine Phillips

Reading level: 10th grade

There is a growing need for a children's day-care policy as more and more women join the work force. As Phillips points out in paragraph 13, several countries already have national systems of day-care and parental leave, but not the U.S. She presents some interesting data (paragraphs 2, 3, 7, 8, and 13) to back up her argument. Once she introduces the need, she establishes a solution (paragraphs 12–17) and then draws a conclusion in her final paragraphs. It makes a good model for explaining the argumentative essay.

In paragraph 3, Phillips discusses some bills being sponsored in the U.S. Congress at the time she wrote. You or your students may know or want to find out if any of the bills have passed since then or whether they are still pending. (Chances are they are still pending!) If so, try assigning a letter-writing project to Congress members supporting or rejecting Phillips's plan, or get students to write for *Newsweek*'s "My Turn" column expressing their personal viewpoints.

A research project on day-care centers and parental leave could be of interest to some students.

"Workers" by Richard Rodriquez

Reading level: 6th grade

Rodriquez basically compares and contrasts the *gringo* construction worker with what Rodriquez calls *los pobres*, the Mexican itinerant worker. But this first-person narrative also uses classification (paragraphs 9 and 16) and description well (paragraphs 5, 10, 12–16), and indirectly defines and contrasts "real work" as known by his father with the type of work he does for the summer. Thus, the essay is a blend of rhetorical modes. However, labeling these passages as such seems to diminish their content, so I prefer first to point out and deal with the content of these passages, then later look at the modes used to say what he says.

Rodriquez has written many essays arguing against affirmative action and bilingual education. In his book, *Hunger of Memory: The Education of Richard Rodriquez,* he recounts how he was offered several university positions after graduating from Stanford, but "he could not withstand the irony of being counted a 'minority' when in fact the irreversibly successful effort of his life had been to become a fully assimilated member of the majority." It may be of interest to students to learn that Rodriquez eventually was rejected by his Mexican-American immigrant parents, who, unable to speak English, thought they had failed in their efforts to educate him because of his stance on these issues.

"My Mother Never Worked" by Bonnie Smith-Yackel

Reading level: 6th grade

The structure of this essay is worth pointing out to students. It opens and closes with a conversation between the author and someone in the Social Security Office. The opening conversation establishes the mother's death through the author's request for a death-benefit check. While she is put on hold, the author reminisces on her mother's hard-working, difficult life. By the time the Social Security clerk gets back on the line, explaining that there will be no death-benefit check because the mother "never worked" a "real job," we feel the irony of the situation.

All the questions under "Looking at Structure and Style" are useful for discussion of the essay's structure.

STUDENT ESSAY: **"Oh, I'm Just a Housewife"** by Roy Wilson

Reading level: 6th grade

For the reasons mentioned in the commentary, the Roy Wilson essay is a good one for class discussion. While not powerful or erudite, it does contain the elements of essay writing taught in composition classes and is rather typical of freshman student fare.

Using Unit 9: Media

Many students are unaware of the media's influence on our thinking and values, so you may want to give some emphasis to the theme. Several informative books mentioned in the unit's preface make useful references for you or for student research projects. In addition, many of the items under "Pursuing Possible Essay Topics" contain leads to sources on various aspects of the media.

Because most students have grown up with television as a natural part of their environment, they seldom evaluate what they have grown accustomed to seeing. As an eye-opener of sorts for students, I play back in class a videotaped broadcast of the national evening news from the night before. I then have the students count the number of commercials, keep track of the actual amount of time devoted to news, note what news is emphasized and evaluate the style of the commentators. This sometimes requires running portions of the tape more than once. For some students, it's the first time they have watched the news; for others, it gives them new viewing eyes.

I also play back some commercials, discussing the audience for whom they are intended, the honesty and values being displayed, the need for the product, and the quality of the presentation. Try turning off the monitor and have students listen to the news without the video portion. Is there much difference? Such activities create some interest in the media theme.

You can also ask students to bring in a particular edition of a newspaper. Go through the paper with them, looking for hard news as opposed to the space devoted to Ann Landers, movie reviews, garden ideas, recipes, advertisements, and other non-news. It's a good opportunity to point out the editorial section, letters to the editor, syndicated columnists, and essay contributions. For some students, it's a revelation to discover that essays appear in places outside of textbooks!

You might wish to compare the depth of news coverage presented in the newspaper with that on the videotape, especially if they both deal with the same day's news. As a way to tease students, ask them why sports coverage gets a section of its own. Why isn't sports coverage included in the business section? What does such an emphasis on sports say about our values?

Ask students to compare some news magazines, such as *TIME* and *Newsweek*. Or, bring in some copies of *Harpers, The Atlantic, Utne Reader,* or *The New Republic,* for example, to expose students to magazines they may not find at supermarket checkout counters. This may also be an appropriate time to look at the sources for the essays in *Viewpoints* by reading the acknowledgments on pages v–viii.

"TV's Crime Coverage Is Too Scary and Misleading"
by Georgette Bennett

Reading level: 9th grade

Some students may have trouble accepting Bennett's thesis that the media's coverage of crime has "robbed" us of our "sense of safety." Before assigning this essay, you may want to ask for a show of hands on such questions as whether or not it's safe to walk the streets, what one's chances of being robbed are, whether or not the crime rate is rising, etc. Then, after they have read it, ask whether or not Bennett's essay has changed their minds and why.

An argumentative essay, it can be used as a model for teaching just that. You can have students evaluate Bennett's argument, examine her sources, and look for bias and weaknesses in her argument.

Bennett cites a recent Gallup poll which revealed that 62 percent of America gets its news from television. Discuss what this might mean in terms of a knowledgeable populace. If students don't think it makes much difference, have them immediately read the following essay by Ben Stein.

"The Media's Regrettable Imitation of the *National Enquirer*" by Ben Stein

Reading level: 11th grade

Despite Stein's anti-communist bias, he does raise the question of what news is and is not important to report. My bias is that he has a point. For instance, when *TIME* magazine's publishers discovered its readers loved the "People" section, it started publishing *People* magazine, which now outsells its parent. *Us* magazine followed shortly after that success. One can't go through a checkout lane at a supermarket without being informed in the various tabloids of the latest gossip regarding media personalities. So you might want to dwell on Stein's last paragraph to discuss whether or not "the news media of this country choose its subjects on the basis of triviality, gossip, herd instinct, ignorance, pro-Soviet feelings, and still more ignorance."

While there are flaws in Stein's caustic comments, the essay deals with a provocative subject worth some class time.

"Red, White, and Beer" by Dave Barry

Reading level: 12th grade

Anyone who watches even a little of television has probably seen the ubiquitous beer commercial. Barry's essay can be taught as a model for taking something with which everyone is familiar and presenting it with a new slant, forcing us to look again with fresh eyes. Of course, not everyone may appreciate Barry's sense of humor, but most students probably will.

The discussion in paragraph 7 is based on the vast media coverage of the 1986 unveiling of the renovated Statue of Liberty. If students missed it, you might need to explain who Lee Iacocca and Mary Lou Retton are, as well as why he selected them to mention. Celebrities in two vastly different areas, both have gone the way of commercials.

Barry's essay is another one that should be read aloud for all the subtle nuances and jibes. The long sentence in paragraph 5 seems to add humor and fit the tone of the story Barry is telling. The reality hidden under Barry's idea for a laxative commercial might move some students to discuss or write on the subject.

"The Issue Isn't Sex, It's Violence" by Caryl Rivers

Reading level: 8th grade

Rivers's essay touches on the negative effects that some rock lyrics may have. With the advent of MTV, rock videos now bring the lyrics to life. Her argument that some rock lyrics incite listeners to violence is not new. But unlike those who call for censorship, Rivers provides her own solution to what she sees as a problem (see paragraph 15 especially). This piece, written for the *Boston Globe*, uses several paragraphs to define the problem and present her view, always anticipating those who may disagree with her by presenting counterarguments.

Some students who disagree with Rivers fail to really look at her arguments because their own bias prevents them from accepting what she presents. Naturally, they don't have to agree with her, but a careful look at her arguments, how she orders and presents them, is worth some class time as an exercise in understanding the argumentative essay. Students may want to know her credentials. Rivers is a professor of journalism at Boston University, a novelist, and frequent essay contributor to newspapers and magazines.

"Censorship in Publishing" by Lynette Lamb

Reading level: 14th grade

Usually when we think of censorship, we think of protests and book burnings. Lamb shows us another type of censorship, one we seldom are privy to: censorship before publication. Lamb provides several examples to back up her thesis, then compares book publishing in the past with what is happening in the present. Present students with the information in paragraph 7 to see if they can connect it with "censorship in publishing." It may be difficult for some to see the implication being made.

"Presenting the Good News About Black College Students" by R. Richard Banks

Reading level: 11th grade

Banks accuses the media of presenting more negative than positive news regarding black college students. Stating that in general the news "harps on the gloom and doom themes," Banks offers at least five good news stories about blacks (see paragraphs 9–13) that he feels should receive the same attention the more publicized racist incidents do. It's worthwhile to look closely at the achievements he mentions. Ask students if they know of more recent ones.

Many people often ask why so much bad news seems to dominate the media. You may want to use this essay as a springboard into the whole area of media sensationalism, tying it in with Stein's viewpoints on the news.

"Reflections Dental" by Phyllis McGinley

This little poem is included mostly for comic relief, but it can be used to get into discussions of the shallowness of most television programs, the values reflected in the description of television entertainment, or even a discussion of analogies, metaphor, or descriptive writing.

STUDENT ESSAY: **"TV News: Journalism or Propaganda?"** by Jim Stone
Reading level: 11th grade
A full commentary appears in the text. Again, you will no doubt want to add your comments.

Using Unit 10: Controversial Issues

As the preface to the unit says, there are three controversial issues presented: bilingual education, capital punishment, and gun control. Two different viewpoints on each of the three issues are presented. Thus, the reading selections should be assigned in pairs so that at least two viewpoints can be read and considered before students attempt to write about their own views.

All three of these issues make excellent topics for research projects. The issues are contemporary ones, and students will have no trouble finding source materials for whatever position they desire to defend or investigate.

"Bilingual Programs: Crucial Vehicles" by Thomas A. Arciniega
Reading level: 14th grade
If some of your students have gone through bilingual education programs you will have some "authorities" on the subject. Try to engage them in class discussion of their attitudes and reactions to bilingual programs. For those students who are not living in areas affected by bilingual education programs and are seemingly disinterested in the subject, you might remind them of those statistics mentioned in Unit 5 regarding the growing number of Spanish-speaking people in Los Angeles, Miami, and other large metropolitan areas.

Arciniega opens with his thesis clearly stated. In paragraphs 2 and 3, he presents the need for and advantages of bilingual education. He states the financial problem in paragraph 5, then proceeds to argue for the continuation of funding for such programs. Because this is an argumentative essay, students should make certain they first understand what his reasons for supporting the programs are, and then discuss the validity of each.

"Bilingualism's Goal" by Barbara Mujica

Reading level: 11th grade

When you discuss this essay, have students reread paragraph 3 in Arciniega's essay, especially the last sentence: "I just can't understand why Chicanos get so worked up about Bilingual Education." Arciniega is mockingly paraphrasing non-Chicanos who disagree with him. Then have them reread paragraph 3 in Mujica's essay. Mujica is a Chicana mother. Ask students how her position differs from Arciniega's. Do they agree on anything? Are they both talking about the same type of bilingual education programs?

Arciniega is involved in bilingual education programs at a political and educational level. Mujica speaks more as a mother, one concerned with her family. Ask which one's viewpoint should be given more credence. You might even connect these selections with the unit on changing social values.

"Death to the Killers" by Mike Royko

Reading level: 8th–9th grade

Royko lets it be known from the first that he has written columns in favor of the death penalty for murderers. Then, stating that he doesn't like to make fun of people who oppose his views (paragraph 3), he spends most of his essay doing just that. He follows a pattern of quoting someone's question or argument, then attacks or ridicules it with sometimes flippant answers, making his opponents sound naive or stupid.

Royko does use a good argumentative technique. He takes his opposition's arguments, then shows or attempts to show why those arguments aren't valid. However, some of Royko's answers need to be examined for their bias and reasoning. Ask students how much of Royko's argument is based on logic and how much on emotion. Such a question can bring on a good class discussion and compositions.

"The Death Penalty Is a Step Back" by Coretta Scott King

Reading level: 15th grade

King looks at capital punishment as both immoral and unconstitutional, but the basis of her argument is built around three "practical reasons" presented in paragraphs 6–9. In paragraphs 10 and 11, she anticipates and states counterarguments and, like Royko, she answers back but more gently. She also makes it clear in paragraph 4 that she has suffered loss of loved ones from murderers. In effect this seems to imply that even though she has cause for favoring the death penalty, she looks at the subject objectively not emotionally.

It helps students if you list both Royko's and King's arguments on the board. Then have them create a list of arguments of their own. As a class or in small groups, have students examine the arguments for and against, take sides and debate the issue.

"United We Stand" by Editor, *The American Rifleman*

Reading level: 12th grade

My own bias will show here, but this editorial is a marvelous example of propaganda. No doubt the National Rifle Association provides many fine firearms safety education programs. But a close look at the emotionally charged language reveals cliched chauvinism hidden among a sales pitch for NRA membership.

"The Right (?) to Bear Arms" by Adam Ribb

Reading level: 10th grade

Ribb's basic concern is why the NRA is opposed to handgun laws. He says that based on the name of the organization, he understands why it might wage campaigns restricting ownership of rifles and shotguns, but wonders why they balk at the restriction of handguns. He enters into the old argument as to whether or not the U.S. Constitution really gives us the "right to bear arms." By quoting from several sources, Ribb tries to establish two major points: the sale of handguns should be regulated and the American Bar Association has implied that the NRA is misusing the "right to bear arms" phrase.

STUDENT ESSAY: **"Ignorant to What Is Sacred"** by Benjamin Little

Reading level: 13th grade

A full commentary appears in the text.